C000233311

THE

EUROPEAN FOOTBALL

CHAMPIONSHIPS

1958-1996

John Robinson

CONTENTS

Acknowledgements

In addition to thanking again those people who helped with the preparation of The European Championship 1958-1992 (the forerunner of this book), I wish to record my thanks to Michael Robinson for page layouts and editorial assistance.

John Robinson

British Library Cataloguing in Publication Data
A catalogue record for this book is available from the British Library

ISBN 0-947808-69-8

Published in Great Britain by Soccer Book Publishing Ltd.
72 St. Peter's Avenue, Cleethorpes, DN35 8HU

Typeset by Marksman Publications

Printed in Great Britain by Redwood Books, Kennet House, Kennet Way, Trowbridge, Wilts.

The European Soccer Championship

A Brief History

ALTHOUGH the European Championship itself did not get underway until 5th April 1958, organised regional international tournaments were already well established throughout Europe.

Way back in 1883 England, Northern Ireland (then just Ireland), Scotland and Wales kicked-off the British Championship (known as the Home International Championship) followed, in 1924, by Denmark, Finland, Norway and Sweden with the Scandinavian Championship (the Nordic Cup). In 1927 Hugo Meisl, that great Austrian champion of the game, originated the Central European Championship between Austria, Czechoslovakia, Hungary, Italy and Switzerland. Indeed, although known as the Dr. Gero Cup from 1955, this tournament was variously called 'The Nations Cup', 'The International Cup' and 'The Europe Cup'!

Just as we have to thank a Frenchman, Jules Rimet, for the conception of the FIFA World Cup in 1930, we are indebted to another Frenchman, Henri Delaunay, for the European Championship. Monsieur Delaunay, the secretary of the French Football Federation, proposed the tournament in the mid-1950's but, sadly, died before the competition got under way, although the trophy still bears his name.

M. Henri Delaunay

LINE-UPS FOR EUROPEAN CHAMPIONSHIP FINALS

1960

USSR: Yashin, Tchekeli, Kroutilov, Voinov, Maslenkin, Netto, Metreveli, Ivanov, Ponedelnik, Bubukin, Meshki.

Yugoslavia: Vidinic, Durkovic, Jusufi, Zanetic, Miladinovic, Perusic, Sekularac, Jerkovic, Galic, Matus, Kostic.

1964

Spain: Iribar, Rivilla, Calleja, Fuste, Olivella, Zoco, Amancio, Pereda, Marcelino, Suarez, Lapetra.

USSR: Yashin, Chustikov, Mudrik, Voronin, Shesterniev, Anitchkin, Chislenko, Ivanov, Ponedelnik, Kornalev, Khusainov.

1968

Italy: Zoff, Burgnich, Facchetti, Ferrini, Guarneri, Castano, Domenghini, Juliano, Anastasi, Lodetti, Prati.

Yugoslavia: Pantelic, Fazlagic, Damjanovic, Pavlovic, Paunovic, Holcer, Petkovic, Acimovic, Musemic, Trivic, Dzajic.

1968 Replay

Italy: Zoff, Burgnich, Facchetti, Rosato, Guarneri, Salvadore, Domenghini, Mazzola, Anastasi, De Sisti, Riva.

Yugoslavia: Pantelic, Fazlagic, Damjanovic, Pavlovic, Paunovic, Holcer, Hosic, Acimovic, Musemic, Trivic, Dzajic.

1972

West Germany: Maier, Hottges, Schwarzenbeck, Beckenbauer, Breitner, Hoeness, Wimmer, Netzer, Heynckes, Muller, Kremers.

USSR: Rudakov, Dzodzuashvili, Khurtsilava, Kaplichny, Istomin, Troshkin, Kolotov, Baidachni, Konkov (Dolmatov), Banishevsky (Kozinkievits), Onishenko.

1976

Czechoslovakia: Viktor, Dobias (F. Vesely), Pivarnik, Ondrus, Capkovic, Gogh, Moder, Panenka, Svehlik (Jurkemik), Masny, Nehoda.

West Germany: Maier, Vogts, Beckenbauer, Schwarzenbeck, Dietz, Bonhof, Wimmer (Flohe), D. Muller, Beer (Bongartz), Hoeness, Holzenbein.

1980

West Germany: Schumacher, Kalz, K.N. Förster, Stielike, Dietz, Schuster, Briegel (Cullmann 55), H. Muller, Rummenigge, Hrubesch, Allofs.

Belgium: Pfaff, Gerets, Millecamps Meeuws, Renquin, Van Moer, Cools, Vandereycken, Van der Elst, Mommens, Ceulemans.

1984

France: Bats, Battiston (Amoros 72), Le Roux, Bossis, Domergue, Fernandez, Giresse, Tigana, Platini, Lacombe (Genghini 79), Bellone, *Le Roux sent off, 84.

Spain: Arconada, Urquiaga, Salva (Roberto 84), Gallego, Senor, Francisco, Victor, Gamacho, Julio Alberto (Sarabia 76), Santillana, Carrasco.

1988

Holland: Breukelen, Aerle, Rijkaard, Tiggelen, Koeman (R), Koeman (E), Muhren, Vanenburg, Wouters, Gullit, Van Basten.

USSR: Dasayev, Khidiatulin, Demianenko, Rats, Aleinikov, Litovchenko, Zavarov, Mikhailichenko, Gotsmanov (Baltacha 67), Protasov (Pasulko 71), Belanov.

1992

Denmark: Schmeichel, Piechnik, Olsen, Nielsen, Sivebaek (Christiansen 66), Vilfort, Jensen, Larsen, Christofte, Povlsen, Laudrup.

Germany: Illgner, Reuter, Kohler, Helmer, Buchwald, Hassler, Effenberg (Thom 80), Sammer (Doll 46), Brehme, Klinsmann, Riedle.

1st Series 1958/60

THEN TITLED 'The European Nations Cup', the first tournament almost failed to get off the ground when, as the deadline for entries approached, less than the required number of 16 countries had applied. Most major European footballing nations (including Italy and several of the sides who appeared in the 1958 World Cup Final England, Northern Ireland, Scotland, Sweden, Wales and West Germany) declined to enter, doubting the potential of such a competition. There were, no doubt, furious behind-the-scenes negotiations before 17 of the 33 European nations eventually applied.

This, in itself, posed a problem as the first round of the competition was to be run on a straight home-and-away knockout basis! That hurdle was overcome by playing a preliminary round to eliminate the 'excess' country and it fell to Eire and Czechoslovakia to compete for the 16th place.

Thus, the very first game of the competition took place between Eire and Czechoslovakia in Dublin on 5th April 1958. The Irish opened the scoring with a well-taken goal by Liam Tuomy and when Noel Cantwell converted a penalty later in the game, they must have thought themselves well on the way to the first round proper. However, it was not to be. In Bratislava five weeks later, the Czechs (who had already qualified for the 1958 World Cup Finals in Sweden) hammered Eire 4-0 to take the tie 4-2 on aggregate.

The draw for the first and second rounds was made in Sweden during the World Cup Finals and passed almost unnoticed by the world's press amidst the excitement of the World Cup itself. The first name out of the hat was that of the USSR who were drawn against Hungary both teams from the last 16 of the current World Cup, and consequently one of the most attractive pairings possible. It was decided that the second round would be between the winners of the first and second pairings, the third and fourth pairings and so on; with Poland drawn against Spain in the second pairing, an interesting second round tie was also in prospect.

The first match of "The European Nations' Cup" tournament proper, was played on 28th September 1958 in Moscow's Central Stadium (a huge bowl of an arena completed only in 1956) before a crowd of 100,572 – the biggest attendance of the series. Neither the USSR nor Hungary had had a very successful World Cup series in Sweden and, as a consequence, both fielded much changed teams. The USSR began with the sort of cavalry charge associated with the mighty Hungarian team of the early fifties and took a fourth-minute lead through Ilyin. The pressure continued and they were unfortunate to be denied a second, six minutes later when the Austrian referee Herr Grill disallowed a seemingly good goal by Simonian. They maintained their momentum, pinning Hungary back in their own half by an endless series of attacks down both flanks, until, inevitably, scoring a second goal when right winger Metreveli cracked in a shot from the edge of the area. Although 2-0 up after only 20 minutes, still the Russians did not ease back and, in the 32nd minute, Valentin Ivanov, the USSR's outstanding player, scored a brilliant solo goal to cap an outstanding first-half display.

At half-time, the Russians left the field 3-0 up, to the rapturous applause of the Soviet supporters, who sensed further domination in the second half.

However, the Magyars pulled themselves together and turned the tables on the Russians after the restart. Playing like a different team, Hungary pushed the USSR on to the defensive but the Russian defence, solidly organised around Maslenkin, held out until the 84th minute when Gorocs scored a consolation goal. Although this gave the score an air of respectability, Hungary had left it too late to come back further and, with the final result of 3-1, left themselves with a mammoth task for the return leg of the tie.

It was almost a year to the day that the second leg was played in Budapest before 78,000 rain-soaked spectators. The Hungarians drafted back keeper Grosics, schemer Bozsik and several other ageing stars from their great side of the early fifties. Russia too, brought back their veterans in the guise of Yashin and Netto and clinched the game and the tie when Voinov scored the only goal in the second half.

Of the countries who had entered the European Nations Cup competition, France had made the best showing in the 1958 World Cup, finishing in third-place (thanks to goal-ace Just Fontaine), with the highest number of goals scored 23. On 1st October 1958, France took the field against Greece for the second game of the first round and continued their goalscoring ways. A crowd of 38,000 crammed into the Parc des Princes Stadium in Paris to see Real Madrid's Raymond Kopa lead an impressive French team on to the attack – and attack they certainly did. Goals by Kopa, Fontaine and Cisowski gave France a comfortable half-time lead and, undeterred by a Greek goal just after the restart, they continued their goal-scoring spree. Cisowski grabbed a hat-trick with two further goals and Vincent and Fontaine made the score a heady 7-1 – the highest of the series. When the return match was played in Athens two months later, the Greeks regained a certain amount of pride with a 1-1 draw, but France, nevertheless, became the first country to qualify for the second round.

The other first round ties produced few surprises with straight wins, home and away for Spain over Poland, Austria over Norway and Portugal over East Germany, while Yugoslavia, won in Belgrade and drew the return leg in Sofia to despatch their neighbours, Bulgaria. The remaining tie, Rumania against Turkey, was the closest of the round, with home wins for each country. Rumania just held out in the second leg, to win the tie 3-2.

The most attractive tie in the second round, the USSR against Spain, was never played. Then still a dictatorship under General Franco, the Spanish Government, unable to forget Russian participation in the Spanish Civil War, vetoed their team's participation. The Spanish and Russian football associations had agreed dates for the two matches (the first leg was scheduled to be played in Moscow in May 1960) but, because the Spanish team were refused permission to travel, the Soviet side were left with a walk-over into the semi-finals.

France, drawn against Austria, continued their goal-scoring ways, winning 5-2 at home in the first of the second round matches and 4-2 away.

Czechoslovakia, too, made short work of Rumania winning both legs of their tie without conceding a goal. Yugoslavia, meanwhile, did not enjoy the same degree of superiority, losing their first leg in Portugal but, committing themselves to outright attack, won the home leg 5-1 to confirm their semi-final place.

France was selected as the venue for the Finals of the first series but attendances for the Final series, unlike the earlier rounds (which had frequently been capacity crowds) were extremely disappointing. The home country was drawn against Yugoslavia in Paris, while the USSR faced Czechoslovakia in Marseille.

Both ties were played on 6th July 1960 and 26,370 fans were in the Parc des Princes to see France (without Kopa, Fontaine or Piantoni) take on the Slavs. Confidence was running high in the French team and they were comfortably 3-1 in the lead by the 52nd minute and 4-2 up ten minutes later. Yugoslavia, however, were far from finished and, in the final quarter of the match, prompted by goal-scoring ace Jerkovic, they stormed through for a 5-4 victory, to send the French fans home disconsolate.

In Marseille, meanwhile, a similar-sized crowd, 25,184, saw the USSR take the honours against Czechoslovakia in a match played in blistering heat. The Russians won 3-0, a scoreline that did not reflect the balance of play in a game which the Czechs controlled for much of the time. Czechoslovakia pressed hard from the kick-off and Lev Yashin, Russia's veteran goalkeeper, thwarted attack after attack. In the midfield for Russia, Netto, Voinov and especially Ivanov (who scored two goals) gradually took control and, although the Czechs continued to fight hard right up to the final whistle, they were still unable to find the net.

A meagre crowd of 9,438 spectators turned up at Marseille's huge oval cycling stadium to see France meet Czechoslovakia in the play-off for third place on 9th July 1960, probably as much a reflection of the futility of such 'also-ran' contests as of French disappointment. On balance, the fans were wise to stay away, because, despite the introduction of five new players by team coach Albert Batteaux, the home side gave an abysmal display. Jonquet, the 35-year-old centre-half, included in the team to bolster the defence, did anything but. In the 58th minute, he slipped to allow Bubernik to put Czechoslovakia into the lead. The Czechoslovakians, through their midfield trio of Bubernik, Masopust and Popluhar, had controlled the game from the kick-off. The French, who were unable to get achieve cohesion, were jeered by their own supporters even before conceding the goal. A second Czech goal by Pavlovic in the 87th minute, ended any lingering French hopes, of a comeback and guaranteed Czechoslovakia's third-place.

Thus, the stage was set for the Final between the USSR and Yugoslavia which was played the following day at the Parc des Princes stadium. Played under floodlights, it attracted only 17,966 spectators, and Yugoslavia began with the same sort of non-stop attack that had enabled them to overcome France the previous Wednesday. Once again, goalkeeper Lev Yashin was the saviour of his country as he thwarted attack after attack, until Yugoslavia's wiry centre-forward, Galic, put his country ahead in the 41st minute. In the second half, it was a very different story as the Russians came right back into the game, equalising through Metreveli within five minutes. Now Yugoslavia were forced on to the defensive and, although little was seen of the Yugoslav attack, the Russians had been unable to increase their score when the English referee, Arthur Ellis, whistled for full-time. So, the first Final went into extra-time and the physical superiority of the Russians began to tell. After twice going near to scoring, the USSR took the lead through Ponedelnik in the 113th minute when he plucked a centre from left-winger Meshki out of the air and hammered the ball into the net. Yugoslavia were too tired to muster an equaliser and the USSR became the first winners of the Henri Delaunay Cup, the first European Champions.

1958/60 Series

Preliminary Round

Eire .... 2 Czechoslovakia .. 0
Czechoslovakia .. 4 Eire 0

First Round

USSR .... 3 Hungary 1
Hungary .... 0 USSR 1

Poland .... 2 Spain 4
Spain .... 3 Poland 0

Denmark .... 2 Czechoslovakia .. 2
Czechoslovakia .. 5 Denmark 1

Romania .... 3 Turkey 0
Turkey .... 2 Romania 0

France .... 7 Greece 1
Greece .... 1 France 1

Norway .... 0 Austria 1
Austria .... 5 Norway 2

Portugal .... 3 East Germany 2
East Germany .... 0 Portugal 2

Yugoslavia .... 2 Bulgaria 0
Bulgaria .... 1 Yugoslavia 1

Quarter-Finals

USSR WALK OVER - SPAIN (WITHDREW)

Romania .... 0 Czechoslovakia .. 2
Czechoslovakia .. 3 Romania 0

France .... 5 Austria 2
Austria .... 2 France 4

Portugal .... 2 Yugoslavia 1
Yugoslavia .... 5 Portugal 1

Semi-Finals

USSR .... 3 Czechoslovakia .. 0
Yugoslavia .... 5 France 4

Third Place Match

Czechoslovakia .. 2 France 0

FINAL

USSR .... 2 Yugoslavia 1
After Extra Time

The Victorious Russians hold aloft the Trophy after winning the first Final in 1960

2nd Series 1962-64

THE SECOND SERIES was organised on the same home-and-away straight knockout basis as the First Series but, with 29 of the 33 European nations agreeing to compete, it was poised, from the outset, to be the all-encompassing tournament of which Henry Delaunay had dreamed. West Germany, Scotland, Finland and Cyprus were the four absentees and their absence went largely unnoticed. This time the draw was wisely scheduled after the completion of the 1962 World Cup Finals. Spain, the host nation for the closing stages, was drawn first and found themselves up against Rumania.

The draw was for the first round only and the absence of seeding threw up only one potentially outstanding tie, England vs France, with the clash between World Cup runners-up Czechoslovakia and on-form East Germany the most attractive of the remainder. The USSR, Austria and Luxembourg received byes to balance out second round numbers to 16.

Almost immediately, politics reared its ugly head again, as Greece found itself drawn against neighbouring Albania. Memories are long in that area of the Mediterranean and the two countries, technically at war since 1912, maintained an uneasy truce in their dealings with each other. Greece refused to play in Albania, no doubt fearing for the safety of its players, and Albania were awarded the tie in consequence.

The French, who had failed to qualify for the 1962 World Cup Finals in Chile, were anxious to restore a little national pride by beating England, and travelled to Sheffield in October 1962 for the first leg of their tie. Their new trainer Henri Guerin had already taken control, whereas this was to be Walter Winterbottom's last game as England team manager and, with Jimmy Adamson having turned down the role as his successor, matters in the English camp were somewhat uncertain. England who had been a little fortunate to reach the quarter-finals of the World Cup in Chile (qualifying on goal-difference) before being beaten by Brazil, felt that they too, had something to prove and the stage was set for a hard game. In the few days before the match, there was much speculation in the French camp as to whether Raymond Kopa, their 31-year-old star (whose son was desperately ill) would be prepared to play. Jimmy Greaves, meanwhile, England's goalscoring genius, who had been injured for several weeks, was also a doubtful starter.

In the event, both Kopa and Greaves were present when the teams took the field before an expectant Hillsborough crowd on 3rd October 1962. Contrary to all expectations, England struggled from the onset to get to grips with their opponent's system of play as the French totally dictated the pace of the game. Employing the same sort of 4-2-4 formation as Brazil had used to annihilate England a few months earlier, the French played a fluent passing game which shunned the man-to-man marking system that the English were anticipating.

Gujon put France ahead in only the eighth minute and England were all at sea as Raymond Kopa, playing with his usual brilliance gave their centre-half, Norman, an absolute roasting. Irresistible on the ball, Kopa, proved to be the key factor in a first-half dominated by the French, which, if they had had a finisher in the class of Just Fontaine, would probably have ended 4-0 or 5-0 in their favour. As it was, the half-time score remained 1-0 and, shortly after the restart, Ron Flowers equalised from the penalty spot. Jimmy Greaves, who had scored four goals for Tottenham in a League match a few days earlier, was clearly still troubled by a knee injury and without his punch up front, England never looked like taking the lead. Indeed, although the final score of 1-1 was regarded almost as a defeat by the home fans, England were in fact fortunate indeed to have avoided a very heavy defeat.

When the return leg was played in Paris five months later, Alf Ramsey had just taken over as team manager and decided to go all out for attack by including five strikers in his front-line Connelly, Tambling, Smith, Greaves and Charlton! This, in itself, proved to be a gamble which failed, but, by far the greatest gamble which Ramsey took was to include Ron Springett (who was desperately lacking in match practice) in goal. The French, were without Raymond Kopa but still required only three minutes to take the lead when Springett's poor form allowed Wisnieski to score an easy goal. Undaunted by this, England took control of the game and their forwards gave the French defenders Lerond and Wendling, a really hard time. Bernard, the French goalkeeper, meanwhile, showed himself to be everything that Springett was not and beat out all that the English forward line threw at him. In the 33rd minute the French broke out of defence for Douis to make the score 2-0 and, on the stroke of half-time, Springett was again seriously at fault in conceding a third goal. After the break, Smith and Tambling both scored to narrow the gap to 2-3 but England's all-out attacking play left gaps at the rear which (assisted by yet another Springett error) the French were able to exploit by scoring two more goals, to run out 5-2 winners. Alf Ramsey returned with the disconsolate English team, to be battery of criticism from the UK press and began reshaping England's squad with an eye firmly fixed on the 1966 World Cup!

In early September 1962, Eire became the first country to qualify for the second round (other than those with a bye) by beating Iceland 5-3 on aggregate.

The biggest shock of the first round occurred, however, on 10th October 1962 in Katowice, Poland, when unrated Northern Ireland had little difficulty in beating the home side 2-0 with goals by Dougan and Humphries. Moreover, having meanwhile suffered a 5-1 thrashing at the hands of Scotland early in November, (thanks to four goals by Denis Law), Northern Ireland were not expected to repeat their achievement when they faced Poland for the return leg of the tie. The man of this match was John Crossan, a player who had served a three-year apprenticeship in Holland and Belgium League football after being exiled from the UK somewhat harshly for an offence committed early in his career. Rehabilitated into English League football with Sunderland FC, Crossan must have savoured his return to Northern Ireland when, in the ninth minute, he put

Hertig scores Switzerland's only goal in their 1st Round game in Holland.
The Dutch won the match 3-1.

his country ahead. In the second half Billy Bingham scored another goal to ensure Poland's early exit from the competition.

Hungary, playing the same formation that had served them relatively well in Chile, had little difficulty in disposing of Wales, winning the home leg 3-1 and drawing 1-1 in Wales. Czechoslovakia, the team that had beaten Hungary in the World Cup Quarter-Finals before progressing to the Final itself, provided the other real shock of the round when they met East Germany. The Czechs were narrowly defeated by the odd goal in three when they played the first leg in East Germany, but observers believed that it would be a different story in Prague on 31st March 1963. Conscious of the 2-1 deficit, Czechoslovakia fielded their strongest team and, with their half-back line of Pluskal, Popluhar and Masopust considered to be the best in the world, clearly expected to redeem themselves. The game itself started as a drab affair as East Germany concentrated so much on defence that it was not until the 30th minute that they got anywhere near the Czech goal. Indeed, the whole of the first half consisted of the Czechoslovakian attack battering against an East German wall of defenders. In the second-half the game opened up with the Germans, now confident in their ability to contain the Czech attack, mounting their own breakaway sorties into the opposing half. Twenty minutes after the restart, Czechoslovakia had their reward when Mazek scored with a good 15-yard shot and, shortly after, seemed certain to score again when he was roughly bundled off the ball in the German penalty area. The Hungarian referee, Mr. Bella, turned down the Czechs' frantic appeals for a penalty and the Germans breathed again. Nine minutes from the end, when the East Germans broke out of defence, Jan Popluhar dithered when he should have cleared and this allowed Roland Ducke to grab the equaliser, dumping Czechoslovakia out of the tournament.

The remaining ties went very much to form as Spain overcame Rumania 7-3 on aggregate (despite losing the away leg 3-1), Holland beat Switzerland 4-2 on aggregate, and Denmark trounced Malta 9-2, winning home and away, a feat emulated by both Yugoslavia (against Belgium) and Italy (against Turkey).

After losing the home game against neighbouring Sweden 2-0, Norway did extremely well to draw the away leg 1-1. Unfortunately this was not enough to give them the chance of the replay that Bulgaria earned against Portugal in the closest tie of the round. Bulgaria won the first leg 3-1 and were trailing 3-0 in the second leg before scoring to level the tie 3-1 again. The play-off was in neutral Rome and a goal by Asparoukov ten minutes from time saw Bulgaria through to the next round.

The draw for the second round on 26th March 1963 threw up one outstanding pairing – Italy v USSR, (a match that many would have chosen for the Final) and the first leg of this clash took place on 13th October 1963 in Moscow.

Since winning the title in Paris in 1960, the new Soviet trainer Konstantin Beskov had introduced several young players into the Russian side, while the Italian coach Edmondo Fabri had also completely rebuilt his side. Despite pouring rain, the stadium was packed and after only 12 minutes, a Russian defender, Dubinski, clashed with Italy's centre-forward Sormani who had to leave the field for treatment to a head injury. Ten minutes later Ivanov and Ponedelnik combined neatly to set up a shot for Khusainov which rebounded back to Ponedelnik the Russian centre-forward, who slotted the ball past three Italian defenders into the net to put the USSR one up. Soon afterwards, tempers flared as Pascutti, who had been brought down by Dubinski, tore into the Russian player, ripping his shirt and head-butting him. The Polish referee Mr. Banksiuk was left with no option but to send Pascutti off the field, leaving the Italians down to only nine

Malta's defence repulse a Danish attack on 16th December 1962. Denmark won 3-1.

men. Sormani, however, returned to the field, his head heavily bandaged, but a further Russian goal seemed inevitable. Just before half-time Chislenko made it 2-0 and in the second-half, the USSR, never seriously troubled by the occasional Italian breakaway, coasted to victory.

A month later, the return leg was played in Rome and trainer Beskov replaced an attacker with a midfielder and played his trump card by recalling, once more, his marvellous veteran goalkeeper Lev Yashin. As in the 1958/60 Series Yashin proved to be a match-winner when, in the first half-hour, the Italians threw everything at him, only for him to throw it back again! In almost their first breakaway the Russians scored through Gusarov and the Italians became increasingly desperate. Twelve minutes into the second-half, Italy were awarded a penalty and the home crowd's hopes were raised, only to be dashed again as Yashin saved Mazzola's weak effort. The Italians were unable to penetrate Russia's solid defence until Rivera scored a face-saving equaliser in the last minute – too late to effect the result of the tie.

The biggest upset of the round and, indeed, of the entire competition to date, had meanwhile taken place in Holland. Luxembourg had elected to play both legs of their tie in the Netherlands, and the first leg, Holland's real 'home' game, was played in Amsterdam on 11th September 1963, before a crowd of 36,000. Prior to this game it had been the custom for the Dutch to field a 'B' team for matches against their neighbours from the Grand Duchy but, because of the

Goussarov hammers the ball past Italian 'keeper Sarti in the second leg of Russia's second round match of the 1962-64 Nations' Cup.

importance of this tie, they put out their strongest team. The result appeared to be a foregone conclusion and, when Nuninga shot them into the lead after only five minutes, the Dutch crowd felt that they were in for a goal avalanche. This, however, never materialised, May equalised for Luxembourg in the 35th minute and, despite constant Dutch pressure, the score remained 1-1. Undaunted by this result, the Dutch clearly expected to hammer Luxembourg in the 'away' leg and fielded a much changed team for that game, which was played in Rotterdam on 30th October 1963. Players from the local team Feyenoord formed the backbone of the Dutch team and the game opened eventfully with first Luxembourg and then Holland, hitting the crossbar in the early stages. After 20 minutes, Dimmer put Luxembourg in front with a well-taken goal and the 'home' crowd (the Dutch crowd that is) began to clamour for a Netherlands' reply. Fifteen minutes later the uproar died down as Kruiver scored the equaliser and, at last realising that they had a real game on their hands, Holland's play became harder and harder. Luxembourg soaked up the pressure of the increasingly desperate Dutch attacks as the second half got under way and Nico Schmitt, their goalkeeper, played a 'blinder' to deny Keizer, Giezen and Kruiver in quick succession. Indeed, after Dimmer had grabbed his second goal for the Grand Duchy, even a collision which put his shoulder out of joint did not prevent Schmitt from denying the Dutch any further goals. The score remained 2-1 to the astonishment of the crowd (and indeed the whole of Europe), and the footballing lesson delivered by Luxembourg that day still rings out clear today – don't underestimate your opponents!

Yugoslavia, runners-up in 1958/60, faced Sweden in the second round on 21st June 1963 and were found wanting in match fitness by the Scandinavians, who were right in the middle of their domestic competition. The result, a 0-0 draw, was a good one for Sweden and left Yugoslavia with a stiff task for the second leg in Stockholm in September. Yugoslavia fielded virtually the same side as in the first leg (their star player Draga Sekularac was still technically under suspension) but the Swedes were forced to make a number of changes because of injury. On paper, at least, Sweden's line-up placed the emphasis on defence but it proved to be anything but a defensive game. Yugoslavia took the lead in the 20th minute when Zambata took advantage of a misunderstanding between the Swedish goalkeeper Nyholm and 'Bajdoff' Johansson, but Sweden equalised through Persson ten minutes later and went ahead, via the same player, a quarter of an hour into the second half. Galic levelled the score five minutes later but Harry Bild soon scored a third for Sweden to unexpectedly, take the tie 3-2.

In the remaining ties, Denmark had little difficulty in disposing of Albania 4-1 on aggregate, despite losing the away leg 1-0, and France overcame Bulgaria 3-2 on aggregate after losing 1-0 in Sofia. Hungary disposed of East Germany 5-4 in two hard-fought ties and Northern Ireland played extremely well to draw 1-1 in Spain, only to throw away their home advantage and lose the return 1-0. The other game in the second round was between Austria and Eire. Austria had been somewhat unlucky when they narrowly failed to qualify for the 1962 World Cup Finals, when they had been, in the opinion of many impartial observers, one of the finest teams in Europe. Since 1961 they had suffered a series of humiliations,

The Irish players celebrate their 0-0 draw in Austria on 25th September 1963

including a 3-1 defeat by Egypt and, indeed, had won only one game in the previous 18 months, when they met Eire in Vienna on 25th September 1963. Although the resulting 0-0 draw was a very acceptable score for the Irish, and well earned to boot, it was perhaps not as surprising an outcome as it would have been two years earlier. The return leg in Ireland two weeks later, a close-fought affair, level at half-time with goals by Cantwell and Koleznik, ended 3-2 in favour of the Irish who just had the edge over their opponents.

The quarter-finals drew the following pairings: Spain v Eire; France v Hungary; Luxembourg v Denmark and Sweden v USSR, and were played on the same home-and-away knockout basis as the first competition. All eyes were on Luxembourg could they repeat their giant-killing act of the second round? Literally playing at home this time, Luxembourg shocked Denmark by taking a first-minute lead through Pilot, clearly signalling that their victory over Holland had been no fluke. Ole Madsen levelled the score for Denmark but Klein then put the Grand Duchy ahead. Fortunately for Denmark, Madsen really had his goal-scoring boots on and he again equalised to level the score 2-2 at half-time and, in the second half, grabbed his hat-trick to give Denmark the lead. Klein came back with Luxembourg's third goal and the final score was 3-3. Denmark were hot favourites for the return leg the following week but, once again, Luxembourg took an early lead, this time through Leonard, before Ole Madsen (almost inevitably) did his stuff again, equalising in the first half and shooting his country into the lead twenty minutes from full-time. Still Luxembourg were not finished – they piled on the pressure as the game became harder with a whole string of fouls and rough play, before Schmidt scored a well-earned equaliser six minutes from the end. The two sides met in Amsterdam for the play-off on 18th December 1963, their third meeting in two weeks. It was a bone-chilling evening with mist and the occasional snow flurry and perhaps fittingly, Ole Madsen, the scorer of all five of Denmark's goals in the previous two games ended Luxembourg's hopes of further glory with the only goal of the match, in the 44th minute.

Max Urbini of "France Football" magazine presents Lev Yashin with the Golden Ball prize he won as European Footballer of the Year just before the Russia-Sweden European Nations Cup game in Moscow.

Spain had little difficulty in disposing of Eire, winning both legs, 5-1 at home and 2-0 away, while Hungary achieved a similar feat over France, winning 3-1 in France and 2-1 at home. The champions Russia, however, faced a much stiffer challenge against Sweden. Unbeaten for almost two years, the Swedes had proved their worth by beating the previous runners-up, Yugoslavia, and the first leg in Stockholm was a really tight game. The USSR came intending to defend and, marshalled brilliantly by Voranin, their back-line held firm against all the Swedish attacks. In the second-half Ivanov shot Russia into the lead and, although Kurre Hamrin grabbed an equaliser three minutes from the end, the home crowd were disappointed with the result.

In the return game in Moscow, two weeks later, Sweden began in dominant form, with Bergmark (playing his 80th international) setting up attack after attack. Yashin, in the Russian goal, kept the Swedish forwards at bay and the USSR came more and more into the game. When Ponedelnik scored in almost the first Russian attack of the game, the roles were reversed with the Swedes forced back onto the defensive. Fifteen minutes into the second-half Ponedelnik scored a second goal before Hamrin pulled one back for Sweden. Yashin, so many times the saviour of the Russian team, the current European Footballer of the Year, could only shake his head in disbelief as he gathered the ball from the net – that man Kurre Hamrin had managed to score against him on every single occasion that they had met one another! Swedish hopes of recovery, however, were quickly dashed as Ivanov and Voronin combined to score a classic third goal which put the issue well and truly beyond doubt.

The semi-finals, played in Spain, matched the USSR against Denmark in Barcelona, while the home country met Hungary in Madrid. In Barcelona, both Denmark and the USSR began cautiously as players struggled to overcome their nerves, but it was the Russians who drew first blood with an early goal by Voronin. Ponedelnik scored a second before half-time and the amateurs of Denmark never seriously troubled the Russians as Ivanov scored the third and final goal of the game in the second-half.

Meanwhile, Real Madrid's Bernabeu Stadium was half-empty for the clash between the hosts and Hungary in the other semi-final – the first meeting between the two for 38 years. The Spaniards soon had the edge over the Hungarians, playing their own characteristic brand of fast, neat attacking football while Hungary, playing a laborious game of short passes, square balls and back passes seemed intent on defence. However, for all their attacking effort, the Spanish forwards rarely got themselves into a threatening position, running out of steam (and ideas) as they reached Hungary's goal area. A rasping shot from Albert, dramatically beaten out by Iribar the Spanish 'keeper, came closer than anything that the Spanish forwards had been able to muster and emphasised Spain's lack of penetration up front. Later in the first-half, the hosts did at last score when Pereda headed them into the lead after an Amancio free-kick had enabled Suarez to get a pin-point cross over. Half-time came and went and Spain, content to defend their single goal lead, were little troubled by the unadventurous Hungarians. Five minutes from the end, when Spain seemed to have the game won, Bene equalised for Hungary and the daunting prospect of extra-time loomed. Neither side relished playing a further 30 minutes in the torrid heat but the Spaniards regained the edge and, in the 115th minute, Amancio, Spain's best forward, scored the winning goal saving the referee the trouble of spinning another coin.

Captains Voronin (USSR) and Olivella (Spain) before the 1964 Final in Madrid

UEFA President Gustav Wiederkehr presents Olivella with the trophy.

On the following Saturday the Hungarians travelled to Barcelona for the third-place match and included six of their reserves – Novak, Ihasz and Solymosi at the back, with Farkas replacing the disappointing Kamora. Sandor was still not fit enough to claim his 75th cup and Varga from Ferencvaros replaced him in company with Bene who took Tichy's place. Denmark (no doubt aware that they had lost their last meeting 6-0) fielded an unchanged team and surprised their stronger opponents (who had taken an 11th minute lead through Bene) by equalising nine minutes from the end of normal time. In extra-time Hungary clinched third place with two goals from full-back Novak, the first a penalty after Albert had been brought down and the second, three minutes later (the 110th minute), with a thunderball free-kick from the edge of the area. Denmark, defeated but far from disgraced, had, without doubt, reaffirmed their position as Europe's leading amateurs.

General Franco attended the Final in Madrid and watched an unchanged Spanish team take on a Russian side in which a defender, Kornaiev, replaced a forward, Gussarov. A huge 120,000 crowd packed the Chamatin stadium and saw Spain take a sixth-minute lead when an Ivanov pass, intercepted by Suarez, was put to the unmarked Pereda in the middle who slashed the ball into the empty net. The crowd's delight soon ended when, a little over a minute later, the Spanish goalkeeper, Iribar, allowed a weak shot from Khusainov to dip beneath his diving body, into the net. Heavy rain began to fall and both sides played cautiously as they struggled to keep their feet on the slippery surface. Of the few clear-cut chances created during the dreary hour that followed the goals, Pereda came closest to scoring for Spain when Yashin acrobatically saved a close-range shot and, minutes later, Iribar pulled off a finger-tip save from Ponedelnik at the other end. Of the two defences, Russia's seemed the most insecure and, in the 84th minute, Pereda, despite the attentions of Mudrik, crossed the ball from the touchline for Marcelino to score with a remarkable diving header. The 2-1 scoreline was a fair result to a dreary game and, not only Russia's first-ever defeat in Spain, but also their first-ever defeat in the European Nations Cup!

1962/64 Series

First Round

Spain	6	Romania	0
Romania	3	Spain	1
Poland	0	Northern Ireland	2
Northern Ireland	2	Poland	0
Eire	4	Iceland	2
Iceland	1	Eire	1
Bulgaria	3	Portugal	1
Portugal	3	Bulgaria	1
Bulgaria	1	Portugal	0
England	1	France	1
France	5	England	2
East Germany	2	Czechoslovakia	1
Czechoslovakia	1	East Germany	1
Hungary	3	Wales	1
Wales	1	Hungary	1
Denmark	6	Malta	1
Malta	1	Denmark	3

ALBANIA WALK OVER - GREECE (WITHDREW)

Holland	3	Switzerland	1
Switzerland	1	Holland	1
Norway	0	Sweden	2
Sweden	1	Norway	1
Yugoslavia	3	Belgium	2
Belgium	0	Yugoslavia	1
Italy	6	Turkey	0
Turkey	0	Italy	1

AUSTRIA, LUXEMBOURG & USSR RECEIVED BYES

Second Round

Spain	1	Northern Ireland	1
Northern Ireland	0	Spain	1
Austria	0	Eire	0
Eire	3	Austria	2
Bulgaria	1	France	0
France	3	Bulgaria	1
East Germany	1	Hungary	2
Hungary	3	East Germany	3
Denmark	4	Albania	0
Albania	1	Denmark	0
Holland	1	Luxembourg	1
Luxembourg	2	Holland	1
Yugoslavia	0	Sweden	0
Sweden	3	Yugoslavia	2
USSR	2	Italy	0
Italy	1	USSR	1

Quarter-Finals

Spain	5	Eire	1
Eire	0	Spain	2
France	1	Hungary	3
Hungary	2	France	1
Luxembourg	3	Denmark	3
Denmark	2	Luxembourg	2
Denmark	1	Luxembourg	0
Sweden	1	USSR	1
USSR	3	Sweden	1

Third Place Match

Hungary	3	Denmark	1

After Extra Time

Semi-Finals

Spain	2	Hungary	1
USSR	3	Denmark	0

FINAL

Spain	2	USSR	1

3rd Series 1966-68

THE 'EUROPEAN NATIONS CUP' competition had its name changed by UEFA Congress to 'The European Championship' before the 3rd series commenced and, with an entry of no less than 31 countries, was now clearly established as Europe's premier tournament. In keeping with the FIFA World Cup and to accommodate the greatly increased number of entrants, the previous knockout system was replaced by one of groups. The 31 entrants were split into eight groups for the first round, with everyone playing each other in the group, both home and away. The eight group winners would then contest the quarter-finals in four home-and-away leg ties, the winners of which would become the semi-finalists.

The four Home Countries, England, Northern Ireland, Scotland and Wales, were allowed to form a separate group played simultaneously with the British Home Championship and for the first time again following the FIFA World Cup routine seeding was applied with one seeded country in each group.

The groupings were as follows:

GROUP 1: Czechoslovakia, Eire, Spain and Turkey
GROUP 2: Bulgaria, Norway, Portugal and Sweden
GROUP 3: Austria, Finland, Greece and the USSR
GROUP 4: Albania, West Germany, Yugoslavia
GROUP 5: Denmark, East Germany, Holland and Hungary
GROUP 6: Cyprus, Italy, Rumania and Switzerland
GROUP 7: Belgium, France, Luxembourg and Poland
GROUP 8: England, Northern Ireland, Scotland and Wales

In Group 1, Spain, the holders, were seeded, and having been the only one of the four countries to qualify for the finals of the 1966 World Cup in England, were expected to qualify without difficulty. The Irish, in their last encounter with Spain (a World Cup qualifying match) had forced a Paris play-off and approached the first game of the group with confidence. In Dublin a crowd of almost 40,000 urged on the home team in a dour defensive game. Even without Charlie Hurley, the Irish defence were more than a match for the uninspired Spanish attack and the 0-0 draw was the inevitable outcome of an uneventful and boring 90 minutes.

Eire registered an unexpected but, nevertheless, useful 2-1 victory over Turkey in the next game of the group before travelling to Spain for the other leg of their encounter. As expected, the Spaniards cantered to an easy 2-0 victory over the understrength Irish but were still sadly lacking in attacking flair – a point again emphasised when they could only scrape a 0-0 draw in their next game in Turkey.

Heartened by their draw with Spain, the Turks kept themselves on par with Eire by beating them 2-1, just as the Irish had done against Turkey in Dublin three months earlier. By the time that Czechoslovakia played their first game in the group in May 1967, they must have felt quietly confident of outpointing Spain in the group table, as Spain had already dropped a point against both Turkey and Eire. The Czechs' first game was away to Eire and having recently drawn against the World Champions England, at Wembley, they were confident of victory. Ireland fielded virtually a reserve team with several key players unavailable for a variety of reasons and then had the audacity to increase prices for admission. Who could blame the fans if they registered their annoyance in the only way possible by staying away? The meagre 9,000 crowd who braved torrential rain to see the game were treated to one of the poorest internationals ever seen in the Republic. Czechoslovakia scored twice in the first-half to win the game but were, in fact, little better than the inept Irish team they faced. The drenched supporters (that is the few that stayed all 90 minutes) jeered and slow-handclapped the lack of effort with total justification. The result, however, was a good one for Czechoslovakia who in their next game (their first at home) thrashed Turkey 3-0, a goal more than Spain had managed to score against Turkey three weeks earlier.

Almost four months later, Czechoslovakia met Spain in Prague in the real fight for the honours in the group. The game was preceded by an embarrassing incident when a Czech band played the wrong national anthem for the Spanish, choosing instead the old republican national anthem, the Hymno de Riego! In a goalless first-half, the home side did most of the attacking but Viktor came closest to scoring for Spain when his free-kick hit the bar and was smothered on the line by the Czechoslovakian keeper. The only goal of the game came early in the second-half when Horvath, the Czech right centre-back, made an upfield sortie and released a shot from outside of the penalty area that should not have troubled the Spanish goalie who was down in good time to take it. To say that Iribar was down in good time is something of an understatement as his mistimed dive took him underneath the ball which continued into the back of the net!

It needed the combined efforts of Eire's 'keeper Alan Kelly, and right-back Joe Kinnear, to beat out this shot from a Czech forward during their match in Prague.

Spain pressed hard for the remainder of the game but were unable to break down the Czechoslovakian defence. Three weeks later the two countries met again in Madrid and Spain fielded a much-changed forward line including 22-year-old Pirri and two Atletico Madrid strikers Luis and Garate. Pirri put Spain ahead in the first-half and Garate (making his international debut) scored a second 15 minutes after the restart. Although Czechoslovakia came back strongly with a goal by Kuna in the 75th minute, they were unable to level the score but, with two more games to play (Spain's fixtures were completed) knew that they needed just two points to top the group. They duly picked up the first point on 15th November 1967 when they played out a goalless match with Turkey in Istanbul and were confident for their final home game against Eire. The Irish had not played a game since their awful 0-0 draw with Czechoslovakia six months earlier and, at the last minute, found themselves short when their Manchester United pair, Tony Dunne and Shay Brennan, pulled out because of injury.

Ray Treacy the young West Brom player was called up as an obvious replacement but the selectors scratched their heads to find a second at such short notice. Eventually they decided on Turloch O'Connor, a Fulham reserve striker who had that day broken into the Cottagers' first team for the game with Sheffield Wednesday. Thus the Irish, fielding four Football League First Division, four Second Division, one Third Division and two reserve players, lined up to face virtually a full-strength Czech team. Perhaps, if the Czechs had needed both points to qualify they would have been more venturesome and coasted to a comfortable victory, but even with the match goalless at half-time they never felt seriously threatened. A quarter of an hour into the second-half they must have been even more confident when Dempsey (who had already suffered a gashed hand and an injured nose) added to his misfortunes by scoring an own goal. With 25 minutes left to play the Irish broke away and Treacy headed home a Dunphy cross to level the scores. Ten minutes later the Czechs found themselves down to ten men when Szikora was stretchered off. Four minutes from the end, Popluhar, the last of the Czech's 'old guard', was dispossessed by Treacy whose pass O'Connor gratefully converted into a goal. In just five days O'Connor had progressed from Fulham reserve to European Championship matchwinner! The Irish victory was greeted with astonishment throughout Europe and nowhere more so than in Spain whose last-ditch qualification (which was to be repeated with a vengeance in 1983 – more later) was the result.

Group 2 which contained Portugal, the third-placed team from the 1966 World Cup, soon yielded its own share of surprises. The first two games in the group were both played on 13th November 1966, one in Sofia resulted in a predictable 4-2 victory for Bulgaria over Norway whereas the other in Lisbon ended anything but as expected. Portugal had not lost a game at home since England had won by the odd goal in seven back in May 1964 and indeed had won fifteen and drawn two of their previous nineteen games. After an unhappy spell in 1965 and early 1966, the Swedes under the direction of Orvar Bergmark (who had come to the end of a long and distinguished playing career) began their autumn campaign with wins over Norway, Austria and Denmark before travelling to Portugal. Portugal who fielded most of their World Cup squad, including Eusebio, opened the scoring in the twentieth minute through Graca and seemed certain to go further ahead. Inge Danielsson, however, had other ideas and equalised five minutes from the interval with a scorching thirty-yard drive. Danielsson, a Second Division player with Bromolla noted for his powerful shot, rounded off an excellent performance with another goal (the winner) three minutes from the end, and earned himself not only wide acclaim, but also a transfer to Halsinborg soon after! No doubt encouraged by Sweden's fine away win, 49,689 fans turned up to see the return game in Stockholm in June 1967 and saw an equally gritty performance by the Swedes who fought back from 1-0 down at half-time to earn a 1-1 draw.

A week later Portugal beat neighbouring Norway 2-1, thanks to two Eusebio goals and, soon after, Sweden's form evaporated as they went down 2-0 at home to Bulgaria. This left Bulgaria at the head of the table with four points which they increased to five two weeks later in Oslo when they drew 0-0 with Norway. The next two games of the group both featured Norway and Sweden and the first, in Oslo, provided a real shock for the Swedes when, before a crowd of 32,000 Norway turned on a stunning second-half performance to win 3-1. Two months later the Swedes (supported by a mere 14,000) turned the tables on Norway by winning the return-leg 5-2 and, the following week, travelled to Bulgaria for their final game of the group. Bulgaria won the game 3-0 and, on the same day, Portugal narrowly defeated Norway 2-1 thanks to a second-half goal by Graca. This left the real battle for the qualifying place (as originally expected) between Bulgaria and Portugal who had yet to play one another. Two weeks later they met in Sofia with the scales very much in Bulgaria's favour as they had seven points (two more than Portugal) and a far superior goal difference. Portugal therefore needed two victories to be certain of qualifying but Bulgaria secured the tie and the ultimate qualifying place, with the only goal of the game by Dermendijev, midway through the second-half. Three weeks later, the return-leg, played in Lisbon before 20,000 disheartened Portuguese fans, emphasised why Portugal had failed to qualify, as the toothless home attack, struggled unsuccessfully to recover some pride by achieving a resounding victory. The final result, a 0-0 draw, left Bulgaria group winners by four clear points – an over-flattering margin due more to the failure of Sweden and Portugal than to the achievement of the Bulgarians.

Group 3 appeared to be a one-horse race (the hot favourite being Russia) and, by the time that the Russians played their first game, the three other countries, Austria, Finland and Greece, had already been in action and lost points. Austria, however, gave the USSR quite a fright when they met in Moscow on 10th June 1967. Russia were in a confident mood, having played and won two testing friendlies in the previous fortnight (Mexico 2-0 in Leningrad and France 4-2 in Paris) and, at half-time were cruising along 3-1 in the lead. Ten minutes after the restart Austria took control with two goals in three minutes, one by Wolny and a cracker by Siever. The Russian defence looked likely to concede a fourth goal as play swung from end to end, but it was Streltzov who scored, nine minutes from the end, to give the home country a 4-3 victory. Russia continued in high-scoring form registering three successive wins against Greece and Finland (twice) and seemed to be cruising towards qualification with eight out of eight points when they faced Austria again in Vienna. The Austrians, by comparison, had fared rather poorly having picked up only three points from four games and, with just two games remaining, were already out of the hunt for the qualifying place. Having lost 4-1 to Greece two weeks earlier the Austrians knew that they had to redeem their pride with their own fans of whom 37,400 had turned up. Content to earn a 0-0 draw, the Russians put little into their attack and, at half-time, the game was goalless and seemed likely to remain so. Austria, however, had other ideas and Grausam scored the only goal, later in the game to give the home country victory.

When Greece met the USSR in Athens two weeks later, they were still in with a chance of qualification themselves but, having lost 4-0 in Tbilisi three months earlier, could not have been too confident. As against Austria, the USSR defended fiercely and at half-time the game was goalless. In the second-half, Russia's free-scoring winger Chislenko gave his country the lead and Greece, try as they would, could not get back into the game. The USSR therefore progressed to the quarter finals and, in the remaining game in the group, Austria and Greece played for the honour of second-place – Greece earning it by a 1-1 draw.

Group 4 was the only group which had less than four teams and, with World Cup runners-up West Germany matched against Yugoslavia and Albania, West Germany's qualification seemed beyond doubt. The West Germans, playing their first ever European Championship game, trounced Albania 6-0 but then lost 1-0 to Yugoslavia the following month and had to wait a further five nervous months before playing the return leg at home in Hamburg. Billed as the 'Match

Gerd Muller dives to score with a superb header and puts West Germany 2-1 up in their European Championship match with Yugoslavia.

of the Year' the game was played before 72,000 fans at the Volksparkstadion and was televised live, in colour, to millions of other German supporters. Pouring rain did little to dampen the enthusiasm of the home fans and after ten minutes Lohr shot West Germany into the lead with a cracking 18-yard drive. A minute after the restart, Zambata hammered home a Dzajic cross for the equaliser and Yugoslavia took control of the game. In the 71st minute, however, Muller put West Germany back into the lead when his spectacular flying header finished off a Patzke free-kick brilliantly and the home side were back in the driving seat. Uwe Seeler, the West German centre-forward headed a third goal in the 86th minute and, with a final score of 3-1, West Germany looked destined for the quarter finals.

Yugoslavia, who had beaten Albania 2-0 away before facing West Germany, then won the home leg 4-0 and, with a superior goal difference, West Germany only had to win their final game in Albania to be sure of qualifying. Although both Uwe Seeler and Franz Beckenbauer were injured and unable to play, nevertheless, West Germany took a strong team to Tirana which should have disposed of the Albanians without difficulty. Albania, an extreme Communist state, still harboured a deep suspicion that West Germany was a bastion of fascism and were determined to avenge their 6-0 thrashing in Germany. Three weeks earlier, on 22nd November 1967, West Germany had played abysmally when losing 1-0 in Rumania and, facing an eleven-man defence, knew that they would have their work cut out to score many goals. As expected the Albanians played defensively, packing their defence, tackling hard and generally preventing the Germans from settling down. The first-half passed goalless and, realising that 0-0 would not be enough, West German's attacking efforts increased after the interval as they became more and more agitated. Still the goal did not come and although the home side never once looked likely to score, the 0-0 result was greeted by the 21,889 fans present, as if it were a resounding victory. The Albanians' neighbours, Yugoslavia, who were already reconciled to second-place in the group, must have thought that Christmas had come early!

In Group 5 Hungary were the seeded country and they began their fixtures with a 2-2 draw in Holland. Cruyff scored one of the Dutch goals but, in fact, Holland were not yet the force that they were to become and the result was a good one for the home country. Following this result, Hungary then recorded three straight wins over Denmark (twice) and Holland, before meeting East Germany for the first time. The East Germans, by comparison had collected only three points from their previous three games and it was clear that a victory for the Hungarians would guarantee them the qualifying place. A crowd of 72,000 were in the Nepstadium in Budapest to see the Russian referee Bakhramov (the linesman whose decision that Geoff Hurst's 1966 World Cup 'goal' had crossed the line probably won England the Cup) blow his whistle for the kick-off. Hungary turned on one of their best footballing displays since the demise of the 'Mighty Magyars' (Puskas and company) and even the notoriously critical home supporters forgot their usual cynicism and gave the home team a tremendous ovation. Janos Farkas scored all three Hungarian goals and although Frenzel replied for East Germany in the second-half, Hungary's domination of the game was such that even a double-figure score would not have flattered them. Thus, just a year after they had drawn with Holland (the first game in the series), Hungry became the first country to reach the last eight of the competition. Three further fixtures remained in the group but the scores became largely academic, East Germany finally pipping Holland for second-place by beating Hungary 1-0 in the return leg of the tie.

Group 6 featured an on-form Italy, intent on redeeming themselves after a humiliating display against North Korea in the World Cup, together with Cyprus, Rumania and Switzerland. Rumania regarded themselves as potential group-winners and, in the first game of the group, scored an easy 4-2 home victory over Switzerland, before losing 3-1 in Italy. They then beat Cyprus home and away to head the group by the middle of May 1967 and travelled to Switzerland for the return tie. There, Rumanian hopes of qualification were dashed when the Swiss avenged their earlier defeat with a resounding 7-1 victory. This left the way clear for Italy who topped the table themselves after beating Cyprus home and away, and then were held to a 2-2 draw in an excellent game in Switzerland.

Two days before Christmas, Switzerland travelled to Italy knowing that a victory would give them a real chance of qualification as their remaining game was against Cyprus (who had lost all five previous games) whereas, Italy had to travel to Rumania for their final game. Italy, however, were in no mood to relinquish their leading position and scored a thoroughly deserved 4-0 victory which clinched the qualifying spot for them. Cyprus beat Switzerland 2-1 in their final game but, one wonders, would the score have been different if Italy had not already qualified?

Group 7 was a much closer-fought affair with three very evenly-matched countries, France, Belgium and Poland facing one another, with Luxembourg a very uneven fourth. The games between the three stronger countries went, predictably in favour of the home sides at first with France beating Poland, Poland beating Belgium, Belgium beating France and all three beating Luxembourg. Then, in September and October 1967, the balance shifted as first Poland (to France) and then Belgium (to Poland) suffered home defeats and, in the next game France dropped a home point to Belgium. This left matters very finely balanced with both France and Poland on seven points and Belgium on five points. Poland's programme was complete and, as a result of losing a point in Luxembourg, they seemed unlikely to qualify.

Both France and Belgium had one game remaining against Luxembourg. Belgium faced the Grand Duchy first and, winning 3-0, moved level with France and Poland on seven points. France, however, had a superior goal difference to the other two and, in the last game in the group, required only a draw to qualify. All eyes were on Luxembourg could they pull off another shock result as in the earlier series? The game was a much closer contest than predicted and, at the interval France lead by a single goal scored by Loubet. In the second-half Loubet notched up his hat-trick to ensure France's qualification and Klein scored a consolation goal – Luxembourg's only goal of the tournament.

Group 8 meanwhile was also the British Home Championship for 1966/67 and 1967/68 and quickly developed into the sort of two-horse race which had become so familiar – England and Scotland competing for the honours. As reigning World Champions, England were, of course, favourites to qualify and, with comfortable victories over both Northern Ireland and Wales already under their belt, they faced Scotland at Wembley on 15th April 1967. Billed as 'Scotland's World Cup Final', the game attracted such a huge number of Scottish supporters intent on supporting a defeat of the 'Old Enemy', that it became virtually a home fixture for the Scottish team.

England fielded almost their World Cup winning side - Jimmy Greaves for Roger Hunt being the only change from the team that had defeated West Germany in the Final, whereas Scotland, under their new manager Bobby Brown, had a much-changed line-up. In goal 36-year-old Ronnie Simpson, Celtic's veteran goalkeeper, became Scotland's oldest debutant, and a formidable selection of other Celtic and Rangers stalwarts liberally mixed with 'Anglo-Scots' gave Scotland a very threatening look indeed. On the wings Scotland fielded Wallace and Lennox, both of whom were to earn European Cup-winners medals with Celtic five weeks later, and right from the kick-off they showed their ability to move down the line and cross the ball for Dennis Law to worry the English defence. When Jackie Charlton limped off with a broken toe early in the game, England struggled even more to contain the lively Scottish attack and, although he bravely returned to play in the centre-forward position, this, undoubtedly gave Scotland the edge. Dennis Law scored for Scotland in the first-half and England, hampered by a further injury to full-back Wilson, looked to be facing the same sort of four or five goal rout inflicted by them on Scotland in 1961. That they were not heavily defeated was due partly to outstanding personal performances by Alan Ball, Nobby Stiles and Bobby Moore but mainly to the inability of the Scottish defence to exploit their advantage to the full. However, although the injured Jackie Charlton and Geoff Hurst both scored for England, Bobby Lennox and Jim McCalliog (who was making his international debut), gave Scotland the victory, which, on balance, they deserved. This win tilted the scales in favour of Scotland who had only to achieve their usual victories over Wales and Northern Ireland to then require just a single point from their last game against England. However, on 21st October 1967, although England achieved an easy three goal victory over Wales, Scotland were defeated in Belfast for the third consecutive time thanks largely to George Best. In fact, Northern Ireland's victory gave them a mathematical, though not realistic,

Injured England centre-half Jackie Charlton is helped from the field by trainer Harold Shepherdson. Charlton returned and scored one of the England goals.

chance of topping the group, but a month later, a 2-0 defeat at Wembley put paid to their hopes and, with Scotland achieving a 3-2 victory over Wales, all eyes turned to the Hampden Park encounter between the 'Old Enemies'. A victory for Scotland would have given them the qualifying place and backed by the biggest-ever European Championship crowd (134,000), the home side had all the support and enthusiasm necessary to pull it off. Sometimes though, support and enthusiasm are not enough and, yet again, Scotland showed their unpredictability by turning in a less than inspired performance. It was, as so often is the case, a game of 'might-have-beens' for the Scots and, time and again, Chelsea's Charlie Cooke, enjoying perhaps the best international performance of his career, carved openings and created chances which were not seized upon by his team-mates. The final result, a 1-1 draw which secured qualification for the World Champions, flattered the English somewhat but was perhaps a fair reflection of the team's overall performance on the day or rather of Scotland's inability to turn in a coherent team display.

In the quarter-finals England faced Spain, in the first ever clash between reigning World Champions and reigning European Champions and, although they achieved a 1-0 victory at Wembley in the first leg, it was a narrower margin than they would have wished to take to Madrid. A massive crowd of 120,000 turned up at Real Madrid's stadium to cheer on the home country to victory over the World Champions but, at half-time the game was scoreless and the English defence in particular had little trouble in subduing the Spanish. The pattern remained the same in the second-half and, with goals by Martin Peters and Norman Hunter, England had little difficulty in achieving a 2-1 victory to earn themselves a semi-final place.

Italy threw away the first leg of their tie with Bulgaria in Sofia when they conceded a stupid goal and found themselves under pressure when they played the return leg in Naples. Here, 84,000 aggressive Italian fans roared their side on and the Bulgarian players were clearly unsettled by the hostile reception they received. In the 14th minute Italy scored, a cracking shot on the run by Prati, and the pressure was on Bulgaria. In the second-half, Domenghini drilled a thundering shot through the Bulgarian defensive wall after receiving Rivera's free-kick pass and Italy were 2-0 ahead. Although Bulgaria attacked continually for the remaining half-hour of the game, they never looked like breaking down the Italian defence and, with the score unchanged, the host country progressed to the semi-finals.

Yugoslavia, meanwhile, drew 1-1 in Marseille and were clearly not prepared to yield their advantage when France travelled to Belgrade almost three weeks later. After the home side had taken an early lead through Petkovic, the French defence disintegrated in panic and, by the 32nd minute, were 4-0 in arrears and facing an even bigger rout. Di Nallo pulled a goal back for France just before half-time and, in the second-half Yugoslavia eased back (probably saving themselves for the forthcoming finals) but still finished comfortable 5-1 victors.

The fourth quarter-final tie was between Hungary and the USSR and brought back memories of their classic first-round encounter in the 1958/60 series. This time, however, the first-leg was played in Budapest and, winning the game 2-0, Hungary were decidedly in with a chance when they travelled to Moscow a week later. At half-time the Hungarians were trailing by a single goal, an own goal conceded by Solymosi, but, nevertheless, looked capable of holding on to their narrow overall lead. The Russians, though, were determined and, willed on by 103,000 of their countrymen, they kept up the pressure and went on to win with goals by Khurtsilava and Byshovets. Italy was selected as the host country for the Finals, and the semi-finals matched Italy with the USSR in Naples and England with Yugoslavia in Florence.

The first of these games could hardly be described as a classic. Russia, having played an Olympic game against Czechoslovakia only four days earlier were without two key players, Chislenko and Khurtsilava, both of whom were injured in the Olympic game. Had they been present, perhaps the outcome of the semi-final would have been different. However, unlike Bulgaria and so many other teams before them, the USSR were not in the least unsettled by the extremely hostile Naples crowd and had little difficulty in containing the Italian attack for the whole of normal time and 30 minutes' extra-time. The problem for the Russians was, that, minus their two key forwards, they too failed to score in one of the most defensive games ever played in the competition. The solution to the impasse was not a replay or a penalty shoot-out but, highly unsatisfactorily, the toss of a coin! Italy won and the home team progressed somewhat undeservedly to their first European Championship Final.

Meanwhile, in Florence, the World Champions took on the young and enthusiastic Yugoslavians before a paltry 21,834 crowd. England had played West Germany in an international in Hanover just four days earlier, which, although it had been a friendly, was an ill-considered move. Both Geoff Hurst and Nobby Stiles were omitted from the team although available to play and their absence unbalanced the English side. Perhaps England should have taken greater note of Yugoslavia's performance against France than they did, but, it soon became apparent that the World Champions would have their work cut out to defeat the lively Yugoslavians, who seemed intent on intimidating the English team. At half-time the game was goalless but, in the second-half of a brutal and irritable game, England suffered a body blow when Alan Mullery became (unjustly) the first-ever England player to be sent off in an International game. His alleged offence against the Yugoslavian attacker Trivic was compounded by a superb display of acting by the Yugoslav, which convinced the referee of the enormity of a relatively innocent encounter. Down to ten men, England struggled against both a feeling of injustice and the lively Yugoslavian forward line and, in the closing minutes, the Slav's brilliant winger Dragan Dzajic scored the only goal of the match to earn his country their first big final appearance.

Three days later, in Rome, England met the USSR in the third-place match, before a good crowd of 50,000. In perhaps the best game of the finals, a game for once free from the spoiling tactics employed by both Italy and Yugoslavia, England and Russia went about the business of playing football and, in the

Geoff Hurst scores England's second goal in the third-place match in Rome.

process, won themselves many friends. Bobby Charlton, recovering from the groin injury which had hampered him against Yugoslavia, crashed home a Geoff Hurst pass to give England a deserved first-half lead. Hurst, himself, scored another in the second half as England finished in overall third place – their best ever achievement in the European Championship.

The final was played in Rome on 8th June 1968 and the Yugoslav' trainer Mitic fielded the same team that had beaten England, except for the introduction of 19-year-old Acimovic for the injured Osim. Valcareggi, the Italian trainer, was forced to make a number of changes amongst which, the absence of Rivera, in particular, unbalanced the home attack. Despite the partisan support of a large Italian crowd, Yugoslavia took the game by the scruff of the neck right from the kick-off and completely outplayed the home side. Italy's renowned defence was in tatters as, time and again, the Yugoslavian attack literally walked through it! Dzajic in particular ran rings around Burgnich and it was he who opened the scoring in the 40th minute. The score remained 1-0 at half-time but then, although they created countless chances, Yugoslavia were quite unable to get the ball past the acrobatic Zoff in Italy's goal. Nine minutes from the end, the unthinkable happened Italy were awarded a free-kick which was crashed into the back of the net by Domenghini just as the Swiss referee Dienst was ordering the Yugoslavian defensive wall back. To everyone's amazement, not least the Italians, the goal was allowed to stand and the match went into extra-time. No further goals were scored and a replay was arranged for two days later.

Italy introduced five new players including Mazzola and Yugoslavia fielded precisely the same team. In the replay Yugoslavia's non-stop enthusiasm evaporated as sheer tiredness took its toll and only Pantelic in goal could be described as having a good game. After struggling so much in the first game,

Italy were amazed to be given so much space and wasted little time in putting pressure on the Yugoslavian goal. Riva, one of Italy's five changes added tremendous punch to the attack and had a superb shot saved after only 11 minutes. Soon after, Domenghini crossed from the right and Riva put Italy ahead. Then, on the half-hour, Anastasi (who had already missed an easy chance) shot on the turn and made it two. The game then petered out as both sides strolled aimlessly around resigned, it would seem, to an Italian victory. So, with the same 2-0 final score the Italian team redeemed its awful performance in the 1966 World Cup by becoming European Champions but, some would say, without impressing anyone – an unsatisfactory end to an unsatisfactory final series.

The Italian team which beat Yugoslavia in the 1968 Final replay in Rome.
Back row, left to right: Salvadore, Zoff, Riva, Rosato, Guarneri, Facchetti;
Front row, left to right: Anastasi, De Sisti, Domenghini, Mazzola, Burgnich.

1966/68 SERIES

Group 1

Eire 0 Spain 0
Eire 2 Turkey 1
Spain 2 Eire 0
Turkey 0 Spain 0
Turkey 2 Eire 1
Eire 0 Czechoslovakia 2
Spain 2 Turkey 0
Czechoslovakia 3 Turkey 0
Czechoslovakia 1 Spain 0
Spain 2 Czechoslovakia 1
Turkey 0 Czechoslovakia 0
Czechoslovakia 1 Eire 2

	P	W	D	L	F	A	P
Spain	6	3	2	1	6	2	8
Czechoslovakia	6	3	1	2	8	4	7
Eire	6	2	1	3	5	8	5
Turkey	6	1	2	3	3	8	4

Group 2

Portugal 1 Sweden 2
Bulgaria 4 Norway 2
Sweden 1 Portugal 1
Norway 1 Portugal 2
Sweden 0 Bulgaria 2
Norway 0 Bulgaria 0
Norway 3 Sweden 1
Sweden 5 Norway 2
Bulgaria 3 Sweden 0
Portugal 2 Norway 1
Bulgaria 1 Portugal 0
Portugal 0 Bulgaria 0

	P	W	D	L	F	A	P
Bulgaria	6	4	2	0	10	2	10
Portugal	6	2	2	2	6	6	6
Sweden	6	2	1	3	9	12	5
Norway	6	1	1	4	9	14	3

Group 3

Finland 0 Austria 0
Greece 2 Finland 1
Finland 1 Greece 1
USSR 4 Austria 3
USSR 4 Greece 0
USSR 2 Finland 0
Finland 2 USSR 5
Austria 2 Finland 1
Greece 4 Austria 1
Austria 1 USSR 0
Greece 0 USSR 1
USSR 4 Greece 1

	P	W	D	L	F	A	P
USSR	6	5	0	1	16	6	10
Greece	6	2	2	2	8	9	6
Austria	6	2	2	2	8	10	6
Finland	6	0	2	4	5	12	2

Group 4

West Germany 6 Albania 0
Yugoslavia 1 West Germany 0
Albania 0 Yugoslavia 2
West Germany 3 Yugoslavia 1
Yugoslavia 4 Albania 0
Albania 0 West Germany 0

	P	W	D	L	F	A	P
Yugoslavia	4	3	0	1	8	3	6
West Germany	4	2	1	1	9	2	5
Albania	4	0	1	3	0	12	1

Group 5

Holland 2 Hungary 2
Hungary 6 Denmark 0
Holland 2 Denmark 0
East Germany 4 Holland 3
Hungary 2 Holland 1
Denmark 0 Hungary 2
Denmark 1 East Germany 1
Holland 1 East Germany 0
Hungary 3 East Germany 1
Denmark 3 Holland 2
East Germany 3 Denmark 2
East Germany 1 Hungary 0

	P	W	D	L	F	A	P
Hungary	6	4	1	1	15	5	9
East Germany	6	3	1	2	10	10	7
Holland	6	2	1	3	11	11	5
Denmark	6	1	1	4	6	16	3

Group 6

Romania 4 Switzerland 2
Italy 3 Romania 1
Cyprus 1 Romania 5
Cyprus 0 Italy 2
Romania 7 Cyprus 0
Switzerland 7 Romania 1
Italy 5 Cyprus 0
Switzerland 5 Cyprus 0
Switzerland 2 Italy 2
Italy 4 Switzerland 0
Cyprus 2 Switzerland 1
Romania 0 Italy 1

	P	W	D	L	F	A	P
Italy	6	5	1	0	17	3	11
Romania	6	3	0	3	18	14	6
Switzerland	6	2	1	3	17	13	5
Cyprus	6	1	0	5	3	25	2

Group 7

Poland 4 Luxembourg 0
France 2 Poland 1
Belgium 2 France 1
Luxembourg 0 France 3
Luxembourg 0 Poland 0
Luxembourg 0 Belgium 5
Poland 3 Belgium 1
Poland 1 France 4
Belgium 2 Poland 4
France 1 Belgium 1
Belgium 3 Luxembourg 0
France 3 Luxembourg 1

	P	W	D	L	F	A	P
France	6	4	1	1	14	6	9
Belgium	6	3	1	2	14	9	7
Poland	6	3	1	2	13	9	7
Luxembourg	6	0	1	5	1	18	1

Group 8

North'n Ireland 0 England 2
Wales 1 Scotland 1
England 5 Wales 1
Scotland 2 North'n Ireland 1
North'n Ireland 0 Wales 0
England 2 Scotland 3
Wales 0 England 3
North'n Ireland 1 Scotland 0
England 2 North'n Ireland 0
Scotland 3 Wales 2
Scotland 1 England 1
Wales 2 North'n Ireland 0

	P	W	D	L	F	A	P
England	6	4	1	1	15	5	9
Scotland	6	3	2	1	10	8	8
Wales	6	1	2	3	6	12	4
North'n Ireland	6	1	1	4	2	8	3

Quarter-Finals

Bulgaria 3 Italy 2
Italy 2 Bulgaria 0
Hungary 2 USSR 0
USSR 3 Hungary 0
England 1 Spain 0
Spain 1 England 2
France 1 Yugoslavia 0
Yugoslavia 5 France 1

Semi-Finals

Italy 0 USSR 0
(Italy won on the toss of a coin)

Yugoslavia 1 England 0

Third Place Match

England 2 USSR 0

FINAL

Italy 1 Yugoslavia 1

FINAL REPLAY

Italy 2 Yugoslavia 0

4th Series 1970-72

THE 9th WORLD CUP in Mexico had seen the European contingent promising much but achieving little. England, fielding what many had thought a better team than in 1966, were outmanoeuvred by West Germany in the quarter-finals. Italy and West Germany then played themselves to a standstill in a titanic semi-final thriller which left the winners, Italy, decidedly disadvantaged in the Final. A less tiring semi-final might have improved the Italians' performance against Brazil but, realistically, the South Americans were by far the best team.

When the groupings were drawn for the fourth European Championship, the four European World Cup quarter-finalists, England, Italy, U.S.S.R. and West Germany were placed in separate groups and, with 32 nations entering, every group, this time, comprised four countries. The same home-and-away straight knockout basis applied for the quarter-finals as in previous competitions.

Group 1 brought together both Rumania and Czechoslovakia who had faced each other in Group 3 in Mexico and, in perhaps the least attractive of all the groupings, they were joined by Wales and Finland. The first game in the group, and in the tournament itself, brought little Finland to Prague where a disappointing 5,000 crowd turned up to watch what was considered to be a formality a Czechoslovakian victory. However, Czechoslovakian football was in turmoil as a result of the banning of most of the World Cup squad for alleged 'commercial activities' and a month earlier, the Czechs had played abysmally when they lost 3-0 in France. Despite introducing two substitutes, (now allowed for the first time) they could manage only a 1-1 draw. Three days later Finland were in action against the Czechs' near-neighbours, Rumania and this time, thanks to a brilliant performance by Dumitrache, the score went according to the form-books with Rumania winning 3-0. Wales entered the fray a month later when they drew 0-0 at home to Rumania and in their next game, at Swansea, turned out a depleted team and in a disappointing match lost 3-1 to Czechoslovakia, whose 'banned' players were then rehabilitated into the side again.

Wales managed to beat Finland away, thanks to a Toshack goal, but the real competition was between Czechoslovakia and Rumania who met in Prague in the next Group 1 game. Watched by head of state Gustav Husak and either 35,000 or 50,000 Czechoslovakian supporters (official attendance figures for communist countries often vary in accordance with the wishes of the country's propaganda ministry!) the Czechs' attacked the packed Rumanian defence without scoring. In the 75th minute Czechoslovakia were awarded a penalty which was blasted over the bar by Adamec and, as the game looked destined to be a goalless draw, Vesely scrambled the ball over the Rumanian line to give the home side victory.

A month later the Czechs travelled to Finland and this time scored an easy 4-0 victory to put themselves four points clear of Rumania and Wales at the head of the Group. Rumania too went on to beat Finland 4-0 in Helsinki and Wales pushed their points tally up to five with a 3-0 home victory over the Finns. Although this left Czechoslovakia, Rumania and Wales each with two games to play against each other, in fact, Rumania, with both games at home had a distinct advantage over the other two. Wales' chances of qualification evaporated on 27th October when they were only able to field a makeshift side in Czechoslovakia because key players were required for 4th round Football League Cup matches. That they lost only 1-0 testifies to the excellence of their reserves but the defeat ended any Welsh hopes and hoisted Czechoslovakia's points tally to nine. This left Rumania requiring two wins to top the table on goal difference because Czechoslovakia had a goal difference of +8 and Rumania a difference of +6 before the two games. A recorded crowd of 100,000 turned up for the first of the two games, against Czechoslovakia, and the home side were forced to fight every inch of the way before they eventually won 2-1. In the final game in the group, the Welsh were determined to make a match of it and, despite going behind to an early Lupescu goal, threatened to equalise until Lucescu scored later in the second half to ensure Rumania's quarter-final place.

Group 2 featured Bulgaria, France, Hungary and Norway, and, as in Group 1, began on 7th October 1970. Norway were the home country and Hungary, whose team had been restructured over the past year under Jozsef Hoffer, were the opponents in a game which went 3-1 in Hungary's favour. A month later France, too, beat Norway by the same margin at home but when Bulgaria could only draw their home tie with Norway 1-1, the group was beginning to look a two-horse race, Hungary and France. Five months later, the result of the next game, a clash between the two in Budapest, seemed to confirm that billing until three weeks later, when Bulgaria resurrected their chances by soundly beating Hungary 3-0 at home. Bulgaria followed up that victory soon after by a 4-1 win in Norway to lead the table with five points a lead that they retained for several months despite losing 2-0 in Hungary. France, in the meantime had won 3-1 in Norway and, by the time that Hungary travelled to France for their fifth game on 10th October 1971, all three countries, Bulgaria, France and Hungary held five points. Although France as the home country should have had the advantage, Hungary were beginning to strike good form having drawn a friendly in Rio before defeating Bulgaria and they were determined to win in Paris. The new Hungarian coach, Illovszky, seemed able to encourage greater commitment from his players than previous coaches and before the game, the Hungarians' confidence surprised everyone. Quite why the French selected the old Colombes Stadium for this vital tie remains a mystery but, coupled with a metro strike, its selection resulted in a crowd of only 25,000 supporting their team. On an exceptionally warm October afternoon, the Hungarians settled quickly into their game and assumed complete control. Of the French forwards, only Lech looked capable of achieving anything and he didn't seem to know when to part with the ball. After 35 minutes Hungary took the lead with a real gem of a goal. Nosko crossed perfectly from the right to centre-forward Dunai who, realising that his shot would be blocked, hooked the ball over his head for the unmarked Bene to blast the ball past the bemused French defence. Zambo, Hungary's brilliant left-winger was undoubtedly the man of the match as, time and again he ran circles around the French defence and, seven minutes after Bene had scored, he fired in

Bene puts Hungary ahead in a Group 2 game in France.

a scorching acute-angled shot which was deflected past the French keeper Carnus into the net. No further goals were scored in the second-half although both sides had seemingly legitimate penalty appeals turned down and Hungary, worthy winners, moved to the top of the table.

Soon after, Hungary played their last game and achieved an easy 4-0 victory over Norway to place themselves in an almost unassailable position on nine points with a +7 goal difference. This left both France and Bulgaria each needing to beat one another twice in the two remaining ties. France won their home game 2-1 but to top the group required an impossible five-goal victory in the final game in Bulgaria. In the event, Bulgaria won 2-1 and Hungary proceeded to the quarter-finals.

Group 3 seemed on the face of it, an easy group for England with Greece, Malta and Switzerland forming the opposition, but the Swiss got off to a superb start by beating both Greece and Malta away before England were in action. Malta and Greece had already drawn 1-1 in the first game and neither team looked up to the standards of either England or Switzerland. England entered the fray in Malta and had a much easier victory than the 1-0 winning scoreline would suggest and then made short work of Greece at Wembley winning 3-0. Both Switzerland and England then coasted to 5-0 victories over Malta, and Switzerland again defeated Greece before they met England in Basle. As usual the British press had been quick to point out to both the English public and the England team that, despite winning three games out of three, anything other than a victory could result in failure to qualify. Switzerland began confidently and, in the first-half, scored two superb goals through Jeandupeux and Kunzli and were unlucky to miss a third when Kuhn's shot beat Banks but rebounded off the far post. Meanwhile Martin Chivers was causing panic in the Swiss defence and he and Hurst both scored to keep the half-time score level. England had been at full-stretch against the lively Swiss forwards and, but for Bobby Moore who had been implacable at the centre of the defence, would have found themselves well in arrears at the interval. In the second-half the Swiss part-timers tired and let England off the hook as Weibel conceded an own goal to give England an undeserved 3-2 victory. This win left England on top of the table for the very first time ahead of Switzerland on goal difference and the two sides met a month later at Wembley. England were forced to field an understrength team because the Football League Cup was regarded by many clubs as being of more importance than a vital European Championship tie and their makeshift side really struggled against the Swiss. Had Switzerland played as well as they had in Basle they would undoubtedly have won, but, possibly overawed by playing in front of 100,000 people at Wembley, they allowed England too much freedom. They did, however, give the home side quite a fright and Odermatt in particular exposed the inadequacies of the England defence scoring once and causing havoc constantly. Mike Summerbee equalised for England and, with the final score remaining tied at 1-1, England looked certain to qualify for the quarter-finals. Mathematically, if Greece had beaten England by four clear goals in the final game of the group, Switzerland would have qualified but the Greek national side was in the doldrums at that time and England won that last game 2-0 to top the group.

Group 4 promised, and delivered much and featured Cyprus, Northern Ireland, Spain and the USSR. Russia had played well in Mexico, topping Final Group 1 before being kicked from the field by Uruguay in the quarter-finals and Spain, having failed to qualify for Mexico, were out to show that they, too, were a side to be reckoned with. Northern Ireland were not a great side but, with George Best in the team, were capable of achieving great things, although their first game in the group, away to Spain, turned into something of a disaster. Kubala, the Spanish coach fielded a curiously changed team and, on the day, his selection proved sensible as, thanks to a brilliant goal by Pirri and two gifts, Spain scored an easy 3-0 victory. Northern Ireland went on to defeat Cyprus, both home and away but it soon became apparent that the USSR were the team to beat. Spain, having strung together a ten-match unbeaten run, travelled to the Lenin Stadium in Moscow to play what was portrayed as a 'revenge' match for their 1964 Final defeat. Two days earlier the stadium had staged Yashin's testimonial game when a World XI captained by England's Bobby Charlton had participated in a super display of footballing skills and despite the media hype for the Championship tie it turned out to be a very pedestrian affair indeed. Without mid-fielder Pirri, the Spanish side seemed totally lost, as the Russians did whatever they wanted and only good work by their defence saved Spain from a hiding. Goalless at half-time, the game finished 2-1 in favour of the USSR with goals from Kolotov and Schevtschenko. Russia went on to beat Cyprus 6-1 before facing Northern Ireland in their next home game when a crowd of 100,000 turned up to see if George Best was as great as claimed. In the event Oleg

Dolmatov marked Best out of the game and Russia won 1-0, Muntjan sending McFaul the wrong way with a 38th minute penalty. The return game, three weeks later, did not feature Best at all and ended 1-1, effectively ending Northern Ireland's slim hopes of qualifying for the quarter-finals. Two weeks later the USSR travelled to Spain earning a point in a dour goalless game, and, shortly afterwards finished their programme with a 3-1 win in Cyprus. This gave Russia the quarter-final place and Spain still had two games to play, the results of which, a 7-0 victory over Cyprus and a 1-1 draw with Northern Ireland, were largely academic.

Group 5 was made up of Belgium, Denmark, Portugal and Scotland. The Danes began disasterously, losing to each of the other teams without so much as scoring a goal and it was clear that they could be discounted in the reckoning for first place. Belgium then faced Scotland at home and handed out a 3-0 thrashing, thanks to a Van Himst hat-trick and two weeks later their opponents were Portugal but the result was the same, another 3-0 victory. This left Belgium as favourites for qualification and Scotland's appalling away form continued as they lost first to Portugal and then to Denmark. Portugal drew level with Belgium by beating Denmark 5-0 in Oporto, Eusebio and Victor Baptista both turning in magnificent performances and Belgium themselves faced Denmark in Copenhagen in their next game. Shortly before, Belgium had beaten Luxembourg 4-0 in a friendly and, with Portugal now breathing down their necks, required at least a point to retain their advantage. Denmark, however, were now on the brink of a resurgence because they had at last adopted a policy of including their professionals who were playing abroad. For an hour, Denmark gave Belgium as good as they got but two quick goals by Devrint put the visitors comfortably in the lead and, although a late Danish rally earned a goal through defender Bjerre, Belgium won the game 2-1.

Scotland, who found themselves languishing just above Denmark with only two points, were in action later in the year, first against Portugal and, a month later, against Belgium. Under the temporary direction of Tommy Docherty, the Scot's showed much more fire than of late and took the game to Portugal with a solid-tackling, free running performance. Although their victory was secured by a hotly-disputed second goal scored by Gemmill, Scotland deserved both points thoroughly. Belgium were thus ensured ultimate qualification unless they lost both of their remaining games heavily and, when they travelled to Glasgow, a month later, they too found themselves outplayed. Jimmy Johnstone laid on an early goal for O'Hare and then gave the Belgian defence a real roasting for the remainder of the game. The final score remained 1-0 as Scotland regained a little respect after their earlier abysmal performances. The last game in the group took Belgium to Portugal and as a three goal victory was the least that Portugal required, they brought back both Eusebio (who was suffering from a leg injury) and Jose Torres. Portugal came close to scoring when the English referee Ken Burns turned down a penalty appeal in the third minute, but although they put the Belgian goal under constant pressure it was Belgium who took the lead in the 61st minute when Van Himst laid on a fine pass which Lambert put away. Portugal became increasingly desperate but never looked like scoring until a

Belgian defender inexplicably handled a high ball in the area. Peres scored from the spot but the home side were unable to score again and Belgium's point was all they needed to proceed to the quarter-finals.

Group 6 was potentially one of the strongest groups with Austria, Eire, Italy and Sweden contesting the qualifying place. The first game of the group was between Eire and Sweden in Dublin and the Irish, in the midst of a pretty lean spell, were not expected to achieve much. They took the lead in the first-half when Carroll scored from the spot but Brzokoupil equalised for Sweden after the interval and the score remained a respectable 1-1. A fortnight later the two met again in an equally close game in Sweden which Sweden won 1-0 with a second-half goal from Turesson. Italy entered the fray four days later when they travelled to Austria and, having struggled in an international against Switzerland a few weeks before, were wary of an Austrian side little impressed by their reputation as World Cup runners-up. Luigi Riva, Italy's left-winger broke a leg but, nevertheless, Italy won the game 2-1. A month later Italy faced Eire in Florence and opened the scoring early in the game with a De Sisti penalty. De Sisti was the centre-forward often described by the World's press as 'Italy's best full-back' but against the weak Irish team, he was able to concentrate on attack. The final score was 3-0 in Italy's favour and, some six months later, Italy travelled to Dublin for the next game in the group. This time, Eire gave a much better account of themselves as their wingers, Heighway and Conway gave the Italian full-backs the run-around. At half-time the game was tied 1-1 with goals by Conway and Boninsegna but, in the second-half Prati scored for Italy to give them both points. Sweden defeated Austria 1-0 in the next game of the group and, four days later, Austria travelled to Ireland for their third game still pointless, at the bottom of the table. Fielding much the same team that had lost in Stockholm, Austria moved up a gear in Dublin and by half-time, were 3-0 ahead. The final score was 4-1 to Austria who then moved into third place in the group. Italy, having won their first three games, were held to a goalless draw in Sweden but, won the return game 3-0 thanks largely to two goals by Riva (fit again after breaking his leg the year before). This win guaranteed Italy the quarter-final place as Austria had, a month earlier, defeated Sweden 1-0. The two remaining games in the group could not effect the ultimate outcome but Austria emphasised their return to form grabbing second-place with a 6-0 victory over Eire and a 2-2 draw in Italy.

Group 7 was another closely-matched affair with East Germany, Holland and Yugoslavia fighting for the qualifying place and Luxembourg making up the numbers. The group opened with Yugoslavia travelling for a hard-fought game in Holland, at the end of which honours were even at 1-1. East Germany then won against both Holland and Luxembourg and moved into the top position in the group before Yugoslavia showed why they were favourites to top the table, by winning three consecutive games, two of which were away.

This left Yugoslavia a point ahead of East Germany who travelled to Holland for the next game in the group. There, Johann Cruyff showed why he was being hailed as the next Pele, by creating openings for Keizer (2) and Hulshoff to give Holland victory. Holland's success virtually handed the quarter-final place to

Rinus Israel sends Yugoslavia's goalkeeper Curkovic the wrong way to score Holland's equaliser on the 11th October 1970.

Yugoslavia who had only to defeat Luxembourg in Belgrade to be certain of qualification, whatever the outcome of Yugoslavia's next home game against East Germany. Football, however, can be a fickle game as Yugoslavia showed – they drew the first game with East Germany 0-0 to ensure their qualification, but could then only draw 0-0 with Luxembourg, the team that had lost all four previous games! Holland secured second place in the group by defeating Luxembourg 8-0 in their 'away' fixture in Eindhoven – no question this time of a repeat of the 1963 result.

The remaining group, Group 8, should have been a walkover for West Germany who faced Albania, Poland and Turkey, but the Germans were in for a shock when they faced Turkey in their first game. Four days earlier Poland had opened the group games with a 3-0 victory over Albania and the West Germans started their game in Cologne, confident of an easy victory over the Turks. Fielding the same team that had defeated Hungary 3-1 barely a month earlier, West Germany were shocked in the 16th minute when Kamarun put Turkey ahead after a bad mistake by Weber. Gerd Muller, the scorer of ten World Cup goals levelled the scores with a 37th minute penalty but otherwise was marked out of the game. Turkey held on to their point as the score remained 1-1 but, jubilant though the Turks were at the result, it arose because West Germany had, (as against Albania three years before) under-estimated their opposition. The next game saw Turkey defeat Albania 2-1 and this enabled them to assume the top position in the group until West Germany travelled to Albania some ten weeks later. Desperate to avoid a repeat of the result in the previous series, West Germany looked to their goal-ace Muller to earn them a result and, sure enough, his first-half goal was sufficient to earn Germany victory. Two months later, the West Germans travelled to Turkey but, this time they were anything but complacent. Muller put them ahead before the interval and scored again in the second-half as West Germany treated the Turkish crowd to a real display of footballing skills. Koppel scored a third goal as West Germany strolled to a 3-0 victory and moved into a comfortable lead at the head of the group. Poland, however, were on the brink of emerging as a major footballing force and were, realistically, the only country in the group likely to pip West Germany for the quarter-final place. After a 1-1 draw in Albania, Poland went on to thrash Turkey 5-1 before meeting West Germany (who had in the meantime, beaten Albania 2-0 at home). Poland, spurred on by a crowd of 100,000, threatened to annihilate West Germany and only the brilliance of Sepp Maier in the German goal kept them at bay. Gadocha managed to beat him in the 29th minute but the cheers had scarcely died down before Gerd Muller levelled the scores. In the second-half the Poles again stormed on to the attack but the West Germans paced themselves better, held out and won the game with a further Muller goal and a third from Grabowski. This victory by West Germany left Poland with a very hard task on their hands, requiring to win their last two games, both away, in West Germany and Turkey. The first of these and the decider, was the return game against West Germany and this developed into a really dour confrontation. Playing in slippery conditions, neither side seemed to have much to offer in the way of attack and any thoughts of Polish victory petered out long before the end of the game. Despite the fact that they had seen their team qualify for the quarter finals, the 62,000 crowd booed West Germany from the field. The final game in the group took Poland to Turkey who won 1-0 and were thus able to avoid the ignominy of finishing bottom, a position which they occupied at the start of the game because they had lost their previous match in Albania 3-0.

The quarter-final draw brought together England and West Germany, Belgium and Italy, Hungary and Rumania and the USSR and Yugoslavia. The first leg of each tie was played on 29th April 1972 and West Germany travelled to Wembley for the most interesting of the games. Because of a bribery scandal involving a number of Bundesliga clubs, Helmut Schon, the West German coach was unable

Poland goalkeeper Tomaszewski intercepts a West German attack in Poland, with Gerd Muller close at hand.

Gordon Banks dives at the feet of Gerd Muller during the Quarter-Final 1st Leg at Wembley. The Germans went on to win 3-1.

to select several regular players but this seemed to have no adverse effect on West Germany's performance. Right from the kick-off, West Germany took control of the game as Beckenbauer and Netzer completely commanded the midfield. England, as usual, relied on their three central defenders and with Bobby Moore out of position at the heart of the defence, struggled against a West German side seemingly able to mount five-man attacks with impunity. Hoeness put the visitors ahead in the first-half and although Francis Lee pulled a goal back after the interval, two further goals, the first a Netzer penalty (after Moore had fouled Sigi Held) and the second by Muller gave the Germans a well-deserved 3-1 victory. The return leg was played in Berlin's 1936 Olympic Stadium before a crowd of 77,000 and, although England fared a little better with Hunter and Storey able to control much of the midfield play, Beckenbauer once more rose to the occasion and marshalled the West German defence brilliantly. England had a few scrambled chances early in the game but the West German defence was little troubled by their toothless attack. Alf Ramsey brought on two substitutes, Mike Summerbee for Rodney Marsh and Martin Peters for Norman Hunter but neither had any real effect on England's inept display. The final result of a boring game was 0-0 and West Germany, quite justifiably, progressed to the semi-finals.

Perhaps the biggest surprise of the other three ties was Belgium's performance against Italy. Refusing to be intimidated by the partisan Italian crowd, Belgium defended stubbornly to earn a 0-0 draw in the first leg before playing the return at Anderlecht's ground, the Park Astrid. The selection of this smaller stadium was something of a master stroke because the capacity crowd of 38,000 close to the pitch, unsettled the already nervous Italians. Belgium never allowed the World Cup finalists to settle down in a sometimes brutal game, indifferently controlled by the Austrian referee Hans Schiller, which ended disasterously for Van Moer who put Belgium ahead in the 23rd minute. On the stroke of half-time Bertini 'went' for Van Moer and the resulting 'tackle' resulted in a broken leg for the Belgian. In the 71st minute Van Himst put Belgium further ahead and although Riva pulled one back for Italy with a late penalty, Belgium ran out worthy, if somewhat battered, winners.

In the other ties Russia held out for a 0-0 draw in Yugoslavia before overwhelming their opponents at home with an effortless 3-0 victory, while Hungary and Rumania were more closely matched. The first game in Hungary ended 1-1 and the return in Rumania ended in a 2-2 draw, thanks to an 82nd minute equaliser by the Rumanian Neagu. The play-off took place in Belgrade and this too was a closely-fought affair with Hungary the eventual victors thanks to a Szoeke goal just two minutes from the end.

Belgium was selected as the venue for the finals and the pairings were West Germany against the hosts and the U.S.S.R. against Hungary. Belgium had hoped that their fans would cheer them on to victory over the West Germans but, so great was the number of German fans who made the short journey to Antwerp that, with their bugles, klaxons and hunting horns, they all but drowned the cheers of the Belgian crowd. The home side began well enough, containing the German attack for over 20 minutes without difficulty but the unpredictable genius of Gerd Muller then played a decisive part as Netzer floated a seemingly innocuous ball into the box. Piot, the Belgium goalkeeper seemed certain to reach the ball first but Muller, to the keeper's surprise, made an incredible leap and headed the ball into the net while Piot froze in disbelief. Early in the second-half, Belgium put the West German goal under pressure but Maier, kept the home forwards at bay with a series of excellent saves. In the final quarter of the game Muller struck again when, once more, he beat both the Belgian defence and Piot to a Netzer long ball and planted the ball firmly into the Belgium net. Soon afterwards Polleunis reduced the arrears when he hooked a hopeful shot round Schwarzenbeck passed the unsighted Maier but West Germany held on to win the tie 2-1.

The other semi-final was played in front of a pitifully small crowd described variously as 1,000 and 3,500 and provided very little entertainment. Hungary had by far the most of the play but their approach work was so slow and cumbersome that they never even looked likely to score. The first-half was goalless but, in the 52nd minute, Konkov rocketed a shot into the Hungarian net and thereafter the game improved immensely. Eight minutes from the end Albert put Dunai through and, when he was charged off the ball, Hungary were, somewhat luckily awarded a penalty. This award, incredibly posed problems for the Hungarians who were in the middle of something of a penalty crisis having missed one after another in vital club and international games in the previous few weeks and Zambo volunteered to take the kick. Rudakov, the Russian 'keeper dived to his left and pushed the shot away and Szoke, following up, hit the side netting. After this, the Russians snuffed out any further Hungarian attacks and progressed to their third final in four competitions.

Three days later Belgium met Hungary in Liege to play-off for the third-place and the size of the crowd (only 10,000) once more emphasised the futility of such games. Belgium's players seemed intent on provoking the Hungarians as, right from the kick-off, they kicked and elbowed their opponents whenever the opportunity arose. This led to what can only be described as a bad-tempered match which, although won 2-1 by Belgium was of little credit to either team.

The real contest was played the next day in Brussels as West Germany, supported by virtually a German crowd, met the USSR. Once more Gerd Muller proved why he was Europe's leading marksman as, time and again, he penetrated the Russian defence. The West German team, controlled by Netzer and Beckenbauer in both midfield and defence, never allowed the Russians to settle down and seemed able to mount their attacks at will. Twice in the first quarter hour, West Germany broke clear through the Russian defence, only to be denied by Rudakov who performed excellently in the Russian goal. Time and again Rudakov kept the Germans at bay until late in the first-half Muller chested a cross down and slid the ball into the Russian net. West Germany were not renowned for their second-half stamina but, this time, they moved up a gear after the interval and Wimmer, playing excellently in mid-field, took a perfect return pass from Heynckes and rifled a shot into the corner of the net. Still the Germans were not finished and, five minutes later, Muller once more, created space for himself to send Rudakov the wrong way for his second goal. The USSR then practically gave up, as West Germany settled on their three-goal lead waiting for the formality of the final whistle to collect their trophy. Few could have challenged the German's right to the title of 'the best team in Europe' and, two years later they went on to prove themselves the best team in the World by winning the FIFA World Cup.

The USSR and West Germany line up for the 1972 Final in Brussels.

1970/72 Series

Group 1

Czechoslovakia	1	Finland	1
Romania	3	Finland	0
Wales	1	Czechoslovakia	3
Czechoslovakia	1	Romania	0
Finland	0	Wales	1
Finland	0	Czechoslovakia	4
Finland	0	Romania	4
Wales	3	Finland	0
Czechoslovakia	1	Wales	0
Romania	2	Czechoslovakia	1
Romania	2	Wales	0

	P	W	D	L	F	A	P
Romania	6	4	1	1	11	2	9
Czechoslovakia	6	4	1	1	11	4	9
Wales	6	2	1	3	5	6	5
Finland	6	0	1	5	1	16	1

Group 2

Norway	1	Hungary	3
France	3	Norway	1
Bulgaria	1	Norway	1
Hungary	1	France	1
Bulgaria	3	Hungary	0
Norway	1	Bulgaria	4
Norway	1	France	3
Hungary	2	Bulgaria	0
France	0	Hungary	2
Hungary	4	Norway	0
France	2	Bulgaria	1
Bulgaria	2	France	1

	P	W	D	L	F	A	P
Hungary	6	4	1	1	12	5	9
Bulgaria	6	3	1	2	10	8	7
France	6	3	1	2	10	8	7
Norway	6	0	1	5	5	18	1

Group 3

Malta	1	Greece	1
Greece	0	Switzerland	1
Malta	1	Switzerland	2
Malta	0	England	1
England	3	Greece	0
Switzerland	5	Malta	0
England	5	Malta	0
Switzerland	1	Greece	0
Greece	2	Malta	0
Switzerland	2	England	3
England	1	Switzerland	1
Greece	0	England	2

	P	W	D	L	F	A	P
England	6	5	1	0	15	3	11
Switzerland	6	4	1	1	12	5	9
Greece	6	1	1	4	3	8	3
Malta	6	0	1	5	2	16	1

Group 4

Spain	3	North'n Ireland	0
Cyprus	0	North'n Ireland	3
North'n Ireland	5	Cyprus	0
Cyprus	0	Spain	2
USSR	2	Spain	1
USSR	6	Cyprus	1
USSR	1	North'n Ireland	0
North'n Ireland	1	USSR	1
Spain	0	USSR	0
Cyprus	1	USSR	3
Spain	7	Cyprus	0
North'n Ireland	1	Spain	1

	P	W	D	L	F	A	P
USSR	6	4	2	0	13	4	10
Spain	6	3	2	1	14	3	8
North'n Ireland	6	2	2	2	10	6	6
Cyprus	6	0	0	6	2	26	0

Group 5

Denmark	0	Portugal	1
Scotland	1	Denmark	0
Belgium	2	Denmark	0
Belgium	3	Scotland	0
Belgium	3	Portugal	0
Portugal	2	Scotland	0
Portugal	5	Denmark	0
Denmark	1	Belgium	2
Denmark	1	Scotland	0
Scotland	2	Portugal	1
Scotland	1	Belgium	0
Portugal	1	Belgium	1

	P	W	D	L	F	A	P
Belgium	6	4	1	1	11	3	9
Portugal	6	3	1	2	10	6	7
Scotland	6	3	0	3	4	7	6
Denmark	6	1	0	5	2	11	2

Group 6

Eire	1	Sweden	1
Sweden	1	Eire	0
Austria	1	Italy	2
Italy	3	Eire	0
Eire	1	Italy	2
Sweden	1	Austria	0
Eire	1	Austria	4
Sweden	0	Italy	0
Austria	1	Sweden	0
Itall	3	Sweden	0
Austria	6	Eire	0
Italy	2	Austria	2

	P	W	D	L	F	A	P
Italy	6	4	2	0	12	4	10
Austria	6	3	1	2	14	6	7
Sweden	6	2	2	2	3	5	6
Eire	6	0	1	5	3	17	1

Group 7

Holland	1	Yugoslavia	1
East Germany	1	Holland	0
Luxembourg	0	East Germany	5
Holland	6	Luxembourg	0
Yugoslavia	2	Holland	0
East Germany	2	Luxembourg	1
East Germany	1	Yugoslavia	2
Luxembourg	0	Yugoslavia	2
Holland	3	East Germany	2
Yugoslavia	0	East Germany	0
Yugoslavia	0	Luxembourg	0
Luxembourg	0	Holland	8

	P	W	D	L	F	A	P
Yugoslavia	6	3	3	0	7	2	9
Holland	6	3	1	2	18	6	7
East Germany	6	3	1	2	11	6	7
Luxembourg	6	0	1	5	1	23	1

Group 8

Poland	3	Albania	0
West Germany	1	Turkey	1
Turkey	2	Albania	1
Albania	0	West Germany	1
Turkey	0	West Germany	3
Albania	1	Poland	1
West Germany	2	Albania	0
Poland	5	Turkey	1
Poland	1	West Germany	3
Albania	3	Turkey	0
West Germany	0	Poland	0
Turkey	1	Poland	0

	P	W	D	L	F	A	P
West Germany	6	4	2	0	10	2	10
Poland	6	2	2	2	10	6	6
Turkey	6	2	1	3	5	13	3
Albania	6	1	1	4	5	9	3

Quarter-Finals

England	1	West Germany	3
West Germany	0	England	0
Italy	0	Belgium	0
Belgium	2	Italy	1
Hungary	1	Romania	1
Romania	2	Hungary	2
Hungary	2	Romania	1
Yugoslavia	0	USSR	0
USSR	3	Yugoslavia	0

Semi-Finals

West Germany	2	Belgium	1
USSR	1	Hungary	0

Third Place Match

Belgium	2	Hungary	1

FINAL

West Germany	3	USSR	0

THE EUROPEAN CHAMPIONSHIP 1958-1988

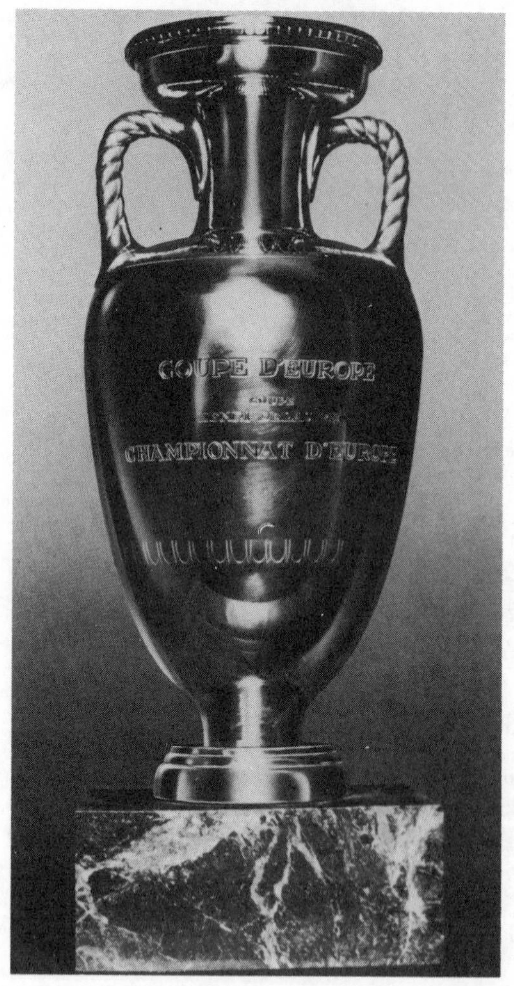

The Henri Delaunay Cup

5th Series 1974-76

EUROPEAN SIDES had fared particularly well in the 1974 World Cup competition with six of the last eight finalists from Europe. The reigning European Champions, West Germany, were also now World Champions and arguably the best team in the world. Holland, were World Cup runners-up and this boosted UEFA's claim that the championship's status was second only to the World Cup.

This claim was emphasised by the fact that Group 1, which was one of the strongest of the eight groups, did not include a single country that had reached the 1974 World Cup Finals. The group featured Czechoslovakia, England and Portugal, all of which were of a similar status, with Cyprus included as the 'no hopers'. England began surprisingly well, when, before a Wembley crowd of 86,000 they hit Czechoslovakia with a second-half goal blast to win 3-0. Now under the managership of Don Revie, England, having failed to qualify for the previous World Cup Finals, were very much on trial and their next game, three weeks later was against Portugal at Wembley. Portugal had been comprehensively beaten 3-0 by Switzerland shortly before and travelled to Wembley intent on achieving a draw. Playing England at their own game, Portugal packed the midfield so well that their twin stoppers, Humberto and Alhinho were only occasionally called upon to break up an English attack, but, so efficiently did they perform, that their goalkeeper Damas only needed to make a couple of saves during the whole match. The final result, a goalless draw, marked the turning point for Portugal who had struggled over the previous couple of years and emphasised, once more, England's inability to break down a determined defence. England were again in action at Wembley in the next game in the group, some five months later, when they faced Cyprus. Shrugging off the draw against Portugal, England were in an ebullient mood having just achieved a thoroughly deserved 2-0 victory over West Germany in their 100th international at Wembley. Although Cyprus could not be described as prime opposition they made a game of it despite losing 5-0 but the tie is best remembered for the fact that 'Supermac', Malcolm Macdonald, scored all five goals.

Four days later on 20th April 1975 Czechoslovakia, too, were in action against Cyprus and they had little difficulty in winning 4-0. Soon after, Portugal were Czechoslovakia's visitors and their revival in fortune suffered something of a setback as the home side strolled to a 5-0 victory. Cyprus continued to struggle, losing first to England (1-0) and then to Portugal (2-0), but the deciding game in the group looked set to be the Czechoslovakia v England clash on 29th October 1975. Don Revie's team were full of confidence, having played nine games without a defeat and, when Mick Channon put them into the lead with a seemingly mishit shot which dipped under the Czech bar, they looked set to collect both points and earn a quarter-final place. Czechoslovakia, however, had other ideas and they moved up a gear to take control of the game and shortly before half-time, levelled the scores. Early in the second-half the Czech's right-winger Masny ran rings round two England defenders before sending over a high cross which Galis headed past Clemence in the English goal. Rarely after that, did England threaten the Czech goal and, clearly rattled by the set-back, England could only watch as Czechoslovakia retained their lead to seriously challenge for the quarter-final place. Two weeks later the Czechs went level with England on seven points, thanks to a 1-1 draw in Portugal, and, a week later, England, too, went to Portugal aware of the fact that they needed to win the game to stand any real chance of finishing in first place. By then, Don Revie's honeymoon with the English press was well and truly over and his team selections and tactical theories were proving to be an increasing embarrassment. England struggled, their attack ran out of ideas and their defence seemed unable to get to grips with the game and, after the 90 minutes were up, they were fortunate to be level 1-1. This result left Czechoslovakia needing two points from their final game in Cyprus which, in view of the fact that Cyprus had failed to score or earn a point in their previous four games, did not seem to be too tall a task. By half-time the Czechs were 3-0 in the lead and threatening a massacre but with both the game and the quarter-final place in the bag, they eased off in the second-half and the score remained the same at the final whistle. Portugal duly defeated Cyprus 1-0 in the final game to finish with a respectable seven points and the knives were out for Don Revie in England.

In Group 2 Wales were matched against Austria, Hungary and Luxembourg and, for once, the Welsh turned in some worthy performances. Firstly they travelled to Austria and played extremely well, taking the lead through Griffiths before going down to two second-half goals. Then they faced Hungary (who had already won 4-2 in Luxembourg) and achieved a well-deserved 2-0 victory thanks to second-half goals from Griffiths and Toshack. Three weeks later they moved to the head of the table with a sparkling 5-0 victory over Luxembourg and retained their lead during the winter break, not being toppled until 2nd April 1975 when Austria, (who had in the meantime defeated Luxembourg), replaced them after drawing 0-0 with Hungary. The Austrians' spell at the top was short-lived because, two

Horvath scores Hungary's first goal in their Group 2 game in Luxembourg

Chris Nicholl of Northern Ireland is beaten to the ball by Sweden's goalkeeper during their 2-1 defeat in Belfast.

weeks later, Wales travelled to play Hungary in Budapest. Enjoying something of an upsurge in their fortunes since the appointment of Mike Smith as their full-time manager, the Welsh held out against early Hungarian pressure and took the lead through John Toshack just before the interval with a close-range shot. In the second-half they went further ahead through Mahoney and, although Hungary pulled a goal back, Wales won the tie 2-1 to move once more to the top of the table.

Two weeks later, Wales moved further ahead with a 3-1 victory in Luxembourg, their fourth consecutive win, and they settled back to await the outcome of further Austrian and Hungarian games. Hungary, by then, were already out of the hunt with only three points secured but Austria on five points still had the potential to overhaul Wales. Lajos Baroti had returned to take control of the Hungarian national team and, in Hungary's 500th full international, and the 120th meeting between the two, the home side were determined to do well. Austria had not won in Budapest for almost 15 years and, within three minutes, were a goal down when the Hungarian left-back Nyilasi opened the scoring. The scoreline ended 2-1 in Hungary's favour so, to take the quarter-final place, Austria faced the prospect of requiring two points from a tough final game in Wrexham. Before then, they had to overcome Luxembourg which they duly did with a 6-2 victory. Hungary then finished their programme with an 8-1 win over Luxembourg which pushed Austria into the third place position when they travelled to meet Wales on 19th November 1975. Wales required just one point to ensure qualification and it was the home crowd's favourite, 34-year-old Arfon Griffiths, the Wrexham striker, who scored the only goal of the match which ensured that Wales became the sole British quarter-finalists.

Group 3 featured Northern Ireland, Norway, Sweden and Yugoslavia and began when the Irish travelled to Norway early in September 1974. The Scandinavians were nearing the end of their league season and, despite trailing 1-0 at half-time, shocked Northern Ireland by storming back to win 2-1.

Yugoslavia were favourites to win the group and they, too, began their programme against Norway but this time, Norway were beaten 3-1 thanks to two second-half goals by Katalinski. Northern Ireland played in Sweden the same day and earned a fine 2-0 victory with goals from Nicholl and O'Neill. These results left the placings evenly balanced and when competition resumed in March 1975 after the winter break, Northern Ireland moved to the head of the group table with a well-deserved 1-0 win over Yugoslavia. Early in June 1975, Yugoslavia travelled to Scandinavia for their games against Sweden and Norway and after winning 2-1 and 3-1 respectively, moved above Northern Ireland with six points. Neighbours, Sweden and Norway then met one another for their two games and Sweden emerged victorious from both, winning 3-1 at home and 2-0 away. Following on from these two wins, the Swedes travelled to Northern Ireland for their next game and despite going behind in the 32nd minute when Allan Hunter scored for the Irish, won comfortably 2-1. This victory put Sweden in with a chance of qualifying for the quarter-finals subject to achieving a good win in their next and last game in Yugoslavia. The Slavs, however, hit peak form against Sweden and put on a really superb display of attacking football which made the Swedish team look very ordinary. Yugoslavia's 3-0 victory ended Sweden's lingering hopes and, all but ended those of Northern Ireland who now required two good victories from their last two games. The first win, over Norway, was duly achieved with a 3-0 scoreline but even this left the Irish needing a victory over Yugoslavia by two clear goals in their last game. In the event, Northern Ireland were totally outplayed by the Yugoslavs who ensured their quarter-final place thanks to an Oblak goal and, only a superb display by Pat Jennings in the Irish goal prevented a much bigger defeat.

Group 4 brought together Denmark, Rumania, Scotland and Spain, and, although they were clear favourites Spain, were made to fight every step of the way. Still smarting from the humiliation of failing to qualify for the 1974 World Cup Finals (because of Yugoslavia) Spain were anxious to excel in the European Championship and began well enough with two away victories, both with a 2-1 scoreline, in Denmark and Scotland. Scotland, typically, having lost at home to Spain, took a first minute lead in the return tie in Valencia and then, for more than an hour, controlled the game so much that their keeper David Harvey was practically a spectator. With luck they could have been four goals up by the 67th minute when Spain scrambled an equaliser but, although the score remained tied at 1-1, Scotland achieved a moral victory and Spain's hopes of an easy passage to the quarter-finals were dashed. Rumania, rightly regarded as one of the least attractive sides in Europe, had drawn their first game in Denmark and, in the next game in the group, they also played out a 1-1 draw in Spain. Amazingly for such a defence-conscious side, Rumania won their next home game over Denmark by a 6-1 margin and were comfortably settled in second place in the group when they met Scotland three weeks later. The official attendance figure of 80,000 probably owed more to propaganda than reality and the game itself was a very drab affair. Rumania took the lead in the first-half and Gordon McQueen equalised for Scotland later in the game. Spain, however, were still the team to beat and Denmark (who had lost to Scotland in September 1975) became their next victims when they lost 2-0 in Spain. This gave Spain eight points from five games and left them requiring just one point from their last game in Rumania, to be sure of reaching the quarter-finals. Scotland had, in the meantime, defeated Denmark 3-1 at home, but their slim hopes, too, rested on a Rumanian victory. In Bucharest Spain seemed to be heading for victory when, with a little over a quarter of an hour left, Rumania trailed 2-0, but, although they pulled back to 2-2, the resulting draw was enough to ensure Spain's quarter-final place. The last game in the group, now a fairly meaningless affair, saw Rumania hold Scotland to a 1-1 draw to pip them for second place in the group.

Group 5 included the World Cup runners-up, Holland, the World Cup third-placed team, Poland, and Italy. As a result, this was perhaps the toughest grouping that the competition had ever seen. Finland made up the numbers and, as expected, fared rather badly against the other three, losing at home firstly to Poland (2-1) and then to Holland (3-1). Poland then beat them again, this time 3-0 and the first decisive clash between the three real contestants took place on 20th November 1974 when Italy travelled to Holland. In only his second game in charge, the new Italian manager, Fulvio Bernardini, introduced a number of younger players and for over an hour it looked as if his gamble would pay off. Italy took an early lead through Boninsegna which Rensenbrink levelled in the 24th minute and the scoreline remained tied until the 65th minute. Holland, cheered on by 62,000 fans, had always looked capable of taking the lead but Italy held out until Cruyff then scored from what seemed to be an offside position. The Russian referee Pavel Kasakov ruled that the goal should stand and the Italians all but went to pieces. Twelve minutes from the end, Cruyff grabbed another goal and Holland went level with Poland at the top of the group table. The next game in the group, some five months later, was played in the Olympic Stadium in Rome when Italy's opponents were Poland. Following numerous crowd disturbances and pitch invasions in Italy, over 4,000 carabinieri were in attendance for the game to ensure that the 90,000 crowd behaved themselves. Sporting their new wonderboy, 21-year-old striker Antognini of Fiorentina, Italy promised much but achieved little and with Poland's goalkeeper Tomaszewski in fine form, never looked like scoring. The resulting goalless draw put Poland clear at the top of the table and there they remained until Holland took over on 20th August 1975 after they had beaten Finland 4-1. Three weeks later Holland travelled to Poland and, there, a crowd of 106,000 saw a remarkable game of football. In an end-to-end game, Poland took the early lead when Lato intercepted a back pass to keeper Van Beveren and scored a simple goal before Gadocha made it two just before the interval. After the restart the Dutch came back strongly but it was Szarmach who scored on the hour to make it 3-0 to Poland. Thirteen minutes from the end, Szarmach was on target again to make the score 4-0 and although Holland pulled a goal back through Rene Van der Kerkhoff, Poland were worthy winners and regained their place at the top of the group. Italy who had managed to notch up a 1-0 win in Finland in June 1975 then disgraced themselves when held by the Finns to a goalless home draw in September. This virtually ended Italy's chances of qualification and all eyes turned to Holland where, following their 4-1 defeat in Poland, the home side were very much on trial for the return game. Cruyff in particular had played awfully in Poland and the Dutch press were on the rampage against him. In the first quarter of the game Cruyff turned on the sort of magic that was expected of him and literally tore the heart out of Poland. Neeskens scored for the home side on the quarter hour and Holland were unlucky not to be further ahead at half-time. In the second-half, first Geels and then Thijssen (who was making his international debut) scored to give the Dutch an impressive victory and to put them, once more, at the head of the group table. Ten days later Poland played Italy in their last game but despite throwing everything into the attack, were unable to penetrate Italy's ten-man defence. The point earned by them virtually gave Holland the quarter-final place as Holland found themselves so far ahead on goal difference that they would have needed to lose their remaining game in Italy by four clear goals. This was a tall order indeed for an Italian team that had only managed to score two goals in their previous five group games and the resulting score (1-0 to Italy) saw Holland through to the next round.

Group 6 had seemed to be an easy ride for the USSR as its three opponents, Eire, Switzerland and Turkey were not exactly formidable challengers but the first game against Eire did not end as expected. Inspired by their player-manager, Johnny Giles, Eire were, for once, able to field their strongest side and the result emphasised what a full-strength Irish squad was capable of. The Queens Park Rangers' forward Don Givens was the Irish hero of the day and he scored all three goals in Eire's 3-0 victory. Three weeks later, the Irish were in action again in Izmir Turkey and freely admitted that they would be more than happy with a draw. Turkey dominated the game right from the kick-off but did not take the lead until Conroy headed into his own net in the 55th minute. Within five minutes Eire were level again when Givens broke out of defence and beat Yasin in the Turkish goal and, with no further score, Eire achieved their objective. Turkey, themselves, were in action in the next game when Switzerland were their visitors and they achieved a notable victory, Mehmet scoring the winning goal, five minutes from the end. After the winter break, Turkey travelled to Russia and were confronted by a Russian side made up of the entire Dynamo Kiev team! The Soviets had taken this unusual step to revive the flagging fortunes of the national side and although it was a successful ploy, the 3-0 winning margin flattered their performance on the day. Undaunted by this defeat, Turkey travelled to Switzerland four weeks later, and came away with a creditable 1-1 draw. Shortly afterwards, the Swiss went to Dublin where a 50,000 crowd turned up to support Eire who were again able to field a strong team. The Irish took an early lead through Manchester United's Martin and Ray Treacy added a second after 30 minutes as Switzerland struggled to stay in the game. In the second-half the Swiss rallied but, although Muller scored in the 75th minute, the Irish ran out 2-1 winners. So it was that Eire were at the top of the table when they travelled to Russia for their next game and, as in the Russian's previous game, the players of Dynamo Kiev were called 'en bloc' to represent their country. Once more the understanding built up as a result of being members of the same club served the Russians in good stead and the Irish were fortunate only to lose the game 2-1. Three days later Eire faced Switzerland in the Wankdorf Stadium in Berne and looked as if they would win a point until, 15 minutes from the end, a goal by the Swiss substitute Elsener, clinched the game for the home side. Several months later the USSR travelled to Switzerland for the next game in the group and once more, Dynamo Kiev provided all but one of the Russian team. Although the Swiss attacked throughout and should have taken both points, the Russians, who seemed to be playing for a draw, broke away late in the game and scored the only goal through Muntjan. Eire beat Turkey 4-0 in their last game and Don Givens was, once more on the mark, scoring all four goals. This result left the USSR one point behind Eire with two games still to play and the first of these was against Switzerland. Again fielding a Dynamo Kiev dominated side and playing in Kiev, the Russians made short work of Switzerland and ran out easy 4-1 winners to clinch their quarter-final place. Although Russia were already sure of the qualifying place a massive crowd of 80,000 turned up to see them when they travelled to Turkey a few days later and the home crowd were, no doubt, delighted to see Turkey win 1-0.

Group 7 brought together Belgium, East Germany, France and Iceland and finished up as the most evenly-matched of all the groups. Iceland, widely regarded as the 'no-hopers', faced Belgium in the first game of the group and were most unfortunate to go down 2-0. In their next game, away to World Cup quarter-finalists East Germany, they again performed well and, to the surprise of everyone, not least the East Germans, earned a point from the resulting 1-1 draw. Belgium met France on the same day and won a close-fought game 2-1 to move to the top of the table and France, themselves, were in action in the next game when East Germany were their visitors. The East Germans, no doubt having taken much criticism after dropping a home point to Iceland, were in a determined mood. A crowd of 35,000 roared the French on, but it was the East Germans who took the lead through Sparwasser in the 25th minute. Twelve minutes after the interval, the Germans went further ahead when Kreische scored his 25th international goal and with ten minutes to play, France looked doomed. In the 81st minute Guillou pulled a goal back and, just on the final whistle, when it looked as if the Germans would hold out, Gallice scored the equaliser. Three weeks later East Germany were at home to group leaders Belgium who came with the sole intention of earning a draw and the tally of corners (11-1 to East Germany) was a fair reflection of the run of play. Piot in the Belgium goal pulled off many spectacular saves and, despite constant East German pressure, the game remained goalless. After the winter break, Iceland were in action again and, in two consecutive home games, proved that their previous performances had been no flukes. Firstly, France were the visitors and, with a little more luck, Iceland could have won the game but eventually had to settle for a 0-0 draw. Then East Germany, victors over their West German neighbours in the World Cup Finals, were the Icelander's guests and the result provided the greatest shock of the competition. Edvaldsson, the Icelandic full-back, who played his football in Denmark, put his country ahead in the 10th minute and, on the half-hour, Sigurvinsson scored a second. So well did the

Icelanders play that they could have been 4-0 up at half-time and, although Pommerenke pulled a goal back early in the second-half, no amount of East German pressure could penetrate Iceland's defence again and they ended worthy 2-1 winners. Three months later Iceland journeyed to France and went down 3-0, a scoreline which flattered the French who had struggled for much of the game. A few days later Iceland met Belgium in their remaining game of the group. Again Iceland played well but were sunk by a Lambert goal just before half-time and Belgium were in action against East Germany three weeks later. After losing to Iceland, East Germany's manager Heorg Buschner gambled on youth and introduced several under 21's into his team which, as a result, played remarkably well. Belgium were without Raoul Lambert, their leading marksman, and, content to play defensively, found themselves 2-1 down with half-an-hour to play. Although the home side then threw everything into attack, keeper Croy kept them at bay until he had to leave the field through injury when his replacement Gtapenthin took over and performed just as well. The 2-1 victory gave East Germany a slender chance of qualifying for the quarter-finals, but they needed to beat France first and then required France to beat Belgium – a tall order indeed! In the event, East Germany won the tie 2-1 but this left Belgium sitting pretty at the head of the table, certain of the quarter-final place subject to avoiding losing the last game in the group (in France) by no more than two goals. France were already doomed to third-place in the group but a large Belgian contingent boosted the crowd to 45,000 when the two neighbours clashed. East German hopes for a French victory soon evaporated as Belgium, by far the better of the two sides pushed the home side on to the defensive. The game, however, remained goalless and Belgium duly took their quarter-final place.

Group 8 featured the World Champions, West Germany, who were matched against Bulgaria, Greece and Malta and began when Greece came back to earn a 3-3 draw in an entertaining game in Bulgaria. Five weeks later, Greece were hosts to West Germany who were now without Gerd Muller and twice they took the lead but were pulled back by the Germans. The 2-2 final scoreline gave an indication that the group was unlikely to be the one-horse race projected and, several weeks later, when West Germany travelled to Malta, this point was emphasised as they struggled before winning 1-0. Greece, in the meantime, had despatched Bulgaria 2-1 in the return tie and were joint group leaders when they travelled to Malta late in February 1975. Boosted by their performance against West Germany, Malta set out to show Greece that they were no pushovers and went ahead in the 32nd minute through their 20-year-old winger Richard Aquilina. Malta continued to control the game and although Greece mounted attack after attack, the home goalkeeper, Gatt, was equal to all that the Greek forwards could muster. Ten minutes from the end, Maxi Magro, put the result beyond doubt when he shot from an impossibly acute angle and beat Konstantinov in the Greek goal to score a second for Malta. The shock result seriously dented Greece's hopes of qualifying for the quarter-finals and, although they moved to the top of the table early in June after beating Malta 4-0 in the return tie (West Germany had only drawn in Bulgaria in the meantime), they required a win in West Germany to stand any realistic chance. West Germany looked anything but World Champions when they faced Greece in the

Yugoslav goalkeeper Enver Maric saves a penalty from Welsh captain Terry Yorath in the 1-1 European Championship draw at Ninian Park.

Rheinstadion, Dusseldorf on 11th October 1975 and were fortunate not to be two goals down when Heynckes put them into the lead in the second-half. Twelve minutes from the end Delikaris equalised for Greece and the point they earned (and richly deserved), left them two points ahead of West Germany who still had home games to play against Bulgaria and Malta. The first of these, five weeks later, was again a scrappy affair with West Germany struggling to regain championship form. Bulgaria, themselves, were only a point behind the Germans with a further game still to play and the pressure was clearly on West Germany. In the second-half Heynckes scored the only goal of the match and West Germany were left requiring only a point against Malta to secure the quarter-final place. Malta lost 2-0 to Bulgaria in December 1975 and were decidedly nervous when they travelled to West Germany two months later for the final game in the group. Their anxiety was soon shown to be justified as West Germany hit them with a goal avalanche and, were four up at the interval. The final score, 8-0 to West Germany, saw them safely through to the quarter-finals, no doubt reflecting upon their good fortune en route.

The quarter-finals brought together neighbours Belgium and Holland, and Czechoslovakia and the USSR plus Yugoslavia against Wales and Spain against West Germany. The tie between Czechoslovakia, conquerors of England, and the USSR quickly put England's performance into perspective as the Czechs won the home leg 2-0 with an impressive performance. The USSR were expected to storm back in the return game but, Moder gave Czechoslovakia a deserved half-time lead and, after Burjak had equalised, scored a second to put the game out of Russia's reach six minutes from time. Blokhin equalised in the 88th minute but the Czechs richly deserved their semi-final place. Champions West Germany had little difficulty in overcoming Spain when, after drawing 1-1 in Madrid, they dominated the second leg to take the tie 3-1 on aggregate and Holland enjoyed an even easier ride against Belgium. Cruyff and Rensenbrink hit tremendous form just at the right time for Holland and, between them they ripped apart Belgium's ultra-defensive lineup.

Rensenbrink scored a superb hat-trick as the Dutch won 5-0 and, when the two sides met in Belgium a month later, Rep and Cruyff were the scorers as Holland cruised to win 7-1 on aggregate. Britain's flag was being flown by Wales and in the first leg in Zagreb, they played only one real forward, John Toshack, concentrating on defence. Still they conceded two goals and, in the return game, found themselves really up against it. Katalinski scored first for Yugoslavia with a well-struck penalty but, although Evans equalised just before the interval, in the second-half the game developed into a dreadfully bad-tempered affair which came close to being abandoned in the 65th minute. Then, several ill-behaved Welsh fans threw beer cans on to the field and the Yugoslavian keeper, Maric, was attacked. The game continued after the troublemakers had been dealt with and the score remained tied at 1-1 to deny Wales a semi-final place. After the final whistle the police were needed to escort the referee from the field, a disgraceful end to a distasteful game. The semi-finals matched Czechoslovakia against Holland and West Germany against Yugoslavia (who were chosen as the host nation for the Finals of the competition) and this quickly lead to speculation that the Final would be a rematch of the previous World Cup Final between West Germany and Holland. First, Czechoslovakia met Holland in Zagreb and the Czechs who brought in an extra defender played with such determination that the elegant Dutch hardly got into the game. Ondrus put Czechoslovakia ahead in the first-half and was then unlucky to deflect a shot into his own net to equalise for Holland. Although the game could not be described as being violent, Pollak for Czechoslovakia and Neeskens and Wim Van Hanegem for Holland were sent off and this gave the Czechs the advantage as the game went into extra-time. Nehoda headed Czechoslovakia into an early extra-time lead and, just before the final whistle Moder made the score 3-1.

The next day Yugoslavia met West Germany in Belgrade and in the first-half, gave such a brilliant account of themselves that they all but annihilated the greatly experienced German defence. Faced with a constant onslaught from the lively Yugoslav forwards, the West German defence was in tatters as, after coming close a number of times, Yugoslavia took the lead. Oblak made a superb run down the left flank and floated a long ball high over the German defence which Popivoda ran on to, holding off Beckenbauer to shoot past Maier. A second came when Maier palmed away a Zungul cross straight to Dzajic who scored from close in but with better finishing, the hosts could have been at least five goals up by the interval. In the second-half the Yugoslavs let West Germany off the hook when they settled back on their two goal lead and, for the first time in the game, allowed their opponents to move onto the attack. The West Germans brought on their substitutes, Heinz Flohe and Dieter Muller and they were soon in the thick of the action as Flohe sent Petrovic the wrong way when his shot cannoned off the chest of Holzenbein into the Slav's net. Muller levelled the scores later in the second-half and, when the game went into extra-time scored two more to give West Germany a victory which at half-time, had seemed an impossibility.

Two days later the hosts faced Holland in Zagreb in the third-place match and the modest crowd of 18,000 were treated to another display of footballing skills. Without Cruyff or Neeskens, who were both suspended, the Dutch set out to win and took the lead through striker Geels early in the game. Willy Van der Kerkhoff scored a second and, just before half-time, when Yugoslavia seemed to have given up the chase, Katalinski pulled one back for the hosts. Yugoslavia took the initiative in the second-half but could not find the form which they had displayed in the semi-final and looked beaten until Jerkovic was fouled on the edge of the Dutch area with a minute left to play. Dzajic chipped the free-kick over the Dutch wall into the net and the game went into extra-time. As play swung from end to end Geels scored his second for Holland and, although the Yugoslavs came close to scoring several times, Holland retained their advantage and claimed third-place.

The following day, the 45,000 crowd at the Final in Belgrade were treated to yet another display of quality football and, unbelievably, as in both Semi-Finals and the Third-Place match, extra-time was required. Czechoslovakia were the first to score after continued pressure, when Svehlik beat Maier and then, the Czechs threatened to run riot as Dobias made it 2-0 when a Masny free-kick was only half cleared by Beckenbauer. Against the run of play, Muller pulled one back for West Germany and the score remained 2-1 at the interval. In the second-half, the pace slackened and the tiring Czechoslovakian defence allowed Holzenbein to head home the equaliser, fouling keeper Viktor in the process. As the game entered extra-time, the Czechs again went on the offensive but, when the final whistle blew, the score was still tied 2-2. Although a penalty-shootout is never a satisfactory way to win a trophy, in the event justice was done. Seven penalties had been on target when Uli Hoeness blazed his kick over the bar and this left Panenka needing to score with his attempt to give Czechoslovakia the title. Maier went the right way and dived a little early if anything, but Panenka's shot, a superb lofted chip, was sufficient to beat any goalkeeper and, at the end of the closest-fought finals since the competition began, Czechoslovakia ran out worthy winners.

The 1976 European Champions from Czechoslovakia - in the shirts of their beaten opponents.

1974/76 Series

Group 1

England	3	Czechoslovakia	0
England	0	Portugal	0
England	5	Cyprus	0
Czechoslovakia	4	Cyprus	0
Czechoslovakia	5	Portugal	0
Cyprus	0	England	1
Cyprus	0	Portugal	2
Czechoslovakia	2	England	1
Portugal	1	Czechoslovakia	1
Portugal	1	England	1
Cyprus	0	Czechoslovakia	3
Portugal	1	Cyprus	0

	P	W	D	L	F	A	P
Czechoslovakia	6	4	1	1	15	5	9
England	6	3	2	1	11	3	8
Portugal	6	2	3	1	5	7	7
Cyprus	6	0	0	6	0	16	0

Group 2

Austria	2	Wales	1
Luxembourg	2	Hungary	4
Wales	2	Hungary	0
Wales	5	Luxembourg	0
Luxembourg	1	Austria	2
Austria	0	Hungary	0
Hungary	1	Wales	2
Luxembourg	1	Wales	3
Hungary	2	Austria	1
Austria	6	Luxembourg	2
Hungary	8	Luxembourg	1
Wales	1	Austria	0

	P	W	D	L	F	A	P
Wales	6	5	0	1	14	4	10
Hungary	6	3	1	2	15	8	7
Austria	6	3	1	2	11	7	7
Luxembourg	6	0	0	6	7	28	0

Group 3

Norway	2	North'n Ireland	1
Yugoslavia	3	Norway	1
Sweden	0	North'n Ireland	2
North'n Ireland	1	Yugoslavia	0
Sweden	1	Yugoslavia	2
Norway	1	Yugoslavia	3
Sweden	3	Norway	1
Norway	0	Sweden	2
North'n Ireland	1	Sweden	2
Yugoslavia	3	Sweden	0
North'n Ireland	3	Norway	0
Yugoslavia	1	North'n Ireland	0

	P	W	D	L	F	A	P
Yugoslavia	6	5	0	1	12	4	10
North'n Ireland	6	3	0	3	8	5	6
Sweden	6	3	0	3	8	9	6
Norway	6	1	0	5	5	15	2

Group 4

Denmark	1	Spain	2
Denmark	0	Romania	0
Scotland	1	Spain	2
Spain	1	Scotland	1
Spain	1	Romania	1
Romania	6	Denmark	1
Romania	1	Scotland	1
Denmark	0	Scotland	1
Spain	2	Denmark	0
Scotland	3	Denmark	1
Romania	2	Spain	2
Scotland	1	Romania	1

	P	W	D	L	F	A	P
Spain	6	3	3	0	10	6	9
Romania	6	1	5	0	11	6	7
Scotland	6	2	3	1	8	6	7
Denmark	6	0	1	5	3	14	1

Group 5

Finland	1	Poland	2
Finland	1	Holland	3
Poland	3	Finland	0
Holland	3	Italy	1
Italy	0	Poland	0
Finland	0	Italy	1
Holland	4	Finland	1
Poland	4	Holland	1
Italy	0	Finland	0
Holland	3	Poland	0
Poland	0	Italy	0
Italy	1	Holland	0

	P	W	D	L	F	A	P
Holland	6	4	0	2	14	8	8
Poland	6	3	2	1	9	5	8
Italy	6	2	3	1	3	3	7
Finland	6	0	1	5	3	13	1

Group 6

Eire	3	USSR	1
Turkey	1	Eire	1
Turkey	2	Switzerland	1
USSR	3	Turkey	0
Switzerland	1	Turkey	1
Eire	2	Switzerland	1
USSR	2	Eire	1
Switzerland	1	Eire	0
Switzerland	0	USSR	1
Eire	4	Turkey	0
USSR	4	Switzerland	1
Turkey	1	USSR	0

	P	W	D	L	F	A	P
USSR	6	4	0	2	10	6	8
Eire	6	3	1	2	11	5	7
Turkey	6	2	2	2	5	10	6
Switzerland	6	1	1	4	5	10	3

Group 7

Iceland	0	Belgium	2
East Germany	1	Iceland	1
Belgium	2	France	1
France	2	East Germany	2
East Germany	0	Belgium	0
Iceland	0	France	0
Iceland	2	East Germany	1
France	3	Iceland	0
Belgium	1	Iceland	0
Belgium	1	East Germany	2
East Germany	2	France	1
France	0	Belgium	0

	P	W	D	L	F	A	P
Belgium	6	3	2	1	6	3	8
East Germany	6	2	3	1	8	7	7
France	6	1	3	2	7	6	5
Iceland	6	1	2	3	3	8	4

Group 8

Bulgaria	3	Greece	3
Greece	2	West Germany	2
Greece	2	Bulgaria	1
Malta	0	West Germany	0
Malta	2	Greece	0
Bulgaria	1	West Germany	1
Greece	4	Malta	0
Bulgaria	5	Malta	0
West Germany	1	Greece	1
West Germany	1	Bulgaria	0
Malta	0	Bulgaria	2
West Germany	8	Malta	0

	P	W	D	L	F	A	P
West Germany	6	3	3	0	14	4	9
Greece	6	2	3	1	12	9	7
Bulgaria	6	2	2	2	12	7	6
Malta	6	1	0	5	2	20	2

Quarter-Finals

Czechoslovakia	2	USSR	0
USSR	2	Czechoslovakia	2
Holland	5	Belgium	0
Belgium	1	Holland	2
Yugoslavia	2	Wales	0
Wales	1	Yugoslavia	1
Spain	1	West Germany	1
West Germany	2	Spain	0

Semi-Finals

Czechoslovakia 3 Holland 1
After Extra Time

West Germany 4 Yugoslavia 2
After Extra Time

Third Place Match

Holland 3 Yugoslavia 2
After Extra Time

FINAL

Czechoslovakia 2 West Germany 2
After Extra Time
(Czechoslovakia won 5-3 on penalties)

6th Series 1978-1980

MAJOR organisational changes were introduced for the 6th series when, for the first time, the host country for the Finals was selected before the commencement of the event. Previously, it had been the policy to choose one of the four semi-finalists as hosts, but because the Finals themselves were also changed to adopt a final grouping system, this was no longer practicable. As in the World Cup Finals, the host country received automatic qualification as one of the eight quarter-finalists who were divided into two final groups of four countries each. The Semi-Final was entirely dispensed with – the winners of each group facing one another in the Final and the runners-up playing-off in the Third Place match instead. Again 32 countries competed in the 6th Series and, because the hosts, Italy, were automatically awarded a final group place, the remaining 31 countries were divided into seven groups. Seven does not divide too well into 31 and, as a consequence, Groups 1, 2 and 4 comprised five countries each and Groups 3, 5, 6 and 7 only four.

Group 1 was a particularly interesting one as, for the first time ever, it brought into International competition the two Irelands, Eire (the Republic of Ireland) and Northern Ireland (Ulster). Although the prospect of such an historic meeting must have intrigued the Irish on both sides of the border, they could not have relished the inclusion of England in their qualifying group! The other two countries in the group were Bulgaria and Denmark and it was the Danes who were Eire's hosts for the first game in the group on 24th May 1978. The Irish surprised Denmark by taking an 11th minute lead through Stapleton and went further ahead in the 25th minute through Grealish before Jensen pulled one back a few minutes later. Daly restored the two-goal margin twenty minutes into the second-half but Denmark stormed back scoring two goals in a minute to tie the game 3-3 and Eire had to be content with one point.

The next game in the group was the historic encounter between Eire and Northern Ireland and a massive crowd of 55,000 turned up to see the fixture in Dublin. Unfortunately, the match itself was an undistinguished affair, as Eire fought tooth and nail to break down the Northern Ireland defensive wall. Northern Ireland held out for a goalless draw and might even have sneaked a winner in the second-half with a little luck. On the same day, England travelled to Copenhagen and by the 23rd minute were two goals ahead through Kevin Keegan, before Denmark hit back with two goals in three minutes to level the scores. Soon after the restart of the second-half, Latchford put England ahead again and Neal made the score 2-4 with five minutes to play. Ruentved made the score 3-4 a minute later but, despite a spirited fight, the Danes were unable to level the scores again. Three weeks later Denmark were in action once more, this time against Bulgaria and they threw away a point when Iliev equalised for the visitors a few minutes from the end. A fortnight later, Denmark travelled to Northern Ireland for their first away game while, on the same day, England travelled to Dublin to face Eire. Once more the Danes gave away a late goal, this time scored by Anderson, and Northern Ireland took the tie 2-1. England,

Northern Ireland goalkeeper Pat Jennings and full-back Sammy Nelson in despair after Tony Woodcock puts England 2-0 ahead in Belfast.

meanwhile took an early lead through Latchford but, after Daly had equalised in the 27th minute, were well held to a 1-1 draw by Eire. Northern Ireland won a surprise 2-0 victory when they travelled to play Bulgaria in Sofia the following month and this put them into the leading place in the group until they travelled to Wembley on 7th February 1979. Then Kevin Keegan turned in one of his best performances for England, when, ably supported by Trevor Brooking, he inspired the resulting 4-0 victory which took England to the top of the table. Three months later, Northern Ireland snatched back the leading position when they defeated Bulgaria 2-0 in Belfast but this victory reinforced England's prospects of qualifying for the quarter-finals as Bulgaria had been seen as their chief rivals for the qualifying place. Eire beat Denmark 2-0 on the same day but England were now in the driving seat and although Bulgaria beat Eire in their next game, (thanks to another late goal) the Bulgaria v England clash was expected to be the key encounter. This took place in Sofia on 6th June 1979 and quickly developed in to a very one-sided affair. Both teams hit the bar in the opening exchanges but it was England who took control after Keegan had scored from a Brooking cross in the 33rd minute. England scored twice more through Watson and Barnes, in the 53rd and 54th minutes respectively and as the game became rougher and rougher, Barnes was substituted seemingly for his own protection after clashing with Grancharov. In the end England could have had several more goals and, the two points earned moved them back into first-place in the group because Northern Ireland, who travelled to Denmark on the same day, were demolished 4-0 thanks to a hat-trick by Elkjaer. England met Denmark at Wembley in the next game in the group and were very fortunate to win 1-0 through a Kevin Keegan goal in the 17th minute. The Danes were unlucky to have three separate penalty appeals turned down but, nevertheless, if their finishing had been better, could have won by two clear goals. England were now in the clear at the head of the table and five weeks later, made certain of the quarter-final place when, on the same day that Eire beat Bulgaria 3-0 in Dublin, they annihilated Northern Ireland 5-1 in Belfast. The four remaining fixtures were duly played and England moved yet further ahead with wins over Bulgaria and Eire while Northern Ireland won the return clash of the Irish with a 1-0 victory in Belfast.

Group 2 featured one country that had reached the 1978 World Cup Finals, Austria, together with Belgium, Norway, Portugal and Scotland. The opening game in the group was played in Norway when Austria were the visitors and they had little difficulty in collecting both points with a 2-0 victory. Three weeks later, Austria were in action again, this time home to Scotland, and a crowd of 70,000 saw them take a three-goal lead when, in the 63rd minute, Kreuz added to goals scored by Pezzey and Schachner. Scotland however, quickly hit back through McQueen and Gray but were unable to prevent Austria moving to the top of the table with four out of four points. Belgium played Norway on the same day and, after falling behind to a Larsen goal early in the game, struggled to level the scores until Cools managed to do so in the 65th minute. Three weeks later Belgium travelled to Portugal and, again, pulled back a goal to earn a 1-1 draw. A fortnight later Norway visited Scotland and began very well by taking a 3rd minute lead which they hung on to until Dalglish equalised on the half-hour. Twenty minutes into the second-half Norway moved ahead again with a goal by Okland and nine minutes from the end Dalglish levelled the scores with his second goal. Three minutes from the end, just when Norway looked as if they would hold out for a point, Scotland were awarded a penalty which Gemmill converted to give Scotland a 3-2 victory. Two weeks later, Portugal met Austria in Vienna and, before a 62,000 crowd, achieved a remarkable victory. The previous meeting in Vienna had been way back in 1953 when Austria had won 9-1 in a qualifying match for the 1954 World Cup and, although the home side did not expect quite such a margin, they did expect to win. Nene put Portugal ahead on the half-hour and Austria equalised through Schachner in the 71st minute

Nene scores for Portugal against Austria in the European Championship match in Vienna, which Portugal won 2-1.

before piling on the pressure for a winner. Right on the final whistle, Alberto, the Benfica full-back, caught the Austrians on the break and scored the winner. Two weeks later Alberto, (who had disgraced himself by being sent off in a UEFA Cup-tie against Borussia Moenchengladbach a few weeks earlier) again scored the winner when Portugal defeated Scotland 1-0 to move to the top of the group throughout the winter break.

The next game in the group took place four months later when Austria travelled to play Belgium in Brussels and they deserved the resulting 1-1 draw which put them joint top with five points. Early in May 1979, the return leg in Vienna finished 0-0 but the point was sufficient to move Austria, briefly, clear of Portugal at the head of the table. A week later Portugal faced Norway in Oslo and although they were very fortunate to win 1-0, thanks to a goal by Alves in the 35th minute, they moved back to the top of the group table. Norway were in action in the next three games in the group and, in the first, Scotland were their visitors when after a bright start Norway faded to let the Scots score an easy 4-0 victory. Austria won the second of the three by the same 4-0 margin but, because they were able to field a stronger team against Belgium in the third game, the Norwegians were most unlucky to go down 2-1. These results left Austria once more at the head of the table but Belgium, who had opened with four consecutive draws, were now coming into contention by registering wins. In their next game Belgium beat Portugal 2-0 to move joint top as the battle for the qualifying place heated up. Austria regained the leading position with a 1-1 draw in Scotland and Portugal grabbed it back by beating Norway 3-1 in their next game. Belgium moved back to the top by beating Scotland 2-0 on 21st November 1979 and, on the same day, Austria completed its programme and in the process dented Portugal's chances, by winning 2-1 in Portugal. These results left Belgium a point clear with one game to play away to Scotland. Portugal also had to play Scotland in their remaining game but needed the Scots to perform well against Belgium first. Scotland's game against Belgium had originally been scheduled February 1979 but was not played until 19th December 1979. Then, Jock Stein's men, having already failed to gain the quarter-final place, were trounced 3-1 by the Belgians who took a 3-0 half-time lead before allowing the Scots back into the game. This result ended Portugal's lingering hopes and the outcome of the last game, a 4-1 score to Scotland, reflected Portugal's loss of interest more than any Scottish resurgence.

In Group 3, Spain were the favourites and, of their three opponents, Cyprus, Rumania and Yugoslavia, the Slavs were regarded as their main challengers. Spain travelled to Yugoslavia for the first match of the group and quickly showed the home side that they meant business by taking a two-goal lead by the 32nd minute. Hodzic pulled a goal back for Yugoslavia just before half-time but the Spanish defence held firm in the second-half to give Spain both points. Three weeks later Yugoslavia travelled to Rumania where they took a 22nd minute lead which they held on to until well into the second-half when, in one quarter hour spell, they were hit for three goals by the Rumanians. They pulled a goal back right on the final whistle but no longer looked serious challengers for the quarter-final place. Spain went on to consolidate their position at the top of the table by beating Rumania 1-0 thanks to a well-taken header by skipper Asensi, in the ninth minute of their next game in Valencia and then went further ahead by beating Cyprus 5-0 in Salamanca. After the winter break Cyprus faced Yugoslavia in Nicosia but posed little threat to the Slavs who ran out easy 3-0 winners. Three days later Spain faced Rumania in Craiova in a rough game which saw five players booked and the Rumanian substitute Crisan and the Spanish full-back San Jose sent off for fighting. The game had originally been scheduled to be played in Bucharest but was switched to the provincial town of Craiova two weeks earlier, presumably as a ploy by the Rumanian manager Kovacs to unsettle the Spanish. Most of the action took place in the second-half and, a few minutes after replacing Lucescu, Crisan was felled by San Jose and Georgescu scored for Rumania from the penalty spot. A minute later mayhem was let loose as San Jose and Crisan scrapped with one another and the Dutch referee, Mr. Van Langenhove, had no hesitation in sending them both off. Spain immediately brought on another full-back in place of an attacker and levelled the score through Dani. Georgescu put Rumania ahead again soon after but, within five minutes, Dani scored his second to give Spain a point. Rumania's slim hopes were dealt a serious blow when they travelled to Limassol the following month and could only manage a 1-1 draw against Cyprus.

The next game in the group was played some five months later on 10th October 1979 when Yugoslavia met Spain in Valencia and, after Surjak had put the Slavs ahead in the 5th minute, the game developed into a very bad-tempered affair. As play progressed, Spain struggled more and more and in the final ten minutes, Yugoslavia were still ahead and the game became very nasty indeed. Two players were sent off in separate incidents (Alesanco for Spain and Primorac for Yugoslavia) and, as the final whistle approached, the game was thrown into pandemonium when a linesman was felled by a missile hurled from the crowd. The score remained 1-0 and within the next few weeks Yugoslavia moved once more into contention by beating first Rumania (2-1) and then Cyprus (5-0) to move to the top of the table. Rumania beat Cyprus 2-0 in their last game in the group but Spain now needed to win the last game in Cyprus to grab the quarter-final place from Yugoslavia. Any doubts about Spain's ability to overcome Cyprus were quickly dispelled as Villar gave the Spaniards an early lead and Santillana scored a second in the 41st minute. Cyprus pulled a goal back midway through the second-half, but never looked seriously capable of causing an upset and Saura scored Spain's third goal a minute from the final whistle to ensure their quarter-final place.

Group 4 contained both the World Cup runners-up Holland, and World Cup quarter-finalists Poland, together with East Germany, Iceland and Switzerland and promised some interesting clashes. Iceland were regarded as the 'rabbits' of the group and proved that billing apt by losing the first three games against Poland (at home) and Holland and East Germany (away). Switzerland, too, were not expected to achieve much and caused Holland little trouble when they faced them in their opening home game which they lost 3-1. This victory put Holland in the clear at the head of the table and, they went further in front by scoring an easy 3-0 win over East Germany in the next match. Poland, however, were determined to show the others that they, too, meant business and, after beating Switzerland 2-0, moved into second place. A further 3-0 victory over Switzerland put Holland four points ahead of Poland who they faced in their next game which took place on 2nd May 1979. Poland had been unfortunate to lose 2-1 in East Germany two weeks earlier and were cheered on by a massive home crowd of 100,000. In steady drizzle, Poland ran at the Dutch from the start and quickly gained the upper hand with an exciting blend of hard, fast, attacking football. Boniek put Poland ahead in the 19th minute and Mazur made it 2-0 with a 64th minute penalty as Holland struggled in vain to get into the game. In the closing minutes the Dutch launched a series of attacks but these came to nothing as Poland finished worthy 2-0 winners. East Germany went level with Poland when they won 2-0 in Switzerland three days later and Switzerland at last notched up some points themselves by beating Iceland home and away in the next two games in the group.

By now the group was clearly a three-horse race and a week later Holland regained their four point lead by beating Iceland 4-0 to move on to eight points. Poland were fortunate to beat Switzerland the same day to share second-place and, two weeks later East Germany travelled to Poland for the crunch game. Grapenthin, East Germany's veteran goalkeeper pulled off a whole series of fine saves to keep his country in the game and after Hafner had scored a breakaway goal in the 61st minute it began to look as if they would take both points. Poland, however, brought on two substitutes and, one of these, Wieczorek, equalised 13 minutes from the end. Two weeks later, Poland moved to the top of the table by beating Iceland 2-0 and, a few days later, East Germany moved onto a similar points total by beating Switzerland 5-2. These results left Holland one point adrift of the other two with a game in hand but, as their first game was against Poland and their second against East Germany, they had a very hard task ahead

Johannes Edvaldson of Iceland in action against Poland.

of them. Poland outplayed Holland for most of the first-half and thoroughly deserved their half-time single-goal lead and it was not until the Dutch boss, Jan Zwartkruis, replaced defender Brandts with an attacker La Ling that Holland's attack came to life and Huub Stevens scored the equaliser in the 64th minute to keep Holland in the chase. The last game in the group was a real cliff-hanger as either of the two participants, East Germany or Holland, could have qualified as a result. Poland were a point clear of the other two but were already out of the reckoning, as any result, draw or win, would push them into second place. East Germany had the advantage of playing at home but Holland needed only a draw whereas East Germany needed a win. Before a Leipzig crowd of 99,000, East Germany took a 17th minute lead through Schnuphase and went further ahead in the 34th minute when Streich converted a dubious penalty, awarded for a foul by Krol on Hafner. Five minutes before the interval, Weiss for East Germany and La Ling for Holland were both sent off for fighting and the consequent disruption upset the East Germans more than Holland, making them lose their command of the game. A minute before half-time Thijssen scored for Holland and, five minutes after the restart, Kist scored the equaliser as Holland took control. A further goal from Rene Van Der Kerkhof in the 67th minute wrapped it up for Holland who progressed to the quarter-finals in Italy.

Group 5 quickly developed into a two-horse race between France and reigning champions Czechoslovakia, despite the fact that Sweden (who had reached the 1978 World Cup Finals) were also in the group. Luxembourg made up the numbers and, although Sweden started well enough by drawing 2-2 in France, they then went down 3-1 to Czechoslovakia at home. As expected France then beat Luxembourg both home and away in the next two games and moved three points clear of Czechoslovakia who they faced in their next game. Although Czechoslovakia had not beaten France for 19 years, they quickly took control of the game in Bratislava on 4th April 1979 but did not manage to score until Panenka's 67th minute penalty shot beat Dropsy in the French goal. Stambachr scored a second, five minutes later and France, despite a belated fight, went down to their first defeat. A few weeks later Czechoslovakia took over the top spot after winning 3-0 in Luxembourg and retained it until France won an easy 3-1 victory in Sweden four months later. Sweden had managed to collect both points when they beat Luxembourg three months before, but, after losing to France, were trounced by Czechoslovakia 4-1 and then, were surprised by Luxembourg who held them to a 1-1 draw in the Scandinavian's last game. Czechoslovakia travelled to Paris on 14th November 1979 already virtually assured of a place in Italy because, whatever the result against France, their remaining game was at home to Luxembourg. France dominated the first-half but failed to find the net in a disappointing game and it was not until the 67th minute that Pecout put them ahead. Rampillon scored a second eight minutes later and although Kozak pulled one back a minute from the end, France, temporarily at least, went to the top of the table. Ten days later, Luxembourg duly made the trip to Prague and the Czechs never contemplated failure as they took control from the start and were three up by the interval. In the second-half it became merely a question of how many the home side would score but, after Vizek had made it 4-0 on the hour, they eased back to save Luxembourg the humiliation of a double-figure defeat.

Group 6 proved to be the most evenly-matched of all and provided some surprising results. The four countries involved were Finland, Greece, Hungary and the USSR and the Finns shocked everyone by beating both Greece (3-0) and Hungary (2-1) in the two opening games. The Soviet Union were expected to grab the qualifying place despite their indifferent international form over the previous two years and they began confidently by beating Greece 2-0. Three weeks later they travelled to Hungary and played defensively intent on achieving a draw. Varadi scored for Hungary in the 26th minute and, after Szokolai had made it 2-0 a quarter of an hour after the restart, the Russians switched on to the attack but could not get back into the game. On the same day that Hungary met Russia, Finland, at the head of the table with four points, travelled to play Greece, who were bottom with none. Mavros who put Greece ahead after 14 minutes had, by half-time, grabbed a hat-trick and Greece were coasting 5-0 in the lead. In the second-half, the rout continued and the 8-1 final score dispelled Finland's brief hopes of glory although they remained at the top of the group table until Greece met Hungary later in the month. Then, the Greek revival continued when, the game which was goalless at half-time, came to life in the second-half. Galakos scored the first on the hour and, with a minute to go, Greece were 4-0 in the lead. Although Martos pulled one back right on the final whistle, it was obvious that Hungary would need to make some changes for the return game in Budapest some six months later. By the time that the game was played, Greece's euphoria at scoring two good wins in the group had evaporated and they had played poorly against both Rumania and Israel in recent internationals. Hungary, on the contrary had recently played well against East Germany and Poland and went into the game intent on grabbing both points. Greece came closest to scoring when Damanakis hit the woodwork in the 25th minute but although Hungary had a goal disallowed for offside, neither team was able to gain the upper hand and the game remained goalless. Russia had only played one game at this stage and were in action in the next three matches in the group. The first of these was played in Tbilisi on 19th May 1979 when Hungary were the opponents. The Russian manager Nikita Simonian fielded an attacking line-up which started well, taking a 23rd minute lead through Chesnokov, but faded after Tatar had equalised ten minutes later. In the second-half Pusztai put the visitors ahead and Hungary looked certain to take both points when the Russian defender Bubnov was sent off in the 72nd minute. Perversely this expulsion lifted the Soviets who equalised through Shengalia, just three minutes later, and, with luck they could have snatched a winner in the closing stages. Russia's next game was away to Finland when Khapsalis put them into the lead after 25 minutes. A quarter of an hour from the final whistle, Ismail Atik (who had recently returned to HJK Helsinki after an unsuccessful six months spell back in his native Turkey) equalised for Finland who moved back to the top of the group table because they had gained five points from four games as against Greece's five points from five games. By the time that the USSR played their next game, away to Greece, Simonian had been replaced as the Russian manager and, after a lively performance against East Germany a week earlier, the Russians were confident of achieving a result. Greece, however, had other ideas and, after taking a 25 minute lead through Nikoloudis, defended successfully for the rest of the game, to grab both points. This result meant that only Finland, who had two games left, could pip Greece for the top place but they lost the first of these 3-1 to Hungary and, when they travelled to the USSR on 31st October 1979 for the last fixture in the group, knew that qualification would be out of the question. Regardless of this, the Finns played extremely well and came back from 2-0 down to earn a point which left Russia languishing at the bottom of the Group 6 table.

Group 7 should have been a walkover for West Germany whose opponents were Malta, Turkey and Wales but, after Wales had stormed to the top of the table by beating Malta 7-0 and Turkey 1-0 in the opening two games, the Germans began very nervously in Valetta. Playing on a sodden pitch against a gale-force wind, the West Germans could be forgiven for their nervousness against no-hopers Malta, but should have played with more authority than they did. The West German goalkeeper, Sepp Maier, playing his 92nd international, was kept busy in the first-half and Malta had two appeals for goals turned down somewhat harshly. In the second-half, West Germany went on to the attack but Sciberras, the Maltese keeper held them at bay and the Germans had to be content with a goalless draw. Just over a month later West Germany travelled to Turkey for their second game and fared little better. Turkey who had beaten Malta 2-1 a fortnight earlier, were forced to defend for much of the game but only looked likely to concede a goal when Zimmermann hit their post in the 11th minute. As the game progressed Turkey moved on to the offensive and they might have snatched a winner when Cemil missed an open goal in the 70th minute but, in the end, were happy to settle for a draw. Leaders Wales played West Germany at Wrexham a month later and were surprised by the uncompromising no-nonsense approach of their visitors. Zimmermann scored from a Manni Kaltz cross on the half-hour and, after Fischer had scored a second soon after the interval the Welsh seemed doomed. Substitute Robbie James came close to scoring for Wales in the 80th minute but they never looked like breaking down the West German defence.

The following month, Wales travelled to Malta and collected both points with goals by Peter Nicholas and Brian Flynn to move two points clear of West Germany at the top of the table. The next game in the group, which was not played until 17th October 1979, took Wales to Köln to play their return fixture against West Germany and the Welsh suffered their heaviest defeat since Mike Smith had taken over as manager. West Germany took complete control right from the kick-off and, by half-time, were 4-0 up and threatening to run riot. Wales held on in the second-half but the 5-1 result was a fair reflection on the run of play. Turkey beat Malta 2-1 in the next game and faced Wales, who were playing their last game in the group, on 21st November 1979. After a first-half in which they came close to scoring several times, Wales were thrown into disarray when Byron Stevenson was sent off in the 69th minute for breaking the cheekbone of Mustapha I. The Turk was replaced by his namesake Mustapha II and Turkey urged on by their now frenzied supporters, scored the only goal of the game through Onal in the 79th minute. This left Turkey at the head of the table with seven points until, a month later, they travelled to Gelsenkirchen to play West Germany. Fischer put the Germans ahead after 16 minutes and the home side totally dominated play winning 2-0 to ensure their quarter-final place in Italy. The one remaining game, West Germany v Malta, was played two months later and the West Germans won 8-0 against a makeshift Maltese side (Malta had initially named 30 players for their squad because they were not sure who could get the time off work to travel to Bremen!).

The eight finalists were split into two groups of four and Group 1 comprised Czechoslovakia, Greece, Holland and West Germany. Both of the opening games in the group were played on 11th June 1980 and were between West Germany and Czechoslovakia in Rome and Holland and Greece in Naples. Except for games featuring Italy, the attendances were, on the whole, very disappointing and only 15,000 turned up to see West Germany take on Czechoslovakia in Rome's massive Olympic Stadium. In the worst tradition of World Cup Finals, the game itself proved an unenterprising start to the final competition and, at half-time, seemed likely to end in a goalless draw. The second-half began little better and it was not until West Germany took the lead through Rummenigge in the 55th minute that the game speeded up as Czechoslovakia took the initiative. The packed West German defence held firm as Panenka and Jurkemik sent in a succession of shots and although the Czech's injured star Masny was brought on later in the game, West Germany held out for both points. Greece, meanwhile, came close to springing a major shock when they outplayed Holland in the first-half of their game in Naples. Ten minutes after the break, the Greek goalkeeper Konstantinou threw away his country's chances by giving away an idiotic penalty, tripping Nanninga when there was absolutely no danger. Kist scored from the spot and Greece were unable to get back onto level terms despite mounting attack after attack.

West Germany faced Holland in Naples in the best attended game in the group when the 50,000 crowd were treated to an excellent display of attacking football. Klaus Allofs was the unlikely West German hero and he opened the scoring on the quarter-hour and went on to net a hat-trick midway through the second-half. As play swung from end to end, the Dutch refused to give up and pulled back to 3-2 through Willy Van Der Kerkhof in the 86th minute. They had, however, left it too late and West Germany moved to the head of the group table with four points. Czechoslovakia defeated Greece 3-1 on the same day and three days later, faced Holland knowing that West Germany were already pretty certain of the place in the Final. Only 11,889 supporters turned up to see the game in Milan's storm-swept Stadio Meazza which soon developed into literally quite a battle. Both Rene Van Der Kerkhof and Dick Nanninga had to be substituted after finding themselves on the wrong end of some harsh Czech tackles after Holland had come close to scoring on numerous occasions. Czechoslovakia opened the scoring in a bizarre manner when the Turkish referee Mr. Ok restarted the game (following Rene Van Der Kerkhof's departure through injury) by dropping the ball at the feet of Krol without a Czech player anywhere near. Nonplussed by this generosity, Krol immediately gave the ball away and the resulting Czech move ended with Nehoda scoring. Kist equalised for Holland on the hour but despite almost continual pressure for the remaining half hour, the Dutch were unable to take the lead and were thus denied second-place in the group.

Belgium players recovering from the effects of tear gas used by Italian police to quell rioting English fans in Turin.

When West Germany lined up to play Greece an hour after the final whistle in Milan, they were already assured of their third consecutive Final place and reorganised their team accordingly, missing out Schuster, Dietz and Allofs to avoid the risk of a second booking and the resulting automatic disqualification from the Final. Greece, however, who had achieved little from their two previous group games, decided to make a game of it and the outcome was quite an enjoyable game of football. Neither side scored but Greece came close on a number of occasions and emerged at least as moral victors.

Group 2 began with a game between England and Belgium in Turin. A meagre 7,000 crowd turned up but, of these, a large number were from the lunatic fringe of English soccer followers. To call these drunken louts 'fans' would be an insult to true fans and their actions that day sowed the seeds of worse excesses which were to follow in later years. The game itself was an uninspired affair and England took the lead in the 32nd minute through Wilkins. Ceulemans scored the equaliser six minutes later and fighting broke out in the crowd when Italians taunted the English. The Italian police, long used to quelling their own domestic soccer riots, quickly dispersed the hoodlums with the use of tear-gas. Play was held up for five minutes as the players fought for their breath, and upon resumption, the game practically fizzled out. Woodcock seemed to have won the game for England in the 73rd minute when he got the ball into the net but his effort was ruled offside and the score remained 1-1. Italy began against Spain in Milan in the wake of a massive domestic bribery scandal which had the Italian fans chanting insults against the home side and their manager. In the light of such a hostile reception, it was hardly surprising that Italy played poorly and against an uninspired Spanish team, were fortunate to earn a goalless draw. Spain took heart at holding Italy in this way and despite going behind in the 17th minute against Belgium, fought back and equalised through Quini in the 35th minute. Belgium came back strongly and, after taking back the lead through Cools twenty minutes into the second-half, threatened to run riot as the Spanish faded. The score remained 2-1 and Belgium moved to the head of the table. England met Italy in Turin on the same day and for most of the opening 45 minutes looked likely to beat the disorganised Italians. Just before half-time, however, Antognoni in the Italian attack, moved up a gear and inspired the sort of penetrative, imaginative attacking play that the home fans had been waiting for. After the interval Italy created numerous good chances but it was not until ten minutes from the end that Tardelli scored the only goal of the match when Graziani beat Neal's imprudent challenge to deliver a simple cross. This result ended England's hopes of a Final place and although they went on to beat Spain 2-1 in their last game, the fight for the first two positions was always going to be between Italy and Belgium who met in Rome later that day. Italy, with a similar goal difference to Belgium, had scored less times and therefore required a win to meet West Germany in the Final but the task proved too great for them. Belgium played Italy at their own game and dished out as many cynical and provocative fouls as the home side. As a result the first-half developed into little short of a bad-tempered brawl which became even worse after the interval when the Italians saw their hopes of glory slipping away. Belgium were never seriously troubled by the lack-lustre Italian attack and could have won the game themselves with a little more effort. The eventual goalless draw ensured Belgium's passage to the Final and Italy's progress to the Third Place match against Czechoslovakia.

Much has been written about the pointlessness of Third-Place matches and, for future series such fixtures were dispensed with. It was unfortunate that this policy was not adopted for the 6th Series as the game between Italy and Czechoslovakia was one of the most tedious of the series. When the final whistle blew after 90 minutes, the game was tied 1-1 and Czechoslovakia won 9-8 on penalties.

The Final was played the next day in the Olympic Stadium in Rome and provided one of the few encounters in Italy that lived up to expectations. Bernd Schuster and Hans-Peter Briegel, 20 and 24 years old respectively, went to Italy, delighted to be in the West German squad, but, in the event, proved to be match-winners. West Germany were first on to the attack and, in only the 4th minute, Pfaff, the Belgium goalkeeper just managed to tip a Muller shot away for a corner. After ten minutes Schuster played a one-two with Allofs before passing the ball to Hrubesch who chested it down before striking a powerful shot into the Belgian net. Belgium struggled to get into the game after going behind and were fortunate to be only a single goal down at the interval. In the first minute of the second-half, Briegel, who had played exceptionally well in the West German midfield, was injured in a collision with Van Der Eychen and left the field for treatment. Three minutes later he hobbled back to resume his place, was immediately felled by Cools, and a few minutes later was substituted by Cullmann. With Briegel out of the game, the German midfield fell apart, their marking disintegrated and for the first time in the match, Belgium grabbed the initiative. In the 71st minute Stielike fouled Van Der Elst on the edge of the area and, although the West Germans argued that the offence had taken place outside the box, a penalty was awarded to Belgium. Van Der Eychen duly equalised from the spot and the game was, once more, wide open. Overcoming his uncertain start after replacing Briegel, Cullmann at last began to get into the game and West Germany deservedly, regained the initiative as play swung from end to end. Then, just as the game seemed to be heading for extra-time, the West Germans took their 11th corner and Hrubesch headed into the Belgium net to break the deadlock. Although the West Germans had left it late, no one could argue that the best team had won on the day and, more importantly, that the Final itself was a victory for the determination and attacking play of West Germany.

Horst Hrubesch is swamped by his team mates after scoring the first of his two goals against Belgium in the Final.

1978/80 Series

Group 1

Denmark	3	Eire	3
Eire	0	North'n Ireland	0
Denmark	3	England	4
Denmark	2	Bulgaria	2
Eire	1	England	1
North'n Ireland	2	Denmark	1
Bulgaria	0	North'n Ireland	2
England	4	North'n Ireland	0
Eire	2	Denmark	0
North'n Ireland	2	Bulgaria	0
Bulgaria	1	Eire	0
Bulgaria	0	England	3
Denmark	4	North'n Ireland	0
England	1	Denmark	0
Eire	3	Bulgaria	0
North'n Ireland	1	England	5
Bulgaria	3	Denmark	0
England	2	Bulgaria	0
North'n Ireland	1	Eire	0
England	2	Eire	0

	P	W	D	L	F	A	P
England	8	7	1	0	22	5	15
North'n Ireland	8	4	1	3	8	14	9
Eire	8	2	3	3	9	8	7
Bulgaria	8	2	1	5	6	14	5
Denmark	8	1	2	5	13	17	4

Group 2

Norway	0	Austria	2
Belgium	1	Norway	1
Austria	3	Scotland	2
Portugal	1	Belgium	1
Scotland	3	Norway	2
Austria	1	Portugal	2
Portugal	1	Scotland	0
Scotland	1	Belgium	3
Belgium	1	Austria	1
Austria	0	Belgium	0
Norway	0	Portugal	1
Norway	0	Scotland	4
Austria	4	Norway	0
Norway	1	Belgium	2
Belgium	2	Portugal	0
Scotland	1	Austria	1
Portugal	3	Norway	1
Belgium	2	Scotland	0
Portugal	1	Austria	0
Scotland	4	Portugal	1

	P	W	D	L	F	A	P
Belgium	8	4	4	0	12	5	12
Austria	8	4	3	1	14	7	11
Portugal	8	4	1	3	10	11	9
Scotland	8	3	1	4	15	13	7
Norway	8	0	1	7	5	20	1

Group 3

Yugoslavia	1	Spain	2
Romania	3	Yugoslavia	2
Spain	1	Romania	0
Spain	5	Cyprus	0
Cyprus	0	Yugoslavia	3
Romania	2	Spain	2
Cyprus	1	Romania	1
Spain	0	Yugoslavia	1
Yugoslavia	2	Romania	1
Yugoslavia	5	Cyprus	0
Romania	2	Cyprus	0
Cyprus	1	Spain	3

	P	W	D	L	F	A	P
Spain	6	4	1	1	13	5	9
Yugoslavia	6	4	0	2	14	6	8
Romania	6	2	2	2	9	8	6
Cyprus	6	0	1	5	2	19	1

Group 4

Iceland	0	Poland	2
Holland	3	Iceland	0
East Germany	3	Iceland	1
Switzerland	1	Holland	3
Holland	3	East Germany	0
Poland	2	Switzerland	0
Holland	3	Switzerland	0
East Germany	2	Poland	1
Poland	2	Holland	0
Switzerland	0	East Germany	2
Switzerland	2	Iceland	0
Iceland	1	Switzerland	2
Iceland	0	Holland	4
Iceland	0	East Germany	3
Switzerland	0	Poland	2
Poland	1	East Germany	1
Poland	2	Iceland	0
East Germany	5	Switzerland	2
Holland	1	Poland	1
East Germany	2	Holland	3

	P	W	D	L	F	A	P
Holland	8	6	1	1	20	6	13
Poland	8	5	2	1	13	4	12
East Germany	8	5	1	2	17	10	11
Switzerland	8	2	0	6	7	18	4
Iceland	8	0	0	8	2	21	0

Group 5

France	2	Sweden	2
Sweden	1	Czechoslovakia	3
Luxembourg	1	France	3
France	3	Luxembourg	0
Czechoslovakia	2	France	0
Luxembourg	0	Czechoslovakia	3
Sweden	3	Luxembourg	0
Sweden	1	France	3
Czechoslovakia	4	Sweden	1
Luxembourg	1	Sweden	1
France	2	Czechoslovakia	1
Czechoslovakia	4	Luxembourg	0

	P	W	D	L	F	A	P
Czechoslovakia	6	5	0	1	17	4	10
France	6	4	1	1	13	7	9
Sweden	6	1	2	3	9	13	4
Luxembourg	6	0	1	5	2	17	1

Group 6

Finland	3	Greece	0
Finland	2	Hungary	1
USSR	2	Greece	0
Hungary	2	USSR	0
Greece	8	Finland	1
Greece	4	Hungary	1
Hungary	0	Greece	0
USSR	2	Hungary	2
Finland	1	USSR	1
Greece	1	USSR	0
Hungary	3	Finland	1
USSR	2	Finland	2

	P	W	D	L	F	A	P
Greece	6	3	1	2	13	7	7
Hungary	6	2	2	2	9	9	6
Finland	6	2	2	2	10	15	6
USSR	6	1	3	2	7	8	5

Group 7

Wales	7	Malta	0
Wales	1	Turkey	0
Malta	0	West Germany	0
Turkey	2	Malta	1
Turkey	0	West Germany	0
Wales	0	West Germany	2
Malta	0	Wales	2
West Germany	5	Wales	1
Malta	1	Turkey	2
Turkey	1	Wales	0
West Germany	2	Turkey	0
West Germany	8	Malta	0

	P	W	D	L	F	A	P
West Germany	6	4	2	0	17	1	10
Turkey	6	3	1	2	5	5	7
Wales	6	3	0	3	11	8	6
Malta	6	0	1	5	2	21	1

Final Group 1

West Germany	1	Czechoslovakia	0
Holland	1	Greece	0
West Germany	3	Holland	2
Czechoslovakia	3	Greece	1
Czechoslovakia	1	Holland	1
West Germany	0	Greece	0

	P	W	D	L	F	A	P
West Germany	3	2	1	0	4	2	5
Czechoslovakia	3	1	1	1	4	3	3
Holland	3	1	1	1	4	4	3
Greece	3	0	1	2	1	4	1

Final Group 2

Belgium	1	England	1
Spain	0	Italy	0
Spain	1	Belgium	2
Italy	1	England	0
Spain	1	England	2
Italy	0	Belgium	0

	P	W	D	L	F	A	P
Belgium	3	1	2	0	3	2	4
Italy	3	1	2	0	1	0	4
England	3	1	1	1	3	3	3
Spain	3	0	1	2	2	4	1

Third Place Match

Czechoslovakia	1	Italy	1

Czechoslovakia won 9-8 on penalties

FINAL

West Germany	2	Belgium	1

7th Series 1982-1984

FURTHER alterations were made in the structure of the 7th Series Finals bringing them into line with changes in the World Cup Finals. By popular demand, straight knockout semi-final games were reintroduced for the top two countries from each final group and the third-place match was entirely dispensed with. France as hosts for the Finals automatically qualified and consequently the other 32 entrants were split into seven qualifying groups, three of four countries and four of five countries.

Group 1 comprised Belgium, East Germany, Scotland and Switzerland and commenced with a visit by Switzerland to Belgium. The Swiss full-back Ludi conceded an own goal in only the 2nd minute and his team never recovered from this early setback. Belgium dominated the play and went further ahead soon after the restart when the Swiss defence were again caught napping. Van Den Bergh scored a third in the closing stages and Belgium were on their way to another successful series. Scotland too (for a change), began well by beating East Germany with two second-half goals but then reverted to their usual European Championship form losing first to Switzerland and then to Belgium in successive games. These results left Belgium clear at the top of the table and several months later, on 30th March 1983, they travelled to Leipzig for a testing game against East Germany. Belgium took a first-half lead through West Ham's Francois Van Der Elst and narrowly avoided conceding two goals before Vandenbergh put them further ahead with twenty minutes to play. Streich pulled one back for East Germany seven minutes from the end but Belgium held on to both points to move further ahead at the top of the table. On the same day, Scotland faced Switzerland at Hampden and after trailing 2-0 fought back in the last 20 minutes to earn a draw. A month later Belgium met East Germany in Brussels and after going behind to an early Streich goal, stormed back to win 2-1 and, in the process, virtually guaranteed their trip to France for the Finals. Only Switzerland was mathematically able to score more points and when East Germany drew 0-0 in Switzerland two weeks later, their slim chances all but evaporated. It was five months before the next games in the group were played and, as Belgium made absolutely sure of the quarter-final place by drawing 1-1 in Scotland, East Germany were thrashing Switzerland 3-0. In the two remaining games, Switzerland beat Belgium 3-1 to grab second place and East Germany overcame Scotland 2-1 to leave the Scots at the foot of the table.

Group 2 brought together Finland, Poland, Portugal and the USSR and began when Poland travelled to Finland. After taking a 3-0 lead, the Poles almost let it slip when Finland scored twice within a minute, five minutes from the end. Portugal were Finland's visitors two weeks later and had little difficulty in winning 2-0 to move above Poland in the table. Poland then travelled to Portugal in the next game and were so shocked by a Nene goal in only the second minute, that they never got into their stride. Gomes scored a second in the 81st minute and, although Poland mounted a late offensive and pulled one back a minute from time, they had left it too late to prevent Portugal from opening a two-point gap at the top of the table. The USSR entered the fray three days later and scored a predictable 2-0 victory over Finland. The next game, some six months later, on 17th April 1983, saw Poland take a 2nd minute lead against Finland which to everyone's surprise was almost immediately levelled when Janas the Polish full-back, deflected a wayward Finnish shot into his own net. After such good fortune, the Finnish goalkeeper Isoaho was equal to the best that the Poles could offer and Finland snatched a deserved point. Two weeks later, Russia signalled its intention of gaining the qualifying place by hammering Portugal 5-0, but a few weeks later, struggled against the jeers and whistles of a hostile Polish crowd and were lucky to obtain a point with a 1-1 draw. The USSR were again less than impressive, when they struggled against Finland in Helsinki a little over a week later. With luck the Finns might have been two goals ahead before half-time but were unfortunate to go down 1-0 to a Blokhin goal in the last quarter of an hour. Portugal closed the gap on Russia by beating Finland 5-0 in their next game, almost four months later and, after Russia had beaten Poland 2-0 in their next fixture, became the only country still in a position to challenge the Soviets for top-place. They travelled to Poland for their next game on 28th October 1983 and must have been surprised by the ease with which they overcame the home side. Poland rarely threatened the Portuguese and the nearest that they came to scoring during the whole match was when Portugal's full-back Inacio mishit a backpass which was cleared off the line by his team-mate Eurico! Carlos Manuel scored Portugal's winner in the 31st minute and the stage was set for a thrilling last game in the group when the USSR travelled to Lisbon two weeks later. Portugal began confidently, no doubt encouraged by their fine performance against Poland and Dassayev in the Soviet goal kept Russia in the game with a sparkling first-half performance. In the 44th minute, however, Borovsky brought down Chalana right on the edge of the Russian box and Portugal were awarded a penalty, much to the consternation of the Russians who argued that the challenge was outside their area. Be that as it may, Jordao scored from the spot and this turned out to be the only goal of the game. Russia, despite protests about the manner in which they went down, could hardly argue that they had deserved to win and, indeed, Portugal might have scored four more goals. Portugal thus qualified for the Finals of a major competition for the first time since the 1966 World Cup in England and, on balance, richly deserved their victory.

Group 3 was made up of Denmark, England, Greece, Hungary and Luxembourg and began when England travelled to Copenhagen to play Denmark on 22nd September 1982. Denmark were no longer the pushovers that they had been in earlier years and although England took an early lead through Francis, they were never able to dominate play and were pinned back for long periods of the game. The Danes equalised via an Allen Hansen penalty midway through the second-half but looked doomed to defeat when Francis scored a second for England ten minutes from the end. In the last minute after a spell of furious activity around the England goalmouth, Olsen scored a much-deserved equaliser and Denmark claimed a share of the points. Luxembourg were not expected to achieve anything in the group and opened with two home defeats at the hands of Greece and Denmark before travelling to Wembley in December. England had, in the meantime, defeated Greece 3-0 in Salonika (new manager Bobby Robson's first

Lars Bastrup harries Bryan Robson during England's 2-2 draw in Copenhagen.

victory) and were determined to knock up a high score to improve their chances of reaching the Finals. Luther Blissett, making his first full appearance for England (he appeared as a substitute against West Germany) equalled Fred Pickering's 1964 record of scoring a debut hat-trick and England dominated the game to win 9-0. The next game in the group was not played until the end of March 1983 when Hungary won 6-2 in Luxembourg and, three days later, England faced Greece at Wembley. After winning 3-0 in Greece, England were expected to achieve an easy victory but the Greeks, encouraged by a large emigree Greek contingent in the crowd, held firm against the best that England's forwards could offer. The match remained goalless and the crowd's constant jeering of 'what a load of rubbish' later in the second-half was well justified. Ten days after Hungary had defeated Luxembourg 6-2 in Budapest, they too travelled to Wembley to play England. After a good opening spell when they could have taken a 2-0 lead but didn't, Hungary fell back on the defensive and, on the half-hour, went behind to a Trevor Francis header. Hungary's attempts to get back into the game were sunk when Withe scored a second in the 70th minute and England had no difficulty in taking the two points to move further ahead at the top of the table. Denmark had only played two games to England's five but were in action the same day in Copenhagen when they earned a 1-0 victory over Greece to move into second place in the group. Hungary suffered a shock home defeat at the hands of the Greeks and travelled to Copenhagen two weeks later to try to redeem themselves against Denmark. Denmark, however, were in no mood to allow Hungary to get in their way and ran out easy 3-1 winners to establish themselves as the only serious challenger to England in the Group.

Denmark travelled to Wembley on 21st September 1983 for the key game in the group, knowing that defeat would probably end their challenge for a place in

France. A fortnight earlier, they had played a friendly against France and achieved a sparkling 3-1 victory to give them confidence for the game against England. In the opening minute at Wembley, Michael Laudrup came close to scoring and clearly underlined Denmark's intention to win the game. Playing a brand of flowing possession football, Denmark dictated the play throughout and, in comparison, England looked a poor side indeed. Yet it was all decided by a penalty when, in the 39th minute, Phil Neal handled a Laudrup cross and Simonsen scored the only goal for Denmark to put his country into the leading position in the group for the first time. Three weeks later, both countries were in action again and although England scored a good 3-0 victory in Hungary, Denmark hammered Luxembourg 6-0 to retain the top-spot. A fortnight later Denmark faltered in Hungary losing 1-0 but, with only one game left to play, remained a point clear of England at the head of the table. Both countries played their last game on 16th November 1983 and Denmark's task was far stiffer than England's because their opponents, Greece, posed a far greater threat than England's opponents, Luxembourg. England duly won 4-0 but Denmark ensured that they took the place in the Finals by running out 2-0 winners in Athens. In the two remaining games in the group, Greece drew with Hungary and defeated Luxembourg to grab third-place.

Group 4 comprised Bulgaria, Norway, Wales and Yugoslavia and began when Wales managed to overcome Norway but only thanks to an own goal by Nygard. Three weeks later, Norway put in a sparkling performance to achieve a shock 3-1 victory over the group favourites, Yugoslavia and, a fortnight later showed that it had been no fluke by drawing 2-2 in Bulgaria. Yugoslavia beat Bulgaria 1-0 in Sofia and, as Wales lined up to face Yugoslavia in Titograd a month later, the group was headed by Norway and looked to be wide open.

The result of this game, a 4-4 draw, emphasised the fact that Yugoslavia would not be the certainties predicted and moved Wales to the top of the table where they remained for some time. In September 1983 Bulgaria picked up their first win with a 2-1 victory in Norway and, a fortnight later, Wales travelled to Norway and were well held to a goalless draw by the home side. Soon afterwards, Yugoslavia moved into second-place by beating Norway 2-1 in Belgrade and, when Bulgaria scored a tight 1-0 victory over Wales a month later, the group was still wide open. On 14th December 1983 Wales met Yugoslavia in Cardiff for their final game knowing that a victory would guarantee them the quarter-final place. Once again, Wales slipped up when they allowed Bazdarevic to equalise ten minutes from the end after leading through a Robbie James goal in the 54th minute. Although Yugoslavia were the best team, Wales would have had the game sewn up by half-time if they had taken their numerous goalscoring chances in the first-half. When Bulgaria travelled to Split to play Yugoslavia four days before Christmas, both sides were in a position to snatch the top place from Wales. Yugoslavia needed a win by two clear goals and the game developed into quite a tussle. Yugoslavia who had missed several easy chances went behind in the 28th minute but Susic levelled the scores on the half-hour and scored a second seven minutes into the second-half. Dimitrov equalised for Bulgaria with half an hour left and both sides pressed for the winner in the closing stages of a dramatic match. Right on the final whistle when almost a minute of injury-time had been played, the Yugoslav defender Radanovic headed the winning goal and snatched the quarter-final place from Wales!

Group 5 was made up of Cyprus, Czechoslovakia, Italy, Rumania and Sweden and, of these, Italy, the reigning World Champions, were expected to grab the place in France. In fact, for once, the draw for the European Championship was made before the 1982 World Cup Finals and, indeed, even the matches in Group 5 began before the World Cup in Spain when Cyprus travelled to Rumania on 1st May 1982. Rumania scored an easy 3-1 victory over Cyprus and went on to defeat Sweden 2-0 in their next game to move to the head of the table. A month later, Sweden travelled to Czechoslovakia and, after being two goals behind for most of the second-half, scored twice in the last two minutes to grab a point. Czechoslovakia, themselves, had to fight back in Milan during their next game against Italy when Chaloupka scored the equaliser for them in the 72nd minute. Cyprus were unlucky to lose 1-0 to Sweden in the next game in the group but delighted their fans when they took the lead against Italy three weeks later. Italy had only managed a goalless draw against Rumania in their previous game and were clearly rattled by Mavri's goal early in the second-half. They were probably not relishing their trip to meet the Italian peacekeeping force in Beirut the following day and were relieved when Patikis conceded an own goal ten minutes later to put Italy level. Although the score remained 1-1, Cyprus were unfortunate to miss several more chances and thoroughly deserved their point. A month later Cyprus surprised the Czechs too, as they attacked straight from the kick-off and forced keeper Zdenek Hruska to make a series of saves before going ahead in the 21st minute through Theophanous. Czechoslovakia came back in the second-half and equalised in the 59th minute but were unable to grab a winner despite late pressure. Italy's indifferent form continued in Bucharest when Rumania scored their first-ever victory over 'the Azzurri' while a changed Czechoslovakian side cruised to a 6-0 home win over Cyprus to move into second-place. Sweden, too, moved into contention by beating Cyprus 5-0 on the same day that Rumania faced Czechoslovakia in Bucharest. Rumania dominated most of that game but it was Czechoslovakia who scored the only goal, a 40th minute disputed penalty. This result left it very close at the top of the group with both Czechoslovakia and Rumania on seven points from five games and, a fortnight later, Sweden beat Italy 2-0 to move on to precisely the same games and points total. Soon afterwards, Sweden faced Rumania in Stockholm and the Rumanians played ultra-defensively after taking a lucky lead in the 29th minute when Catamaru pounced on a misdirected clearance. This was the first goal that Sweden had conceded in four games, but, although they were unable to break through Rumania's massed defence to get back into the game, they beat Czechoslovakia 1-0 in their next game and moved to the top of the table on goal difference. The Swedes last game in the group was against Italy in Naples and they inflicted Italy's worst home defeat in a representative international game since 1955 when winning 3-0 and, in the process, moved two points clear at the top of the table. Rumania beat Cyprus 1-0 in Limassol in their next game to move onto a similar points total and, when Czechoslovakia beat Italy 2-0 four days later, they moved within two points of Sweden and Rumania. The deciding game of the group was fought out two weeks later when Rumania met

Czechoslovakia in Bratislava. In a tight match, Rumania took the lead in the 63rd minute but, after Czechoslovakia had equalised five minutes from the end, the Czechs threw everyone, including goalkeeper Hruska, into the attack in a desperate final fling to win the game. Rumania held firm and took the qualifying place with twelve points.

Group 6 was expected to be an easy one for reigning champions and World Cup runners-up West Germany, yet it proved to be anything but. Albania, Austria, Northern Ireland and Turkey formed the opposition and it was Austria who made the early running by beating Albania 5-0 in their opening match before beating Northern Ireland 2-0 in their second game. After Turkey had scored a narrow victory over Albania with a goal in the closing minutes, Northern Ireland met West Germany in Belfast. The West Germans came close to scoring when Littbarski headed wide in the 2nd minute but the determination of the Irish was asserted and, after coming close several times, Stewart put them ahead in the 18th minute. West Germany never got to grips with the heavy conditions and pouring rain and Northern Ireland had little difficulty in becoming only the second European country to beat them in four years.

Austria beat Turkey 4-0 on the same day and moved four points clear at the top of the table. Playing the same team that beat West Germany 1-0, Northern Ireland were lucky to avoid defeat at the hands of Albania in their next game when they struggled to a goalless draw in Tirana but, with three points, maintained their second place in the group.

After the winter break, Northern Ireland had little difficulty in disposing of Turkey, despite the 2-1 scoreline and, on the same day, West Germany picked up their first points with a 2-1 win in Albania. The following month, the Germans were in action again when they beat Turkey 3-0 in Izmir and, only four days later, faced group leaders Austria in Vienna. In a disappointing game, both sides missed easy chances and had goals disallowed by the Scottish referee Mr. McGinlay. The match remained goalless and West Germany moved into contention for the quarter-final place at last. Northern Ireland met Albania the same day and moved level with Austria on seven points with a 1-0 victory. Albania next earned a point by drawing 1-1 with Turkey in Tirana but, three weeks later, went down 2-1 to Austria who moved two points clear of Northern Ireland from the same number of games. Austria were Northern Ireland's opponents in the next game in the group three months later on 21st September 1983. The Northern Ireland goalkeeper, Pat Jennings, was playing his 100th international game that day, but, such was Northern Ireland's superiority, that he had little to do. Martin O'Neill played his best game ever in the Irish midfield and after Billy Hamilton had opened the scoring in the first-half, Norman Whiteside scored his first international goal twenty minutes after the break, to make it 2-0. Felix Gasselich pulled one back for Austria in the 82nd minute but O'Neill capped his brilliant performance by scoring a third with a minute to go. This 3-1 victory moved Northern Ireland level with Austria on nine points and rekindled Irish hopes of qualification for France although, West Germany, with four games remaining, was still a serious threat. A fortnight later, Austria found just how serious a threat the Germans were when, after only 21 minutes of their game in

Gelsenkirchen, they were 3-0 down to their German neighbours. West Germany eased off for the rest of the game but Austria never looked like getting back into the match and the score remained 3-0. A week later, Turkey pulled off a surprise 1-0 victory over Northern Ireland in Ankara (only their second win in 18 internationals) but a little over a week later, reverted to their normal form when losing 5-1 against West Germany in Berlin. This victory put West Germany level with both Northern Ireland and Austria but with a game in hand over their rivals and a superior goal difference. Three weeks later, Austria's hopes of qualification were shattered when they were defeated 3-1 in Turkey and, on the same day, Northern Ireland played West Germany in their last game and achieved a remarkable result. West Germany had not been defeated at home by a European nation since losing 1-0 to their East German brothers nine years before but the Irish were not overawed by this. Thanks to a brilliant display by Pat Jennings the game was goalless at half-time and when Schumacher failed to hold an Ian Stewart shot five minutes after the interval, Norman Whiteside slid the ball home to put the Irish ahead. The West German pressure in the closing stages was intense but the Irish held on to claim both points. Ironically, West Germany were still favourites to win the group but to do so required a victory over Albania in their last game four days later. Thoughts of an easy West German victory were soon dispelled as the resilient Albanian defence held firm and the visitors even took a 23rd minute lead through Tomori. Rummenigge equalised with a deflected shot within a minute but the West Germans were made to struggle by the Albanian's tenacious tackling and resolute defending. Despite having scorer Tomori sent off for a foul on Voller, the Albanians held firm until the West German full-back, Strack, headed the winner with just ten minutes to play, as the reigning champions came through to deny Northern Ireland a place in France.

Group 7 between Eire, Holland, Iceland, Malta and Spain provided an even closer final game which astounded the whole of the world's footballing community and prompted suggestions of game-fixing. It began on 5th June 1982 when Malta defeated Iceland 2-1 at home and quickly provided a surprise when Iceland held Holland to a 1-1 draw in the next game. Three weeks later, Holland took a first-minute lead against Eire and dominated the game, winning 2-1 but, soon after, Eire picked up their first two points by defeating Iceland 2-0. Spain entered the fray a fortnight later when they struggled to beat Iceland 1-0 and, three weeks later, faced Eire in Dublin. The Irish got off to a good start when Ashley Grimes put them ahead in only the 2nd minute but Spain hit back and, on the hour, were 3-1 up before Frank Stapleton grabbed two goals as the Irish stormed back to earn a point. Malta were banned from playing their next game against Holland at home and had intended to switch it to Southern Italy or Sicily instead. Holland, however, offered the Maltese FA £20,000 to move the game north and, always short of funds, the Maltese switched the tie to Aachen in West Germany. The outcome of the match was never in doubt and the 6-0 winning scoreline concealed the fact that the Maltese goalkeeper John Benello played brilliantly making half-a-dozen superb saves. Holland were at the top of the table with five points when they travelled to Seville to play Spain two months later and, fielding six defenders, they were intent on earning a draw. The game was evenly-balanced throughout and it needed a penalty by Senor to break the deadlock for Spain in the 43rd minute. No further goals were scored and Spain moved level with Holland on five points. Eire moved on to a similar points tally by beating Malta 1-0 thanks to a Stapleton goal in the final minute but, a month later went down 2-0 in Zaragoza as Spain moved clear at the top of the table.

Spain were greatly annoyed that Malta had played their home fixture against Holland in Aachen and protested to UEFA that either they should be given a similar advantage or that the previous result should be declared void. Their protest was rejected but when they saw the new Ta'Qali pitch which was little better than the previous awful surfaces that had precipitated the original ban, they were rightly annoyed at the apparent injustice. However, they overcame their annoyance and after being 2-1 down came back to win 3-2 and moved four points clear of Holland. Two weeks later, Spain further increased their lead at the top of the group by winning 1-0 in Iceland and the following week, Iceland themselves scored their first win by beating Malta 1-0.

Holland moved back into contention beating Iceland 3-0 at home and Eire 3-2 in Dublin, and Eire, who had won a comfortable 3-0 victory in Iceland three weeks earlier, were no longer in with a chance of winning the group. It then became a two-horse race between Holland and Spain and on 16th November 1983, as Eire routed Malta 8-0 in Dublin, Spain faced Holland in Rotterdam. In a tight game Holland took the lead in the 26th minute through Houtman but Spain equalised four minutes before half-time. Rudd Gullit scored the winner in the 63rd minute and Holland moved into first place on goal difference. This left both Holland and Spain on the same number of points with each having a home tie against Malta to play. Holland played Malta first and achieved a respectable 5-0 victory which seemed to virtually guarantee their trip to France because of a far superior goal difference. When Spain faced Malta four days later they needed to win by 11 clear goals to displace Holland in the finals and, as Spain had only scraped a 3-2 victory in the first game, this seemed an impossibility. Indeed, Spain had not scored even as many as five goals since 1978 and the Dutch remained quietly confident of their top-spot. Malta were offended when they turned up for a training session the night before only to find themselves locked out of the unlit stadium, and they allowed this affront to destroy their confidence. They started nervously and conceded a penalty in the 3rd minute but Senor missed his spot-kick and it was not until the 16th minute that Santillana scored the first for Spain. Digiorgio equalised eight minutes later but within five minutes Santillana had scored twice more to complete his hat-trick. At half-time the score was still 3-1 but Rincon scored a fourth two minutes into the second-half despite goalkeeper Bonello's protests that he had been showered with missiles by the Spanish crowd. Bonello's annoyance rose and, soon after, he was booked for time-wasting as he allowed his anger to get the better of him. Then the whole of the Maltese defence lost heart at the way the game was going and conceded four goals in a terrible seven-minute spell. With 13 minutes remaining Spain were still three goals short of their target when Digiorgio, who had been booked for time-wasting in the opening minutes, was sent off for taking too long over a throw-in. This had a devastating effect on the Maltese morale, just as they were getting back into the game and Spain scored three more in the closing period to win the game 12-1. Ironically, Senor who had missed the early penalty, scored the twelfth of these with just four minutes remaining. Spain were through to the finals and although eyebrows were raised and UEFA studied a videotape of the match, the result was allowed to stand.

In the finals France, the host country, were in Group 1 together with Belgium, Denmark and Yugoslavia while, in Group 2 Portugal, Rumania, Spain and West Germany were the contenders. The opening game was played at the Parc des Princes in Paris on 12th June 1984 when France lined up against Denmark. A splendid crowd of 47,750 packed into the stadium and, unlike the previous series, the Finals began with a really thrilling game as both sides played a delightful blend of open attacking football. The first-half provided an exciting mixture of bustling attack and over-enthusiastic tackling which should have been stamped on by the German referee Herr Roth and, in the 43rd minute, this culminated in an unfortunate incident. Leroux lunged at Simonsen in the midfield and he went down with a crack that reverberated around the ground and lay frantically signalling for assistance. For over a minute Simonsen's pleas for help were ignored by the referee and it was only when the Danes had kicked the ball into touch that he was able to receive attention for a badly broken leg. In the second-half the French gained the upperhand and, after missing a number of chances, went ahead 13 minutes from the end when Platini, the European Footballer of the Year, blasted the ball past Qvist in the Danish goal. Jesper Olsen was immediately brought on as substitute to add fire to the attack and, three minutes from the end, he was involved in an unsavoury incident with the French defender Amoros. Olsen fouled Amoros who responded firstly by throwing the ball at him and, when this missed, by head-butting him to the ground. Needless to say, Amoros was sent-off and subsequently suspended for the next three games, but France held on to their one goal advantage for the remaining three minutes.

In the second game, Belgium, who were without no fewer than four of their regular defenders, were fortunate to have 18-year-old Enzo Scifo in their team and his delightful midfield artistry won them the game against Yugoslavia. Vandenbergh scored Belgium's first goal in the 27th minute then, just on the stroke of half-time, Georges Grun, who was making his international debut, headed a second. After the break, Yugoslavia struggled in vain to get back into the game but the score remained 2-0 in Belgium's favour. France were in action against Belgium in Nantes two days later when a crowd of 51,287 saw them take an early lead through Platini. Fielding a more attacking line-up, the French pressured the suspect Belgian defence and were 3-0 ahead by half-time. In the second-half, France threatened to run riot as they completely overwhelmed Belgium but it was not until the 74th minute that Platini scored his second and France's fourth goal with a well struck penalty. Two minutes from the end, Platini completed his hat-trick and, went clear of Just Fontaine's record of scoring 27 international goals for France which he had equalled with his goal in the opening game. The fourth game in the group took place the same day, in Lyon, when Denmark and Yugoslavia were involved in one of the most thrilling internationals ever seen. The final score, 5-0 to Denmark, belies the splendid performance put up by the Slavs and a 12-7 final result would have been a fairer reflection on the play. Ivkovic, the Yugoslav goalkeeper pushed the ball into his own net to put Denmark ahead in only the 7th minute and the Danish stopper Berggren made it 2-0 a few minutes later but the Slavs refused to give up. Susic in particular could have scored several times in the first-half and a number of his team-mates also threw away good chances as play swung from end to end. After the break, Yugoslavia kept up the pressure on the Danish goal but it was Denmark who got the goals and they hoisted the scoreline to 5-0. Michel Platini returned to his former home ground, the Stade Geoffroy-Guichard at St. Etienne for France's next game against Yugoslavia three days later. As France were already assured of a semi-final place and Yugoslavia were certain of elimination, the game was played in a rather more relaxed atmosphere than previous ties but this probably added to the standard of football on display. Yugoslavia took the lead through Sestic on the half-hour but France seemed to sense that they would pull back and refused to be panicked by the deficit. A quarter of an hour into the second-half Platini moved up a gear and, in a 17 minute spell scored another brilliant hat-trick to give France the lead. Yugoslavia pulled a goal back with an 80th minute penalty but were unable to level the scores. The game was marred by the death of the Yugoslavian team doctor Bozhidar Milenovic who collapsed on the touch-line early in the second-half. The other game in the group was played the same day in Strasbourg when Denmark played Belgium for the remaining semi-final place. Once again, the game provided just the right combination of high quality football and nail-biting drama which had typified the previous games in the group. Denmark needed only to draw the game to grab the remaining semi-final place, but instead of pulling onto the defensive, they thrilled the crowd with a display of their usual open attacking football. After Belgium had taken a 25th minute lead through Ceulemans, they went further ahead through Vercauteren seven minutes later and Denmark began to look vulnerable. Ninety seconds later they were back in the game when Arnesen converted a penalty following a foul on Elkjaer and, on the hour, equalised through substitute Brylle. Belgium came close to scoring several times before Elkjaer scored in the 83rd minute when he spooned a remarkable angled shot over Pfaff's head to give Denmark a 3-2 victory.

Group 2 began when West Germany met Portugal in Strasbourg. Portugal clearly signalled their intention of playing defensively when they lined up with just one recognised striker. Because of the absence of Bernd Schuster (injured) and Hansi Muller (sulking), West Germany pulled skipper Rummenigge back into midfield with very negative effects and it was only in the second-half when he returned to the attack that West Germany began to threaten Portugal. The Portuguese, however, managed to hold firm and West Germany had to settle for a goalless draw. Later the same day Spain and Rumania met in St. Etienne in front of the smallest crowd of the whole of the finals. Rumania played their usual blend of rugged unimaginative football and, in the least entertaining of all the games in France, Spain were little better. The resulting score of 1-1 was a fair reflection on the play which inspired no-one. West Germany have a reputation for timing their performances in important competitions to perfection and against Rumania in the next game they certainly improved upon their showing against Portugal. One up after 24 minutes, West Germany could have had a bagful by half-time but, at

Spain's Santillana foiled by Portugal goalkeeper Bento.

the start of the second-half, conceded an equaliser against the run of play. Then they stepped up a gear, regained the lead twenty minutes later and when the final whistle sounded, seemed to be en route to the semi-finals. Later the same day Portugal and Spain met in Marseille when, after a goalless first-half, Portugal took the lead soon after the restart through Sousa. Santillana scored the equaliser twenty minutes later and with the score remaining 1-1, all four countries went into the last games in the group with a chance of a semi-final place. West Germany faced Spain in Paris at the same time as Portugal met Rumania in Nantes. There, Portugal suffered a serious blow in the 17th minute when their star player Chalana was stretchered off the field after a vicious tackle by Irimescu, but this did not deter the Portuguese who mounted attack after attack. Midway through the second-half, Rumania started to gain the upper hand and Portugal, in response, brought on their veteran striker Nene for his record-breaking 65th international appearance. Rumania came close to scoring in the 76th minute but, four minutes later, Nene scored the only goal of the match for Portugal, an unstoppable volley from the edge of the area, to give his country a semi-final place. In Paris, meanwhile, the game between Spain and West Germany was also goalless at half-time and the Germans seemed to be cruising to another semi-final, when, with only a minute left, the score remained the same. Right up to the last half-hour West Germany had the edge over Spain and seemed likely to score, but the Spanish held on stubbornly. Then, encouraged by their performance this far, Spain began to harass the West Germans and, by the closing stages had them back on the defensive. As the game entered injury-time, Spain launched one last desperate attack and Macedo headed Senor's cross into the West German net to give his country victory.

In the semi-finals France played Portugal in Marseille and Spain faced Denmark in Lyon. The first of these was yet another outstanding game of football ranking alongside Portugal's 1966 World Cup semi-final match and France's 1982 World

Cup semi-final for sheer excitement, skill and enthusiasm. France took a 24th minute lead through Domergue as Platini dominated the game but Jordao equalised in the 73rd minute and the game went into extra-time. Despite the exertions of the previous 90 minutes, extra-time began at an even more frantic pace and Jordao grabbed a second goal in the 97th minute to give Portugal the lead for the first time. Still the French were not finished and with only six minutes remaining Domergue scored his second and the hosts were level again. In the final minute, just as a penalty shootout seemed inevitable, superstar Platini struck a Tigana cross firmly into the Portuguese net to give France victory and a place in the Final.

The other semi-final took place the next day and, although it was not able to match the first for skill and sheer excitement, it came pretty close. Denmark took an early lead when Lerby scored in the 6th minute and for much of the first-half, the Danes seemed likely to go further ahead. In the 51st minute, Spain came close to scoring when the Danish defence hesitated, waiting for an offside whistle and thereafter piled the pressure on Denmark. Maceda levelled the scores in the 66th minute and in the final 25 minutes, the game became harder and harder. Extra-time was required to break the deadlock but, although neither side scored further, Denmark suffered a serious blow to their confidence when Berggren was sent off for an innocuous challenge on Camacho in the 106th minute. The tie went into a penalty shootout which, in the absence of Berggren, Spain won 5-4 to ensure their Final place.

Three days later, the Parc des Princes in Paris was the venue for the Final and the French were the first to show as Giresse rifled in a shot within the first minute. Play flowed from end to end as first France and then Spain moved on to the attack but, at half-time, the game was still goalless. Early in the second-half, the French grew increasingly anxious as they laboured to break down the Spanish defence and Le Roux was booked for a foul on Santillana. Up to this point in the game there was little to choose between the two teams but, in the 56th minute disaster struck for Spain. The Spanish captain, goalkeeper Luis Arconada had played dismally in the 1982 World Cup Finals but, over the succeeding two years, had resurrected his reputation with a string of fine saves including a number in earlier games in the series. France were awarded a free kick on the edge of the Spanish area in the 56th minute and Michel Platini curled his shot around Spain's defensive wall. Arconada saw the ball early and met it perfectly but seemed to take it too deep and it squeezed out of his grip over the goal-line as he flapped after it. From then on Spain were completely out of it as their morale collapsed. In the 84th minute Le Roux was sent off after another bookable offence and, for the first time since conceding the goal, Spain moved onto the offensive. Seconds before the final whistle Tigana cleared the ball as practically the whole of the Spanish team moved into the French half and Bellone ran on to it and chipped the ball over the advancing Arconada to ensure France's victory. Michel Platini was, of course, the man of the series but France's triumph was more of a victory for the game of football itself than for an individual country. The European Championship, enthusiastically supported by splendid crowds, had now clearly signalled its arrival as one of the game's premier events.

Above: Michel Platini - the man of the 1984 Finals.

Left: Spain's luckless captain and goalkeeper, Luis Arconada

1982/84 Series

Group 1

Belgium 3 Switzerland 0
Scotland 2 East Germany 0
Switzerland 2 Scotland 0
Belgium 3 Scotland 2
Scotland 2 Switzerland 2
East Germany 1 Belgium 2
Belgium 2 East Germany 1
Switzerland 0 East Germany 0
Scotland 1 Belgium 1
East Germany 3 Switzerland 0
Switzerland 3 Belgium 1
East Germany 2 Scotland 1

	P	W	D	L	F	A	P
Belgium	6	4	1	1	12	8	9
Swizterland	6	2	2	2	7	9	6
East Germany	6	2	1	3	7	7	5
Scotland	6	1	2	3	8	10	4

Group 2

Finland 2 Poland 3
Finland 0 Portugal 2
Portugal 2 Poland 1
USSR 2 Finland 0
Poland 1 Finland 1
USSR 5 Portugal 0
Poland 1 USSR 1
Finland 0 USSR 1
Portugal 5 Finland 0
USSR 2 Poland 0
Poland 0 Portugal 1
Portugal 1 USSR 0

	P	W	D	L	F	A	P
Portugal	6	5	0	1	11	6	10
USSR	6	4	1	1	11	2	9
Poland	6	1	2	3	6	9	4
Finland	6	0	1	5	3	14	1

Group 3

Denmark 2 England 2
Luxembourg 0 Greece 2
Luxembourg 1 Denmark 2
Greece 0 England 3
England 9 Luxembourg 0
Luxembourg 2 Hungary 6
England 0 Greece 0
Hungary 6 Luxembourg 2
England 2 Hungary 0
Denmark 1 Greece 0
Hungary 2 Greece 3
Denmark 3 Hungary 1
England 0 Denmark 1
Hungary 0 England 3
Denmark 6 Luxembourg 0
Hungary 1 Denmark 0
Greece 0 Denmark 2
Luxembourg 0 England 4
Greece 2 Hungary 2
Greece 1 Luxembourg 0

	P	W	D	L	F	A	P
Denmark	8	6	1	1	17	5	13
England	8	5	2	1	23	3	12
Greece	8	3	2	3	8	10	8
Hungary	8	3	1	4	18	17	7
Luxembourg	8	0	0	8	5	36	0

Group 4

Wales 1 Norway 0
Norway 3 Yugoslavia 1
Bulgaria 2 Norway 2
Bulgaria 0 Yugoslavia 1
Yugoslavia 4 Wales 4
Wales 1 Bulgaria 0
Norway 1 Bulgaria 2
Norway 0 Wales 0
Yugoslavia 2 Norway 1
Bulgaria 1 Wales 0
Wales 1 Yugoslavia 1
Yugoslavia 3 Bulgaria 2

	P	W	D	L	F	A	P
Yugoslavia	6	3	2	1	12	11	8
Wales	6	2	3	1	7	6	7
Bulgaria	6	2	1	3	7	8	5
Norway	6	1	2	3	7	8	4

Group 5

Romania 3 Cyprus 1
Romania 2 Sweden 0
Czechoslovakia 2 Sweden 2
Italy 2 Czechoslovakia 2
Cyprus 0 Sweden 1
Italy 0 Romania 0
Cyprus 1 Italy 1
Cyprus 1 Czechoslovakia 1
Romania 1 Italy 0
Czechoslovakia 6 Cyprus 0
Sweden 5 Cyprus 0
Romania 0 Czechoslovakia 1
Sweden 2 Italy 0
Sweden 0 Romania 1
Sweden 1 Czechoslovakia 0
Italy 0 Sweden 3
Cyprus 0 Romania 1
Czechoslovakia 2 Italy 0
Czechoslovakia 1 Romania 1
Italy 3 Cyprus 1

	P	W	D	L	F	A	P
Romania	8	5	2	1	9	3	12
Sweden	8	5	1	2	14	5	11
Czechoslovakia	8	3	4	1	15	7	10
Italy	8	1	3	4	6	12	5
Cyprus	8	0	2	6	4	21	2

Group 6

Austria 5 Albania 0
Austria 2 North'n Ireland 0
Turkey 1 Albania 0
North'n Ireland 1 West Germany 0
Austria 4 Turkey 0
Albania 0 North'n Ireland 0
North'n Ireland 2 Turkey 1
Albania 1 West Germany 2
Turkey 0 West Germany 3
Austria 0 West Germany 0
North'n Ireland 1 Albania 0
Albania 1 Turkey 1
Albania 1 Austria 2
North'n Ireland 3 Austria 1
West Germany 3 Austria 0
Turkey 1 North'n Ireland 0
West Germany 5 Turkey 1
West Germany 0 North'n Ireland 1
Turkey 3 Austria 1
West Germany 2 Albania 1

	P	W	D	L	F	A	P
West Germany	8	5	1	2	15	5	11
North'n Ireland	8	5	1	2	8	5	11
Austria	8	4	1	3	15	10	9
Turkey	8	3	1	4	8	16	7
Albania	8	0	2	6	4	14	2

Group 7

Malta 2 Iceland 1
Iceland 1 Holland 1
Holland 2 Eire 1
Eire 2 Iceland 0
Spain 1 Iceland 0
Eire 3 Spain 3
Malta 0 Holland 6
Spain 1 Holland 0
Malta 0 Eire 1
Spain 2 Eire 0
Malta 2 Spain 3
Iceland 0 Spain 1
Iceland 1 Malta 0
Holland 3 Iceland 0
Iceland 0 Eire 3
Eire 2 Holland 3
Holland 2 Spain 1
Eire 8 Malta 0
Holland 5 Malta 0
Spain 12 Malta 1

	P	W	D	L	F	A	P
Spain	8	6	1	1	24	8	13
Holland	8	6	1	1	22	6	13
Eire	8	4	1	3	20	10	9
Iceland	8	1	1	6	3	13	3
Malta	8	1	0	7	5	37	2

Final Group 1

France 1 Denmark 0
Belgium 2 Yugoslavia 0
France 5 Belgium 0
Denmark 5 Yugoslavia 0
France 3 Yugoslavia 0
Denmark 3 Belgium 2

	P	W	D	L	F	A	P
France	3	3	0	0	9	2	6
Denmark	3	2	0	1	8	3	4
Belgium	3	1	0	2	4	8	2
Yugoslavia	3	0	0	3	2	10	0

Final Group 2

West Germany 0 Portugal 0
Spain 1 Romania 1
West Germany 2 Romania 1
Portugal 1 Spain 1
West Germany 0 Spain 1
Portugal 1 Romania 0

	P	W	D	L	F	A	P
Spain	3	1	2	0	3	2	4
Portugal	3	1	2	0	2	1	4
West Germany	3	1	1	1	2	2	3
Romania	3	0	1	2	2	4	1

Semi-Finals

France 3 Portugal 2
After Extra Time
Spain 1 Denmark 1
After Extra Time
Spain won 5-4 on Penalties

Final

France 2 Spain 0

8th Series 1986-1988

WEST GERMANY was selected as the venue for the Finals of the 8th Series and, as in the 7th Series, West Germany received an automatic bye into the Finals whilst the other 32 entrants were split into seven groups, four of five countries and three of four countries.

Group 1 was made up of Albania, Austria, Rumania and Spain and began on 10th September 1986 when Austria journeyed to Bucharest and were convincingly beaten 4-0 by Rumania. A little over a month later, Austria were in action again when their visitors were Albania and they had little difficulty in achieving an easy 3-0 victory. Spain, who were favourites to win the group, entered the action in Seville a month later when they were hard pressed to beat their at times brutal visitors, Rumania, 1-0. Three weeks later, Spain journeyed to Albania and were shocked to find themselves trailing 1-0 at the interval. Indeed, it was not until 21 minutes into the second-half that Spain's attacking pressure came to anything when Arteche notched up the equaliser. Seven minutes from the end, Joaquin scored the winner for Spain and they moved to the top of the group, remaining there until the next game was played over three months later. This was played in Bucharest and Albania who were once more involved, achieved as little success as they had in their previous two games. Rumania took a 1st-minute lead through Piturca but Albania fought back well and equalised through Muca in the 34th minute. Just before half-time, the Albanians seemed to lose their concentration, conceded two quick goals and were never in the game afterwards. In the second-half, Rumania scored twice more to register an easy 5-1 victory which hoisted them above Spain on goal difference. A week later, Spain were in action against Austria in Vienna and achieved a remarkable last-ditch victory. After taking the lead through Eloy in the 31st minute, Austria came back and levelled the scores 1-1 at half-time. Eloy scored a second very much against the run of play in the 58th minute but, after having an appeal for a penalty turned down on the hour, Austria equalised through Polster in the 64th minute. Polster, Europe's leading league scorer was causing the Spanish defence all kinds of problems and with 13 minutes remaining, Chendo was sent off for fouling him. This really put the pressure on Spain and Polster came close to scoring in the 80th minute when he hit the bar. After weathering continual pressure for the last ten minutes, Spain broke out of defence and Carrasco grabbed a last-minute winner to put them back to the top of the group table. Austria were in action again later that month when they travelled to play Albania in Tirana. Toni Polster scored the only goal of the match with a 7th-minute free-kick but Austria were very lucky indeed to beat the Albanians, who pushed them back into their own half for most of the game. On the same day, group leaders Spain faced Rumania in Bucharest and were subjected to their own brand of brutal, crashing tackling by their opponents. Their noted exponents of hard play, Camacha and Goicoechea were helped from the field injured in the first-half as Rumania gave Spain a taste of their own medicine and, by half-time, Spain were 3-0 down. In the second-half Spain came back into the game but were only able to reduce the arrears to 3-1 via an 81st-minute Caldere goal. This result put Rumania back to the top of the table until

Spain played the next game in the group, some six months later, when they defeated Austria 2-0 in Seville. A fortnight afterwards, Rumania grabbed the top position back again by beating Albania 1-0 away but required a win in their last game against Austria in Vienna, to be certain of the qualifying place. In the event they could only manage a 0-0 draw and Spain, who were playing Albania at the same time, clinched their place in West Germany with a 5-0 victory.

Group 2 featured Italy, Malta, Portugal, Sweden and Switzerland and began when Sweden scored a 2-0 victory over the Swiss. The following month, Sweden travelled to Portugal and were held to a 1-1 draw by the home team and Portugal, themselves, were fortunate to scrape a 1-1 draw in Switzerland when Fernandes scored an 86th-minute equaliser. Italy entered into the action on 15th November 1986 when they met Switzerland in Milan and immediately took the lead through Milan's Roberto Donadoni. In only the 8th minute the Italian captain Cabrini was replaced because of injury and this unsettled the home defence which looked decidedly shaky after Switzerland had equalised through Brigger in the 31st minute. World Cup survivor Altobelli scored two excellent goals for Italy to ensure their victory but in the final minute Weber once more exposed Italy's defence when he scored Switzerland's second goal. The following day, Sweden played Malta in Valletta and scored an impressive 5-0 victory to move well clear at the top of the group table but, soon after, Italy scored a 2-0 victory in Valletta themselves to close the gap. Six weeks later, Italy played Malta again and took over the top place with an easy 5-0 win, and two weeks after moved further in front by achieving a hard-fought 1-0 victory in Portugal. Portugal's slim hopes of reaching the 1988 finals were shattered when Malta held them to a 2-2 draw in Funchal, Madeira, and in the process gained their first-ever away point in the championship. A fortnight afterwards, Switzerland scored their only victory in the group when they defeated Malta 4-1 and, six weeks later, Sweden beat Malta 1-0 to move within a point of Italy who they next faced in Stockholm. Italy had not posed many problems for Norway in a friendly a few days before they travelled to Sweden and they began against Sweden in precisely the same uninspired manner. On the quarter hour Mancini missed a penalty for Italy but, ten minutes later, Peter Larsson made no mistake for Sweden when he was put through by Ekstrom. Just before half-time, Vialli hit the Swedish bar with a fine shot but, after that, Italy never looked like scoring as they slumped to their first defeat under the management of Azeglio Vicini and, in the process, found themselves toppled from the leading spot in the group. Sweden dropped a point when they played Switzerland in Lausanne a fortnight later but moved two points clear of Italy as a result. Portugal were Sweden's opponents when they next played three months later and they ended the Swedes' run of 12 consecutive victories with a goal by Gomes in the 35th minute. Italy picked up a point from a goalless draw in Switzerland and faced Sweden in Naples when they next played. Both sides were well aware that the outcome of this game would probably decide the place in the finals and began very cautiously. Sweden went close in the 20th minute when Pettersson headed wide but it was Italy who took the lead through Vialli in the 27th minute. Larsson equalised 11 minutes later but, seconds before the half-time whistle, Vialli volleyed his second goal into the Swedish net. In the second-half Italy went back on the defensive and, because Sweden were unable

Mordt celebrates Norway's opening goal against France.

to equalise, secured their place in the finals with three games still to play. In these games Portugal, who had earlier drawn 0-0 at home to Switzerland, went down 3-0 in Italy and won 1-0 in Malta whilst Switzerland drew 1-1 in Malta.

Group 3 featured the reigning champions and World Cup third-placed team, France, together with East Germany, Iceland, Norway and the USSR and began with a shock result when France were held to a goalless draw in Iceland. Two weeks later, the Icelanders proved that the opening game had been no fluke by drawing 1-1 with the USSR and as East Germany had struggled to earn a goalless draw against Norway the same day, the group began to look very open indeed. Russia, however, had other ideas and, after gaining a marvellous 2-0 victory over France in Paris, they trounced Norway 4-0 to move clear at the top of the table. East Germany then moved into contention by beating Iceland 2-0 and drawing 0-0 with France before the winter break. France picked up two points from a 2-0 victory over Iceland on 29th April 1987 but, on the same day, the USSR beat East Germany 2-0 in Kiev to move three points clear at the top of the table. East Germany inflicted Iceland's worst-ever home defeat (6-0) when they played their next game but, because Russia won 1-0 in Norway the same day, could not close the gap at the top of the table.

The inconsistency of the French team was highlighted when, playing their first game after the retirement of Michel Platini, they were easily defeated 2-0 by Norway and, in their next game, they came close to beating the USSR in Moscow. After leading through Toure for over an hour, France allowed the Russian substitute Mikhailichenko to snatch a 77th-minute equaliser and this goal gave Russia the point that they needed to resist France's challenge for the top spot. Only East Germany could still catch Russia who they faced at home the following month and, once again, the Soviets trailed for much of the match but snatched a late equaliser to win a point. A little over two weeks later, the USSR ensured their place in the Finals by winning a comfortable 2-0 victory over Iceland on the same day that East Germany defeated Norway 3-1. In the remaining game, France, who had earlier been held to a draw by Norway, lost 1-0 at home to East Germany and only pipped Iceland for third-place in the group on goal difference.

Group 4 featured England, Northern Ireland, Turkey and Yugoslavia and began at Wembley on 15th October 1986. Then, Gary Lineker showed why he had been the 1986 World Cup's leading goalscorer as he put England into the lead against Northern Ireland in the 33rd minute. Waddle scored a second in the 78th minute and Lineker grabbed another, two minutes later, as England cruised to an easy victory. A fortnight afterwards, Yugoslavia scored an equally emphatic 4-0 win over Turkey and the group was already beginning to look like a two-horse race. England went on to record an easy 2-0 victory over Yugoslavia at Wembley on 12th November 1986 and, the same day, the two also-rans, Turkey and Northern Ireland, played out a goalless draw in Izmir. England retained their lead at the top of the group and went further ahead with a comfortable 2-0 win in Belfast when the group matches resumed in April 1987. Four weeks later Yugoslavia, too, won in Belfast (2-1) and with only one point from four games, the best that the Irish could hope for was third place.

England were up against Turkey in Izmir on the same day but they faltered and could only take one point from the resulting goal-less draw. The next games in the group were not played until 14th October 1987 when Northern Ireland faced Yugoslavia in Sarajevo and England played Turkey at Wembley. While the Yugoslavs won a comfortable 3-0 victory over the Irish, England ran riot against the Turks at Wembley. Barnes put England into the lead in the opening minute and, after Lineker had made it 2-0 a few minutes later, the Turks looked a beaten side. The combination of a heavy pitch, driving rain and a chilling wind were sufficient in themselves to put Turkey onto the defensive but, with Lineker in goalscoring form too, the visitors did not stand a chance and were lucky to be only 4-0 down at half-time. After the interval Turkey rallied for a brief spell but the 8-0 closing scoreline was a fair reflection on the play. This result meant that England required only a draw against Yugoslavia in Belgrade in their next game to be certain of reaching the finals but the English forward line hit peak form and, after only 25 minutes were 4-0 ahead and virtually home and dry. Yugoslavia pulled a goal back with ten minutes left to play but never recovered from England's early onslaught and England booked their ticket to West Germany. In the two remaining games both Northern Ireland and Yugoslavia beat Turkey who finished at the bottom of the group with only two points.

The favourites in Group 5 were Holland and, on paper at least, their opponents Greece, Hungary, Poland and Cyprus posed a relatively formidable challenge to them. The group kicked-off on 15th October 1986 when Greece faced Poland in Poznan and Holland took on Hungary in Budapest. Marco Van Basten scored the winner for Holland in Hungary to set the favourites on the right road and

Dziekanowski converted two first-half penalties to give Poland victory over Greece. Four weeks later Greece earned two points by defeating Hungary 2-1 in Athens and, after Poland had held Holland to a goalless draw a week later, the group looked to be wide open. Cyprus were the 'minnows' of the group and they were in action in all of the next four games and lost the lot – 4-2 and 3-1 against Greece, 2-0 against Holland and 1-0 against Hungary. These results left Greece at the top of the group and they shocked Holland by taking a 1-0 half-time lead when they travelled to Rotterdam in the next game. Van Basten equalised in the second-half but the Dutch were fortunate to take a point and Greece remained at the head of the group. In mid-April 1987, Poland slipped up badly as they were held to a goalless home draw by Cyprus and, later in the month, both Greece and Holland registered home wins over Poland and Hungary respectively to move further in front at the top of the group table. Three weeks later, Poland travelled to Hungary where a meagre 8,000 fans turned up to see if the home side could reverse their recent decline. Lajos Detari the Hungarian forward whose name had been linked with several Western European clubs was under particular scrutiny and, after a string of disappointing games, the notoriously critical home crowd were desperately hoping for a worthwhile performance. Hungary made five changes from the side beaten in Holland but, it was not until the last half-hour that they got their act together and scored four goals in 21 minutes to come back from 2-1 down to win the game 5-3. The return game in Poland four months later went 3-2 to Poland and when Hungary next played at home, against Greece, another abysmal 8,000 gate was recorded which was unfortunate because Hungary trounced the Greeks 3-0. A number of Greek fans who made the journey to Budapest, were so enraged by Greece's inept performance that they attacked members of their team later that night! Holland were now firmly in the driving seat as they had beaten Poland 2-0 the same day to move to the top of the group and required only a win against Cyprus two weeks later to secure the place in the finals. When the game was played in Rotterdam, Holland took a first minute lead through Bosman but soon after, the hooligan element amongst Holland's followers asserted themselves and pandemonium broke out when the Cypriot goalkeeper Charitou was injured by a smokebomb. As he was carried off with concussion and an eye injury, his team-mates walked off in protest and were only persuaded to return an hour later. Clearly shaken, they went down 8-0 but the result was not allowed to stand. UEFA's initial decision was to award the game to Cyprus with a 3-0 scoreline but, after the Dutch appealed, they did an about-turn and ruled that the game should be replayed behind closed doors. Eventually Holland had no difficulty in taking the rematch 4-0 to secure their place in the Finals. Holland beat Greece 3-0 in the last game in the group but, if UEFA had not reversed their decision on the Cyprus incident would they still have won in Rhodes?

Group 6 featured Czechoslovakia, Denmark, Finland and Wales and began in Finland on 10th September 1986 when Wales scored an equaliser in the 68th minute after trailing to a Hjelm goal for most of the game. Five weeks later, Finland were in action again when they travelled to Brno to face Czechoslovakia who had little difficulty in winning the game 3-0. Denmark were widely regarded as being the favourites to win the group but they did not begin very impressively and were quite lucky to defeat Finland 1-0 in Copenhagen in the next game in the group. Two weeks later Denmark travelled to play Czechoslovakia in Bratislava and were again lucky to come away with a goalless draw. After the winter break, Wales were in action against Finland at Wrexham and after Ian Rush had put them into the lead with an early goal, were little troubled by the Finns and ran out easy 4-0 winners. Finland were having a hard time of it and, on the same day that Czechoslovakia drew 1-1 in Wales, Denmark beat them 1-0 in Helsinki to go to the top of the table for the first time. Five weeks later the Czechs held Denmark to a 1-1 draw in Copenhagen but nevertheless, the Danes remained at the top of the group. Three months later Denmark faced Wales in Cardiff in a bruising if not downright vicious encounter. Ian Rush, Wales's exiled striker, was refused permission to play by his new Italian masters and the Welsh struggled to find the net in his absence. Encouraged by the news from Helsinki where Finland had scored a remarkable 3-0 victory over Czechoslovakia earlier in the day, Wales fought tooth and nail to overcome the Danes and went ahead through Mark Hughes in the 19th minute. Denmark tried to get back into the game but received very harsh treatment from the Welsh who were determined to remain ahead. A sterner referee might well have sent off at least three Welshmen for dangerous play but the score remained 1-0 in favour of the Welsh who moved above Denmark with the same six points but a better goal difference. Denmark had only one game remaining, against Wales, but Wales also had an away fixture in Czechoslovakia. When the Welsh travelled to Copenhagen, five weeks later, they were subject to much the same brand of physical excess as they inflicted on the Danes in Cardiff and the result, too, was the same, 1-0 to the home side. This meant that in the last game in the group Wales had to beat Czechoslovakia in Prague to grasp the qualifying place from Denmark. Czechoslovakia had nothing to play for and were pinned back in their own half for most of the game, but, although the Welsh forwards had numerous easy scoring chances, they just could not find the net. Knoflicek put the home side ahead in the 32nd minute and then Bilek scored another in the final minute to give the Czechs an undeserved 2-0 victory and Denmark a place in the finals.

Group 7 was made up of Belgium, Bulgaria, Eire, Luxembourg and Scotland and, with the exception of Luxembourg, they proved to be very evenly-matched. The group opened on 10th September 1986 when Scotland and Bulgaria played out a goalless draw at Hampden and Eire snatched a late equaliser against Belgium in Brussels when Liam Brady scored a last minute penalty. Five weeks later, Belgium were little troubled when they beat their neighbours Luxembourg 6-0, Nico Claesen scoring a hat-trick in the process and, the following day, Scotland and Eire played out a goalless draw in Dublin. A month later, Scotland defeated Luxembourg 3-0 at Hampden and the following week Belgium met Bulgaria in Brussels. Goalkeeper Jean-Marie Pfaff who had been dropped for the game against Luxembourg because he criticised manager Guy Thys's team selection, was restored into the Belgian team and he made a number of fine saves to keep the home country in the game. The match was goalless at half-time, and Spurs' Nico Claesen put Belgium ahead two minutes after the restart with a scrambled goal. After Bulgaria had equalised a quarter of an hour later, the visitors pressured for a winner but, thanks to Pfaff, Belgium held on for a point.

The manager of Eire, Jack Charlton came in for quite a lot of criticism when he included Mark Lawrenson in his team to play Scotland at Hampden on 18th February 1987 but, in the 8th minute, Lawrenson silenced the critics when he scored via an Aldridge free-kick. This was the first goal that the Scots had conceded in four games under manager Andy Roxburgh and although they piled on the pressure for an equaliser, Eire held resolutely on to their lead and, with luck, might have been three up by the final whistle. A few weeks later, both Scotland and Eire were in away action in the group and while Scotland were being thrashed 4-1 by Belgium, thanks to another Nico Claesen hat-trick, the Irish were unlucky to lose 2-1 in Bulgaria where they looked as if they would take a point. Belgium were now two points clear at the top of the table, and remained in front despite losing a point to Eire when they were held to a goalless draw later that month in Dublin. A day later, Bulgaria moved into second-place with a 4-1 win in Luxembourg and, three weeks later beat Luxembourg once again, this time 3-0, to move to the top of the group with eight points. Eire, too, then played Luxembourg twice in consecutive group games and, winning 2-0 and 2-1 respectively, moved to the top of the table with nine points. Bulgaria and Belgium, however, had played two games less than Eire and they faced each other in Sofia on 23rd September 1987 in the next game in the group. Sirakov put Bulgaria ahead in the 19th minute and as the second-half opened, Belgium pressed for an equaliser, the tackling grew fiercer, and five players were booked. Belgium came close several times but, after Tanev had scored Bulgaria's second goal in the 70th minute, the Belgian attacks petered out. Bulgaria were now a point clear of Eire with a game in hand and were favourites to win the group. On the day that Scotland beat Belgium 2-0 at Hampden to end their faint hopes of the top-spot, Eire played Bulgaria in Dublin. Eire attacked injury-hit Bulgaria without reward for the whole of the first-half but it was not until the 52nd minute that Manchester United's Paul McGrath gave the Irish the lead. In the 83rd minute Liam Brady became the first Irishman to be sent off in an international since Mick Martin and Noel Campbell both received their marching orders 11 years earlier … against Bulgaria. Kevin Moran notched up a second goal for the Irish five minutes from the end to ensure both points. This result put the Irish back to the top of the table but Bulgaria who had a superior goal difference needed only a point from their last home game against Scotland, to win the group. Scotland travelled to Sofia four weeks later with an understrength team because of injury and were not expected to dent Bulgaria's near-four-year unbeaten home record. The Bulgarians, however, played into the Scots' hands by choosing a defensive line-up and in the dying minutes the game was still goalless. Although Jim Leighton had played superbly in the Scottish goal his services had not been required often as Bulgaria settled back content with a draw. With three minutes remaining, Scotland's two substitutes Gordon Durie and Gary Mackay got into the action as Mackay put Durie's pass into the Bulgarian net. The Bulgarians tried to get the equaliser but there was just no time and the home crowd jeered them from the field. Back in Dublin the news was greeted with astonishment and delight as Eire progressed to the Finals of their first major tournament for years. The last game in the group summed up Scotland's unpredictable record in the European Championship they struggled to a goalless draw against Luxembourg.

In West Germany, the host country and England were both seeded, in Groups 1 and 2 respectively and in Group 1, the Germans faced Denmark, Italy and Spain. The finals kicked-off on 10th June 1988 at the Rheinstadion in Dusseldorf when West Germany faced Italy. The Italians went straight on to the attack and Giannini should have opened the scoring in the very first minute when the German full-back Herget lost possession on the edge of his area, but Immel pushed the ball away for a corner. More Italian attacks followed as the West Germans were pushed back into their own half and so it continued for most of the first 45 minutes. At times one or two of the home defenders looked decidedly nervous but the Italians were not exactly brimful of confidence either. The West German counter attacks threatened more than all the Italian's continuing pressure and, after Klinsmann had headed over the bar in the 32nd minute, Matthaus, one of the greatest 'divers' in the game, went down appealing for a penalty in the 39th minute. English referee Keith Hackett was not impressed and, at half-time, the game remained goalless. After the restart Matthaus was in action again when his 30-yard shot was only just off target but, a few minutes later, he and Herget slipped up badly to let the Italians in for the opening goal. Donadoni capitalised upon their misunderstanding and Robert Mancini scored his first goal for his country, at long last. The Italian joy was short-lived when, four minutes later, their goalkeeper Zenga was penalised for taking too many steps. Littbarski touched his free-kick to Brehme and his drive was deflected into the bottom corner of the net. This goal encouraged the hosts to take the initiative but their defence still looked very suspect at times. In the closing stages Italy reverted to form, pulled back on to the defensive and the score remained 1-1.

Italy's Vialli holds off Herget's challenge.

The following day, Denmark played Spain in Hanover, hoping to avenge their dreadful performance against the Spaniards in the World Cup in Mexico. Spain took an early lead when Michel finished off a one-two with Gellego, placing his shot past Rasmussen and it was not until 20 minutes later that Laudrup equalised for the Danes. Still the Spaniards always looked the more dangerous and the Danish defence were so lacking in pace that it seemed only a question of time before Spain regained the lead. Michel was in action again when he was tripped in the area but he spoiled an otherwise superb display when he missed the resulting spot-kick. After the interval, Spain went ahead again when Butragueno received a Baquero pass in an obviously offside position, found the net and to the surprise of impartial observers was awarded a goal. To their credit, the Danes did not allow the injustice to upset their game but after Gordillo had scored a third, fifteen minutes later, they looked a beaten side. Povlsen pulled a goal back for Denmark five minutes from the end but the Spaniards held out and were well worth their two points.

West Germany met Denmark in the next match and, Herget, who had run the gauntlet of the German press as a result of his problems against Italy, was given the opportunity to redeem himself. Manager Beckenbauer, too, had found himself the centre of attention of the German media and he needed a better performance from the home side to relieve the pressure. Denmark made panic changes and brought in a different sweeper and goalkeeper but, after only nine minutes, found themselves trailing to a goal by Klinsmann. The West German side played with immensely more purpose and effort than in their first game and at half-time remained comfortably in the lead. On the hour, Laudrup, who had been unable to get into the game to any effect, was replaced by John Eriksen but he, too, was easily suppressed by the none too gentle German defence. Lerby, whose sliced clearance had paved the way for West Germany's goal, came into the game in the last minutes and provided the first real Danish threat, firing in a number of useful long-range shots which tested Immel in the German goal. In the 85th minute Littbarski sent over a superb corner-kick which soared to the back of the penalty box and Thon headed West Germany's second goal to put them en route to the semi-finals. Later the same day, Italy faced Spain in Frankfurt and never allowed Spain time to get into the game. After only nine minutes Vialli should have put Italy ahead when his shot went over the bar and, two minutes later, he had another goalbound shot deflected for a corner. At half-time the game was still goalless although Italy had the upper hand and it was not until the 73rd minute that Vialli, who had missed another easy chance three minutes before, scored the deciding goal for Italy.

Three days later West Germany, much relieved after the triumph over Denmark, set about Spain and, after resisting early pressure, assumed complete control of the midfield through Matthaus. Voller put West Germany ahead after half an hour (his first goal in 618 minutes of international football) and as the game progressed, the home side became more dominant. Matthaus created West Germany's second goal five minutes after the restart when he dashed half the length of the field, before backheeling the ball to Voller who had no hesitation in finding the net again. West Germany settled back on their lead and had no difficulty in holding the few uninspired attacks that the Spaniards were able to muster in the last 40 minutes.

When Italy faced Denmark in Cologne, they knew that a draw would be sufficient to see them through to the semi-finals, while all that the Danes could hope for was a little self respect. The Danish goalkeeper, Schmeichel, began very shakily and in only the 2nd minute completely mistimed an attempt to gather a Maldini cross, presenting Mancini, with a virtual open goal, but the Italian somehow managed to miss it. Thereafter Schmeichel became almost a liability as he mishandled everything that came his way but, it was not until the 65th minute that Altobelli put Italy ahead, only seconds after being brought on as substitute for the ineffectual Mancini. Three minutes from the end De Agostini, the other Italian substitute, who had been on the field for no more than a minute emulated Altobelli's feat and scored a second goal to kill off Denmark's hopes of a comeback.

Group 2 began in Stuttgart on 12th June 1988 with a match between England and Eire. Eire's late qualification by courtesy of the Scots had come as quite a surprise in the Republic and, as underdogs, Jackie Charlton's men were excused the media-hype and pressure to which the English squad were subjected. After only five minutes, the unthinkable happened, as England's shaky defence were cruelly exposed by the lively Irish attack. Blunders by both Kenny Sansom and Gary Stevens left John Aldridge clear to lay on a pass to Ray Houghton who had no difficulty in beating Shilton in the English goal. England nominally went onto the attack but were badly let down by their supposed star forward line in which Barnes in particular excelled by his mediocrity. Nor were things happy in the defence and, whenever the Irish moved on to the offensive, they caused problems. Hoddle replaced Webb after an hour and largely prompted by this substitution the second-half developed into one-way traffic as England attacked the Irish goal. The Irish defence stood firm, Bonner in goal pulled off a number of good saves, and England squandered several chances before Mr. Kirschen the East German referee blew for time. After the game, predictably, Bobby Robson, England's manager, expressed the opinion that England could have won the game 4-1. He was no doubt also aware that England's defence were so inept that it would not be long before they started to concede goals – in quantity.

England's Gary Lineker and Eire's Mick McCarthy tussle for the ball.

Later the same day, Holland faced the USSR in Cologne and were surprised when, in the 53rd minute, after soaking up almost continual Dutch pressure, the Russians broke out of defence and took the lead through Rats. Holland played some delightful football but when they got the ball into the Russian area, Dasayev the Soviet goalkeeper was there. As the game progressed, the Dutch efforts seemed less and less likely to come to anything and the Russians always posed more danger on the break and held on to their lead with relative ease. The next game in the group was the key clash between England and Holland in Dusseldorf and was preceded, the night before, by a near riot as neo-Nazi German youths (believed to be followers of Schalke and Borussia Dortmund) attacked both English and Dutch fans at the railway station. When the game was played, the atmosphere was tense but, fielding a slightly different team, England played the more direct football throughout the first-half and were unlucky to be a goal down at the break. In the 53rd minute Robson put England level after playing a one-two with Lineker and for a brief spell, England took command. England's defence, however, still looked shaky and, in the 71st minute, failed to clear a Muhren free-kick and Van Basten (who had opened the scoring in the 23rd minute) grabbed a second goal. Four minutes later he completed his hat-trick

Arnold Muhren congratulates Marco van Basten after scoring for Holland against England.

and England were virtually out of the reckoning for the semi-finals.

Later the same day, the Irish faced the USSR and quickly dispelled any thoughts that their performance against England had been a flash-in-the-pan. The Russians played the same sort of game that had served them so well against Holland and were content to defend and counterattack the Irish for the first half-hour when they began to apply the pressure themselves. Then, in the 38th minute, the Irish went ahead with one of the finest goals of the finals when Ronnie Whelan superbly volleyed a McCarthy long-throw into the Russian net. The score remained unchanged at the interval and then, for almost half-an-hour, the Irish held firm and, on occasions, looked as if they might go further ahead. In the 74th minute Protasov equalised for the USSR and the resulting draw meant that Eire had only to take a point from their last game to reach the semi-finals. On the same day that England played the USSR and performed abysmally, losing 3-1, Eire met Holland in Gelsenkirchen. The game was played in the packed Parkstadion and the atmosphere was simply electric. At half-time the match was goalless, although both sides had come near to scoring, and it was the Irish who threatened most as the second-half began. The Dutch substitute Kieft, replaced Erwin Koeman five minutes after the interval and Holland gained the initiative and pushed the Irish back onto the defensive. With only nine minutes left, Kieft deflected a mishit shot past Bonner and as the Irish were unable to level the scores again, Holland progressed, somewhat fortunately, to the semi-finals.

Holland faced West Germany in the first semi-final which was played three days later in Hamburg, aware of the fact that they had not beaten the Germans in a full international for 32 years. The Germans were forced to make a last minute change when Littbarski suffered stomach pains in the pre-match warm-up and was replaced by Frank Mill. This late change upset the Germans' rhythm a little but, nevertheless, the goalless first-half was fairly evenly balanced although the Dutch should have scored through Van Basten. Herget was injured in a collision with Ruud Gullit and was replaced on half-time by Pflugler. Just as the Dutch had gained the upper hand after the break, they were set back on their heels when Matthaus scored from the penalty spot in the 54th minute after Klinsmann had allegedly been tripped by Frank Rijkaard. To that point Rijkaard had been the man of the match and he did not let the harsh penalty decision effect his game but carried on supplying a flow of passes to Ruud Gullit whose performance was at last beginning to match up to pre-match expectations. A little under 20 minutes later Holland were back in the game when Ronald Koeman converted an even more dubious penalty award after Van Basten had tumbled over the outstretched leg of Kohler. This goal gave Holland the boost that they needed and they took control of the game for the last quarter of an hour, mounting a series of attacks. Just as the match seemed poised to go into extra-time, Wouters found Marco Van Basten with a defence-splitting pass and his sliding shot gave Immel no chance. The Dutch held out for the remaining couple of minutes and progressed to the Final.

The USSR faced Italy in Stuttgart the following day only too aware that no less than seven of their team had been booked in previous games and that a second booking for any of them would mean automatic exclusion from the Final if they beat Italy. This did not, however, stop the Russians from treating their opponents to a liberal helping of crashing tackles right from the off and, in only the 2nd minute, Kuznetsov, their key defender was booked and consequently suspended for the next game. If the Russians were concerned about this, they did not show it and wasted no time in getting to grips with the Italians whenever the chance arose. At half-time, the game was goalless although the Italians had come closest to scoring and it was not until 14 minutes into the second-half that the deadlock was broken. Kuznetsov started the move when he broke from defence and, after some hesitation, Litovchenko stabbed the ball past Zenga into the Italian net. Just over two minutes later, the man of the match, Zavarov, tore down the left flank and found Protasov as the Italians floundered, and his first-time shot whistled beyond Zenga, into the Italian net. The Italians attacked for the remaining half-hour but, despite one or two scrambles in the Russian goalmouth, they achieved nothing and the USSR progressed to yet another European Championship Final.

Three days later, the Dutch played the USSR in the Olympic Stadium in Munich before a crowd of 72,308, most of whom were their own supporters. Forgetting their 1-0 defeat at the hands of the Russians 13 days earlier, Holland were determined to win and knew that the absence of Kuznetsov would enable them to open up the centre of the Russian defence as they had been unable to do before. In the 6th minute, Ronald Koeman showed the tremendous velocity of his shooting when he blasted a free-kick over the bar and over the next 25 minutes the play swung from end to end. On the half-hour the Russians should have gone ahead when Litovchenko shot straight at Van Breukelen but two minutes later the Dutch took the lead. Erwin Koeman took a return pass from a corner and crossed to Van Basten who nodded the ball for Gullit to head past Dasayev. The Soviets came back on to the attack and, a few minutes later, should have equalised when the unmarked Belanov ballooned his shot over the Dutch bar. After the interval the Dutch weathered further Russian attacks before moving further ahead in the 53rd minute. In the crowning moment of the entire competition Van Tiggelen collected a loose ball in midfield, passed to Arnold Muhren on the left, and his superb cross to the back of the penalty area found Van Basten whose brilliant right-foot volley beat Dasayev to make the score 2-0. Six minutes later, Van Breukelen stupidly gave away a penalty when there was absolutely no danger but redeemed himself by scrambling Belanov's spot-kick clear. In the remaining half-hour, the Russians attacked with decreasing enthusiasm and the Dutch always seemed to pose the greater threat when they had the ball. In the dying minutes they came close to making it 3-0 through Frank Rijkaard. When the closing whistle sounded, a thunderous cheer went up as the Dutch fans celebrated their country's first-ever major championship win, a fitting ending to an outstanding Final Series.

1986/88 Series

Group 1

Home		Away	
Romania	4	Austria	0
Austria	3	Albania	0
Spain	1	Romania	0
Albania	1	Spain	2
Romania	5	Albania	1
Austria	2	Spain	3
Albania	0	Austria	1
Romania	3	Spain	1
Spain	2	Austria	0
Albania	0	Romania	1
Spain	5	Albania	0
Austria	0	Romania	0

	P	W	D	L	F	A	P
Spain	6	5	0	1	14	6	10
Romania	6	4	1	1	13	3	9
Austria	6	2	1	3	6	9	5
Albania	6	0	0	6	2	17	0

Group 2

Home		Away	
Sweden	2	Switzerland	2
Portugal	1	Sweden	1
Switzerland	1	Portugal	1
Italy	3	Switzerland	2
Malta	0	Sweden	5
Malta	0	Italy	2
Italy	5	Malta	0
Portugal	0	Italy	1
Portugal	2	Malta	2
Switzerland	4	Malta	1
Sweden	1	Malta	0
Sweden	1	Italy	0
Switzerland	1	Sweden	1
Sweden	0	Portugal	1
Switzerland	0	Italy	0
Portugal	0	Switzerland	0
Italy	2	Sweden	1
Malta	1	Switzerland	1
Italy	3	Portugal	0
Malta	0	Portugal	1

	P	W	D	L	F	A	P
Italy	8	6	1	1	16	4	13
Sweden	8	4	2	2	12	5	10
Portugal	8	2	4	2	6	8	8
Switzerland	8	1	5	2	9	9	7
Malta	8	0	2	6	4	21	2

Group 3

Home		Away	
Iceland	0	France	0
Iceland	1	USSR	1
Norway	0	East Germany	0
France	0	USSR	2
USSR	4	Norway	0
East Germany	2	Iceland	0
East Germany	0	France	0
France	2	Iceland	0
USSR	2	East Germany	0
Norway	0	USSR	1
Iceland	0	East Germany	6
Norway	2	France	0
USSR	1	France	1
Iceland	2	Norway	1
Norway	0	Iceland	1
East Germany	1	USSR	1
France	1	Norway	1
USSR	2	Iceland	0
East Germany	3	Norway	1
France	0	East Germany	1

	P	W	D	L	F	A	P
USSR	8	5	3	0	14	3	13
East Germany	8	4	3	1	13	4	11
France	8	1	4	3	4	7	6
Iceland	8	2	2	4	4	14	6
Norway	8	1	2	5	5	12	4

Group 4

Home		Away	
England	3	North'n Ireland	0
Yugoslavia	4	Turkey	0
England	2	Yugoslavia	0
Turkey	0	North'n Ireland	0
North'n Ireland	0	England	2
North'n Ireland	1	Yugoslavia	2
Turkey	0	England	0
Yugoslavia	3	North'n Ireland	0
England	8	Turkey	0
Yugoslavia	1	England	4
North'n Ireland	1	Turkey	0
Turkey	2	Yugoslavia	0

	P	W	D	L	F	A	P
England	6	5	1	0	19	1	11
Yugoslavia	6	4	0	2	13	9	8
North'n Ireland	6	1	1	4	2	10	3
Turkey	6	0	2	4	2	16	2

Group 5

Home		Away	
Hungary	0	H[illegible]	1
Poland	2	[illegible]	1
Greece	2	Hu[illegible]	1
Holland	0	Poland	0
Cyprus	2	Greece	4
Cyprus	0	Holland	2
Greece	3	Cyprus	
Cyprus	0	Hungary	1
Holland	1	Greece	1
Poland	0	Cyprus	0
Greece	1	Poland	0
Holland	2	Hungary	0
Hungary	5	Poland	3
Poland	3	Hungary	2
Hungary	3	Greece	0
Poland	0	Holland	2
Cyprus	0	Poland	1
Hungary	1	Cyprus	0
Greece	0	Holland	3
Holland	4	Cyprus	0

	P	W	D	L	F	A	P
Holland	8	6	2	0	15	1	14
Greece	8	4	1	3	12	13	9
Poland	8	3	2	3	9	11	8
Hungary	8	4	0	4	13	11	8
Cyprus	8	0	1	7	3	16	1

Group 6

Home		Away	
Finland	1	Wales	1
Czechoslovakia	3	Finland	0
Denmark	1	Finland	0
Czechoslovakia	0	Denmark	0
Wales	4	Finland	0
Finland	0	Denmark	1
Wales	1	Czechoslovakia	1
Denmark	1	Czechoslovakia	1
Wales	1	Denmark	0
Finland	3	Czechoslovakia	0
Denmark	1	Wales	0
Czechoslovakia	2	Wales	0

	P	W	D	L	F	A	P
Denmark	6	3	2	1	4	2	8
Czechoslovakia	6	2	3	1	7	5	7
Wales	6	2	2	2	7	5	6
Finland	6	1	1	4	4	10	3

Group 7

Home		Away	
Scotland	0	Bulgaria	0
Belgium	2	Eire	2
Luxembourg	0	Belgium	6
Eire	0	Scotland	0
Scotland	3	Luxembourg	0
Belgium	1	Bulgaria	1
Scotland	0	Eire	1
Bulgaria	2	Eire	1
Belgium	4	Scotland	1
Eire	0	Belgium	0
Luxembourg	1	Bulgaria	4
Bulgaria	3	Luxembourg	0
Luxembourg	0	Eire	2
Eire	2	Luxembourg	1
Bulgaria	2	Belgium	0
Scotland	2	Belgium	0
Eire	2	Bulgaria	0
Belgium	3	Luxembourg	1
Bulgaria	0	Scotland	1
Luxembourg	0	Scotland	0

	P	W	D	L	F	A	P
Eire	8	4	3	1	10	5	11
Bulgaria	8	4	2	2	12	6	10
Belgium	8	3	3	2	16	8	9
Scotland	8	3	3	2	7	5	9
Luxembourg	8	0	1	7	2	23	1

Final Group 1

Home		Away	
West Germany	1	Italy	1
Denmark	2	Spain	3
West Germany	2	Denmark	0
Italy	1	Spain	0
West Germany	2	Spain	0
Italy	2	Denmark	0

	P	W	D	L	F	A	P
West Germany	3	2	1	0	5	1	5
Italy	3	2	1	0	4	1	5
Spain	3	1	0	2	3	6	2
Denmark	3	0	0	3	2	7	0

Final Group 2

Home		Away	
England	0	Eire	1
Holland	0	USSR	1
England	1	Holland	3
Eire	1	USSR	1
England	1	USSR	3
Eire	0	Holland	1

	P	W	D	L	F	A	P
USSR	3	2	1	0	5	2	5
Holland	3	2	0	1	4	2	4
Eire	3	1	1	1	2	2	3
England	3	0	0	3	2	7	0

Semi-Finals

Home		Away	
West Germany	1	Holland	2
USSR	2	Italy	0

FINAL

Home		Away	
Holland	2	USSR	0

9th Series 1990-92

The 9th Series began at a time of momentous change throughout Europe with the collapse of communism, and the re-emergence of many small sovereign states out of its ashes. The first change, however, was not caused by the splintering of countries into their original component states but by precisely the opposite chain of events. This was the re-unification of East and West Germany into a single 'Germany' and it came, in footballing terms, just as the West Germans had won the FIFA World Cup for the third time. Against the backdrop of this new spirit of nationalism, 33 countries set out on the 'road to Sweden', (which had been selected as the host country) and they were divided into seven qualifying groups - five of five countries and two of four countries.

Group 1 was made up of Albania, Czechoslovakia, France, Iceland and Spain and began on 30th May 1990, even before the commencement of the FIFA World Cup in Italy. The first game brought together the group's two outsiders, Iceland and Albania and proved an unfortunate experience for the Albanian players whose arrival in Reykjavik was delayed at Heathrow by the London Police, after a confrontation about alleged shoplifting offences. In the game itself, they fared little better and were fortunate to lose only 2-0. The next game, some three months later, was again in Reykjavik but this time the opposition was France, unbeaten in ten games, who took an early lead through Papin. Cantona scored a peculiar second goal for France, heading the ball into the net whilst on his hands and knees and the game ended 2-1 to the visitors. Iceland also featured in the next two games in the group and by 10th October 1990 had already played half of their eight fixtures! The scores 1-0 to Czechoslovakia and 2-1 to Spain reflected the closeness of both games and highlighted the progress made by the Icelanders in the late 1980's.

France nosed ahead in the group with a 2-1 home win over Czechoslovakia who, a month later, faced Spain in Prague. In a lively game, Czechoslovakia took an early lead but, ten minutes into the second-half, went 1-2 down after Carlos had scored his third goal in consecutive games. The home side, however, fought back well, equalising when Danek beat the Spanish offside-trap and stealing the winner 13 minutes from the end. Three days later, France moved to the head of the group with a 1-0 victory over Albania in Tirana and the scene was set for a classic encounter between France and Spain, when, in their next game, Spain hammered nine goals past a hapless Albania to give themselves a commanding goal difference (Emilio Butraguenos's four goal tally in the game enabled him to push his personal total of international goals to 27, one ahead of Alfredo De Stefano's all-time record). Before a crowd of 45,000, the French team struggled to get their game together in a disjointed first-half, which saw Spain snatch an early lead before Sauzee equalised via a Durand free-kick. Manager Michel Platini's half-time talk must have done the trick because the French moved up a gear in the second-half and finished comfortable 3-1 winners.

A month later, the French maintained their 100% record with an easy 5-0 victory over Albania. Albania also featured in the next two games, losing 0-2 at home to Czechoslovakia, before gaining their first points of the series with a 1-0 victory over Iceland. A week later, Iceland lost at home to Czechoslovakia who, on eight points, then seemed to be France's main rival for the top-place. These two countries met in Prague in the next game of the group and it was the Czechs (who were unable to field several of their first-team regulars because of illness) who took the lead through Nemecek. The French came back well in the second half equalising through Papin, who went on to snatch the winner in the last minute of the game. This victory virtually guaranteed France's place in Sweden as they then only required a draw from their last two games against Spain and Iceland, who, in fact, played one another in Reykjavik in the next game in the group. Spain still had a faint chance of qualifying (aided by their 9-0 victory over Albania) and they dominated the first-half which, nonetheless, remained goalless. In the second-half, however, the Icelanders, inspired by midfielder Sigurdur Gretarsson, took control as the Spanish faltered. No doubt assisted by the cold, stormy weather, Iceland took the lead in the 71st minute through the ex-Nottingham Forest player Orlygsson and wrapped it up soon after with a second goal from Sverrisson. The victory was one of the few real shocks of the series and heralded a further upsurgence of Icelandic football under new manager Eliasson.

When the French faced Spain in Seville, they took control of the game with two early goals, from Fernandez and Papin and were never seriously troubled, thereafter, as they recorded their seventh successive victory. This win virtually ended the group contest and France went on to qualify with a 100% record – the only country to achieve full points. Spain and Albania, already doomed to third and bottom-place respectively, did not even bother to play their last game in the group.

Group 2 featured Bulgaria, Rumania, San Marino, Scotland and Switzerland and began on 12th September 1990 when Bulgaria travelled to Switzerland and Rumania travelled to Scotland. Switzerland, under their coach Uli Stielike, took an early lead through Marc Hottinger but very nearly threw the game away during a poor spell at the start of the second-half. After Bulgaria had squandered several easy chances, the Swiss reasserted their dominance and ended comfortable 2-0 winners. Meanwhile, at Hampden, a very small crowd (only 12,801) saw the Scots struggle at first against a well-organised Rumanian team who took an early lead with a hotly-disputed 13th minute goal by Camataru. Shortly before half-time, the Hearts' player, John Robertson, equalised and, in the second-half, Scotland dominated play for much of the time. Ally McCoist snatched the winner in the last 15 minutes as Scotland embarked upon their best-ever European Championship campaign. A month later, the Scots were in action again, this time at home to Switzerland, when Robertson opened the scoring with a first-half penalty kick. In the second-half, McAllister scored another goal, as the home side moved to the top of the group table with a 2-1 victory. Rumania and Bulgaria met in Bucharest on the same day when Bulgaria trounced their arch-rivals 3-0.

A month later, the minnows of the group, San Marino, went into action for the first time and the game ended in a predictable 4-0 win to their opponents, Switzerland. Scotland were also in action the same day when they faced Bulgaria in Sofia and retained their top-place with a commendable 1-1 draw. On 5th December 1990, Rumania beat San Marino 6-0 and the next game in the group was not until almost four months later when leaders, Scotland, again played Bulgaria, this time at Hampden Park. Few chances were created by either side and, when Scotland took the lead through substitute Collins six minutes from the end, they seemed to have wrapped it up. However, in the final minute, with the Scottish defence appealing for offside, Kostadinov was allowed to play the ball into an empty net to steal an equaliser. Rumania beat San Marino 3-1 but unbeaten Scotland were still the clear leaders. Switzerland played out a goalless draw with Rumania in early April and on May-Day pulled off a remarkable comeback when they met Bulgaria in Sofia. Trailing 2-0 at half-time, the Swiss pulled back to 2-1 but, with only two minutes remaining, seemed to be heading for defeat until Knup headed them level from a free-kick. In injury-time, Kubilay Turkyilmaz made a solo-run from his own half and scored the winner for Switzerland. Scotland retained their leading place with a 2-0 victory in San Marino but found themselves trailing the Swiss when they met in September because Switzerland had themselves, in the meantime, chalked up a 7-0 victory over San Marino. At half-time the Swiss were 2-0 ahead but the Scots fought back well to earn a 2-2 draw to put themselves in line for their first-ever final series. Their next game, however, away to Rumania nearly proved their undoing as they went down 1-0 after Durie was penalised for handling the ball in his own area. Then, on the same day that Scotland duly won their last game against San Marino 4-0, Switzerland could have made certain of their qualifying place against Rumania but, losing 1-0, left Rumania themselves with a chance of the top place. All depended upon the last game of the group which was played a week later between Bulgaria and Rumania. Rumania needed to win, scoring at least two goals, and they took a first-half lead through Popescu after Hagi had missed a penalty kick. Bulgaria, however, who had won the first group game 3-0 in Bucharest levelled the score 1-1 which effectively ended their neighbour's hopes of finishing in first place. Scotland thus qualified for their first-ever European Championship finals, by courtesy of Bulgaria (the same country that they, themselves, had beaten two years earlier to give Eire a World Cup Finals place!).

Group 3 was made up of Cyprus, Hungary, Italy, Norway and the USSR and began on 12th September 1990 when Norway travelled to Moscow to face the 1988 runners-up. Norway seemed intent upon defending to earn a draw and, even after Russia had taken the lead through Kanchelskis in the 22nd minute, they continued to defend and tamely handed the tie to Russia, 2-0. A month later, Norway were in action again when Hungary travelled to Bergen and this time they attacked throughout the game. Zsolt Petry in the Hungarian goal made a string of superb saves to deny the Norwegians the victory that they richly deserved and the game ended goalless. A week later, Hungary faced Italy in Budapest and took an early lead, controlling the play for the whole of the first-half. After the interval, the Italians went on to the offensive and were rewarded with a 54th minute penalty which Baggio duly put away. For the remainder of the game, the Hungarians attacked without success against a ten-man Italian defence and were unlucky to be denied penalties on at least two occasions. A fortnight later, a tiny Budapest crowd of about 3,000 saw Hungary take a first-minute lead against Cyprus, who, 20 minutes later were trailing 3-1 and seemed to be heading for a big defeat. The final scoreline of 4-2 flattered the Cypriots who could not have objected if the game had ended 7-2.

Italy faced the USSR in Rome in what many believed would be the most decisive confrontation of the group. Russia, playing their usual defensive game, were rarely troubled by the under-par Italians who looked vulnerable to their opponents' counter-attacks. The game ended 0-0 – a poor result for Italy but, as Protasov missed an easy chance in the dying minutes of the game, they could have feared worse. Cyprus were at home in the following three group games when their opponents, Norway, Italy and Hungary, all recorded easy victories by 3-0, 4-0 and 2-0 respectively. The USSR travelled to Budapest in April 1991 to play the group leaders, Hungary, and, after Mikhailichenko had put them ahead on half-an-hour, held out for a 1-0 victory. Two weeks later on May Day, Hungary's lingering hopes of taking the qualifying place were finally crushed when they played Italy in Salerno. Italian manager Vicini, under pressure as a result of reports that he was to be replaced by Sacchi, recalled Roberto Donadoni and Gianluca Vialli into the Italian side and, within a quarter of an hour, Donadoni had scored two goals. Vialli missed a penalty in the 22nd minute but made amends by scoring early in the second-half to leave Italy with an easy 3-1 victory. On the same day, Norway recorded a 3-0 win over Cyprus who then went down 4-0 to the USSR later in the month.

When Italy met Norway in Oslo the following week, they presented the Scandinavians with a gift goal in the 4th minute when Dahlum was left with an easy header. Twenty minutes later, a suicidal attempted backpass by Crippa gave Bohinen the chance to make it 2-0 and Norway took complete control of the game. In the 79th minute Schillachi pulled a goal back, but in the closing minutes, the Italians lost their self-control and went to pieces. Within seconds of coming on, Bergomi, an 89th minute substitute, fouled Lydersen and then Sorloth and was sent off (without even touching the ball) as Italy crashed to a 2-1 defeat. There was no repeat of this shock result when the USSR travelled to Norway in August, (although the Norwegians had the greater number of scoring chances), and the Russians achieved a 1-0 win.

In the next game in the group, Hungary faced the USSR in Moscow against a background of rumours (hotly denied by the Italians) that under-the-counter payments had been made to encourage the Hungarians to play better. Whether they had, or not, Hungary certainly played their best football in the group and, somewhat fortunately, held the Russians to a 2-2 draw. Two weeks later, Italy themselves travelled to Moscow to play the deciding game in the group and a tense, dour game it proved to be. In front of a huge crowd of over ninety thousand, the nervous Russians made little headway against the massed Italian defence and, in a game in which virtually no scoring chances were created by either side, had to be content with a 0-0 draw. This draw put the USSR only one point away from certain qualification and, to boot, resulted in the dismissal of the Italian manager Vicini who was replaced by Sacchi. Sacchi, himself, discovered the realities of International management when, for his first game, Norway travelled to Genoa and outplayed Italy for most of the game. Jakobsen put Norway ahead on the hour and it was not until eight minutes from the end that Italy equalised to earn a point. The qualifying place, thus went to the USSR who, although requiring only one point from their final game against Cyprus, took both with a 3-0 victory.

Group 4 was made up of Austria, Denmark, the Faroe Islands, Northern Ireland and Yugoslavia and started with one of the all-time shock results of the Championship when the Faroe Islands met Austria in their first-ever Championship game. Played at Landskrona in Sweden, because there were no turf pitches available on any of the 18 islands, the Faroes braced themselves for a heavy defeat as they faced Austrian strikers Polster and Rodax whose joint transfer fees to Sevilla and Athletico Madrid amounted to £5 million! Indeed, Jakoksen the Faroes' skipper, who supplemented his earnings as a dental surgery manager by part-time folk singing, was quoted as saying "We know we will suffer heavy defeats. But we are proud to represent our country". Austria, confident of scoring five or six goals, failed to make any head way against the Faroes' determined defence behind which keeper Knudsen (wearing a knitted 'bobble-hat') played a solid, reliable game and, in the 63rd minute Torkil Nielsen scored the shock winning goal. After the game, the Austrian manager relinquished his job in favour of Alfred Riedl after commenting "We have just seen a world sensation – I can't explain it!" His counterpart from the Faroe Islands, Gudlaugsson, summed up the victory rather better – "My boys live on barren islands in the middle of the Atlantic. They're used to hard work and they have to fight for their living. That was the spirit which worked for us tonight".

On the same day, Yugoslavia took control of their game against Northern Ireland in Belfast and had little trouble in taking both points with a 2-0 victory. A month later, the Faroe Islanders were brought down to earth when they faced 'big brothers' Denmark in Copenhagen, who ran out easy 4-1 victors. The Danes travelled to Belfast a week later and were held to a draw by the determined Irish but Yugoslavia were already showing signs that their rating (as favourites to qualify) was justified, when they thumped Austria 4-1 in the next group game. A fortnight later, the group seemed to be a 'one-horse' race as the Yugoslavs maintained their 100% record with a 2-0 win over the Danes in Copenhagen as Austria and Northern Ireland played out a goalless draw in Vienna. After a four month break, Yugoslavia were in action again when they thrashed Northern Ireland 4-1 and it was not until their next game, at home to Denmark, that they suffered a setback. Denmark, weakened by the absence of the Laudrup brothers because of a dispute with the manager Richard Moller, nevertheless dominated the game and took the lead after half an hour through Bent Christiansen. Although Pancev equalised five minutes into the second-half, Christiansen scored a second soon after and Denmark took the points. Meanwhile, in Belfast, the Faroe Islands gave the Irish a fright as they snatched a point with a 1-1 draw and the group was clearly becoming little more than a contest between Denmark and Yugoslavia. Yugoslavia moved five points clear with a 7-0 thrashing of the Faroe Islands but Denmark, with two games in hand, were beginning to get into their stride and faced the prospect of three group games before Yugoslavia saw action again. With two victories over Austria and another over the Faroe Islands, Denmark climbed a point ahead of Yugoslavia who faced the Faroe Islands in the next game. The dissolution of Yugoslavia into its various states was by now well under way, with a virtual state of war existing between Serbia and Montenegro on one hand and Croatia, Bosnia and Slovenia on the other. This resulted in the Yugoslavs fielding a 'Belgrade XI' which consisted mainly of players from Red Star and Partizan, but, against the Faroes, they proved more than adequate, winning the game 2-0 and putting their country back at the top of the table. This meant that everything depended upon the two final group games which were both played on 13th November 1991. Denmark, playing in Odense, duly won their game against the Irish but to little avail as Yugoslavia easily defeated an experimental Austrian side in Vienna – to clinch the qualifying place.

Unfortunately for the Yugoslavians, events away from the football field were to snatch this feat from them when, shortly before the finals were to be played in Sweden, the United Nations Security Council imposed sanctions upon Serbia which resulted in the disqualification of the Yugoslav team. The outshot of this action was that, at a very late stage, Denmark were called upon to fill the vacancy – with startling results!

Group 5 consisted of just four countries, Belgium, Germany, Luxembourg and Wales. Germany, playing their first competition since unification, were the reigning World Champions – a fact that failed to cut much ice with either Belgium or Wales. The group commenced when Belgium travelled to the new Welsh National Stadium, (alias Cardiff Arms Park), to play a Welsh side which had recorded only one victory in its previous 12 games. A goal down after 24 minutes, the Welsh hit back through Ian Rush (his first international goal for over two years) and earned a very creditable victory with further goals from Saunders and Hughes in the closing minutes.

The next game in the group featured Germany and Luxembourg and was played in the newly-renovated municipal stadium in Luxembourg. The day started badly when scores of Germany 'fans', bristling with weapons and missiles were turned back at the border. Both on and off the field, it was a very bad day indeed for the Germans as the hooligan elements among the German supporters then fought (literally) to impose a reign of terror upon the home fans. Police baton-charged these thugs and the game itself went ahead. Germany took an early lead through Klinsmann and were 3-0 up soon after half-time when Voller struck home a Brehme cross. Luxembourg, however, hit back to 3-2 and deserved to equalise in the closing minutes as they overran the disorganised German defence. The result, two points for Germany, brought little credit to the World Champions and heralded worse hooligan problems which were to follow in the group. Luxembourg's next opponents were Wales who came (despite the contrivances of the British press) without hooligans, and, once more, the home team put up a splendid display and were unfortunate to lose 1-0. Wales, however, down to 10 men after the expulsion of Clayton Blackmore in the 11th minute, could have argued with some justification that they deserved both points.

The next game in the group, played some three months later, saw Belgium beat Luxembourg 3-0 in Brussels but the really interesting game came a month later when Wales travelled to Brussels. Needing to win to keep alive any real hopes of qualification, Belgium went ahead soon after the start of the second-half but, ten minutes later, Dean Saunders equalised and Wales held on for a point.

Germany's hooligan 'fans' went on the rampage again when Belgium travelled to Hannover for the next game and the German police found themselves fighting a running battle with a mob of 500 missile-throwing, flare-firing thugs. When the match eventually started, the 56,000 crowd saw another under-par performance by Germany who were fortunate to scrape a 1-0 win. This left Germany one point behind Wales (their next opponents) with a game in hand. When the Germans travelled to the Welsh National Stadium early in June, they did so with some trepidation, more than aware of the threat posed by the Welsh attacking trio of Rush, Saunders and Hughes. Fielding a defensive side, Germany lost their captain, Matthaus, with an injury half-way through the hard, and at times, dirty, game and never settled back into their stride. On the hour the German player Berthold lost control and was dismissed for trampling all over Radcliffe and his absence increased pressure on an already shaky defence. In the 69th minute, Rush sprinted on to a long through-ball from Bodin and scored to give Wales both points and an unexpected boost to their aspirations of qualifying for Sweden. Belgium, by this time, were virtually out of the running although they duly beat Luxembourg in their next game. The deciding game in the group was played on 16th October 1991 when Wales travelled to Nurnberg to face Germany, needing just one point to be certain of qualifying. A very different looking Germany attacked from the offset and it seemed to be only a question of time before they took the lead as the Welsh struggled to stay in the game. Moller put Germany ahead in the 34th minute and by half-time they were leading 3-0. On the hour, Wales were reduced to ten men when Dean Saunders committed an atrocious foul on Doll and the game ended 4-1 to Germany. This result left Germany a point behind Wales with a game in hand and, when Wales had beaten Luxembourg 1-0 in their last game, the pressure was on Germany when they travelled to Brussels a week later. Once again, Germany's hoodlum fringe of supporters travelled with the sole intention of causing trouble and, forewarned, the Belgian security forces arrested over 300 and despatched them back to Germany. Nevertheless, Brussels became something of a battlefield as fighting broke out extensively. As for the game – the Germans did just enough to win 1-0, dominating the first-half but hanging on grimly in the second, as the Belgians fought back. This left Germany with the simple task of securing a point from their final game against Luxembourg which they duly did, comfortably winning the game 4-0.

Group 6 was made up of the reigning champions, Holland, together with Finland, Greece, Malta and Portugal. The first game was between Finland and Portugal in Helsinki when an under-strength Portuguese side should have lost heavily to the unfancied Finns (who missed five good chances) but, instead, held out for a 0-0 draw. Holland, minus both Rijkaard and Koeman, then travelled to Lisbon five weeks later and struggled against a lively Portuguese side. Goalless at half-time, Portugal went ahead early in the second-half via an Aguas header and held on to win 1-0. A fortnight later, Greece and Malta entered the action and the Greeks gained an easy 4-0 victory to put them in second-place in the group behind Portugal. The next game in the group saw a confident Greek side, with an eight-game unbeaten run to their credit, face a tense, under-strength Dutch team in Rotterdam. The problems for the home side arose mainly from the fact that the players had not welcomed the return of manager Rinus Michels and, for one reason or another, Gullitt, Rijkaard, Koeman, Kieft and Van Aerle were all absent from the Dutch line-up. Despite their problems, however, Holland played well and took the lead in only the 7th minute when Dennis Bergkamp headed a fine goal. Van Basten made it 2-0 twelve minutes later and Holland then cruised to their first victory. The group outsiders, Malta and Finland shared the points in the next game but Holland moved to the top of the group with a crushing 8-0 win over Malta on 19th December 1990, Van Basten, with five goals, doing most of the damage. Greece, too, moved on to four points with Holland when they beat Portugal 3-2 in the next group game and two weeks later Portugal, themselves, went to the top of the group with a rather fortunate 1-0 win in Malta. The return game was played in Oporto, just eleven days later, when Portugal won 5-0 to move three points clear of Holland.

Portugal's success, however, was short-lived as Holland won the next two games (1-0 against Malta and 2-0 against Finland) to regain the lead. Holland's next opponents, Finland, aided and abetted by an appalling footballing pitch in Helsinki, gave them quite a fright when they equalised in the 78th minute and pressed for a winner. Joop Hiele in the Dutch goal performed magnificently in the closing minutes as Holland hung on for a point. This left Portugal two points behind Holland with a game in hand and, a 1-0 victory over Finland in their next game put Portugal on level-pegging with the champions. Fittingly, Portugal travelled to play Holland in the next game in what proved to be the deciding match in the group. Frank Rijkaard sorted out his differences with manager Michels and was back in the Dutch team after his self-imposed 'retirement' and his presence bolstered Holland. Fielding a full-strength side for the first time in the series, Holland took a 20th minute lead through Witschge and, despite a few late scares, held on to win 1-0 to put themselves into pole position for the qualifying place. Although Portugal beat Greece 1-0 in their last game, to go onto eleven points also, the Dutch were already virtually assured of qualification because of their superior goal difference. Theoretically, Greece could have qualified, but the Dutch easily beat them 2-0 in their closing game to ensure their trip to Sweden.

Group 7 was made up of Eire, England, Poland and Turkey and kicked-off with the first-ever all-seated international game at Wembley Stadium. This was new manager Graham Taylor's first important game (his first was a friendly against Hungary) and a near capacity crowd of over 77,000 saw his team make hard work of beating an inept Polish side. Gary Lineker scored the opening goal in the 39th minute and Peter Beardsley made it 2-0 just before the end but a more determined opposition might have achieved better against an unsettled-looking England. Jack Charlton's Irish Republic team, despite an injury crisis, gave their opponents, Turkey, no chance in the next game in the group in Dublin. The partisan crowd of 46,000 which crammed into Landsdowne Road were treated to a brand of lively attacking football of a standard rarely achieved by an Irish team. With John Aldridge scoring his first-ever international hat-trick, Ireland ran out easy 5-0 victors to send out a warning to England that they would have a fight on their hands when the countries met a month later. Manager Taylor, determined to assert his own individual management-style upon the England team, dropped Paul Gascoigne for the game in Dublin, to the amazement and disappointment of the English press. Deprived of 'Gazza's' inventive talent, the game proved to be just as dour and unenterprising a game a when the two sides had met in Italy in the Summer. With chances few and far between, the game ended 1-1 – a result which pleased Taylor and appeared to vindicate his uninspired team selection. On the same night, Poland snatched a 1-0 win in Turkey with a Dziekanowski goal and action in the group did not resume until 27th March 1991 when the Irish travelled to Wembley to face England again. Once more lacking Gascoigne (this time through injury), England, short of imagination, struggled to overcome the lively Irish but in only their second real attack, were fortunate to take the lead when a Lee Dixon shot was deflected into the Irish net. Ireland hit back and the England defence, in sheer panic at times, always seemed vulnerable to the aerial strength of their opponents. When the Irish equalised in the 28th minute it was, inevitably, via the head of Niall Quinn and the game remained stalemated to end without further score or much entertainment for the spectators.

The next game in the group saw Poland move into second-place on the same number of points as both Eire and England, after they had beaten the Turks 3-0. Two weeks later, Poland travelled to Dublin to face Eire on such an appalling pitch that neither team were able to string together more than a couple of passes before the ball went astray. The resulting goalless draw left the door open to England who, on the same day, played Turkey in Izmir. Despite their position in the group (bottom, without a point), Turkey showed England that they should not be underrated on home soil, as they had the best of the play in a scrappy game. Much against the run of play, Dennis Wise put England ahead with a scrambled 32-minute goal and they held on to the points to go top of the group.

Almost five months later, both England and Turkey, and Eire and Poland were in action again as the group moved to it's climax. At Wembley, England again had a lucky 1-0 win, by courtesy of a goal from Alan Smith while, over in Poznan, a far more exciting game was underway. The Irish took an early lead through McGrath and, by the 68th minute, were 3-1 ahead and cruising towards victory. Uncharacteristically, the Irish defence then lost their grip and allowed Furtok and Urban to snatch back goals to earn a 3-3 draw. This left England (two points clear of Poland and Eire) needing to win at least a point in their final game in Poland, to be certain of qualifying. Poland, themselves, were virtually out of the running already, but this did not stop them from making a game of it as they took a 32nd minute lead. England pressed hard without success and could have gone further behind on several occasions. Then, with just 13 minutes remaining, their captain, Gary Lineker, scored the equaliser and England were through to the Finals in Sweden, one point ahead of the Irish who had won 3-1 in Turkey.

As the various countries travelled to Sweden, events in Yugoslavia took a sinister turn as open warfare raged between Serbia, Croatia and Bosnia. A UN Security Council meeting imposed severe restrictions upon Serbia and, to the disappointment of the Yugoslav side which had been in Sweden for some time, Yugoslavia were expelled from the Finals. This totally unprecedented action led to their replacement by second-placed Denmark who stepped into the breach little more than a week before the commencement.

On 10th June, the first game in Group 1 brought together the host country, Sweden, and the 1984 champions France. Sweden who were not expected to achieve a great deal in the Finals, surprised the French whose 100 per cent record in the qualifying competition had put them among the favourites. Playing the highest standard of football that they had achieved for some years, Sweden outplayed the disorganised French team and could have taken an early lead when, in the tenth minute, a quickly-taken free-kick created a goalscoring chance for Schwarz. A quarter of an hour later, Sweden took the lead from a corner when Eriksson powered a header past the French 'keeper Martini and for the rest of the first-half, France struggled to stay in the game. Sweden could have gone further ahead, on two occasions when Martini, at full stretch, saved the day. In the second-half, the French forward Vahirua was replaced by Perez, who, 13 minutes later, started the move which gave France an equaliser. After drawing the Swedish defence forward, Perez aimed an angled cross towards Papin who just beat the offside trap, nodded the ball forward and turned it into the corner of the Swedish net. After this equaliser, both sides seemed to be content with a draw as the game finished 1-1.

Next to go in Group 1 were latecomers Denmark and England who met in Malmo the following day. England were without five key players because of injury and their late unavailability seemed to leave manager Taylor in a state of confusion. After holding a prolonged press conference in which he eulogised about the benefits of a sweeper system, the absence of one player (Mark Wright) resulted in an immediate reversion to a flat back-four. Without a single recognised right-back in the entire squad, Taylor drafted Keith Curle into the position and, despite his enthusiasm, he soon showed that he was not cut out to be a full-back as he struggled against Povlsen and Andersen. The England midfield, looking totally unsettled, fought well enough but never asserted any real control over a Danish team who, at first, seemed rather bemused with the whole affair. As the game progressed, the Danes began to pose more of a threat, particularly along the English right flank, but it was England who came closest to scoring in the first-half when the Danish keeper, Schmeichel, saved well from Platt and Smith. In the second-half, Denmark took control of midfield as John Jensen moved up a gear and it was he who came closest to scoring when he beat Chris Woods in the 61st minute. His angled shot seemed to be heading for the net but struck the inside of the post and spun out. This prompted manager

England's Carlton Palmer challenges France's Eric Cantona

Taylor to bring on a substitute and he replaced the struggling Curle with a forward, Tony Daley, and reorganised his back four. Daley was immediately into his stride, unsettling the Danish defence and, within a couple of minutes, he should have scored twice but after receiving a caution just six minutes later, he ran out of steam as the game wound down to a goalless draw.

Three days later, England faced France, again in Malmo, determined (as were their opponents) not to lose the game. Fielding a defensive line-up, France seemed unwilling to enter the English half of the field, while England seemed incapable of breaking down the French defence. The resulting spectacle was far from entertaining and it was not until France were urged to attack by Platini, that England posed any threat. Then, Shearer dispossessed Canosi on the English left-wing and raced for the French goal, where, instead of passing to the supporting Lineker, he tried a shot which was turned away for a corner. As the first-half progressed, France took control of midfield and began to pressurise the English defence. Des Walker, given the task of controlling Papin, was in good form and at half-time the game was goalless. After half-time, the injured Sauzee was replaced by Angloma and his introduction unsettled the French midfield and almost lead to a goal when Shearer headed a Sinton cross wide of the post. The French responded with an Angloma header which Andy Sinton cleared off the line and, with a quarter of an hour left, Perez replaced midfielder Fernandez. A few minutes later, a squabble broke out in the English penalty area during which Stuart Pearce was head-butted by the French full-back Boli for no apparent reason. Referee Puhl and his linesmen failed to spot the culprit but with blood flowing from a cut on Pearce's face, knew that something had happened. Almost immediately, England were awarded a free-kick on the edge of the French penalty area and Pearce came tremendously close to scoring when his thunderous shot struck the bar. After the game which ended goalless, the French manager Platini shrugged as he admitted that his team had been instructed to play defensively but the English fans summed it up with a closing chant of 'What a load of rubbish!'

On the same day, Sweden were in action against their neighbours Denmark in Stockholm where a very different game emerged. Free from the 'don't lose at all costs' paranoia which had taken over the English and French sides, the Scandinavians' approach was like a breath of fresh air. The Swedes would have been the first to admit that their's was not the strongest squad in the competition but they attacked from the offset and in the opening minutes almost scored when Dahlin's header flashed wide of the post. Piling on the pressure, the home side went close again when Dahlin, with only keeper Schmeichel to beat, struck the ball over the bar and, five minutes before half-time, the Danes produced their best move of the game when Povlsen and Sivebaek combined to feed Vilfort with a superb opening. Unfortunately for the Danes, the ball bounced awkwardly and the Swedish keeper, Ravelli, was able to gather the ball without difficulty. Early in the second-half, the Danes brought on Torben Frank in place of their attacker Christensen but it was their opponents who made the breakthrough when Thern threaded a delightful pass through the Danish defence. Dahlin latched on to the ball, beat Nielsen and crossed to Brolin who thumped it into the net to put Sweden ahead. Not prepared to sit on their lead, the Swedes continued to attack the Danish goal and came close to scoring a second in the 7th minute when Limpar's shot was acrobatically saved by Schmeichel. Soon after, the Danes themselves went close through Frank but, just three minutes from the end, Brolin should have scored a second when Olsen blocked his goalbound shot. The game ended 1-0 much to the delight of the home crowd and this left all four countries in the group with a chance of reaching the semi-finals.

The last two games in the group were played three days later, Sweden and England in Stockholm and France and Denmark in Malmo. Sweden, requiring just a point to be certain of qualifying, struggled in the first-half after David Platt had given England a 3rd minute lead when he volleyed home a Lineker cross. England controlled much of the play and Lineker, Sinton, Platt and Daley all went close although the Swedes still counterattacked, gamely. Brolin had two strong penalty appeals turned down and the score remained 1-0 at half-time. Johnny Ekstrom replaced Limpar at the start of the second-half and his presence pressurised the unsteady English defence as the game progressed. In the 51st minute the Swedish defender Eriksson headed Sweden level from a corner-kick and England, overrun at the back, struggled to stay in the game. Then the England manager, Taylor, completely misreading the game, replaced his most dangerous striker, Gary Lineker, with Arsenal's Alan Smith. The move was greeted by stunned silence from the English team and supporters alike and heralded the virtual collapse of the England team's morale. Sweden completely dominated the rest of the game and deservedly scored a winner, through Brolin in the 82nd minute. After the game, Taylor, seemingly unaware of his appalling handling of the team throughout the series (he never even used his skillful midfield ace Nigel Clough) held his usual press conference. In this he glibly blamed (amongst other things) the half-time whistle for his team's defeat but failed even to be aware of his own miserable role in the event.

Meanwhile in Malmo, the French put on an even more inept display against Denmark when, trailing to an eighth-minute Larsen goal, they failed to take the game to their opponents. Indeed, it was the Danes who threatened to go further ahead as France had three players booked in a bad-tempered first-half. After the interval, France brought on midfielder Fernandez in place of attacker Vahirua – a strange move for a team 1-0 down and one which summed up the French attitude to the game. Nevertheless, it began to look as if it had paid off when Papin equalised on the hour but, by then, Denmark were clearly in control of the game. Twelve minutes from the final whistle, Denmark deservedly took the lead again through Elstrup, and the French went out with a whimper. Unlike the English manager, Platini soon took the honourable course and resigned.

In Group 2, the first game was played on 12th June in Gothenburg and featured Holland and Scotland. Widely regarded as the no-hopers of the group, Scotland had nothing to lose and, refusing to be overawed by Holland's star-studded team, were determined to make a game of it. The Dutch, however, at full-strength and playing their best football for years attacked the robust Scottish defence throughout the first-half without ever really looking as if they would break them down. With big Richard Gough suppressing van Basten effectively, the Scots relied upon Stuart McCall to chase and harry the Dutch midfield and, alongside him, Paul McStay provided the drive and direction. Gullit was in fine form for Holland and provided some delightful crosses which Bergkamp failed to convert but it was Frank Rijkaard who came closest to scoring in the 39th minute when Goram pushed his well-struck shot for a corner.

After the interval, Jan Wouters was replaced by Jonk and Scotland came more into the game as it progressed. The Scots, sensing that the Dutch were fading (van Basten was completely stifled by Gough and Gullit was hardly touching the ball) went on to the attack and McStay and Gough both came close to scoring. As the game entered the final quarter of an hour, Bergkamp struck Gullit's corner into the Scottish net and the holders breathed a sigh of relief. Gallacher then came on for Ally McCoist who had had a very quiet game and Ferguson replaced McClair – but to no avail. The game ended 1-0 but Scotland, their spirits raised by such a bright performance, looked eagerly to their next game against World Champions, Germany.

On the same day, Germany faced the CIS (alias the USSR) in Norrkoping and were shaken by the standard of play of the Russian team. The Germans attacked from the offset but had little success against the Russians whose naturally-defensive style of play, soaked up their attacks without many problems. In a full-blooded physical scrap, neither side shirked any tackles and in the 20th minute Germany's Rudi Voller suffered a broken arm in a collision with Kuznetsov but gamely played on until half-time. Germany had little to show for all of their pressure and the CIS (fielding Dobrovolski as their sole winger and Kolivanov in a roaming attacking role) had them baffled with their unusual tactics. Indeed, whenever the CIS mounted an attack, they broke quickly with midfielders and defenders streaming up in support of their two attackers and the German back four seemed to be in near panic every time. At half-time, Voller was replaced by midfielder Moller, an odd substitution as this left Germany with even less firepower and, not surprisingly, it was the CIS who took the lead in the 62nd minute. Kanchelskis put over a superb cross from the Russian right-wing and Reuter clumsily bundled Dobrovolski to the ground as he went for the ball. Dobrovolski scored the penalty himself and the German manager, Vogts, responded by substituting Reuter immediately with striker Jurgen Klinsmann. On the brink of panic, Germany threw everything into the attack, lobbing a succession of high balls towards Klinsmann's head – without any real success. In the 75th minute the Russians came close to scoring a second when, mounting another of their lightning attacks, Dobrovolski's centre bounced back into play off the German bar. The CIS held off the German pressure without much difficulty until the final minute when Klinsmann's apparent dive on the edge of the Russian area, earned the World Champions a free-kick. Midfielder Hassler struck the ball round the end of the Russian wall and it curled into the net to the relief of Germany.

Three days later, Germany were in action against Scotland in Norrkoping in a most unusual game. Scotland manager Andy Roxburgh, fielded the same team that had come so close against Holland and Berti Vogts fielded a more attacking side with Klinsmann and Moller in from the start. In an open, flowing game, both teams seemed intent upon scoring, as first Scotland (through Gough) and then Germany threatened to score in the opening minutes. Within the first ten minutes, Illgner, in the German goal had made three fine saves and then both McAllister and McPherson had good strikes at goal. Scotland, unfortunate not to be in the lead, had a lucky escape when Klinsmann's goalbound header struck keeper Goram's legs but in the 28th minute found themselves behind when their defence stood back from Klinsmann and Riedle thundered in on the blind side and struck an unstoppable blindside shot low into their net. Undaunted, the Scots continued to take the play to Germany and went close on several occasions.

Just a minute into the second-half, Germany struck again when a seemingly harmless cross from Effenberg was deflected by Malpas over the stranded Goram who lost his footing and could only watch in dismay as the ball looped into the Scottish net. Undaunted, Scotland fought even harder and, when Durie was substituted by Nevin, a few minutes later, began to give their opponents all sorts of problems, particularly during set-piece play. In the 57th minute, Gough had a header saved and Germany struggled to hold the aggressive Scots. Reuter was brought on in place of Riedle in the 68th minute to bolster the German defence but, only five minutes later, was injured in a clash of heads with McCall and was himself substituted by Schulz. Soon after, Buchwald was also forced to leave the field with a similar head wound and, for the last few minutes, Germany were reduced to ten men. Scotland, despite coming close on several occasions, were held by the Germans who must have counted themselves fortunate indeed to win 2-0.

Meanwhile, in Gothenburg, Holland were being held by the CIS in the other group game. Employing exactly the same tactics as worked so well against Germany, the CIS completely stifled the Dutch attack who were denied the space which they badly needed to pose a threat. Nonetheless, Holland did have two reasonable first-half chances, both as a result of Russian defensive errors. These, in the 10th minute when Bergkamp broke away and, in the 38th minute when a Koeman free-kick flashed wide, were all that Holland could muster and at half-time the game remained goalless. The CIS themselves posed no mean threat when they broke in numbers on two occasions in the first-half and, after the interval, the game continued with more of the same cat-and-mouse play. In the second-half, the CIS keeper Kharin was tested much more and Rijkaard and Van Basten drew fine saves from him. Both sides played aggressively and the Russians, Yuran and Aleinikov together with Holland's Gullitt and Bergkamp were substituted because of injury. Late in the second-half Van Basten headed into the CIS net but his seemingly good goal was ruled offside by the linesman and the game ended 0-0.

The last two matches in the group were played on 18th June when Holland and Germany met in Gothenburg while Scotland faced the CIS in Norrkoping.

In Gothenburg, the Dutch fans made their feelings known before the game when they whistled and jeered the German national anthem so loudly that the Germans began to limber up before it had finished! Germany, as a result of their bruising encounter with Scotland, were without both Buchwald and Reuter and their combined absence left the German defence in tatters. In only the second minute, Van Basten was fouled by Kohler and Koeman's lofted free-kick was headed into the net by Rijkaard. After an escape in the 8th minute, Germany went further behind in the 14th minute when Witschge struck a low drive just inside their post. Germany were totally dominated by the Dutch who controlled the game so effectively that, by half-time they could have had another two or three goals. After half-time, buoyed by the news that Scotland were 2-0 ahead of the CIS, Germany replaced Binz with Sammer and reorganised their struggling defence. Within ten minutes, Germany had assumed the offensive and, through a Klinsmann goal, pulled the score back to 2-1. De Boer found himself struggling against the aerial power of Klinsmann and Brehme and Dutch manager Michels wisely reorganised his defence and brought Winter on in his place. The Dutch reassumed the upper hand and minutes later scored a third goal through Dennis Bergkamp and coasted to a 3-1 victory and a semi-final place.

In Norrkoping, Scotland, a team that had deserved much more from their previous games against Germany and Holland faced a jaded-looking CIS team. Adopting their usual 'defend and break' tactics, the CIS team were unfortunate to go behind in only the sixth minute and, once behind, seemed to lack the imagination to get back into the game. Scotland, with nothing to lose, pushed forward against the Russians and pressurised their defence. but after scoring a second through McClair in the 17th minute, settled down to leave the attacking to their opponents. Unfamiliar with the aggressor's role, the CIS created only a

The Scottish team celebrate a fine victory over the CIS.

couple of half-chances which were not capitalised upon and, at half-time, the score remained 2-0.

After half-time, the Russians brought on two substitutes and, for a while, threatened to get back into the game but their threat was effectively countered by the substitution of McCoist and Gallacher. In the 83rd minute, Scotland scored a third when McAllister put away a penalty kick and the CIS had to settle for a 3-0 defeat, leaving Holland and Germany with the semi-final places.

The first of the semi-finals brought the host country, Sweden, against Germany in Stockholm. Memories of Sweden's 1958 World Cup semi-final defeat of West Germany in Stockholm, were not exactly fresh in the mind, but the Germans were aware that they needed to play much better than they had in their previous games. With both Buchwald and Reuter back in the team after recovering from the head wounds incurred during the Scottish match, the German defence looked much steadier. Sweden, on the contrary, were without Andersson and Schwarz who had been cautioned in two of the group games and the absence of Schwarz, in particular, unbalanced the Swedish midfield. As in their match against England, Sweden went behind in the early stages (when Hassler beat the defensive wall with a free-kick that went low into the Swedish net) and were fortunate to hold the half-time score to 1-0. After the interval, Sweden changed their formation to push the tall Kennet Andersson up into the attack but the only real chance which he created was pushed over the bar by Illgner. Germany, somewhat against the run of the play, went further ahead in the 58th minute when Riedle scored from a Sammer cross and Sweden immediately brought on Anders Limpar to replace Nilsson. Within five minutes Sweden pulled a goal back when Helmer brought down Ingesson in the German box and Brolin converted the penalty. However, the Swedes now made little progress against the steadfast German defence and, indeed, it was the German forwards who looked most threatening, even when, in the 72nd minute, Ekstrom came on in place of Dahlin. Effenberg went close for Germany in the 84th minute and, just two minutes from the end, Germany made sure of their place in the Final when Riedle scored a simple goal from Helmer's delightful through ball. The Swedish fans, who had expected little from their team when the Championships commenced, applauded their players and World Champions Germany, predictably moved to the Final in Gothenburg.

Holland, favourites to retain their European crown, met Denmark in Gothenburg the following day and in the 5th minute found themselves trailing to a Larsen goal. Danish striker Brian Laudrup, playing his best game of the Finals, beat his marker on the right and lofted the perfect centre over Van Breukelen for Larsen to head a simple goal. The Dutch came back strongly but found Peter Schmeichel in the Danish goal in a determined mood as he scattered Dane and Dutchman alike in his drive to get the ball whenever he could. Danish midfielder, Henrik Andersen, received his second booking of the series for a tackle on Gullit and played on knowing that, if his team were successful, he would miss the Final. Meanwhile, the Dutch created the odd opening but never seriously threatened the Danish goals until Bergkamp finished off a move which had involved Wouters, Witschge and Rijkaard by scoring in the 23rd minute. Although this equaliser was much against the run of play, the Danes did not let it upset them and, within ten minutes, went back into the lead when Larsen struck Koeman's poor clearance into the Dutch net. As half-time approached, Denmark maintained the upper-hand and came closer to scoring than the Dutch.

After half-time, Wim Kieft, an attacker, was brought on instead of defender De Boer as Holland went on to the attack. Although they spent most of the second-half in the Danish section of the field, the Dutch created few opportunities and found themselves outplayed by the Danish midfielders, Andersen and Jensen. In the 70th minute Andersen suffered a serious knee injury and was substituted by Christiansen. The limping Sivebaek was forced to play on in the attack as the Danes had already used their other substitute when Elstrup replaced the injured Laudrup in the 57th minute. Still Holland had nothing to show for their pressure and it was not until the 85th minute that the Dutch equalised when Rijkaard scored from a corner.

As the game went into extra-time, the Dutch seemed certain to overcome the struggling Danes but, against the odds, Denmark held out to take the game to a penalty shoot out. Then, after both sides had scored their opening penalties, Van Basten (who had failed to score at all during the finals) had his shot saved and, when the other Danes maintained their 100% record, Denmark, to everyone's surprise, progressed to the Final.

Ironically, eight years earlier, after Denmark had been knocked out by Spain in the semi-finals, as a result of a penalty shoot out, their Captain Mort Olsen had said that "Luck evens itself out in the long term" – how right he was!

Four days later, the underdogs, Denmark, faced the World Champions, Germany at the Ullevi stadium in Gothenburg. Without the injured Andersen, who had been the team's midfield powerhouse for the three group matches and most of the semi-final, Denmark were expected to struggle against the Germans, but his absence merely served to bring other Danish players to the fore. Germany assumed the offensive right from the kick-off and had most of the possession throughout the game. As early as the 4th minute, Schmeichel was in the action to snatch a cross off Klinsmann's head and, a couple of minutes later, Denmark had an escape when Christofte blocked a shot from Sammer. Despite the early German pressure, it was Denmark who took the lead in the 18th minute. Brondby's Kim Vilfort took the ball off Brehme and backheeled it down the line on Germany's left flank for Povlsen to cut it back to Jensen who drove the ball home.

Germany immediately reassumed the offensive and, minutes later, Schmeichel tipped away a goal-bound shot for a corner. On the half-hour, Illgner was called into action twice within a minute and, the Danish fan's chorus of 'Auf Wiedersehen' rang throughout the stadium drowning the unusually quiet German supporters. As the Germans became increasingly anxious, first Effenberg and then Hassler were cautioned for bad tackles. The Germans continued to camp out in the Danish half of the field but had little to show for all of their efforts other than an Effenberg shot which Schmeichel tipped over the bar seconds before the half-time whistle.

After the interval, Germany restarted the game with Doll replacing Sammer in the German midfield, and within a couple of minutes, he was involved in a scuffle with Povlsen after fouling Jensen. The German spoiling tactics continued and in the 54th minute, Reuter was cautioned for yet another unnecessary foul. As the game progressed, Germany pressed Denmark continually, pinning them back in their own half of the field, but the pressure created few real chances other than a 73rd minute Klinsmann header which was acrobatically tipped over the bar by Schmeichel. With twelve minutes of the match remaining, it was Denmark, however, who went further ahead through Vilfort when substitute Claus Christiansen headed back a poorly cleared free-kick. Germany protested that Vilfort had controlled the ball with his hand (which he obviously had) but their objections were brushed aside by referee Galler who was on Vilfort's blind side. During the last twelve minutes of the game, the Germans went to pieces and collected two further yellow cards (Doll and Klinsmann) bringing their match total to five bookings. The score remained 2-0 to Denmark whose win provided the greatest shock that the competition had ever known and a fitting climax to a splendid European Championship.

1990/92 SERIES

Group 1

Iceland	2	Albania	0
Iceland	1	France	2
Czechoslovakia	1	Iceland	0
Spain	2	Iceland	1
France	2	Czechoslovakia	1
Czechoslovakia	3	Spain	2
Albania	0	France	1
Spain	9	Albania	0
France	3	Spain	1
France	5	Albania	0
Albania	0	Czechoslovakia	2
Albania	1	Iceland	0
Iceland	0	Czechoslovakia	1
Czechoslovakia	1	France	2
Iceland	2	Spain	0
Spain	1	France	2
Czechoslovakia	2	Albania	1
Spain	2	Czechoslovakia	1
France	3	Iceland	1

Albania vs Spain was Cancelled

	P	W	D	L	F	A	P
France	8	8	0	0	20	6	16
Czechoslovakia	8	5	0	3	12	9	10
Spain	7	3	0	4	17	12	6
Iceland	8	2	0	6	7	10	4
Albania	7	1	0	6	2	21	2

Group 2

Switzerland	2	Bulgaria	0
Scotland	2	Rumania	1
Rumania	0	Bulgaria	3
Scotland	2	Switzerland	1
Bulgaria	1	Scotland	1
San Marino	0	Switzerland	4
Rumania	6	San Marino	0
Scotland	1	Bulgaria	1
San Marino	1	Rumania	3
Switzerland	0	Rumania	0
Bulgaria	2	Switzerland	3
San Marino	0	Scotland	2
San Marino	0	Bulgaria	3
Switzerland	7	San Marino	0
Switzerland	2	Scotland	2
Bulgaria	4	San Marino	0
Rumania	1	Scotland	0
Scotland	4	San Marino	0
Rumania	1	Switzerland	0
Bulgaria	1	Rumania	1

	P	W	D	L	F	A	P
Scotland	8	4	3	1	14	7	11
Switzerland	8	4	2	2	19	7	10
Rumania	8	4	2	2	13	7	10
Bulgaria	8	3	3	2	15	8	9
San Marino	8	0	0	8	1	33	0

Group 3

USSR	2	Norway	0
Norway	0	Hungary	0
Hungary	1	Italy	1
Hungary	4	Cyprus	2
Italy	0	USSR	0
Cyprus	0	Norway	3
Cyprus	0	Italy	4
Cyprus	0	Hungary	2
Hungary	0	USSR	1
Italy	3	Hungary	1
Norway	3	Cyprus	0
USSR	4	Cyprus	0
Norway	2	Italy	0
Norway	0	USSR	1
USSR	2	Hungary	2
USSR	0	Italy	0
Hungary	0	Norway	0
Italy	1	Norway	1
Cyprus	0	USSR	3
Italy	2	Cyprus	0

	P	W	D	L	F	A	P
USSR	8	5	3	0	13	2	13
Italy	8	3	4	1	12	5	10
Norway	8	3	3	2	9	5	9
Hungary	8	1	1	6	6	14	3
Cyprus	8	0	0	8	2	25	0

Group 4

N.Ireland	0	Yugoslavia	2
Faroe Islands	1	Austria	0
Denmark	4	Faroe Islands	1
N.Ireland	1	Denmark	1
Yugoslavia	4	Austria	1
Denmark	0	Yugoslavia	2
Austria	0	N.Ireland	0
Yugoslavia	4	N.Ireland	1
Yugoslavia	1	Denmark	2
N.Ireland	1	Faroe Islands	1
Yugoslavia	7	Faroe Islands	0
Austria	3	Faroe Islands	0
Denmark	2	Austria	1
Faroe Islands	0	N.Ireland	5
Faroe Islands	0	Denmark	4
Austria	0	Denmark	3
Faroe Islands	0	Yugoslavia	2
N.Ireland	2	Austria	1
Denmark	2	N.Ireland	1
Austria	0	Yugoslavia	2

	P	W	D	L	F	A	P
Yugoslavia	8	7	0	1	24	4	14
Denmark	8	6	1	1	18	7	13
N.Ireland	8	2	3	3	11	11	7
Austria	8	1	1	6	6	14	3
Faroe Islands	8	1	1	6	3	26	3

Group 5

Wales	3	Belgium	1
Luxembourg	2	Germany	3
Luxembourg	0	Wales	1
Belgium	3	Luxembourg	0
Belgium	1	Wales	1
Germany	1	Belgium	0
Wales	1	Germany	0
Luxembourg	0	Belgium	2
Germany	4	Wales	1
Wales	1	Luxembourg	0
Belgium	0	Germany	1
Germany	4	Luxembourg	0

	P	W	D	L	F	A	P
Germany	6	5	0	1	13	4	10
Wales	6	4	1	1	8	6	9
Belgium	6	2	1	3	7	6	5
Luxembourg	6	0	0	6	2	14	0

Group 6

Finland	0	Portugal	0
Portugal	1	Holland	0
Greece	4	Malta	0
Holland	2	Greece	0
Malta	1	Finland	1
Malta	0	Holland	8
Greece	3	Portugal	2
Malta	0	Portugal	1
Portugal	5	Malta	0
Holland	1	Malta	0
Holland	2	Finland	0
Finland	2	Malta	0
Finland	1	Holland	1
Portugal	1	Finland	0
Finland	1	Greece	1
Holland	1	Portugal	0
Greece	2	Finland	0
Portugal	1	Greece	0
Greece	0	Holland	2
Malta	1	Greece	1

	P	W	D	L	F	A	P
Holland	8	6	1	1	17	2	13
Portugal	8	5	1	2	11	4	11
Greece	8	3	2	3	11	9	8
Finland	8	1	4	3	5	8	6
Malta	8	0	2	6	2	23	2

Group 7

England	2	Poland	0
Eire	5	Turkey	0
Eire	1	England	1
Turkey	0	Poland	1
England	1	Eire	1
Poland	3	Turkey	0
Turkey	0	England	1
Eire	0	Poland	0
Poland	3	Eire	3
England	1	Turkey	0
Turkey	1	Eire	3
Poland	1	England	1

	P	W	D	L	F	A	P
England	6	3	3	0	7	3	9
Eire	6	2	4	0	13	6	8
Poland	6	2	3	1	8	6	7
Turkey	6	0	0	6	1	14	0

Final Group 1

Sweden	1	France	1
Denmark	0	England	0
France	0	England	0
Sweden	1	Denmark	0
Sweden	2	England	1
France	1	Denmark	2

	P	W	D	L	F	A	P
Sweden	3	2	1	0	4	2	5
Denmark	3	1	1	1	2	2	3
France	3	0	2	1	2	2	2
England	3	0	2	1	1	2	2

Final Group 2

Holland	1	Scotland	0
CIS	1	Germany	1
Scotland	0	Germany	2
Holland	0	CIS	0
Holland	3	Germany	1
Scotland	3	CIS	0

	P	W	D	L	F	A	P
Holland	3	2	1	0	4	1	5
Germany	3	1	1	1	4	4	3
Scotland	3	1	0	2	3	3	2
CIS	3	0	2	1	1	4	2

Semi-Finals

Sweden	2	Germany	3
Holland	2	Denmark	2

(Denmark won on Penalties)

FINAL

Germany	0	Denmark	2

1994/96 Qualifiers

Group 1

Home		Away	
Israel	2	Poland	1
Slovakia	0	France	0
Romania	3	Azerbaijan	0
France	0	Romania	0
Israel	2	Slovakia	2
Poland	1	Azerbaijan	0
Romania	3	Slovakia	2
Poland	0	France	0
Azerbaijan	0	Israel	2
Azerbaijan	0	France	2
Israel	1	Romania	1
Romania	2	Poland	1
Israel	0	France	0
Slovakia	4	Azerbaijan	1
Poland	4	Israel	3
France	4	Slovakia	0
Azerbaijan	1	Romania	4
Poland	5	Slovakia	0
Romania	2	Israel	1
France	1	Poland	1
Azerbaijan	0	Slovakia	1
France	10	Azerbaijan	0
Slovakia	1	Israel	0
Poland	0	Romania	0
Romania	1	France	3
Israel	2	Azerbaijan	0
Slovakia	4	Poland	1
Slovakia	0	Romania	2
Azerbaijan	0	Poland	0
France	2	Israel	0

	P	W	D	L	F	A	P
Romania	10	6	3	1	18	8	21
France	10	5	5	0	22	2	20
Slovakia	10	4	2	4	14	18	14
Poland	10	3	4	3	14	12	13
Israel	10	3	3	4	13	11	12
Azerbaijan	10	0	1	9	2	29	1

Group 2

Home		Away	
Cyprus	1	Spain	2
Macedonia	1	Denmark	1
Belgium	2	Armenia	0
Armenia	0	Cyprus	0
Denmark	3	Belgium	1
Macedonia	0	Spain	2
Belgium	1	Macedonia	1
Spain	3	Denmark	0
Cyprus	2	Armenia	0
Belgium	1	Spain	4
Macedonia	3	Cyprus	0
Spain	1	Belgium	1
Cyprus	1	Denmark	1
Armenia	0	Spain	2
Belgium	2	Cyprus	0
Denmark	1	Macedonia	0
Armenia	2	Macedonia	2
Denmark	4	Cyprus	0
Macedonia	0	Belgium	5
Spain	1	Armenia	0
Armenia	0	Denmark	2
Belgium	1	Denmark	3
Spain	6	Cyprus	0
Macedonia	1	Armenia	2
Armenia	0	Belgium	2
Denmark	1	Spain	1
Cyprus	1	Macedonia	1
Spain	3	Macedonia	0
Cyprus	1	Belgium	1
Denmark	3	Armenia	1

	P	W	D	L	F	A	P
Spain	10	8	2	0	25	4	26
Denmark	10	6	3	1	19	9	21
Belgium	10	4	3	3	16	12	15
Macedonia	10	1	4	5	9	18	7
Cyprus	10	1	4	5	5	19	7
Armenia	10	1	2	7	5	17	5

Group 3

Home		Away	
Iceland	0	Sweden	1
Hungary	2	Turkey	2
Turkey	5	Iceland	0
Switzerland	4	Sweden	2
Switzerland	1	Iceland	1
Sweden	2	Hungary	0
Turkey	1	Switzerland	2
Turkey	2	Sweden	1
Hungary	2	Switzerland	2
Hungary	1	Sweden	0
Switzerland	1	Turkey	2
Sweden	1	Iceland	1
Iceland	2	Hungary	1
Iceland	0	Switzerland	2
Sweden	0	Switzerland	0
Turkey	2	Hungary	0
Switzerland	3	Hungary	0
Iceland	0	Turkey	0
Hungary	1	Iceland	0
Sweden	2	Turkey	2

	P	W	D	L	F	A	P
Switzerland	8	5	2	1	15	7	17
Turkey	8	4	3	1	16	8	15
Sweden	8	2	3	3	9	10	9
Hungary	8	2	2	4	7	13	8
Iceland	8	1	2	5	3	12	5

Group 4

Home		Away	
Estonia	0	Croatia	2
Slovenia	1	Italy	1
Ukraine	0	Lithuania	2
Estonia	0	Italy	2
Croatia	2	Lithuania	0
Ukraine	0	Slovenia	0
Ukraine	3	Estonia	0
Slovenia	1	Lithuania	2
Italy	1	Croatia	2
Italy	4	Estonia	1
Croatia	4	Ukraine	0
Slovenia	3	Estonia	0
Ukraine	0	Italy	2
Lithuania	0	Croatia	0
Lithuania	0	Italy	1
Croatia	2	Slovenia	0
Estonia	0	Ukraine	1
Lithuania	2	Slovenia	1
Estonia	1	Slovenia	3
Ukraine	1	Croatia	0
Estonia	0	Lithuania	1
Croatia	7	Estonia	1
Italy	1	Slovenia	0
Lithuania	1	Ukraine	3
Croatia	1	Italy	1
Slovenia	3	Ukraine	2
Lithuania	5	Estonia	0
Italy	3	Ukraine	0
Slovenia	1	Croatia	2
Italy	4	Lithuania	0

	P	W	D	L	F	A	P
Croatia	10	7	2	1	22	5	23
Italy	10	7	2	1	20	6	23
Lithuania	10	5	1	4	13	12	16
Ukraine	10	4	1	5	11	15	13
Slovenia	10	3	2	5	13	13	11
Estonia	10	0	0	10	3	31	0

Group 5

Home		Away	
Czech Rep.	6	Malta	1
Luxembourg	0	Holland	4
Norway	1	Byelorussia	0
Malta	0	Czech Rep.	0
Byelorussia	2	Luxembourg	0
Norway	1	Holland	1
Byelorussia	0	Norway	4
Holland	0	Czech Rep.	0
Malta	0	Norway	1
Holland	5	Luxembourg	0
Malta	0	Luxembourg	1
Czech Rep	4	Byelorussia	2
Luxembourg	0	Norway	2
Holland	4	Malta	0
Byelorussia	1	Malta	1
Czech Rep.	3	Holland	1
Norway	6	Luxembourg	0
Byelorussia	1	Holland	0
Luxembourg	1	Czech Rep.	0
Norway	2	Malta	0
Norway	1	Czech Rep.	1
Czech Rep.	2	Norway	0
Luxembourg	1	Malta	0
Holland	1	Byelorussia	0
Byelorussia	0	Czech Rep.	2
Malta	0	Holland	4
Luxembourg	0	Byelorussia	0
Malta	0	Byelorussia	2
Czech Rep.	3	Luxembourg	0
Holland	3	Norway	0

	P	W	D	L	F	A	P
Czech Republic	10	6	3	1	21	6	21
Holland	10	6	2	2	23	5	20
Norway	10	6	2	2	17	7	20
Byelorussia	10	3	2	5	8	13	11
Luxembourg	10	3	1	6	3	21	10
Malta	10	2	2	8	2	22	2

Group 6

Home		Away	
North'n Ireland	4	Liechtenstein	1
Liechtenstein	0	Austria	4
North'n Ireland	1	Portugal	2
Latvia	0	Eire	3
Latvia	1	Portugal	3
Austria	1	North'n Ireland	2
Eire	4	Liechtenstein	0
Portugal	1	Austria	0
Liechtenstein	0	Latvia	1
North'n Ireland	0	Eire	4
Portugal	8	Liechtenstein	0
Eire	1	North'n Ireland	1
Austria	5	Latvia	0
Eire	1	Portugal	0
Latvia	0	North'n Ireland	1
Austria	7	Liechtenstein	0
Portugal	3	Latvia	2
Liechtenstein	0	Eire	0
North'n Ireland	1	Latvia	2
Eire	1	Austria	3
Liechtenstein	0	Portugal	7
Latvia	3	Austria	2
Portugal	1	North'n Ireland	1
Austria	3	Eire	1
Latvia	1	Liechtenstein	0
Eire	2	Latvia	1
Austria	1	Portugal	1
Liechtenstein	0	North'n Ireland	4
Portugal	3	Eire	0
North'n Ireland	5	Austria	3

	P	W	D	L	F	A	P
Portugal	10	7	2	1	28	7	23
Eire	10	5	2	3	17	11	17
North'n Ireland	10	5	2	3	21	15	17
Austria	10	5	1	4	29	14	16
Latvia	10	4	0	6	11	20	12
Liechtenstein	10	0	1	9	1	40	1

Group 7

Home		Away	
Wales	2	Albania	0
Georgia	0	Moldova	1
Moldova	3	Wales	2
Bulgaria	2	Georgia	0
Albania	1	Germany	2
Georgia	5	Wales	
Bulgaria	4	Moldova	
Wales	0	Bulgaria	
Moldova	0	Germany	
Albania	0	Georgia	
Germany	2	Albania	
Georgia	0	Germany	
Bulgaria	3	Wales	
Albania	3	Moldova	
Germany	1	Wales	
Moldova	0	Bulgaria	
Georgia	2	Albania	
Bulgaria	3	Germany	
Wales	0	Georgia	
Moldova	2	Albania	
Germany	4	Georgia	
Wales	1	Moldova	
Albania	1	Bulgaria	
Bulgaria	3	Albania	
Germany	6	Moldova	
Wales	1	Germany	
Georgia	2	Bulgaria	
Germany	3	Bulgaria	
Albania	1	Wales	
Moldova	3	Georgia	

	P	W	D	L	F	A	P
Germany	10	8	1	1	27	10	[illegible]
Bulgaria	10	7	1	2	24	10	[illegible]
Georgia	10	5	0	5	14	13	[illegible]
Moldova	10	3	0	7	11	27	[illegible]
Wales	10	2	2	6	9	19	[illegible]
Albania	10	2	2	6	10	16	[illegible]

Group 8

Home		Away	
Finland	0	Scotland	
Faroe Islands	1	Greece	
Scotland	5	Faroe Islands	
Greece	4	Finland	
Russia	4	San Marino	
Scotland	1	Russia	
Greece	2	San Marino	
Finland	5	Faroe Islands	
Finland	4	San Marino	
Greece	1	Scotland	
Russia	0	Scotland	
San Marino	0	Finland	
San Marino	0	Scotland	
Greece	0	Russia	
Faroe Islands	0	Finland	
Russia	3	Faroe Islands	
Faroe Islands	3	San Marino	
Faroe Islands	0	Scotland	
San Marino	0	Russia	
Finland	2	Greece	
Scotland	1	Greece	
Finland	0	Russia	
Scotland	1	Finland	
Faroe Islands	2	Russia	
San Marino	0	Greece	
Russia	2	Greece	
San Marino	1	Faroe Islands	
Scotland	5	San Marino	
Russia	3	Finland	
Greece	5	Faroe Islands	

	P	W	D	L	F	A	P
Russia	10	8	2	0	34	5	26
Scotland	10	7	2	1	19	3	23
Greece	10	6	0	4	23	9	18
Finland	10	5	0	5	18	18	15
Faroe Islands	10	2	0	8	10	35	6
San Marino	10	0	0	10	2	36	0

Play-Off

Home		Away	
Holland	2	Eire	[illegible]

FULL COUNTRY-BY-COUNTRY MATCH RECORD

ALBANIA

1962/64 SERIES

First Round

ALBANIA W.O. GREECE (WITHDREW)

GREECE & ALBANIA TECHNICALLY AT WAR SINCE 1912

Second Round

29/6/63 **DENMARK** (3) **4** **ALBANIA** (0) **0** 25200
J. Peterson, O. Madsen, Clausen, Enoksen

30/10/63 **ALBANIA** (1) **1** **DENMARK** (0) **0** 27765
Pano

1966/68 SERIES

GROUP MATCHES - GROUP 4

9/4/67 **WEST GERMANY** (2) **6** **ALBANIA** (0) **0** 30000
Muller (4), Lohr (2)

14/5/67 **ALBANIA** (0) **0** **YUGOSLAVIA** (1) **2** 35000
Zambata (2)

12/11/67 **YUGOSLAVIA** (1) **4** **ALBANIA** (0) **0** 30000
Sprecic, Osim (2), Lazarevic

17/12/67 **ALBANIA** (0) **0** **WEST GERMANY** (0) **0** 21889

1970/72 SERIES

GROUP MATCHES - GROUP 8

14/10/70 **POLAND** (1) **3** **ALBANIA** (0) **0** 15000
Gadocha, Lubanski, Szoltysik

9/12/70 **TURKEY** (2) **2** **ALBANIA** (1) **1** 45000
Metin, Cemil — *Ziu*

17/2/71 **ALBANIA** (0) **0** **WEST GERMANY** (1) **1** 20000
Muller

12/5/71 **ALBANIA** (1) **1** **POLAND** (1) **1** 20000
Zegha — *Banas*

12/6/71 **WEST GERMANY** (2) **2** **ALBANIA** (0) **0** 46000
Netzer, Grabowski

4/11/71 **ALBANIA** (1) **3** **TURKEY** (0) **0** 15000
Pernaska (2), Pano

DID NOT COMPETE IN THE 1974/76 OR 1978/80 CHAMPIONSHIPS

1982/84 SERIES

GROUP MATCHES - GROUP 6

22/9/82 **AUSTRIA** (2) **5** **ALBANIA** (0) **0** 9000
Hagmayr (23), Gasselich (40), Kola (og 64) Weber (66), Brauneder (81)

27/10/82 **TURKEY** (0) **1** **ALBANIA** (0) **0** 35000
Arif (86)

15/12/82 **ALBANIA** (0) **0** **NORTHERN IRELAND** (0) **0** 30000

30/3/83 **ALBANIA** (0) **1** **WEST GERMANY** (0) **2** 30000
Targaj (Pen 81) — *Voeller (54), Rummenigge (Pen 67)*

27/4/83 **NORTHERN IRELAND** (0) **1** **ALBANIA** (0) **0** 14000
Stewart (54)

11/5/83 **ALBANIA** (0) **1** **TURKEY** (1) **1** 30000
Rashit (og 73) — *Metin (34)*

8/6/83 **ALBANIA** (0) **1** **AUSTRIA** (1) **2** 25000
Targaj (Pen 83) — *Schacner (6, 58)*

20/11/83 **WEST GERMANY** (1) **2** **ALBANIA** (1) **1** 40000
Rummenigge (24), Strack (80) — *Tomori (23)*

1986/88 SERIES

GROUP MATCHES - GROUP 1

15/10/86 **AUSTRIA** (1) **3** **ALBANIA** (0) **0** 8000
Orgris (19), Polster (65), Linzmaier (76)

3/12/86 **ALBANIA** (1) **1** **SPAIN** (0) **2** 20000
Muca (27) — *Arteche (66), Joaquin (83)*

25/3/87 **ROMANIA** (3) **5** **ALBANIA** (1) **1** 15000
Piturca (1), Holoni (42), Hagi (Pen 44) Belodedici (54), Bumbescu (69) — *Muca (34)*

29/4/87 **ALBANIA** (0) **0** **AUSTRIA** (1) **1** 13000
Polster (7)

28/10/87 **ALBANIA** (0) **0** **ROMANIA** (0) **1** 18000
Klein (61)

18/11/87 **SPAIN** (3) **5** **ALBANIA** (0) **0** 50000
Baquero (5, 31, 74), Michel (Pen 36) Llorente (67)

1990/92 SERIES

GROUP MATCHES - GROUP 1

30/5/90 **ICELAND** (1) **2** **ALBANIA** (0) **0** 6500
Gudjohnsen (41), Edvaldsson (82)

17/11/90 **ALBANIA** (0) **0** **FRANCE** (1) **1** 15000
Boli (25)

19/12/90 **SPAIN** (4) **9** **ALBANIA** (0) **0** 27600
Amor (9), Carlos (22, 63), Butragueno (30, 57, 66, 75) Hierro (37), Baquero (86)

30/3/91 **FRANCE** (4) **5** **ALBANIA** (0) **0** 24181
Sauzee (1, 19), Papin (pen 34, 43), Lekbello (o.g. 82)

1/5/91 **ALBANIA** (0) **0** **CZECHOSLOVAKIA** (0) **2** 10000
Kubik (47), Kuka (67)

26/5/91 **ALBANIA** (0) **1** **ICELAND** (0) **0** 5000
Abazi (65)

16/10/91 **CZECHOSLOVAKIA** (0) **2** **ALBANIA** (0) **1** 2366
Kula (36), Lancz (40) — *Zmijani (62)*

18/12/91 **ALBANIA** vs **SPAIN** Cancelled

1994/96 SERIES

GROUP MATCHES - GROUP 7

7/9/94 **WALES** (1) **2** **ALBANIA** (0) **0** 6500
Coleman (9), Giggs (67)

16/11/94 **ALBANIA** (1) **1** **GERMANY** (1) **2** 23000
Zmijani (32) — *Klinsmann (18), Kirsten (46)*

14/12/94 **ALBANIA** (0) **0** **GEORGIA** (1) **1** 15000
Arveladze (17)

18/12/94 **GERMANY** (2) **2** **ALBANIA** (0) **1** 20310
Matthaus (Pen, 8), Klinsmann (17) — *Rraklli (58)*

29/3/95 **ALBANIA** (2) **3** **MOLDOVA** (0) **0** 15000
Kushta (32, 79), Kacaj (42)

26/4/95 **GEORGIA** (2) **2** **ALBANIA** (0) **0** 25000
S. Arveladze (3), Ketsbaia (42)

7/6/95 **MOLDOVA** (2) **2** **ALBANIA** (2) **3** 7000
Curteanu (10), Kleshchenko (15) — *Kushta (8), Bellai (25), Vata (71)*

6/9/95 **ALBANIA** (1) **1** **BULGARIA** (1) **1** 10000
Rraklli (16) — *Stoichkov (8)*

7/10/95 **BULGARIA** (1) **3** **ALBANIA** (0) **0** 35000
Letchkov (15), Kostadinov (80, 82)

15/11/95 **ALBANIA** (1) **1** **WALES** (1) **1** 5500
Kushta (Pen, 4) — *Pembridge (43)*

ARMENIA

1994/96 SERIES

GROUP MATCHES - GROUP 2

7/9/94 **BELGIUM** (1) **2** **ARMENIA** (0) **0**
Krbashian (Og, 4), Degryse (73)

8/10/94 **ARMENIA** (0) **0** **CYPRUS** (0) **0** 6000

16/11/94 **CYPRUS** (1) **2** **ARMENIA** (0) **0** 8000
Soteriou (7), Fasouliotis (87)

26/4/95 **ARMENIA** (0) **0** **SPAIN** (0) **2** 40000
Amavisca (49), Goikoetxea (63)

10/5/95 **ARMENIA** (1) **2** **MACEDONIA** (0) **2** 12500
Grigorian (23), Shakhgeldyan (50) — *Hristov (60), Markovski (69)*

7/6/95 **SPAIN** (0) **1** **ARMENIA** (0) **0** 17000
Hierro (Pen, 64)

16/8/95 **ARMENIA** (0) **0** **DENMARK** (1) **2** 22000
M. Laudrup (32), Allan Nielsen (46)

6/9/95 **MACEDONIA** (1) **1** **ARMENIA** (0) **2** 10000
Micevski (10) — *Razmik (61), Armen (78)*

7/10/95 **ARMENIA** (0) **0** **BELGIUM** (2) **2** 5000
Nilis (28, 39)

15/11/95 **DENMARK** (2) **3** **ARMENIA** (0) **1** 40208
Schjonberg (19), Beck (35), M. Laudrup (58) — *Artur Petrossian (47)*

AUSTRIA

1958/60 SERIES

First Round

20/5/59 **NORWAY** (0) **0** **AUSTRIA** (1) **1** 27566
Hof

23/9/59 **AUSTRIA** (3) **5** **NORWAY** (2) **2** 37000
Nemic (2), Hof (2), Skerlan

Quarter-Finals

13/12/59 **FRANCE** (3) **5** **AUSTRIA** (1) **2** 43775
Fontaine (3), Vincent (2) — *Horak, Pichler*

27/3/60 **AUSTRIA** (0) **2** **FRANCE** (1) **4** 38000
Nemec, Probst — *Marcel, Rahis, Heutte, Kopa (Pen)*

1962/64 SERIES

First Round

AUSTRIA RECEIVED A BYE

Second Round

Date	Home	HT	FT	Away	HT	FT	Att.
25/9/63	**AUSTRIA**	(0)	**0**	**EIRE**	(0)	**0**	26800
13/10/63	**EIRE**	(1)	**3**	**AUSTRIA**	(1)	**2**	40000
	Cantwell (2), Fogarty			*Koleznik, Floegel*			

1966/68 SERIES

GROUP MATCHES - GROUP 3

Date	Home	HT	FT	Away	HT	FT	Att.
2/10/66	**FINLAND**	(0)	**0**	**AUSTRIA**	(0)	**0**	10000
10/6/67	**USSR**	(3)	**4**	**AUSTRIA**	(1)	**3**	103000
	Malafeev, Byshovets, Chislenko, Streltzov			*Hof, Wolny, Sieber*			
24/9/67	**AUSTRIA**	(1)	**2**	**FINLAND**	(0)	**1**	27000
	Floegel, Grausam			*Peltonen*			
4/10/67	**GREECE**	(2)	**4**	**AUSTRIA**	(0)	**1**	45000
	Sideris (3, 1 Pen), Papaioannu			*Grausam*			
15/10/67	**AUSTRIA**	(0)	**1**	**USSR**	(0)	**0**	37400
	Grausam						
5/11/67	**AUSTRIA**	(1)	**1**	**GREECE**	(0)	**1**	25000
	Siber			*Sideris*			

1970/72 SERIES

GROUP MATCHES - GROUP 6

Date	Home	HT	FT	Away	HT	FT	Att.
1/11/70	**AUSTRIA**	(1)	**1**	**ITALY**	(2)	**2**	60000
	Parits			*De Sisti, Mazzola*			
26/5/71	**SWEDEN**	(0)	**1**	**AUSTRIA**	(0)	**0**	10000
	Olsson						
30/5/71	**EIRE**	(0)	**1**	**AUSTRIA**	(3)	**4**	16000
	Rogers (Pen)			*Schmidradner (Pen), Kodat, Ettmayer, Stare*			
5/9/71	**AUSTRIA**	(1)	**1**	**SWEDEN**	(0)	**0**	42000
	Stering						
10/10/71	**AUSTRIA**	(3)	**6**	**EIRE**	(0)	**0**	25000
	Parits (3), Jara (2), Pirkner						
20/11/71	**ITALY**	(1)	**2**	**AUSTRIA**	(2)	**2**	85000
	Riva, De Sisti			*Jara, Santarini (og)*			

1974/76 SERIES

GROUP MATCHES - GROUP 2

Date	Home	HT	FT	Away	HT	FT	Att.
4/9/74	**AUSTRIA**	(0)	**2**	**WALES**	(1)	**1**	35000
	Kreuz, Krankl			*Griffiths*			
16/3/75	**LUXEMBOURG**	(1)	**1**	**AUSTRIA**	(0)	**2**	6000
	Braun			*Koglberger, Krankl*			
2/4/75	**AUSTRIA**	(0)	**0**	**HUNGARY**	(0)	**0**	70000
24/9/75	**HUNGARY**	(2)	**2**	**AUSTRIA**	(1)	**1**	30000
	Nyilasi, Pusztai			*Krankl (Pen)*			
15/10/75	**AUSTRIA**	(3)	**6**	**LUXEMBOURG**	(2)	**2**	14500
	Welzl (2), Krankl (2), Jara, Prohaska			*Braun, Phillipp*			
19/11/75	**WALES**	(1)	**1**	**AUSTRIA**	(0)	**0**	30000
	Griffiths						

1978/80 SERIES

GROUP MATCHES - GROUP 2

Date	Home	HT	FT	Away	HT	FT	Att.
30/8/78	**NORWAY**	(0)	**0**	**AUSTRIA**	(2)	**2**	12000
				Pezzey (23), Krankl (43)			
20/9/78	**AUSTRIA**	(1)	**3**	**SCOTLAND**	(0)	**2**	70000
	Pezzey (27), Schachnwe (47), Kreuz (63)			*McQueen (64), Gray (78)*			
15/11/78	**AUSTRIA**	(0)	**1**	**PORTUGAL**	(1)	**2**	62000
	Schachner (71)			*Nene (30), Alberto (90)*			
28/3/79	**BELGIUM**	(1)	**1**	**AUSTRIA**	(0)	**1**	9900
	Vandereycken (Pen, 21)			*Krankl (61)*			
2/5/79	**AUSTRIA**	(0)	**0**	**BELGIUM**	(0)	**0**	40000
29/8/79	**AUSTRIA**	(1)	**4**	**NORWAY**	(0)	**0**	37000
	Jara (42), Prohaska (Pen, 46), Kreuz (75), Krankl (86)						
17/10/79	**SCOTLAND**	(0)	**1**	**AUSTRIA**	(1)	**1**	72700
	Gemmill (75)			*Krankl (40)*			
21/11/79	**PORTUGAL**	(1)	**1**	**AUSTRIA**	(1)	**2**	80000
	Reinaldo (42)			*Welzl (36), Schachner (51)*			

1982/84 SERIES

GROUP MATCHES - GROUP 6

Date	Home	HT	FT	Away	HT	FT	Att.
22/9/82	**AUSTRIA**	(2)	**5**	**ALBANIA**	(0)	**0**	9000
	Hagmayr (23), Gasselich (40)						
13/10/82	**AUSTRIA**	(2)	**2**	**NORTHERN IRELAND**	(0)	**0**	11500
	Schachner (3, 39)						
17/11/82	**AUSTRIA**	(3)	**4**	**TURKEY**	(0)	**0**	10500
	Polster (10), Pezzey (34), Prohaska (Pen, 36), Schachner (54)						
27/4/83	**AUSTRIA**	(0)	**0**	**WEST GERMANY**	(0)	**0**	60000
8/6/83	**ALBANIA**	(0)	**1**	**AUSTRIA**	(1)	**2**	25000
	Targaj (Pen, 83)			*Schachner (6, 58)*			
21/9/83	**NORTHERN IRELAND**	(1)	**3**	**AUSTRIA**	(0)	**1**	25000
	Hamilton (28), Whiteside (65), O'Neill (89)			*Gasselich (82)*			
5/10/83	**WEST GERMANY**	(3)	**3**	**AUSTRIA**	(0)	**0**	70000
	Rummenigge (4), Voller (19, 21)						
16/11/83	**TURKEY**	(0)	**3**	**AUSTRIA**	(0)	**1**	30000
	Ilyas (62), Selcuk (69, (Pen, 76))			*Baumeister (71)*			

1986/88 SERIES

GROUP MATCHES - GROUP 1

Date	Home	HT	FT	Away	HT	FT	Att.
10/9/86	**ROMANIA**	(1)	**4**	**AUSTRIA**	(0)	**0**	20000
	Iovan (44, 63), Lacatus (61), Hagi (89)						
15/10/86	**AUSTRIA**	(1)	**3**	**ALBANIA**	(0)	**0**	8000
	Orgris (19), Polster (65), Linzmaier (76)						
1/4/87	**AUSTRIA**	(1)	**2**	**SPAIN**	(1)	**3**	41000
	Linzmaier (39), Polster (64)			*Eloy (31, 58), Carrasco (89)*			
29/4/87	**ALBANIA**	(0)	**0**	**AUSTRIA**	(1)	**1**	13000
				Polster (7)			
14/10/87	**SPAIN**	(0)	**2**	**AUSTRIA**	(0)	**0**	70410
	Michel (Pen, 58), Sanchis (63)						
18/11/87	**AUSTRIA**	(0)	**0**	**ROMANIA**	(0)	**0**	6200

1990/92 SERIES

GROUP MATCHES - GROUP 4

Date	Home	HT	FT	Away	HT	FT	Att.
12/9/90	**FAROE ISLANDS**	(0)	**1**	**AUSTRIA**	(0)	**0**	1265
	Nielsen (61)						
31/10/90	**YUGOSLAVIA**	(2)	**4**	**AUSTRIA**	(1)	**1**	17500
	Pancev (32, 52, 85), Katanec (43)			*Ogris (15)*			
14/11/90	**AUSTRIA**	(0)	**0**	**N. IRELAND**	(0)	**0**	7000
22/5/91	**AUSTRIA**	(1)	**3**	**FAROE ISLANDS**	(0)	**0**	13000
	Pfeifenberger (13), Streiter (48), Wetl (69)						
5/6/91	**DENMARK**	(1)	**2**	**AUSTRIA**	(0)	**1**	12521
	Christensen (2, 77)			*Ogris (83)*			
9/10/91	**AUSTRIA**	(0)	**0**	**DENMARK**	(3)	**3**	10000
				Artner (o.g. 10), Povlsen (16), Christensen (37)			
16/10/91	**N. IRELAND**	(2)	**2**	**AUSTRIA**	(1)	**1**	8000
	Dowie (17), Black (40)			*Lainer (44)*			
13/11/91	**AUSTRIA**	(0)	**0**	**YUGOSLAVIA**	(2)	**2**	8000
				Lukic (19), Savicevic (39)			

1994/96 SERIES

GROUP MATCHES - GROUP 6

Date	Home	HT	FT	Away	HT	FT	Att.
7/9/94	**LIECHTENSTEIN**	(0)	**0**	**AUSTRIA**	(3)	**4**	5800
				Polster (21, 45, 83), Aigner (22)			
12/10/94	**AUSTRIA**	(1)	**1**	**NORTHERN IRELAND**	(2)	**2**	20000
	Polster (Pen, 25)			*Gillespie (3), P. Gray (36)*			
13/11/94	**PORTUGAL**	(1)	**1**	**AUSTRIA**	(0)	**0**	46000
	Figo (37)						
29/3/95	**AUSTRIA**	(2)	**5**	**LATVIA**	(0)	**0**	4000
	Herzog (17, 59), Pfeifenberger (40), Polster ((Pen, 70), 90)						
26/4/95	**AUSTRIA**	(3)	**7**	**LIECHTENSTEIN**	(0)	**0**	5500
	Kuhbauer (7), Polster (10, (Pen, 54)), Sabitzer (17), Purk (84), Hutter (87, 89)						
11/6/95	**EIRE**	(0)	**1**	**AUSTRIA**	(0)	**3**	33000
	Houghton (65)			*Polster (69, 78), Ogris (72)*			
16/8/95	**LATVIA**	(1)	**3**	**AUSTRIA**	(0)	**2**	2000
	Rimkus (13, 59), Zeiberlins (88)			*Polster (68), Ramusch (78)*			
6/9/95	**AUSTRIA**	(1)	**3**	**EIRE**	(0)	**1**	24000
	Stoger (3, 64, 77)			*McGrath (74)*			
11/10/95	**AUSTRIA**	(1)	**1**	**PORTUGAL**	(0)	**1**	44000
	Stoger (21)			*Paulinho Santos (49)*			
15/11/95	**NORTHERN IRELAND**	(2)	**5**	**AUSTRIA**	(0)	3	8400
	Dowie (Pen, 32), Gray (64), Hunter (53), O'Neill (27, 78)			*Schopp (56), Stumpf (70), Wetl (81)*			

AZERBAIJAN

1994/96 SERIES

GROUP MATCHES - GROUP 1

Date	Home	HT	FT	Away	HT	FT	Att.
7/9/94	**ROMANIA**	(1)	**3**	**AZERBAIJAN**	(0)	**0**	10000
	Belodedici (43), Petrescu (58), Raducioiu (88)						

12/10/94 **POLAND** (1) **1** **AZERBAIJAN** (0) **0** 10000
Juskowiak (45)

16/11/94 **AZERBAIJAN** (0) **0** **ISRAEL** (1) **2** 3000
R. Harazi (29), Rosenthal (51)

13/12/94 **AZERBAIJAN** (0) **0** **FRANCE** (1) **2** 4000
Papin (24), Loko (55)

29/3/95 **SLOVAKIA** (3) **4** **AZERBAIJAN** (0) **1** 12450
Tittel (35), Timko (40, 52), Dubovsky (Pen, 45) — *Suleimanov (Pen, 80)*

26/4/95 **AZERBAIJAN** (1) **1** **ROMANIA** (2) **4** 1000
Suleimanov (35) — *Raducioiu (2, 69, 76), Dumitrescu (39)*

16/8/95 **AZERBAIJAN** (0) **0** **SLOVAKIA** (0) **1** 1000
Jancula (60)

6/9/95 **FRANCE** (3) **10** **AZERBAIJAN** (0) **0** 15000
Desailly (13), Djorkaeff (18, 79), Guerin (33), Pedros (49), Leboeuf (53, 70), Dugarry (66), Zidane (68), Cocard (90)

11/10/95 **ISRAEL** (1) **2** **AZERBAIJAN** (0) **0** 5000
R. Harazi (30, 50)

15/11/95 **AZERBAIJAN** (0) **0** **POLAND** (0) **0** 1000

BELGIUM

1962/64 SERIES

First Round

4/11/62 **YUGOSLAVIA** (2) **3** **BELGIUM** (2) **2** 25500
Skoblar (2), Vasovic — *Stockman, Jurion*

31/3/63 **BELGIUM** (0) **0** **YUGOSLAVIA** (1) **1** 24600
Samardzic

1966/68 SERIES
GROUP MATCHES - GROUP 7

11/11/66 **BELGIUM** (0) **2** **FRANCE** (0) **1** 45000
Van Himst (2) — *Lech*

19/3/67 **LUXEMBOURG** (0) **0** **BELGIUM** (3) **5** 10000
Van Himst (2), Stockman (3)

21/5/67 **POLAND** (2) **3** **BELGIUM** (0) **1** 70000
Lubanski (2), Szoltysik — *Puis*

8/10/67 **BELGIUM** (2) **2** **POLAND** (2) **4** 30000
Devrindt (2) — *Smijevski (3), Brychczy*

28/10/67 **FRANCE** (0) **1** **BELGIUM** (1) **1** 18000
Herbin — *Claessen*

22/11/67 **BELGIUM** (0) **3** **LUXEMBOURG** (0) **0** 8000
Thio (2), Claessen

1970/72 SERIES
GROUP MATCHES - GROUP 5

25/11/70 **BELGIUM** (2) **2** **DENMARK** (0) **0** 11000
Devrindt (2)

3/2/71 **BELGIUM** (1) **3** **SCOTLAND** (0) **0** 25000
Van Himst (3, 1 Pen)

17/2/71 **BELGIUM** (2) **3** **PORTUGAL** (0) **0** 25000
Lambert, Van Himst, Denul

26/5/71 **DENMARK** (0) **1** **BELGIUM** (0) **2** 30000
Bjerre — *Devrindt (2)*

10/11/71 **SCOTLAND** (1) **1** **BELGIUM** (0) **0** 36000
O'Hare

21/11/71 **PORTUGAL** (0) **1** **BELGIUM** (0) **1** 53600
Peres (Pen) — *Lambert*

Quarter-Finals

29/4/72 **ITALY** (0) **0** **BELGIUM** (0) **0** 70000

13/5/72 **BELGIUM** (1) **2** **ITALY** (0) **1** 38000
Van Moer, Van Himst — *Riva (Pen)*

Semi-Finals

14/6/72 **WEST GERMANY** (1) **2** **BELGIUM** (0) **1** 60000 Antwerp
Muller (2) — *Polleunis*

Third Place Match

17/6/72 **BELGIUM** (1) **2** **HUNGARY** (0) **1** 10000 Liege
Lambert, Van Himst — *Ku (Pen)*

1974/76 SERIES
GROUP MATCHES - GROUP 7

8/9/74 **ICELAND** (0) **0** **BELGIUM** (1) **2** 10000
Van Moer (2, 1 Pen)

12/10/94 **BELGIUM** (1) **2** **FRANCE** (1) **1** 50000
Martens, Van Der Elst — *Coste*

7/12/74 **EAST GERMANY** (0) **0** **BELGIUM** (0) **0** 35000

6/9/75 **BELGIUM** (1) **1** **ICELAND** (0) **0** 9000
Lambert

27/9/75 **BELGIUM** (0) **1** **EAST GERMANY** (0) **2** 26000
Puis — *Ducke, Hafner*

15/11/75 **FRANCE** (0) **0** **BELGIUM** (0) **0** 45000

Quarter-Finals

25/4/76 **HOLLAND** (2) **5** **BELGIUM** (0) **0** 58000
Rijsbergen, Rensenbrink (3), Neeskens (Pen)

22/5/76 **BELGIUM** (1) **1** **HOLLAND** (0) **2** 45000
Van Gool — *Rep, Cruyff*

1978/80 SERIES
GROUP MATCHES - GROUP 2

20/9/78 **BELGIUM** (0) **1** **NORWAY** (1) **1** 7000
Cools (65) — *Larsen (8)*

11/10/78 **PORTUGAL** (1) **1** **BELGIUM** (1) **1** 35000
Gomes (31) — *Vercauteren (37)*

28/3/79 **BELGIUM** (1) **1** **AUSTRIA** (0) **1** 9900
Vandereycken (Pen, 21) — *Krankl (61)*

2/5/79 **AUSTRIA** (0) **0** **BELGIUM** (0) **0** 40000

12/9/79 **NORWAY** (1) **1** **BELGIUM** (1) **2** 11665
Jacobsen (7) — *Janssens (31), Van Der Elst (75)*

17/10/79 **BELGIUM** (0) **2** **PORTUGAL** (0) **0** 10000
Van Moer (46), Van Der Elst (55)

21/11/79 **BELGIUM** (1) **2** **SCOTLAND** (0) **0** 12000
Van Der Elst (5), Voordeckers (47)

19/12/79 **SCOTLAND** (0) **1** **BELGIUM** (3) **3** 30000
Robertson (55) — *Vandenbergh (18), Van Der Elst (23, 28)*

FINALS - GROUP 2

12/6/80 **BELGIUM** (1) **1** **ENGLAND** (1) **1** 7000
Ceulemans (38) — *Wilkins (32)*

15/5/80 **SPAIN** (1) **1** **BELGIUM** (1) **2** 11000
Quini (35) — *Gerets (17), Cools (64)*

18/6/80 **ITALY** (0) **0** **BELGIUM** (0) **0** 69000

Final

22/6/80 **WEST GERMANY** (1) **2** **BELGIUM** (0) **1** 47864 Rome
Hrubesch (10, 89) — *Vandereycken (Pen, 71)*

1982/84 SERIES
GROUP MATCHES - GROUP 1

6/10/82 **BELGIUM** (1) **3** **SWITZERLAND** (0) **0** 16808
Ludi (og, 2), Coeck (48), Vandenbergh (82)

15/12/82 **BELGIUM** (2) **3** **SCOTLAND** (2) **2** 48877
Vandenbergh (25), Van Der Elst (38, 63) — *Dalglish (13, 35)*

30/3/83 **EAST GERMANY** (0) **1** **BELGIUM** (1) **2** 75000
Streich (83) — *Van Der Elst (36), Vandenbergh (69)*

27/4/83 **BELGIUM** (2) **2** **EAST GERMANY** (1) **1** 43894
Ceulemans (18), Coeck (38) — *Streich (9)*

12/10/83 **SCOTLAND** (0) **1** **BELGIUM** (1) **1** 23000
Nicholas (50) — *Vercauteren (30)*

9/11/83 **SWITZERLAND** (1) **3** **BELGIUM** (0) **1** 10000
Schallibaum (24), Brigger (76), Geiger (82) — *Vandenbergh (64)*

FINALS - GROUP 1

13/6/84 **BELGIUM** (2) **2** **YUGOSLAVIA** (0) **0** 45000
Vandenbergh (27), Grun (44)

16/6/84 **FRANCE** (3) **5** **BELGIUM** (0) **0** 51287
Platini (3, (Pen, 74), 88), Giresse (32), Fernandez

19/6/84 **DENMARK** (1) **3** **BELGIUM** (2) **2** 36911
Arnesen (Pen, 40), Brylle (60), Elkjaer (83) — *Ceulemans (25), Vercauteren (38)*

1986/88 SERIES
GROUP MATCHES - GROUP 7

10/9/86 **BELGIUM** (1) **2** **EIRE** (1) **2** 22212
Claesen (14), Scifo (71) — *Stapleton (18), Brady (Pen, 89)*

14/10/86 **LUXEMBOURG** (0) **0** **BELGIUM** (3) **6** 15000
Gerets (6), Claesen (9, 54, (Pen, 88)), Vercauteren (41), Ceulemans (87)

19/11/86 **BELGIUM** .... (0) **1** **BULGARIA** .... (0) **1** 33000
Janssen (47) — *Tanev (63)*

1/4/87 **BELGIUM** .... (1) **4** **SCOTLAND** .... (1) **1** 26650
Claesen (8, 55, 85), Vercauteren (75) — *McStay (13)*

29/4/87 **EIRE** .... (0) **0** **BELGIUM** .... (0) **0** 49000

23/9/87 **BULGARIA** .... (1) **2** **BELGIUM** .... (0) **0** 60000
Sirakov (19), Tanev (70)

14/10/87 **SCOTLAND** .... (1) **2** **BELGIUM** .... (0) **0** 20052
McCoist (14), McStay (79)

11/11/87 **BELGIUM** .... (1) **3** **LUXEMBOURG** .... (0) **0** 15000
Ceulemans (17), Degryse (55), Creve (81)

1990/92 SERIES

GROUP MATCHES - GROUP 5

17/10/90 **WALES** .... (1) **3** **BELGIUM** .... (1) **1** 12000
Rush (29), Saunders (86), Hughes (88) — *Versavel (24)*

27/2/91 **BELGIUM** .... (3) **3** **LUXEMBOURG** .... (0) **0** 24500
Vandenburgh (7), Ceulemans (17), Scifo (36)

27/3/91 **BELGIUM** .... (0) **1** **WALES** .... (0) **1** 27500
Degryse (47) — *Saunders (58)*

1/5/91 **GERMANY** .... (1) **1** **BELGIUM** .... (0) **0** 56000
Matthaus (3)

11/9/91 **LUXEMBOURG** .... (0) **0** **BELGIUM** .... (1) **2** 9000
Scifo (25), Degryse (49)

20/11/91 **BELGIUM** .... (0) **0** **GERMANY** .... (1) **1** 26000
Voller (15)

1994/96 SERIES

GROUP MATCHES - GROUP 2

7/9/94 **BELGIUM** .... (1) **2** **ARMENIA** .... (0) **0**
Krbashian (Og, 4), Degryse (73)

12/10/94 **DENMARK** .... (1) **3** **BELGIUM** .... (1) **1** 40075
Vilfort (35), Jensen (70), Strudal (85) — *Degryse (30)*

16/11/94 **BELGIUM** .... (1) **1** **MACEDONIA** .... (0) **1** 17000
Verheyen (31) — *Boskovski (54)*

17/12/94 **BELGIUM** .... (1) **1** **SPAIN** .... (1) **4** 21000
Degryse (6) — *Hierro (29), Donato (Pen, 56), Julio Salinas (68), Luis Enrique (89)*

29/3/95 **SPAIN** .... (1) **1** **BELGIUM** .... (1) **1** 27000
Guerrero (24) — *Degryse (26)*

26/4/95 **BELGIUM** .... (1) **2** **CYPRUS** .... (0) **0** 14000
Karagiannis (20), Schepens (47)

7/6/95 **MACEDONIA** .... (0) **0** **BELGIUM** .... (4) **5**
Grun (15), Scifo (18, 59), Schepens (27), Versavel (43)

Match played behind closed doors as a disciplinary punishment

6/9/95 **BELGIUM** .... (1) **1** **DENMARK** .... (2) **3** 40000
Grun (25) — *M. Laudrup (19), Beck (21), Vilfort (65)*

7/10/95 **ARMENIA** .... (0) **0** **BELGIUM** .... (2) **2** 5000
Nilis (28, 39)

15/11/95 **CYPRUS** .... (1) **1** **BELGIUM** .... (0) **1** 8000
Agathocleous (18) — *De Bilde (76)*

BULGARIA

1958/60 SERIES

First Round

31/5/59 **YUGOSLAVIA** .... (1) **2** **BULGARIA** .... (0) **0** 40000
Galic, Tasic

25/10/59 **BULGARIA** .... (0) **1** **YUGOSLAVIA** .... (0) **1** 45000
Diev — *Mujic*

1962/64 SERIES

First Round

7/11/62 **BULGARIA** .... (0) **3** **PORTUGAL** .... (0) **1** 50000
Asparoukhov (2), Diev — *Eusebio*

16/12/62 **PORTUGAL** .... (2) **3** **BULGARIA** .... (0) **1** 25900
Hernani (2), Coluna — *Iliev*

23/1/63 **BULGARIA** .... (0) **1** **PORTUGAL** .... (0) **0** 15000
Asparoukov — Replay, Rome

Second Round

29/9/63 **BULGARIA** .... (1) **1** **FRANCE** .... (0) **0** 26000
Diev

26/10/63 **FRANCE** .... (1) **3** **BULGARIA** .... (0) **1** 32223
Goujon (2), Herbin — *Jamikov*

1966/68 SERIES

GROUP MATCHES - GROUP 2

13/11/66 **BULGARIA** .... (3) **4** **NORWAY** .... (0) **2** 2000
Tzanev (2), Jekov (2) — *Hasund (2)*

11/6/67 **SWEDEN** .... (0) **0** **BULGARIA** .... (1) **2** 2427
Jekov, Dermendjiev

29/6/67 **NORWAY** .... (0) **0** **BULGARIA** .... (0) **0** 2000

12/11/67 **BULGARIA** .... (2) **3** **SWEDEN** .... (0) **0** 3500
Kotkov, Mitkov, Asparoukov

26/11/67 **BULGARIA** .... (0) **1** **PORTUGAL** .... (0) **0** 6000
Dermendijev

17/12/67 **PORTUGAL** .... (0) **0** **BULGARIA** .... (0) **0** 2000

Quarter-Finals

6/4/68 **BULGARIA** .... (1) **3** **ITALY** .... (0) **2** 5500
Jekov (2, 1 Pen), Dermendijev — *Penev (og), Prati*

20/4/68 **ITALY** .... (1) **2** **BULGARIA** .... (0) **0** 8400
Prati, Domenghini

1970/72 SERIES

GROUP MATCHES - GROUP 2

15/11/70 **BULGARIA** .... (1) **1** **NORWAY** .... (0) **1** 25000
Atanson — *Fuglset*

19/5/71 **BULGARIA** .... (1) **3** **HUNGARY** .... (0) **0** 45000
Kolev, Petkov, Velickov

9/6/71 **NORWAY** .... (0) **1** **BULGARIA** .... (4) **4** 22000
Iversen — *Bonev (2, 1 Pen), Zhekov, Vassilev*

22/9/71 **HUNGARY** .... (0) **2** **BULGARIA** .... (0) **0** 70000
Juhasz, Vidats

10/11/71 **FRANCE** .... (0) **2** **BULGARIA** .... (0) **1** 10000
Loubet (2) — *Bonev (Pen)*

4/12/71 **BULGARIA** .... (0) **2** **FRANCE** .... (0) **1** 15000
Zhekov, Michailov — *Blanchet*

1974/76 SERIES

GROUP MATCHES - GROUP 8

13/10/74 **BULGARIA** .... (3) **3** **GREECE** .... (1) **3** 35000
Bonev, Denev (2) — *Antoniadis, Papaioannou, Glenzos*

18/12/74 **GREECE** .... (2) **2** **BULGARIA** .... (0) **1** 30000
Sarafis, Antoniadis — *Kolev*

27/4/75 **BULGARIA** .... (0) **1** **WEST GERMANY** .... (0) **1** 50000
Kolev (Pen) — *Ritschel (Pen)*

11/6/75 **BULGARIA** .... (3) **5** **MALTA** .... (0) **0** 35000
Dimitrov, Denev, Panov, Bonev (Pen), Milanov

19/11/75 **WEST GERMANY** .... (0) **1** **BULGARIA** .... (0) **0** 73000
Heynckes

21/12/75 **MALTA** .... (0) **0** **BULGARIA** .... (0) **2** 7000
Panov, Jordanov

1978/80 SERIES

GROUP MATCHES - GROUP 1

11/10/78 **DENMARK** .... (1) **2** **BULGARIA** .... (1) **2** 16000
B. Nielsen (17), Lerby (63) — *Panov (34), Iliev (84)*

29/11/78 **BULGARIA** .... (0) **0** **NORTHERN IRELAND** . (1) **2** 30000
Armstrong (17), J. Nicholl (83)

2/5/79 **NORTHERN IRELAND** . (2) **2** **BULGARIA** .... (0) **0** 18700
C. Nicholl (16), Armstrong (33)

19/5/79 **BULGARIA** .... (0) **1** **EIRE** .... (0) **0** 20000
Tzvetkov (80)

6/6/79 **BULGARIA** .... (0) **0** **ENGLAND** .... (1) **3** 47500
Keegan (33), Watson (53), Barnes (54)

17/10/79 **EIRE** .... (1) **3** **BULGARIA** .... (0) **0** 22000
Martin (39), Grealish (46), Stapleton (83)

31/10/79 **BULGARIA** .... (1) **3** **DENMARK** .... (0) **0** 7000
Jeliaskov (21), Tzvetkov (51, 88)

22/11/79 **ENGLAND** .... (1) **2** **BULGARIA** .... (0) **0** 71491
Watson (9), Hoddle (68)

1982/84 SERIES

GROUP MATCHES - GROUP 4

27/10/82 **BULGARIA** .... (1) **2** **NORWAY** .... (1) **2** 37500
Velichkov (13), Nikolov (68) — *Thoresen (17), Oekland (67)*

17/11/82 **BULGARIA** .... (0) **0** **YUGOSLAVIA** .... (1) **1** 25000
Stojkovic

27/4/83 **WALES** .... (0) **1** **BULGARIA** .... (0) **0** 9006
Charles (79)

7/9/83 **NORWAY** (1) **1** **BULGARIA** (1) **2** 15515
Hareide (4) — *Mladenov (12), Sirakov (50)*

16/11/83 **BULGARIA** (0) **1** **WALES** (0) **0** 8000
Gochev (54)

21/12/83 **YUGOSLAVIA** (1) **3** **BULGARIA** (1) **2** 37500
Susic (30, 52), Radanovic (90) — *Iskrenov (28), Dimitrov (60)*

1986/88 SERIES
GROUP MATCHES - GROUP 7

10/9/86 **SCOTLAND** (0) **0** **BULGARIA** (0) **C** 35070

19/11/86 **BELGIUM** (0) **1** **BULGARIA** (0) **1** 33000
Janssen (47) — *Tanev (63)*

1/4/87 **BULGARIA** (1) **2** **EIRE** (0) **1** 38000
Sadkov (41), Tanev (Pen, 82) — *Stapleton (52)*

30/4/87 **LUXEMBOURG** (0) **1** **BULGARIA** (0) **4** 1500
Langers (59) — *Sadkov (49), Sirakov (55), Tanev (62), Kolev (82)*

20/5/87 **BULGARIA** (2) **3** **LUXEMBOURG** (0) **0** 20000
Sirakov (35), Vordanov (Pen, 41), Kolev (57)

23/9/87 **BULGARIA** (1) **2** **BELGIUM** (0) **0** 60000
Sirakov (19), Tanev (70)

14/10/87 **EIRE** (0) **2** **BULGARIA** (0) **0** 26000
McGrath (52), Moran (85)

11/11/87 **BULGARIA** (0) **0** **SCOTLAND** (0) **1** 60000
Mackay

1990/92 SERIES
GROUP MATCHES - GROUP 2

12/9/90 **SWITZERLAND** (1) **2** **BULGARIA** (0) **0** 12500
Hottiger (19), Bickel (63)

17/10/90 **ROMANIA** (0) **0** **BULGARIA** (1) **3** 25000
Sirakov (28), Todorov (48, 76)

14/11/90 **BULGARIA** (0) **1** **SCOTLAND** (1) **1** 42000
Todorov (74) — *McCoist (9)*

27/3/91 **SCOTLAND** (0) **1** **BULGARIA** (0) **1** 33119
Collins (84) — *Kostadinov (89)*

1/5/91 **BULGARIA** (2) **2** **SWITZERLAND** (0) **3** 55000
Kostadinov (11), Sirakov (25) — *Knup (58, 88), Turkyil Maz (90)*

22/5/91 **SAN MARINO** (0) **0** **BULGARIA** (2) **3** 612
Ivanov (13), Sirakov (20), Penev (70)

16/10/91 **BULGARIA** (3) **4** **SAN MARINO** (0) **0** 8000
Valentini (o.g. 20), Stoichkov (pen 37), Yankov (41), Iliev (85)

20/11/91 **BULGARIA** (0) **1** **ROMANIA** (1) **1** 20000
Sirakov (56) — *Popescu (30)*

1994/96 SERIES
GROUP MATCHES - GROUP 7

12/10/94 **BULGARIA** (0) **2** **GEORGIA** (0) **0** 45000
Kostadinov (56, 62)

16/11/94 **BULGARIA** (1) **4** **MOLDOVA** (0) **1** 50000
Stoichkov (45, 85), Balakov (64), Kostadinov (87) — *Kleshchenko (59)*

14/12/94 **WALES** (0) **0** **BULGARIA** (2) **3** 20000
Ivanov (5), Kostadinov (15), Stoichkov (51)

29/3/95 **BULGARIA** (1) **3** **WALES** (0) **1** 65000
Balakov (37), Penev (70, 82) — *Saunders (83)*

26/4/95 **MOLDOVA** (0) **0** **BULGARIA** (1) **3** 20500
Balakov (29), Stoichkov (54, 67)

7/6/95 **BULGARIA** (1) **3** **GERMANY** (2) **2** 60000
Stoichkov (Pens, (45, 66)), Kostadinov (69) — *Klinsmann (18), Strunz (44)*

6/9/95 **ALBANIA** (1) **1** **BULGARIA** (1) **1** 10000
Rraklli (16) — *Stoichkov (8)*

7/10/95 **BULGARIA** (1) **3** **ALBANIA** (0) **0** 35000
Letchkov (15), Kostadinov (80, 82)

11/10/95 **GEORGIA** (1) **2** **BULGARIA** (0) **1** 45000
Arveladze (3), Kinkladze (48) — *Stoichkov (88)*

15/11/95 **GERMANY** (0) **3** **BULGARIA** (0) **1** 75841
Klinsmann (50, (Pen, 76)), Hassler (56) — *Stoichkov (47)*

BYELORUSSIA
1994/96 SERIES
GROUP MATCHES - GROUP 5

7/9/94 **NORWAY** (0) **1** **BYELORUSSIA** (0) **0** 16739
Frigaard (88)

12/10/94 **BYELORUSSIA** (0) **2** **LUXEMBOURG** (0) **0** 8500
Romashchenko (67), Gerasimets (76)

16/11/94 **BYELORUSSIA** (0) **0** **NORWAY** (2) **4** 7500
Berg (34), Leonhardsen (39), Bohinen (52), Rekdal (Pen, 83)

29/3/95 **CZECH REPUBLIC** (2) **4** **BYELORUSSIA** (1) **2** 5549
Kadlec (5), Berger (18, 63), Kuka (69) — *Gerasimets (Pen, 44), Gurinovich (88)*

26/4/95 **BYELORUSSIA** (0) **1** **MALTA** (0) **1** 9250
Taikov (57) — *Carabott (71)*

7/6/95 **BYELORUSSIA** (1) **1** **HOLLAND** (0) **0** 22000
Gerasimets (27)

6/9/95 **HOLLAND** (0) **1** **BYELORUSSIA** (0) **0** 17000
Mulder (83)

7/10/95 **BYELORUSSIA** (0) **0** **CZECH REPUBLIC** (1) **2** 20000
Frydek (25), Berger (84)

11/10/95 **LUXEMBOURG** (0) **0** **BYELORUSSIA** (0) **0** 4500

12/11/95 **MALTA** (0) **0** **BYELORUSSIA** (0) **2** 4000
Gerasimets (82, 85)

CROATIA
1994/96 SERIES
GROUP MATCHES - GROUP 4

4/9/94 **ESTONIA** (0) **0** **CROATIA** (1) **2** 1250
Suker (44, 75)

9/10/94 **CROATIA** (0) **2** **LITHUANIA** (0) **0** 12000
Jerkan (56), Kozniku (61)

16/11/94 **ITALY** (0) **1** **CROATIA** (1) **2** 39000
D. Baggio (90) — *Suker (32, 60)*

25/3/95 **CROATIA** (2) **4** **UKRAINE** (0) **0** 25000
Boban (13), Suker (21, 76), Prosinecki (70)

29/3/95 **LITHUANIA** (0) **0** **CROATIA** (0) **0** 9000

26/4/95 **CROATIA** (1) **2** **SLOVENIA** (0) **0** 25000
Prosinecki (17), Suker (90)

11/6/95 **UKRAINE** (1) **1** **CROATIA** (0) **0** 10000
Kalitvintsev (13)

3/9/95 **CROATIA** (4) **7** **ESTONIA** (1) **1** 25000
Mladenovic (3), Suker (19, 38, 90), Boksic (29), Boban (42), Stimac (81) — *Reim (17)*

8/10/95 **CROATIA** (0) **1** **ITALY** (1) **1** 40000
Suker (Pen, 47) — *Albertini (29)*

15/11/95 **SLOVENIA** (1) **1** **CROATIA** (1) **2** 10000
Gliha (36) — *Suker (41), Jurcevic (55)*

CYPRUS
1966/68 SERIES
GROUP MATCHES - GROUP 6

3/12/66 **CYPRUS** (1) **1** **ROMANIA** (0) **5** 20000
Kostakis — *Dridea (2), Lucescu, Fratila (2)*

22/3/67 **CYPRUS** (0) **0** **ITALY** (0) **2** 11105
Domenghini, Facchetti

23/4/67 **ROMANIA** (3) **7** **CYPRUS** (0) **0** 20000
Dimitriu (3), Ionescu (2), Martinovic, Lucescu

1/11/67 **ITALY** (2) **5** **CYPRUS** (0) **0** 24000
Fogli, Mazzola, Riva (3)

8/11/67 **SWITZERLAND** (2) **5** **CYPRUS** (0) **0** 4000
Blattler (2), Kunzli, Durr, Odermatt

17/2/67 **CYPRUS** (1) **2** **SWITZERLAND** (0) **1** 8000
Melis, Bamboulis — *Odermatt*

1970/72 SERIES
GROUP MATCHES - GROUP 4

3/2/71 **CYPRUS** (0) **0** **NORTHERN IRELAND** (0) **3** 12000
Nicholson, Dougan, Best (Pen)

21/4/71 **NORTHERN IRELAND** (2) **5** **CYPRUS** (0) **0** 35000
Best (3), Dougan, Nicholson

15/11/71 **CYPRUS** (1) **1** **USSR** (2) **3** 8000
Charalambos — *Koloton, Evryuzhikhin, Sherchenko*

9/5/71 **CYPRUS** (0) **0** **SPAIN** (1) **2** 10000
Pirri, Violeta

7/6/71 **USSR** (3) **6** **CYPRUS** (0) **1** 50000
Fedoton (2), Evryuzhikhin (2), Koloton, Banischevsky — *Mikail*

24/11/71 **SPAIN** (3) **7** **CYPRUS** (0) **0** 68000
Pirri (2, 1 Pen), Quino (2), Aquilar, Loro, Rojo

1974/76 SERIES
GROUP MATCHES - GROUP 1

16/4/75 **ENGLAND** (2) **5** **CYPRUS** (0) **0** 68000
Macdonald (5)

20/4/75 **CZECHOSLOVAKIA** (2) **4** **CYPRUS** (0) **0** 5000
Panenka (3), Masny

11/5/75 **CYPRUS** .... (0) **0** **ENGLAND** .... (1) **1** 20000
Keegan

8/6/75 **CYPRUS** .... (0) **0** **PORTUGAL** .... (1) **2** 11000
Nene (2)

23/11/75 **CYPRUS** .... (0) **0** **CZECHOSLOVAKIA** .... (3) **3** 15000
Nehoda, Bicovsky, Masny

3/12/75 **PORTUGAL** .... (1) **1** **CYPRUS** .... (0) **0** 4000
Alves

1978/80 SERIES

GROUP MATCHES - GROUP 3

13/12/78 **SPAIN** .... (2) **5** **CYPRUS** .... (0) **0** 17500
Asensi (9), Delbosque (10), Santillana (52, 77), R. Cano (65)

1/4/79 **CYPRUS** .... (0) **0** **YUGOSLAVIA** .... (1) **3** 4500
Vujovic (40, 79), Surjak (82)

13/5/79 **CYPRUS** .... (1) **1** **ROMANIA** .... (1) **1** 8000
Kaiafas (31) — *Ankustia (30)*

14/11/79 **YUGOSLAVIA** .... (1) **5** **CYPRUS** .... (0) **0** 22500
Kranjcar (32, 50), Vujovic (60), Petrovic (75), Savic (87)

18/11/79 **ROMANIA** .... (1) **2** **CYPRUS** .... (0) **0** 10000
Multescu (40), Radacanu (75)

9/12/79 **CYPRUS** .... (0) **1** **SPAIN** .... (2) **3** 15000
Vrahimis (69) — *Villar (5), Santillana (41), Saura (89)*

1982/84 SERIES

GROUP MATCHES - GROUP 5

1/5/82 **ROMANIA** .... (2) **3** **CYPRUS** .... (1) **1** 20000
Vaetus (16), Camataru (19), Boloni (71) — *Vrachmis (29)*

13/11/82 **CYPRUS** .... (0) **0** **SWEDEN** .... (1) **1** 3000
Corneliusson (34)

12/2/83 **CYPRUS** .... (0) **1** **ITALY** .... (0) **1** 25000
Mavris (47) — *Patikis (og, 57)*

27/3/83 **CYPRUS** .... (1) **1** **CZECHOSLOVAKIA** .... (0) **1** 12000
Theophanous (21) — *Bicovsky (59)*

16/4/83 **CZECHOSLOVAKIA** .... (3) **6** **CYPRUS** .... (0) **0** 6750
Danek (4, 71), Vizek (21, 48) Prokes (37), Jurkemik (56)

15/5/83 **SWEDEN** .... (0) **5** **CYPRUS** .... (0) **0** 19801
Prytz (52, 75), Corneliusson (57), Hysen (60), A. Ravelli (71)

12/11/83 **CYPRUS** .... (0) **0** **ROMANIA** .... (0) **1** 13000
Boloni (77)

22/12/83 **ITALY** .... (0) **3** **CYPRUS** .... (0) **1** 20773
Altobelli (53), Cabrini (82), Rossi (Pen, 86) — *Tsinghis (Pen, 68)*

1986/88 SERIES

GROUP MATCHES - GROUP 5

3/12/86 **CYPRUS** .... (2) **2** **GREECE** .... (1) **4** 10000
Christofi (28), Savvides (41) — *Antoniou (13), Papaioannu (48)*

21/12/86 **CYPRUS** .... (0) **0** **HOLLAND** .... (1) **2** 10000
Gullit (19), Bosman (73)

14/1/87 **GREECE** .... (0) **3** **CYPRUS** .... (0) **1** 35000
Anastopoulos (54, 66), Bonovas (63) — *Savva (60)*

8/2/87 **CYPRUS** .... (0) **0** **HUNGARY** .... (0) **1** 8000
Boda (49)

12/4/87 **POLAND** .... (0) **0** **CYPRUS** .... (0) **0** 25000

28/10/87 **HOLLAND** .... (4) **8** **CYPRUS** .... (0) **0** 55000
Bosman (1, 38, 52, 60, 67), Gullit (20), Spelbos (3), Vant Schip (46)

GAME DECLARED VOID DUE TO ATTACK ON CYPRIOT GOALKEEPER

Replay : -

9/12/87 **HOLLAND** .... (2) **4** **CYPRUS** .... (0) **0** Closed Doors
Bosman (35, 44, 66), R. Koeman (Pen, 63)

11/11/87 **CYPRUS** .... (0) **0** **POLAND** .... (0) **1** 8000
Lesniak (74)

1/12/87 **HUNGARY** .... (0) **1** **CYPRUS** .... (0) **0** 2000
Kiprich (89)

1990/92 SERIES

GROUP MATCHES - GROUP 3

31/10/90 **HUNGARY** .... (3) **4** **CYPRUS** .... (1) **2** 3000
Lorincz (1), Christodolou (o.g. 19) Kiprich (pen 20, pen 67)) — *Xiurupas (13), Tsolakis (89)*

14/11/90 **CYPRUS** .... (0) **0** **NORWAY** .... (1) **3** 3000
Sorloth (39), Bohinen (50), Brandhaug (64)

22/12/90 **CYPRUS** .... (0) **0** **ITALY** .... (3) **4** 10(
Vierchowod (15), Serena (22, 50), Lombardo (44)

3/4/91 **CYPRUS** .... (0) **0** **HUNGARY** .... (2) **2** 3(
Szalma (15), Kiprich (40)

1/5/91 **NORWAY** .... (0) **3** **CYPRUS** .... (0) **0** 7
Lydersen (pen 49), Dahlum (65), Sorloth (90)

29/5/91 **USSR** .... (1) **4** **CYPRUS** .... (0) **0** 200
Mostovoi (29), Mikhailichenko (51), Korneyev (84), Aleinikov (88)

13/11/91 **CYPRUS** .... (0) **0** **USSR** .... (1) **3** 4(
Protasov (27), Yuran (79), Kanchelskis (82)

21/12/91 **ITALY** .... (1) **2** **CYPRUS** .... (0) **0** 260
Vialli (27), Baggio (55)

1994/96 SERIES

GROUP MATCHES - GROUP 2

7/9/94 **CYPRUS** .... (1) **1** **SPAIN** .... (2) **2** 100
Soteriou (36) — *Higueras (15, 25)*

8/10/94 **ARMENIA** .... (0) **0** **CYPRUS** .... (0) **0** 60

16/11/94 **CYPRUS** .... (1) **2** **ARMENIA** .... (0) **0** 80
Soteriou (7), Fasouliotis (87)

17/12/94 **MACEDONIA** .... (2) **3** **CYPRUS** .... (0) **0** 160
Bosko Djurovski (16, 26, 90)

29/3/95 **CYPRUS** .... (1) **1** **DENMARK** .... (1) **1** 150
Agathocleous (45) — *Schjonberg (2)*

26/4/95 **BELGIUM** .... (1) **2** **CYPRUS** .... (0) **0** 140
Karagiannis (20), Schepens (47)

7/6/95 **DENMARK** .... (1) **4** **CYPRUS** .... (0) **0** 4019
Vilfort (45, 50), B. Laudrup (59), M. Laudrup (76)

6/9/95 **SPAIN** .... (1) **6** **CYPRUS** .... (0) **0** 160
Guerrero (45), Alfonso (51), Pizzi (75, 80), Hierro (78), Caminero (83)

11/10/95 **CYPRUS** .... (0) **1** **MACEDONIA** .... (1) **1** 1200
Agathocleous (90) — *Perides (Og, 30)*

15/11/95 **CYPRUS** .... (1) **1** **BELGIUM** .... (0) **1** 800
Agathocleous (18) — *De Bilde (76)*

CZECHOSLOVAKIA

1958/60 SERIES

Preliminary Round

5/4/59 **EIRE** .... (2) **2** **CZECHOSLOVAKIA** ... (0) **0** 4200
Tuohy, Cantwell (Pen)

10/5/59 **CZECHOSLOVAKIA** .... (1) **4** **EIRE** .... (0) **0** 6000
Dolinsky, Pavlovic, Bubernik, Stacho (Pen)

First Round

23/9/59 **DENMARK** .... (2) **2** **CZECHOSLOVAKIA** ... (2) **2** 3420
P. Pedersen, B. Hansen — *Kacani, Dolinsky*

18/10/59 **CZECHOSLOVAKIA** .... (1) **5** **DENMARK** .... (1) **1** 3000
Bubernik (2), Scherer (2), Dolinsky — *J. Kramer*

Quarter-Finals

22/5/60 **ROMANIA** .... (0) **0** **CZECHOSLOVAKIA** ... (2) **2** 100000
Masopust, Bubnik

29/5/60 **CZECHOSLOVAKIA** .... (3) **3** **ROMANIA** .... (0) **0** 4500
Bubernik (2), Bubnik

Semi-Final

6/7/60 **USSR** .... (1) **3** **CZECHOSLOVAKIA** ... (0) **0** 25184
Ivanov (2), Ponedelnik — Marseille

Third Place Match

9/7/60 **CZECHOSLOVAKIA** .... (0) **2** **FRANCE** .... (0) **0** 9438
Bubnik, Pavlovic — Marseille

1962/64 SERIES

First Round

21/11/62 **EAST GERMANY** ..... (0) **2** **CZECHOSLOVAKIA** ... (0) **1** 22100
Erler, Liebrecht (Pen) — *Kucera*

31/3/63 **CZECHOSLOVAKIA** .... (0) **1** **EAST GERMANY** ..... (0) **1** 20000
Mazek — *Ducke*

1966/68 SERIES

GROUP MATCHES - GROUP 1

21/5/67 **EIRE** .... (0) **0** **CZECHOSLOVAKIA** ... (2) **2** 9000
Finucane (og), Masny

18/6/67 **CZECHOSLOVAKIA** . . . . (1) **3** **TURKEY** . . . . (0) **0** 20000
Adamec (2), Jurkanin

1/10/67 **CZECHOSLOVAKIA** . . . . (0) **1** **SPAIN** . . . . (0) **0** 40000
Horvath

2/10/67 **SPAIN** . . . . (1) **2** **CZECHOSLOVAKIA** . . . . (0) **1** 40000
Pirri, Garate — *Kuna*

5/11/67 **TURKEY** . . . . (0) **0** **CZECHOSLOVAKIA** . . . . (0) **0** 52000

2/11/67 **CZECHOSLOVAKIA** . . . . (0) **1** **EIRE** . . . . (0) **2** 8000
Dempsey (og) — *Treacy, O'Connor*

1970/72 SERIES

GROUP MATCHES - GROUP 1

7/10/70 **CZECHOSLOVAKIA** . . . . (1) **1** **FINLAND** . . . . (1) **1** 5000
Albrecht — *Paatalainen*

21/4/71 **WALES** . . . . (0) **1** **CZECHOSLOVAKIA** . . . . (0) **3** 20000
R. Davies (Pen) — *Capkovic (2), Taborsky*

16/5/71 **CZECHOSLOVAKIA** . . . . (0) **1** **ROMANIA** . . . . (0) **0** 50000
Vesely

12/6/71 **FINLAND** . . . . (0) **0** **CZECHOSLOVAKIA** . . . . (2) **4** 4500
Capkovic, Pollak, Karko (2)

:7/10/71 **CZECHOSLOVAKIA** . . . . (0) **1** **WALES** . . . . (0) **0** 32000
Kuna

4/11/71 **ROMANIA** . . . . (1) **2** **CZECHOSLOVAKIA** . . . . (0) **1** 100000
Dembrovski, Dobrin — *Capkovic*

1974/76 SERIES

GROUP MATCHES - GROUP 1

30/10/74 **ENGLAND** . . . . (0) **3** **CZECHOSLOVAKIA** . . . . (0) **0** 86000
Channon, Bell (2)

20/4/75 **CZECHOSLOVAKIA** . . . . (2) **4** **CYPRUS** . . . . (0) **0** 5000
Panenka (3), Masny

30/4/75 **CZECHOSLOVAKIA** . . . . (3) **5** **PORTUGAL** . . . . (0) **0** 25000
Bicovsky (2), Nehoda (2), Petras

29/10/75 **CZECHOSLOVAKIA** . . . . (1) **2** **ENGLAND** . . . . (1) **1** 45000
Nehoda, Galis — *Channon*

12/11/75 **PORTUGAL** . . . . (1) **1** **CZECHOSLOVAKIA** . . . . (1) **1** 45000
Nene — *Ondrus*

23/11/75 **CYPRUS** . . . . (0) **0** **CZECHOSLOVAKIA** . . . . (3) **3** 15000
Nehoda, Bicovsky, Masny

Quarter-Finals

24/4/76 **CZECHOSLOVAKIA** . . . . (1) **2** **USSR** . . . . (0) **0** 52000
Moder, Panenka

22/5/76 **USSR** . . . . (0) **2** **CZECHOSLOVAKIA** . . . . (1) **2** 100000
Burjak, Blokhin — *Moder (2)*

Semi-Final

16/6/76 **CZECHOSLOVAKIA** . . . . (1) **3** **HOLLAND** . . . . (0) **1** 40000
Ondrus, Nehoda, Moder — *Ondrus (og)* — Zagreb

(After Extra Time)

Final

20/6/76 **CZECHOSLOVAKIA** . . . . (2) **2** **WEST GERMANY** . . . . . (1) **2** 45000
Svehlik, Dobias — *Muller, Holzenbein* — Belgrade

(After Extra Time)
(CZECHOSLOVAKIA WON 5-3 ON PENALTIES)

1978/80 SERIES

GROUP MATCHES - GROUP 5

4/10/78 **SWEDEN** . . . . (1) **1** **CZECHOSLOVAKIA** . . . . (1) **3** 12000
Borg (Pen, 15) — *Kroupa (17), Masny (47), Nehoda (85)*

4/4/79 **CZECHOSLOVAKIA** . . . . (0) **2** **FRANCE** . . . . (0) **0** 50000
Panenka (Pen, 67), Stambachr (72)

1/5/79 **LUXEMBOURG** . . . . (0) **0** **CZECHOSLOVAKIA** . . . . (1) **3** 3500
Masny (22), Gajdusek (67), Stambachr (68)

10/10/79 **CZECHOSLOVAKIA** . . . . (3) **4** **SWEDEN** . . . . (0) **1** 35000
Nehoda (20), Kozak (34), Visek (41, 78) — *Jan Svensson*

14/11/79 **FRANCE** . . . . (0) **2** **CZECHOSLOVAKIA** . . . . (0) **1** 39973
Pecout (67), Rampillon (75) — *Kozak (89)*

24/11/79 **CZECHOSLOVAKIA** . . . . (3) **4** **LUXEMBOURG** . . . . (0) **0** 15000
Panenka (37), Masny (39, 44), Visek (60)

FINALS - GROUP 1

11/6/80 **WEST GERMANY** . . . . . (0) **1** **CZECHOSLOVAKIA** . . . . (0) **0** 15000
Rummenigge (55)

14/6/80 **CZECHOSLOVAKIA** . . . . (2) **3** **GREECE** . . . . (1) **1**
Panenka (5), Visek (35), Nehoda (63) — *Anastopoulos (11)*

17/6/80 **CZECHOSLOVAKIA** . . . . (1) **1** **HOLLAND** . . . . (0) **1** 11889
Nehoda (38) — *Kist (59)*

Third Place Match

21/6/80 **CZECHOSLOVAKIA** . . . . (0) **1** **ITALY** . . . . (0) **1** 25000
Jurkemik — *Graziani* — Naples

(CZECHOSLOVAKIA WON 9-8 ON PENALTIES)

1982/84 SERIES

GROUP MATCHES - GROUP 5

6/10/82 **CZECHOSLOVAKIA** . . . . (0) **2** **SWEDEN** . . . . (0) **2** 17500
Janecka (48, 53) — *Jingblad (88), Eriksson (89)*

13/11/82 **ITALY** . . . . (1) **2** **CZECHOSLOVAKIA** . . . . (1) **2** 80000
Altobelli (13), Kapko (og, 66) — *Sloup (22), Chaloupka (72)*

27/3/83 **CYPRUS** . . . . (1) **1** **CZECHOSLOVAKIA** . . . . (0) **1** 12000
Theophanous (21) — *Bicovsky (59)*

16/4/83 **CZECHOSLOVAKIA** . . . . (3) **6** **CYPRUS** . . . . (0) **0** 6750
Danek (4, 71), Visek (21, 48)
Prokes (37), Jurkemik (56)

15/5/83 **ROMANIA** . . . . (0) **0** **CZECHOSLOVAKIA** . . . . (1) **1** 60000
Visek (Pen, 40)

21/9/83 **SWEDEN** . . . . (1) **1** **CZECHOSLOVAKIA** . . . . (0) **0** 22000
Corneliusson (14)

16/11/83 **CZECHOSLOVAKIA** . . . . (0) **2** **ITALY** . . . . (0) **0** 40000
Rada (64, (Pen, 77))

30/11/83 **CZECHOSLOVAKIA** . . . . (0) **1** **ROMANIA** . . . . (0) **1** 48000
Luhovy (85) — *Geolgau (63)*

1986/88 SERIES

GROUP MATCHES - GROUP 6

15/10/86 **CZECHOSLOVAKIA** . . . . (2) **3** **FINLAND** . . . . (0) **0** 26000
Janecka (38), Knoflicek (43), Kula (67)

12/11/86 **CZECHOSLOVAKIA** . . . . (0) **0** **DENMARK** . . . . (0) **0** 30000

29/4/87 **WALES** . . . . (0) **1** **CZECHOSLOVAKIA** . . . . (0) **1** 14150
Rush (83) — *Knoflicek (74)*

4/6/87 **DENMARK** . . . . (1) **1** **CZECHOSLOVAKIA** . . . . (0) **1** 45000
Molby (17) — *Hasek (48)*

9/9/87 **FINLAND** . . . . (1) **3** **CZECHOSLOVAKIA** . . . . (0) **0** 6430
Hjelm (29), Lius (72), Tiainen (82)

11/11/87 **CZECHOSLOVAKIA** . . . . (1) **2** **WALES** . . . . (0) **0** 6443
Knoflicek (32), Bilek (89)

1990/92 SERIES

GROUP MATCHES - GROUP 1

26/9/90 **CZECHOSLOVAKIA** . . . . (1) **1** **ICELAND** . . . . (0) **1** 35000
Danek

13/10/90 **FRANCE** . . . . (0) **2** **CZECHOSLOVAKIA** . . . . (0) **1** 38249
Papin (60, 83) — *Skuhravy (89)*

14/11/90 **CZECHOSLOVAKIA** . . . . (1) **3** **SPAIN** . . . . (1) **2** 35000
Danek (16, 67), Moravcik (77) — *Roberto (30), Carlos (55)*

1/5/91 **ALBANIA** . . . . (0) **0** **CZECHOSLOVAKIA** . . . . (0) **2** 10000
Kubik (47), Kuka (67)

5/6/91 **ICELAND** . . . . (0) **0** **CZECHOSLOVAKIA** . . . . (1) **1** 5000
Hasek (15)

4/9/91 **CZECHOSLOVAKIA** . . . . (1) **1** **FRANCE** . . . . (0) **2** 50000
Nemecek (19) — *Papin (53, 89)*

16/10/91 **CZECHOSLOVAKIA** . . . . (2) **2** **ALBANIA** . . . . (0) **1** 2366
Kula (36), Lancz (40) — *Zmijani (62)*

13/11/91 **SPAIN** . . . . (1) **2** **CZECHOSLOVAKIA** . . . . (0) **1** 24500
Abelardo (10), Michel (pen 79) — *Nemecek (59)*

CZECH REPUBLIC

1994/96 SERIES

GROUP MATCHES - GROUP 5

6/9/94 **CZECH REPUBLIC** . . . . . (3) **6** **MALTA** . . . . (0) **1** 10226
Smejkal (6), Kubik (33), — *Laferla (75)*
Siegl (35, 49, 81), Berger (89)

12/10/94 **MALTA** . . . . (0) **0** **CZECH REPUBLIC** . . . . (0) **0** 4000

16/11/94 **HOLLAND** . . . . (0) **0** **CZECH REPUBLIC** . . . . (0) **0** 45000

29/3/95 **CZECH REPUBLIC** . . . . . (2) **4** **BYELORUSSIA** . . . . (1) **2** 5549
Kadlec (5), Berger (18, 63), Kuka (69) — *Gerasimec (Pen, 44), Gurinovich (88)*

26/4/95 **CZECH REPUBLIC** . . . . . (0) **3** **HOLLAND** . . . . (1) **1** 17463
Skuhravy (49), Nemecek (57), Berger (62) — *Jonk (7)*

7/6/95 **LUXEMBOURG** . . . . (0) **1** **CZECH REPUBLIC** . . . . (0) **0** 1500
Hellers (89)

16/8/95 **NORWAY** . . . . (1) **1** **CZECH REPUBLIC** . . . . (0) **1** 22054
Berg (27) — *Suchoparek (84)*

6/9/95 **CZECH REPUBLIC** . . . . . (1) **2** **NORWAY** . . . . (0) **0** 19522
Skuhravy (Pen, 6), Drulak (87)

7/10/95 **BYELORUSSIA** . . . . (0) **0** **CZECH REPUBLIC** . . . . (1) **2** 20000
Frydek (25), Berger (84)

15/11/95 **CZECH REPUBLIC** (1) **3** **LUXEMBOURG** (0) **0** 22530
Drulak (35, 46), Berger (57)

DENMARK

1958/60 SERIES

First Round

23/9/59 **DENMARK** (2) **2** **CZECHOSLOVAKIA** (2) **2** 34200
P. Pedersen, B. Hansen — *Kacani, Dolinsky*

18/10/59 **CZECHOSLOVAKIA** (1) **5** **DENMARK** (1) **1** 30000
Bubernik (2), Scherer (2), Dolinsky — *J. Kramer*

1962/64 SERIES

First Round

28/6/62 **DENMARK** (3) **6** **MALTA** (0) **1** 11200
O. Madsen (3), Enoksen, Berthelsen, Clausen — *Theobald*

16/12/62 **MALTA** (1) **1** **DENMARK** (2) **3** 6987
Urpani — *Madsen, Christiansen, Berthelsen*

Second Round

29/6/63 **DENMARK** (3) **4** **ALBANIA** (0) **0** 25200
J. Petersen, O. Madsen, Clausen, Enoksen

30/10/63 **ALBANIA** (1) **1** **DENMARK** (0) **0** 27765
Pano

Quarter-Finals

4/12/63 **LUXEMBOURG** (2) **3** **DENMARK** (2) **3** 6921
Pilot, H. Klein (2) — *O. Madsen (3)*

10/12/63 **DENMARK** (1) **2** **LUXEMBOURG** (1) **2** 39400
O. Madsen (2) — *Leonard, H. Schmidt*

18/12/63 **DENMARK** (1) **1** **LUXEMBOURG** (0) **0** 5700
O. Madsen

Semi-Final

17/6/64 **USSR** (2) **3** **DENMARK** (0) **0** 38000
Voronin, Ponedelnik, Ivanov — Barcelona

Third Place Match

20/6/64 **HUNGARY** (1) **3** **DENMARK** (0) **1** 4000
Bene, Novak (2, 1 Pen) — *Berthelsen*

(After Extra Time)

1966/68 SERIES

GROUP MATCHES - GROUP 5

21/9/66 **HUNGARY** (5) **6** **DENMARK** (0) **0** 20000
Albert (2), Meszoly (Pen), Bene, Farkas, Varga

30/11/66 **HOLLAND** (0) **2** **DENMARK** (0) **0** 23000
Van De Kuyen, Swart

25/5/67 **DENMARK** (0) **0** **HUNGARY** (1) **2** 35200
Sandvad (og), Bene

4/6/67 **DENMARK** (0) **1** **EAST GERMANY** (1) **1** 23000
Bjerre — *Lowe*

4/10/67 **DENMARK** (1) **3** **HOLLAND** (0) **2** 34500
Bjerre (2, 1 Pen), Sondergaard — *Suurbier, Israel*

11/10/67 **EAST GERMANY** (1) **3** **DENMARK** (2) **2** 25000
Koerner (Pen), Pankau (2) — *Dyreborg, Sondergaard*

1970/72 SERIES

GROUP MATCHES - GROUP 5

14/10/70 **DENMARK** (0) **0** **PORTUGAL** (1) **1** 18000
Joao Jacinto

11/11/70 **SCOTLAND** (1) **1** **DENMARK** (0) **0** 24000
O'Hare

25/11/70 **BELGIUM** (2) **2** **DENMARK** (0) **0** 11000
Devrindt (2)

9/6/71 **DENMARK** (1) **1** **SCOTLAND** (0) **0** 38600
Laudrup

12/5/71 **PORTUGAL** (2) **5** **DENMARK** (0) **0** 20000
Rodrigues, Eusebio, Baptista (2), Sandvad (og)

26/5/71 **DENMARK** (0) **1** **BELGIUM** (0) **2** 30000
Bjerre — *Devrindt (2)*

1974/76 SERIES

GROUP MATCHES - GROUP 4

25/9/74 **DENMARK** (0) **1** **SPAIN** (2) **2** 27300
Nygaard (Pen) — *Claramunt (Pen), Martinez*

13/10/74 **DENMARK** (0) **0** **ROMANIA** (0) **0** 157

11/5/75 **ROMANIA** (2) **6** **DENMARK** (0) **1** 6000
Georgescu (2), Cristan (2), Lucescu, Dinu — *Dahl*

3/9/75 **DENMARK** (0) **0** **SCOTLAND** (0) **1** 403
Harper

12/10/75 **SPAIN** (1) **2** **DENMARK** (0) **0** 2000
Pirri, Capon

29/10/75 **SCOTLAND** (0) **3** **DENMARK** (1) **1** 480
Dalglish, Rioch, McDougall — *Bastrup*

1978/80 SERIES

GROUP MATCHES - GROUP 1

24/5/78 **DENMARK** (1) **3** **EIRE** (2) **3** 1200
Jensen (32), B. Nielsen (Pen, 79), Lerby (80) — *Stapleton (11), Grealish (25), Daly (65)*

20/9/78 **DENMARK** (2) **3** **ENGLAND** (2) **4** 4800
Simonsen (Pen, 25), Arnesen (28), Roentved (86) — *Keegan (17, 23), Latchford (50), Neal (85)*

11/10/78 **DENMARK** (1) **2** **BULGARIA** (1) **2** 1600
B. Nielsen (17), Lerby (63) — *Panov (34), Iliev (84)*

25/10/78 **NORTHERN IRELAND** (0) **2** **DENMARK** (0) **1** 3000
Spence (63), Anderson (85) — *Jensen (51)*

2/5/79 **EIRE** (1) **2** **DENMARK** (0) **0** 2600
Daly (44), Givens (66)

6/6/79 **DENMARK** (2) **4** **NORTHERN IRELAND** (0) **0** 1680
Elkjaer (30, 33, 83), Simonsen (63)

12/9/79 **ENGLAND** (1) **1** **DENMARK** (0) **0** 8500
Keegan (17)

31/10/79 **BULGARIA** (1) **3** **DENMARK** (0) **0** 700
Jeliaskov (21), Tsvetkov (51, 88)

1982/84 SERIES

GROUP MATCHES - GROUP 3

22/9/82 **DENMARK** (0) **2** **ENGLAND** (1) **2** 4430
Allen Hansen (Pen, 69), Ilsen (89) — *Francis (7, 80)*

10/11/82 **LUXEMBOURG** (0) **1** **DENMARK** (1) **2** 205
Di Domenico (54) — *Lerby (Pen, 29), Berggren (67)*

27/4/83 **DENMARK** (0) **1** **GREECE** (0) **0** 4500
Busk (76)

1/6/83 **DENMARK** (1) **3** **HUNGARY** (1) **1** 4480
Elkjaer (4), J. Olsen (81), Simonsen (42) — *Nyilasi (30)*

21/9/83 **ENGLAND** (0) **0** **DENMARK** (1) **1** 8205
Simonsen (Pen, 39)

12/10/83 **DENMARK** (4) **6** **LUXEMBOURG** (0) **0** 4470
Laudrup (17, 24, 69), Elkjaer (37, 58), Simonsen (42)

26/10/83 **HUNGARY** (0) **1** **DENMARK** (0) **0** 1000
Kiss (56)

16/1183 **GREECE** (0) **0** **DENMARK** (1) **2** 3000
Elkjaer (16), Simonsen (47)

FINALS - GROUP 1

12/6/84 **FRANCE** (0) **1** **DENMARK** (0) **0** 4775
Platini (77)

16/6/84 **DENMARK** (2) **5** **YUGOSLAVIA** (0) **0** 2500
Ivkovic (og, 7), Berggren (16), Arnesen (Pen, 68), Elkjaer (81), Lauridsen (83)

19/6/84 **DENMARK** (1) **3** **BELGIUM** (2) **2** 36911
Arnesen (Pen, 40), Brylle (60), Elkjaer (83) — *Ceulemans (25), Vercauteren (38)*

Semi-Final

24/6/84 **SPAIN** (0) **1** **DENMARK** (1) **1** 48000 Lyon
Maceda (66) — *Lerby (6)*

(After Extra Time)
SPAIN WON 5-4 ON PENALTIES

1986/88 SERIES

GROUP MATCHES - GROUP 6

29/10/86 **DENMARK** (0) **1** **FINLAND** (0) **0** 40300
Bertelsen (68)

12/11/86 **CZECHOSLOVAKIA** (0) **0** **DENMARK** (0) **0** 30000

29/4/87 **FINLAND** (0) **0** **DENMARK** (0) **1** 29197
Molby (53)

4/6/87 **DENMARK** (1) **1** **CZECHOSLOVAKIA** (0) **1** 45000
Molby (17) — *Hasek (48)*

9/9/87 **WALES** (1) **1** **DENMARK** (0) **0** 20535
Hughes (19)

14/10/67 **DENMARK** (0) **1** **WALES** (0) **0** 44500
Elkjaer (49)

FINALS - GROUP 1

1/6/68 **DENMARK** .... (1) **2** **SPAIN** .... (1) **3** 60000
Laudrup (25), Povlsen (85) — *Michel (5), Butragueno (52), Gordillo (67)*

4/6/88 **WEST GERMANY** ..... (1) **2** **DENMARK** .... (0) **0** 70000
Klinsmann (9), Thon (85)

7/6/88 **ITALY** .... (0) **2** **DENMARK** .... (0) **0** 60500
Altobelli (65), De Agostini (87)

1990/92 SERIES

GROUP MATCHES - GROUP 4

/10/90 **DENMARK** .... (2) **4** **FAROE ISLANDS** ...... (1) **1** 38563
M. Laudrup (8, 48), Elstrup (37) Povlsen (89) — *Morkore (21)*

/10/90 **N. IRELAND** .... (0) **1** **DENMARK** .... (1) **1** 10000
Clarke (58) — *Bartram (pen 11)*

/11/90 **DENMARK** .... (0) **0** **YUGOSLAVIA** .... (0) **2** 39700
Bazdarevic (77), Jarni (84)

1/5/91 **YUGOSLAVIA** .... (0) **1** **DENMARK** .... (1) **2** 26000
Pancev (50) — *Christensen (31, 62)*

5/6/91 **DENMARK** .... (1) **2** **AUSTRIA** .... (0) **1** 12521
Christensen (2, 77) — *Ogris (83)*

5/9/91 **FAROE ISLANDS** ...... (0) **0** **DENMARK** .... (2) **4** 2589
Christofte (pen 2), Christensen (8) Pingel (71), Vilfort (76)

/10/91 **AUSTRIA** .... (0) **0** **DENMARK** .... (3) **3** 10000
Artner (o.g. 10), Povlsen (16), Christensen (37)

/11/91 **DENMARK** .... (2) **2** **N. IRELAND** .... (0) **1** 10881
Povlsen (22, 36) — *Taggart (71)*

FINALS - GROUP 1

enmark qualified for the Finals after Yugoslavia were excluded
cause of UN sanctions against Serbia.

1/6/92 **DENMARK** .... (0) **0** **ENGLAND** .... (0) **0** 26385

4/6/92 **SWEDEN** .... (0) **1** **DENMARK** .... (0) **0** 29902
Brolin (58)

7/6/92 **FRANCE** .... (0) **1** **DENMARK** .... (1) **2** 25763
Papin (60) — *Larsen (8), Elstrup (78)*

emi Final

22/6/92 **HOLLAND** .... (1) **2** **DENMARK** .... (2) **2** 37450
Bergkamp (23), Rijkaard (85) — *Larsen (5, 32)*

Denmark won on penalties after extra-time

nal

26/6/92 **GERMANY** .... (0) **0** **DENMARK** .... (1) **2** 37800
Jensen (18), Vilfort (78)

1994/96 SERIES

GROUP MATCHES - GROUP 2

7/9/94 **MACEDONIA** .... (1) **1** **DENMARK** .... (0) **1** 25000
Stojkovski (4) — *Povlsen (87)*

2/10/94 **DENMARK** .... (1) **3** **BELGIUM** .... (1) **1** 40075
Vilfort (36), Jensen (70), Strudal (85) — *Degryse (30)*

6/11/94 **SPAIN** .... (1) **3** **DENMARK** .... (0) **0** 38000
Nadal (41), Donato (57), Luis Enrique (87)

29/3/95 **CYPRUS** .... (1) **1** **DENMARK** .... (1) **1** 15000
Agathocleous (45) — *Schjonberg (2)*

26/4/95 **DENMARK** .... (0) **1** **MACEDONIA** .... (0) **0** 38888
P. Nielsen (70)

7/6/95 **DENMARK** .... (1) **4** **CYPRUS** .... (0) **0** 40199
Vilfort (45, 50), B. Laudrup (59), M. Laudrup (76)

16/8/95 **ARMENIA** .... (0) **0** **DENMARK** .... (1) **2** 22000
M. Laudrup (32), Allan Nielsen (46)

6/9/95 **BELGIUM** .... (1) **1** **DENMARK** .... (2) **3** 40000
Grun (25) — *M. Laudrup (19), Beck (21), Vilfort (65)*

1/10/95 **DENMARK** .... (0) **1** **SPAIN** .... (1) **1** 40260
Vilfort (47) — *Hierro (Pen, 17)*

15/11/95 **DENMARK** .... (2) **3** **ARMENIA** .... (0) **1** 40208
Schjonberg (19), Beck (35), M. Laudrup (58) — *Artur Petrossian (47)*

EAST GERMANY

1958/60 SERIES

irst Round

28/6/59 **PORTUGAL** .... (1) **3** **EAST GERMANY** ..... (0) **2** 35000
Columa (2), Cavem — *Vogt, Kohle*

21/6/59 **EAST GERMANY** ..... (0) **0** **PORTUGAL** .... (1) **2** 25000
Matateu, Coluna

1962/64 SERIES

First Round

21/11/62 **EAST GERMANY** ..... (0) **2** **CZECHOSLOVAKIA** .... (0) **1** 22100
Erler, Liebrecht (Pen) — *Kucera*

31/3/63 **CZECHOSLOVAKIA** .... (0) **1** **EAST GERMANY** ..... (0) **1** 20000
Mazek — *Ducke*

Second Round

20/10/63 **EAST GERMANY** ..... (0) **1** **HUNGARY** .... (1) **2** 33400
Noeldner — *Bene, Rakosi*

3/11/63 **HUNGARY** .... (2) **3** **EAST GERMANY** ..... (2) **3** 35400
Bene, Sandor, Solymosi (Pen) — *Heine, R. Ducke, Erler*

1966/68 SERIES

GROUP MATCHES - GROUP 5

5/4/67 **EAST GERMANY** ..... (0) **4** **HOLLAND** .... (2) **3** 40000
Vogel, Frenzel (3) — *Keizer (2), Mulder*

4/6/67 **DENMARK** .... (0) **1** **EAST GERMANY** ..... (1) **1** 23000
Bjerre — *Lowe*

13/6/67 **HOLLAND** .... (0) **1** **EAST GERMANY** ..... (0) **0** 45000
Cruyff

27/9/67 **HUNGARY** .... (1) **3** **EAST GERMANY** ..... (0) **1** 72000
Farkas (3) — *Frenzel*

11/10/67 **EAST GERMANY** ..... (1) **3** **DENMARK** .... (2) **2** 25000
Koerner (Pen), Pankau (2) — *Dyreborg, Sondergaard*

29/10/67 **EAST GERMANY** ..... (0) **1** **HUNGARY** .... (0) **0** 60000
Frenzel

1970/72 SERIES

GROUP MATCHES - GROUP 7

11/11/70 **EAST GERMANY** ..... (0) **1** **HOLLAND** .... (0) **0** 36000
Ducke

15/11/70 **LUXEMBOURG** .... (0) **0** **EAST GERMANY** ..... (4) **5** 3000
Vogel, Kreische (4)

25/4/71 **EAST GERMANY** ..... (1) **2** **LUXEMBOURG** .... (0) **1** 15000
Kreische, Frenzel — *Dussier*

9/5/71 **EAST GERMANY** ..... (0) **1** **YUGOSLAVIA** .... (2) **2** 100000
Lowe — *Filipovic, Dzajic*

10/10/71 **HOLLAND** .... (1) **3** **EAST GERMANY** ..... (1) **2** 50000
Keizer (2), Hulshoff — *Vogel (2)*

17/10/71 **YUGOSLAVIA** .... (0) **0** **EAST GERMANY** ..... (0) **0** 4000

1974/76 SERIES

GROUP MATCHES - GROUP 7

12/10/74 **EAST GERMANY** ..... (1) **1** **ICELAND** .... (1) **1** 15000
Hoffman — *Hallgrimsson*

16/11/74 **FRANCE** .... (0) **2** **EAST GERMANY** ..... (1) **2** 50000
Guillou, Gallice — *Sparwasser, Kreische*

7/12/74 **EAST GERMANY** ..... (0) **0** **BELGIUM** .... (0) **0** 35000

5/6/75 **ICELAND** .... (2) **2** **EAST GERMANY** ..... (0) **1** 4500
Edvaldsson, Sigurvinsson — *Pommerenke*

27/9/75 **BELGIUM** .... (0) **1** **EAST GERMANY** ..... (0) **2** 26000
Puis — *Ducke, Hafner*

11/10/75 **EAST GERMANY** ..... (0) **2** **FRANCE** .... (0) **1** 30000
Streich, Vogel (Pen) — *Bathenay*

1978/80 SERIES

GROUP MATCHES - GROUP 4

4/10/78 **EAST GERMANY** ..... (2) **3** **ICELAND** .... (1) **1** 12000
Peter (6), Riedieger (29), Hoffman (72) — *P. Pettursson (Pen, 14).*

15/11/78 **HOLLAND** .... (1) **3** **EAST GERMANY** ..... (0) **0** 47000
Kische (og, 17), Geels ((Pen, 73), 88)

18/4/79 **EAST GERMANY** ..... (0) **2** **POLAND** .... (1) **1** 55000
Streich (50), Lindemann (63) — *Boniek (8)*

5/5/79 **SWITZERLAND** .... (0) **0** **EAST GERMANY** ..... (1) **2** 9000
Lindemann (44), Streich (89)

12/9/79 **ICELAND** .... (0) **0** **EAST GERMANY** ..... (0) **3** 10000
Weber ((Pen, 64), 70), Streich (77)

26/9/79 **POLAND** .... (0) **1** **EAST GERMANY** ..... (0) **1** 90000
Wieczorek (77) — *Hafner (61)*

13/10/79 **EAST GERMANY** ..... (3) **5** **SWITZERLAND** ...... (1) **2** 45000
Weber (1), Haffmann (9, 75, 85) — *Barberis (19), Pfister (72)*

21/11/79 **EAST GERMANY** ..... (2) **2** **HOLLAND** .... (1) **3** 99000
Schuphase (17), Streich (Pen, 34) — *Thijssen (44), Kist (50), R.Van Der Kerkhof (67)*

1982/84 SERIES
GROUP MATCHES - GROUP 1

13/10/82 **SCOTLAND** (0) **2** **EAST GERMANY** (0) **0** 40300
Wark (53), Sturrock (75)
30/3/83 **EAST GERMANY** (0) **1** **BELGIUM** (1) **2** 75000
Streich (83) — *Van Der Elst (36), Van Den Bergh (69)*
27/4/83 **BELGIUM** (2) **2** **EAST GERMANY** (1) **1** 43894
Ceulemans (18), Coeck (38) — *Streich (9)*
14/5/83 **SWITZERLAND** (0) **0** **EAST GERMANY** (0) **0** 32000
12/10/83 **EAST GERMANY** (1) **3** **SWITZERLAND** (0) **0** 12000
Richter (44), Ernst (73), Streich (89)
16/11/83 **EAST GERMANY** (2) **2** **SCOTLAND** (0) **1** 18000
Kreer (33), Streich (42) — *Bannon (78)*

1986/88 SERIES
GROUP MATCHES - GROUP 3

24/9/86 **NORWAY** (0) **0** **EAST GERMANY** (0) **0** 10142
29/10/86 **EAST GERMANY** (1) **2** **ICELAND** (0) **0** 18000
Thom (4, 89)
19/11/86 **EAST GERMANY** (0) **0** **FRANCE** (0) **0** 52000
29/4/87 **USSR** (1) **2** **EAST GERMANY** (0) **0** 95000
Zavarov (41), Belanov (49)
3/6/87 **ICELAND** (0) **0** **EAST GERMANY** (2) **6** 10000
Minge (15), Thom (37, 69, 88), Doll (49), Doschner (85)
10/10/87 **EAST GERMANY** (1) **1** **USSR** (0) **1** 25000
Kirsten (44) — *Aleinikov (80)*
28/10/87 **EAST GERMANY** (2) **3** **NORWAY** (1) **1** 10000
Kirsten (15, 53), Thom (34) — *Fjaerestad (32)*
18/11/87 **FRANCE** (0) **0** **EAST GERMANY** (0) **1** 20000

EIRE

1958/60 SERIES

Preliminary Round

5/4/89 **EIRE** (2) **2** **CZECHOSLOVAKIA** (0) **0** 42000
Tuohy, Cantwell (Pen)
10/5/59 **CZECHOSLOVAKIA** (1) **4** **EIRE** (0) **0** 60000
Dolinsky, Pavlovic, Bubernik, Stacho (Pen)

1962/64 SERIES

First Round

12/8/62 **EIRE** (2) **4** **ICELAND** (1) **2** 25000
Cantwell (2), Tuohy, Fogarty — *Jonsson (2)*
2/9/62 **ICELAND** (0) **1** **EIRE** (1) **1** 9100
Arnason — *Tuohy*

Second Round

25/9/63 **AUSTRIA** (0) **0** **EIRE** (0) **0** 26800
13/10/63 **EIRE** (1) **3** **AUSTRIA** (1) **2** 40000
Cantwell (2), Fogarty — *Koleznik, Floegel*

Quarter-Finals

11/3/64 **SPAIN** (4) **5** **EIRE** (1) **1** 27200
Amancio (2), Marcellino (2), Fuste — *McEvoy*
8/4/64 **EIRE** (0) **0** **SPAIN** (1) **2** 38100
Zaballa (2)

1966/68 SERIES
GROUP MATCHES - GROUP 1

23/10/66 **EIRE** (0) **0** **SPAIN** (0) **0** 38000
16/11/66 **EIRE** (0) **2** **TURKEY** (0) **1** 20000
O'Neill, McEvoy — *Ogun*
7/12/66 **SPAIN** (2) **2** **EIRE** (0) **0** 25000
Garcia, Pirri
22/2/67 **TURKEY** (1) **2** **EIRE** (0) **1** 35000
Ayhan, Ogun — *Cantwell*
21/5/67 **EIRE** (0) **0** **CZECHOSLOVAKIA** (2) **2** 9000
Finucane (og), Masny
22/11/67 **CZECHOSLOVAKIA** (0) **1** **EIRE** (0) **2** 8000
Treacy, O'Connor

1970/72 SERIES
GROUP MATCHES - GROUP 6

14/10/70 **EIRE** (1) **1** **SWEDEN** (0) **1** 30000
Carroll (Pen) — *Brzokoupil*
28/10/70 **SWEDEN** (0) **1** **EIRE** (0) **0** 120
Turesson
9/12/70 **ITALY** (2) **3** **EIRE** (0) **0** 550
De Sisti (Pen), Boninsegna, Prati
11/5/71 **EIRE** (1) **1** **ITALY** (1) **2** 250
Conway — *Boninsegna, Prati*
30/5/71 **EIRE** (0) **1** **AUSTRIA** (3) **4** 160
Rogers (Pen) — *Schmidradner (Pen), Kodat, Eddmeyer, Starek*
10/10/71 **AUSTRIA** (3) **6** **EIRE** (0) **0** 250
Parits (3), Jara (2), Pirkner

1974/76 SERIES
GROUP MATCHES - GROUP 6

30/10/74 **EIRE** (2) **3** **USSR** (0) **0** 320
Givens (20, 30, 60)
20/11/74 **TURKEY** (0) **1** **EIRE** (0) **1** 670
Conroy (og) — *Givens*
11/5/75 **EIRE** (2) **2** **SWITERLAND** (0) **1** 500
Martin, Treacy — *Muller*
18/5/75 **USSR** (2) **2** **EIRE** (0) **1** 1000
Blokhin, Kolotov — *Hand*
21/5/75 **SWITZERLAND** (0) **1** **EIRE** (0) **0** 150
Elsener
29/10/75 **EIRE** (3) **4** **TURKEY** (0) **0** 250
Givens (4)

1978/80 SERIES
GROUP MATCHES - GROUP 1

24/5/78 **DENMARK** (1) **3** **EIRE** (2) **3** 120
Jensen (32), B. Nielsen (Pen, 79), Lerby (80) — *Stapleton (11), Grealish (25), Daly (65)*
20/9/78 **EIRE** (0) **0** **NORTHERN IRELAND** (0) **0** 550
25/10/78 **EIRE** (1) **1** **ENGLAND** (1) **1** 500
Daly (27) — *Latchford (8)*
2/5/79 **EIRE** (1) **2** **DENMARK** (0) **0** 260
Daly (44), Givens (66)
19/5/79 **BULGARIA** (0) **1** **EIRE** (0) **0** 200
Tzvetkov (80)
17/10/79 **EIRE** (1) **3** **BULGARIA** (0) **0** 220
Martin (39), Grealish (46), Stapleton (83)
21/11/79 **NORTHERN IRELAND** (0) **1** **EIRE** (0) **0** 150
Armstrong (54)
6/2/80 **ENGLAND** (1) **2** **EIRE** (0) **0** 902
Keegan (34, 74)

1982/84 SERIES
GROUP MATCHES - GROUP 7

22/9/82 **HOLLAND** (1) **2** **EIRE** (0) **1** 190
Schoenaker (1), Gullit (65) — *Daly (80)*
13/10/82 **EIRE** (1) **2** **ICELAND** (0) **0** 200
Stapleton (35), Grealish (63)
17/11/82 **EIRE** (1) **3** **SPAIN** (1) **3** 390
Grimes (2), Stapleton (64, 76) — *Maceda (31), Martin (og, 47), Victor (60)*
30/3/83 **MALTA** (0) **0** **EIRE** (0) **1** 100
Stapleton (89)
27/4/83 **SPAIN** (0) **2** **EIRE** (0) **0** 450
Santillana (51), Rincon (89)
21/9/83 **ICELAND** (0) **0** **EIRE** (2) **3** 120
Waddock (17), Robinson (21), Walsh (82)
12/10/83 **EIRE** (2) **2** **HOLLAND** (0) **3** 350
Waddock (6), Brady (Pen, 34) — *Gullit (51, 76), Van Basten (67)*
16/11/83 **EIRE** (3) **8** **MALTA** (0) **0** 100
Lawrenson (24, 64), Stapleton (Pen, 27), O'Callaghan (33), Sheedy (77), Brady (78, 86) Daly (87)

1986/88 SERIES
GROUP MATCHES - GROUP 7

10/9/86 **BELGIUM** (1) **2** **EIRE** (1) **2** 2221
Claesen (14), Scifo (71) — *Stapleton (18), Brady (Pen, 89)*
15/10/86 **EIRE** (0) **0** **SCOTLAND** (0) **0** 4800
18/2/87 **SCOTLAND** (0) **0** **EIRE** (1) **1** 4508
Lawrenson (8)
1/4/87 **BULGARIA** (1) **2** **EIRE** (0) **1** 3800
Sadkov (41), Tranev (Pen, 82) — *Stapleton (52)*
29/4/87 **EIRE** (0) **0** **BELGIUM** (0) **0** 4900
28/5/87 **LUXEMBOURG** (0) **0** **EIRE** (1) **2** 150
Galvin (44), Whelan (64)
9/9/87 **EIRE** (1) **2** **LUXEMBOURG** (1) **1** 1800
Stapleton (31), McGrath (74) — *Krings (28)*
14/10/87 **EIRE** (0) **2** **BULGARIA** (0) **0** 2600
McGrath (52), Moran (85)

FINALS - GROUP 2

12/6/88 **ENGLAND** (0) **0** **EIRE** (1) **1** 53000
Houghton (5)

15/6/88 **EIRE** (1) **1** **USSR** (0) **1** 52000
Whelan (38) — *Protasov (74)*

18/6/88 **EIRE** (0) **0** **HOLLAND** (0) **1** 70800
Kieft (81)

1990/92 SERIES
GROUP MATCHES - GROUP 7

7/10/90 **EIRE** (2) **5** **TURKEY** (0) **0** 46000
Aldridge (15, 58, 73), O'Leary (40), Quinn (66)

4/11/90 **EIRE** (0) **1** **ENGLAND** (0) **1** 46000
Cascarino (79) — *Platt (67)*

27/3/91 **ENGLAND** (1) **1** **EIRE** (1) **1** 77000
Dixon (9) — *Quinn (27)*

1/5/91 **EIRE** (0) **0** **POLAND** (0) **0** 48000

6/10/91 **POLAND** (0) **3** **EIRE** (1) **3** 17000
Czachowski (55), Furtok (77), Urban (86) — *McGrath (10), Townsend (62), Cascarino (68)*

3/11/91 **TURKEY** (1) **1** **EIRE** (1) **3** 42000
Riza (pen 12) — *Byrne (7, 58), Cascarino (55)*

1994/96 SERIES
GROUP MATCHES - GROUP 6

7/9/94 **LATVIA** (0) **0** **EIRE** (2) **3** 3000
Aldridge (16, (Pen, 75)), Sheridan (29)

2/10/94 **EIRE** (3) **4** **LIECHTENSTEIN** (0) **0** 32980
Coyne (2, 4), Quinn (30, 82)

6/11/94 **NORTHERN IRELAND** (0) **0** **EIRE** (3) **4** 10336
Aldridge (6), Keane (11), Sheridan (38), Townsend (54)

29/3/95 **EIRE** (0) **1** **NORTHERN IRELAND** (0) **1** 32200
Quinn (47) — *Dowie (72)*

26/4/95 **EIRE** (1) **1** **PORTUGAL** (0) **0** 25000
Vitor Baia (Og, 44)

3/6/95 **LIECHTENSTEIN** (0) **0** **EIRE** (0) **0** 4500

11/6/95 **EIRE** (0) **1** **AUSTRIA** (0) **3** 33000
Houghton (65) — *Polster (69, 78), Ogris (72)*

6/9/95 **AUSTRIA** (1) **3** **EIRE** (0) **1** 24000
Stoger (3, 64, 77) — *McGrath (74)*

1/10/95 **EIRE** (0) **2** **LATVIA** (0) **1** 33000
Aldridge ((Pen, 61), 64) — *Rimkus (78)*

5/11/95 **PORTUGAL** (0) **3** **EIRE** (0) **0** 80000
Rui Costa (59), Helder (78), Cadete (89)

Play-Off Match

13/12/95 **EIRE** (0) **0** **HOLLAND** (1) **2** 40000
Kluivert (29, 88) — Liverpool

ENGLAND

1962/64 SERIES

First Round

3/10/62 **ENGLAND** (0) **1** **FRANCE** (1) **1** 35380
Flowers (Pen) — *Goujon*

27/2/63 **FRANCE** (3) **5** **ENGLAND** (0) **2** 23986
Wisnieski (2), Cossou (2), Douis — *Smith, Tambling*

1966/68 SERIES
GROUP MATCHES - GROUP 8

22/10/66 **NORTHERN IRELAND** (0) **0** **ENGLAND** (1) **2** 48600
Hunt, Peters

16/11/66 **ENGLAND** (3) **5** **WALES** (1) **1** 76000
Hurst (2), J. Charlton, R. Charlton, Hennessey (og) — *W. Davies*

15/4/67 **ENGLAND** (0) **2** **SCOTLAND** (1) **3** 100000
J. Charlton, Hurst — *Law, Lennox, McCalliog*

21/10/67 **WALES** (0) **0** **ENGLAND** (1) **3** 45000
Peters, R. Charlton, Ball

22/11/67 **ENGLAND** (1) **2** **NORTHERN IRELAND** (0) **0** 85000
Hurst, R. Charlton

24/2/68 **SCOTLAND** (1) **1** **ENGLAND** (1) **1** 134000
Hughes — *Peters*

Quarter-Finals

3/4/68 **ENGLAND** (0) **1** **SPAIN** (0) **0** 100000
R. Charlton

8/5/68 **SPAIN** (0) **1** **ENGLAND** (0) **2** 120000
Amancio — *Peters, Hurst*

Semi-Final

5/6/68 **YUGOSLAVIA** (0) **1** **ENGLAND** (0) **0** 21834
Dzajic — *Florence*

Third Place Match

8/6/68 **ENGLAND** (1) **2** **USSR** (0) **0** 50000
R. Charlton, Hurst — *Rome*

1970/72 SERIES
GROUP MATCHES - GROUP 3

3/2/71 **MALTA** (0) **0** **ENGLAND** (1) **1** 30000
Peters

21/4/71 **ENGLAND** (1) **3** **GREECE** (0) **0** 55000
Chivers, Hurst, Lee

12/5/71 **ENGLAND** (2) **5** **MALTA** (0) **0** 35000
Chivers (2), Lee, Clarke (Pen), Lawler

13/10/71 **SWITZERLAND** (2) **2** **ENGLAND** (2) **3** 55000
Jeandupeux, Kunzli — *Hurst, Chivers, Weibel (og)*

10/11/71 **ENGLAND** (1) **1** **SWITZERLAND** (1) **1** 100000
Summerbee — *Odermatt*

1/12/71 **GREECE** (0) **0** **ENGLAND** (0) **2** 45000
Hurst, Chivers

Quarter-Finals

29/4/72 **ENGLAND** (0) **1** **WEST GERMANY** (1) **3** 100000
Lee — *Hoeness, Netzer (Pen), Muller*

13/5/72 **WEST GERMANY** (0) **0** **ENGLAND** (0) **0** 77000

1974/76 SERIES
GROUP MATCHES - GROUP 1

30/10/74 **ENGLAND** (0) **3** **CZECHOSLOVAKIA** (0) **0** 86000
Channon, Bell (2)

20/11/74 **ENGLAND** (0) **0** **PORTUGAL** (0) **0** 85700

16/4/75 **ENGLAND** (2) **5** **CYPRUS** (0) **0** 68000
Macdonald (5)

11/7/75 **CYPRUS** (0) **0** **ENGLAND** (1) **1** 20000
Keegan

29/10/75 **CZECHOSLOVAKIA** (1) **2** **ENGLAND** (1) **1** 45000
Nehoda, Galis — *Channon*

19/11/75 **PORTUGAL** (1) **1** **ENGLAND** (1) **1** 40000
Rodrigues — *Channon*

1978/80 SERIES
GROUP MATCHES - GROUP 1

20/9/78 **DENMARK** (2) **3** **ENGLAND** (2) **4** 48000
Simonsen (Pen, 25), Arnesen (28), Roentved (86) — *Keegan (17, 23), Latchford (50), Neal (85)*

25/10/78 **EIRE** (1) **1** **ENGLAND** (1) **1** 50000
Daly (27) — *Latchford (8)*

7/2/79 **ENGLAND** (1) **4** **NORTHERN IRELAND** (0) **0** 92000
Keegan (24), Latchford (46, 63), Watson (49)

6/6/79 **BULGARIA** (0) **0** **ENGLAND** (1) **3** 47500
Keegan (33), Watson (53), Barnes (54)

12/9/79 **ENGLAND** (1) **1** **DENMARK** (0) **0** 85000
Keegan (17)

17/10/79 **NORTHERN IRELAND** (0) **1** **ENGLAND** (2) **5** 25000
Moreland (Pen, 50) — *Francis (18, 62), Woodcock (34), J. Nicholl (og, 74)*

22/11/79 **ENGLAND** (1) **2** **BULGARIA** (0) **0** 71491
Watson (9), Hoddle (68)

6/2/80 **ENGLAND** (1) **2** **EIRE** (0) **0** 90299
Keegan (34, 74)

FINALS - GROUP 2

12/6/80 **BELGIUM** (1) **1** **ENGLAND** (1) **1** 7000
Ceulemans (38) — *Wilkins (32)*

15/6/80 **ITALY** (0) **1** **ENGLAND** (0) **0** 59649
Tardelli (80)

18/6/80 **SPAIN** (0) **1** **ENGLAND** (1) **2** 14440
Dani (Pen, 48) — *Brooking (18), Woodcock (62)*

1982/84 SERIES
GROUP MATCHES - GROUP 3

22/9/82 **DENMARK** (0) **2** **ENGLAND** (1) **2** 44300
Allen Hansen (Pen, 69), Olsen (89) — *Francis (7, 80)*

17/11/82 **GREECE** (0) **0** **ENGLAND** (1) **3** 45000
Woodcock (2, 63), Lee (68)

15/12/82	**ENGLAND**	(4)	**9**	**LUXEMBOURG**	(0)	**0**	35000
	Moes (og, 17), Coppell (21), Woodcock (34) Blissett (43, 63, 86), Chamberlain (72) Hoddle (88)						
30/3/83	**ENGLAND**	(0)	**0**	**GREECE**	(0)	**0**	48500
27/4/83	**ENGLAND**	(1)	**2**	**HUNGARY**	(0)	**0**	55000
	Francis (31), Withe (70)						
21/9/83	**ENGLAND**	(0)	**0**	**DENMARK**	(1)	**1**	82050
				Simonsen (Pen, 39)			
12/10/83	**HUNGARY**	(0)	**0**	**ENGLAND**	(3)	**3**	15000
				Hoddle (14), Lee (19), Mariner (40)			
16/11/83	**LUXEMBOURG**	(0)	**0**	**ENGLAND**	(2)	**4**	12000
				Robson (11, 56), Mariner (39), Butcher (50)			

1986/88 SERIES

GROUP MATCHES - GROUP 4

15/10/86	**ENGLAND**	(1)	**3**	**NORTHERN IRELAND**	(0)	**0**	35300
	Lineker (33, 80), Waddle (78)						
12/11/86	**ENGLAND**	(1)	**2**	**YUGOSLAVIA**	(0)	**0**	60000
	Mabbutt (21), Anderson (57)						
1/4/87	**NORTHERN IRELAND**	(0)	**0**	**ENGLAND**	(2)	**2**	23000
				Robson (19), Waddle (43)			
29/4/87	**TURKEY**	(0)	**0**	**ENGLAND**	(0)	**0**	25000
14/10/87	**ENGLAND**	(4)	**8**	**TURKEY**	(0)	**0**	42528
	Barnes (1, 28), Lineker (8, 42, 71), Robson (59), Beardsley (62), Webb (88)						
11/11/87	**YUGOSLAVIA**	(0)	**1**	**ENGLAND**	(4)	**4**	70000
	Katanec (80)			*Beardsley (4), Barnes (17), Robson (20), Adams (25)*			

FINALS - GROUP 2

12/6/88	**ENGLAND**	(0)	**0**	**EIRE**	(1)	**1**	53000
				Houghton (5)			
15/6/88	**ENGLAND**	(0)	**1**	**HOLLAND**	(1)	**3**	65000
	Robson (53)			*Van Basten (23, 71, 75)*			
18/6/88	**ENGLAND**	(1)	**1**	**USSR**	(2)	**3**	53000
	Adams (16)			*Aleinikov (3), Mikhailichenko (28), Pasulko (72)*			

1990/92 SERIES

GROUP MATCHES - GROUP 7

7/10/90	**ENGLAND**	(1)	**2**	**POLAND**	(0)	**0**	77040
	Lineker (pen 39), Beardsley (89)						
14/11/90	**EIRE**	(0)	**1**	**ENGLAND**	(0)	**1**	46000
	Cascarino (79)			*Platt (67)*			
27/3/91	**ENGLAND**	(1)	**1**	**EIRE**	(1)	**1**	77000
	Dixon (9)			*Quinn (27)*			
1/5/91	**TURKEY**	(0)	**0**	**ENGLAND**	(1)	**1**	25000
				Wise (32)			
16/10/91	**ENGLAND**	(1)	**1**	**TURKEY**	(0)	**0**	50896
	Smith (21)						
13/11/91	**POLAND**	(1)	**1**	**ENGLAND**	(0)	**1**	15000
	Szewczyk (32)			*Lineker (77)*			

FINALS - GROUP 1

11/6/92	**DENMARK**	(0)	**0**	**ENGLAND**	(0)	**0**	26385
14/6/92	**FRANCE**	(0)	**0**	**ENGLAND**	(0)	**0**	26535
17/6/92	**SWEDEN**	(0)	**2**	**ENGLAND**	(1)	**1**	30126
	Eriksson (51), Brolin (82)			*Platt (3)*			

ESTONIA

1994/96 SERIES

GROUP MATCHES - GROUP 4

4/9/94	**ESTONIA**	(0)	**0**	**CROATIA**	(1)	**2**	1250
				Suker (44, 75)			
8/10/94	**ESTONIA**	(0)	**0**	**ITALY**	(1)	**2**	4000
				Panucci (20), Casiraghi (77)			
13/11/94	**UKRAINE**	(2)	**3**	**ESTONIA**	(0)	**0**	500
	Konovalov (30), Kirs (Og, 45), Guseinov (76)						
25/3/95	**ITALY**	(1)	**4**	**ESTONIA**	(0)	**1**	33000
	Zola (45, 65), Albertini (58), Ravanelli (82)			*Reim (72)*			
29/3/95	**SLOVENIA**	(1)	**3**	**ESTONIA**	(0)	**0**	12000
	Zahvic (40), Gliha (53), Kokol (90)						
26/4/95	**ESTONIA**	(0)	**0**	**UKRAINE**	(1)	**1**	1600
				Guseinov (16)			
11/6/95	**ESTONIA**	(1)	**1**	**SLOVENIA**	(1)	**3**	2000
	Reim (26)			*Novak (38, 69), Zahovic (79)*			
16/8/95	**ESTONIA**	(0)	**0**	**LITHUANIA**	(0)	**1**	1750
				Maciulevicius (48)			
3/9/95	**CROATIA**	(4)	**7**	**ESTONIA**	(1)	**1**	250
	Mladenovic (3), Suker (19, 58, 90), Boksic (29), Boban (42), Stimac (81)			*Reim (17)*			
11/10/95	**LITHUANIA**	(4)	**5**	**ESTONIA**	(0)	**0**	25
	Maciulevicius (8), Shuka (13, 39), Slekys (44), Ivanauskas (61)						

FAROE ISLANDS

1990/92 SERIES

GROUP MATCHES - GROUP 4

12/9/90	**FAROE ISLANDS**	(0)	**1**	**AUSTRIA**	(0)	**0**	12
	Nielsen (61)						
10/10/90	**DENMARK**	(2)	**4**	**FAROE ISLANDS**	(1)	**1**	385
	M. Laudrup (8, 48), Elstrup (37) Povlsen (89)			*Morkore (21)*			
1/5/91	**N. IRELAND**	(1)	**1**	**FAROE ISLANDS**	(0)	**1**	100
	Clarke (44)			*Reynheim (65)*			
16/5/91	**YUGOSLAVIA**	(2)	**7**	**FAROE ISLANDS**	(0)	**0**	80
	Najdoski (21), Prosinecki (24) Pancev (51, 72), Vulic (65), Boban (68) Suker (85)						
22/5/91	**AUSTRIA**	(1)	**3**	**FAROE ISLANDS**	(0)	**0**	130
	Pfeifenberger (13), Streiter (48) Wetl (69)						
11/9/91	**FAROE ISLANDS**	(0)	**0**	**N. IRELAND**	(3)	**5**	16
				Wilson (8), Clarke (12, 51, Pen 68), McDonald (14)			
25/9/91	**FAROE ISLANDS**	(0)	**0**	**DENMARK**	(2)	**4**	25
				Christofte (Pen 2), Christensen (8) Pingel (71), Vilfort (76)			
16/10/91	**FAROE ISLANDS**	(0)	**0**	**YUGOSLAVIA**	(1)	**2**	24
				Yugovic (17), Savicevic (79)			

1994/96 SERIES

GROUP MATCHES - GROUP 8

7/9/94	**FAROE ISLANDS**	(0)	**1**	**GREECE**	(2)	**5**	241
	Rasmussen (89)			*Saravakos (12), Tsalouhidis (16, 86), Alexandris (55, 65)*			
12/10/94	**SCOTLAND**	(3)	**5**	**FAROE ISLANDS**	(0)	**1**	208
	McGinlay (4), Booth (34), Collins (40, 72), McKinley (61)			*Muller (75)*			
16/11/94	**FINLAND**	(1)	**5**	**FAROE ISLANDS**	(0)	**0**	500
	Sumiala (37), Litmanen ((Pen 51), 71), Paatelainen (75, 85)						
26/4/95	**FAROE ISLANDS**	(0)	**0**	**FINLAND**	(0)	**4**	100
				Hjelm (55), Paatelainen (75), Lindberg (78), Helin (83)			
6/5/95	**RUSSIA**	(0)	**3**	**FAROE ISLANDS**	(0)	**0**	950
	Kechinov (53), Pisarev (72), Moukhamadiev (80)						
25/5/95	**FAROE ISLANDS**	(2)	**3**	**SAN MARINO**	(0)	**0**	345
	J.C. Hansen (6), J.E. Rasmussen (9), J. Johnsson (62)						
7/6/95	**FAROE ISLANDS**	(0)	**0**	**SCOTLAND**	(2)	**2**	388
				McKinlay (25), McGinlay (29)			
6/9/95	**FAROE ISLANDS**	(1)	**2**	**RUSSIA**	(1)	**5**	185
	H. Jarnskor (2), T. Jonsson (55)			*Mostovoi (10), Kiriakov (60), Kolivanov (65), Tsimbalar (84), Shalimov (87)*			
11/10/95	**SAN MARINO**	(0)	**1**	**FAROE ISLANDS**	(2)	**3**	100
	Valentini (52)			*Todi Jonsson (42, 45, 59)*			
15/11/95	**GREECE**	(0)	**5**	**FAROE ISLANDS**	(0)	**0**	1100
	Alexandris (58), Nikolaides (62), Mahlas (66), Donis (75), Tsartas (80)						

FINLAND

1966/68 SERIES

GROUP MATCES - GROUP 3

2/10/66	**FINLAND**	(0)	**0**	**AUSTRIA**	(0)	**0**	1000
16/10/66	**GREECE**	(1)	**2**	**FINLAND**	(0)	**1**	3200
	Alexiades (2)			*Makipaa*			
10/5/67	**FINLAND**	(1)	**1**	**GREECE**	(1)	**1**	1403
	Peltonen			*Haitas*			
30/8/67	**USSR**	(1)	**2**	**FINLAND**	(0)	**0**	2059
	Khurtsilava, Chislenko						
6/9/67	**FINLAND**	(2)	**2**	**USSR**	(3)	**5**	779
	Peltonen, Kilponen			*Sabo (2), Masslov, Banischevsky, Malafeev*			
24/9/67	**AUSTRIA**	(1)	**2**	**FINLAND**	(0)	**1**	2700
	Flogel, Grausam			*Peltonen*			

1970/72 SERIES

GROUP MATCHES - GROUP 1

7/10/70	**CZECHOSLOVAKIA**	(1)	**1**	**FINLAND**	(1)	**1**	500
	Albrecht			*Paatalainen*			

Date	Home	HT	FT	Away	HT	FT	Att
0/10/70	**ROMANIA**	(2)	**3**	**FINLAND**	(0)	**0**	50000
	Dumitrache (2), Nunweiller						
26/5/71	**FINLAND**	(0)	**0**	**WALES**	(0)	**1**	6000
				Toshack			
12/6/71	**FINLAND**	(0)	**0**	**CZECHOSLOVAKIA**	(2)	**4**	4500
				Capkovic, Pollak, Karko (2)			
22/9/71	**FINLAND**	(0)	**0**	**ROMANIA**	(2)	**4**	2084
				Jordanescu, Lupescu, Dembrovski, Lucescu (Pen)			
3/10/71	**WALES**	(1)	**3**	**FINLAND**	(0)	**0**	10000
	Durban, Toshack, Reece						

1974/76 SERIES

GROUP MATCHES - GROUP 5

Date	Home	HT	FT	Away	HT	FT	Att
1/9/74	**FINLAND**	(1)	**1**	**POLAND**	(1)	**2**	19000
	Rahja			*Szarmach, Lato*			
25/9/74	**FINLAND**	(1)	**1**	**HOLLAND**	(2)	**3**	20379
	Rahja			*Cruyff (2), Neeskens*			
9/10/74	**POLAND**	(2)	**3**	**FINLAND**	(0)	**0**	50000
	Kasperczak, Gadocha (Pen), Lato						
5/6/75	**FINLAND**	(0)	**0**	**ITALY**	(0)	**1**	17700
				Chinaglia (Pen)			
20/8/75	**HOLLAND**	(2)	**4**	**FINLAND**	(1)	**1**	28000
	Van Der Kuylen (3), Lubse			*Paatelainen*			
27/9/75	**ITALY**	(0)	**0**	**FINLAND**	(0)	**0**	29000

1978/80 SERIES

GROUP MATCHES - GROUP 6

Date	Home	HT	FT	Away	HT	FT	Att
24/5/78	**FINLAND**	(1)	**3**	**GREECE**	(0)	**0**	6000
	Ismail Atik (35, 82), Nieminen (80)						
20/9/78	**FINLAND**	(1)	**2**	**HUNGARY**	(0)	**1**	4797
	Ismail Atik (30), Pyykko (53)			*Tieber (74)*			
11/10/78	**GREECE**	(5)	**8**	**FINLAND**	(0)	**1**	8000
	Mavros (14, 39, 44, (Pen, 74)), Nikoloudis (20), Delikaris (23, 47), Galakos (80)			*Heiskanen (60)*			
4/7/79	**FINLAND**	(0)	**1**	**USSR**	(1)	**1**	12000
	Ismail Atik (55)			*Khapsalis (25)*			
17/10/79	**HUNGARY**	(2)	**3**	**FINLAND**	(0)	**1**	15000
	Fekete (23, 43), Tatar (51)			*Toivola (50)*			
31/10/79	**USSR**	(0)	**2**	**FINLAND**	(0)	**2**	1000
	Andreyev (50), Gavrilov (68)			*Himanka (75), Hasivi (82)*			

1982/84 SERIES

GROUP MATCHES - GROUP 2

Date	Home	HT	FT	Away	HT	FT	Att
8/9/82	**FINLAND**	(0)	**2**	**POLAND**	(2)	**3**	3526
	Valvee (84), Kousa (85)			*Smolarek (Pen, 16), Dziekanowski (20), Kupcewicz (73)*			
22/9/82	**FINLAND**	(0)	**0**	**PORTUGAL**	(1)	**2**	3132
				Nene (15), Oliveira (89)			
13/10/82	**USSR**	(1)	**2**	**FINLAND**	(0)	**0**	20000
	Baltacha (2), Andreyev (59)						
17/4/83	**POLAND**	(1)	**1**	**FINLAND**	(1)	**1**	8000
	Smolarek (Pen, 2)			*Janes (og, 5)*			
1/6/83	**FINLAND**	(0)	**0**	**USSR**	(1)	**1**	16996
				Blokhin (75)			
21/9/83	**PORTUGAL**	(2)	**5**	**FINLAND**	(0)	**0**	7500
	Jordao (18), C. Manuel (23), Ikalainen (og, 46), J. Luis (48), Oliveira (51)						

1986/88 SERIES

GROUP MATCHES - GROUP 6

Date	Home	HT	FT	Away	HT	FT	Att
10/9/86	**FINLAND**	(1)	**1**	**WALES**	(0)	**1**	9840
	Hjelm (11)			*Slatter (68)*			
15/10/86	**CZECHOSLOVAKIA**	(2)	**3**	**FINLAND**	(0)	**0**	26000
	Janecka (38), Knoflicek (43), Kula (67)						
29/10/86	**DENMARK**	(0)	**1**	**FINLAND**	(0)	**0**	40300
	Bertelsen (68)						
1/4/87	**WALES**	(2)	**4**	**FINLAND**	(0)	**0**	7696
	Rush, Hodges, Philips (64), A. Jones						
29/4/87	**FINLAND**	(0)	**0**	**DENMARK**	(0)	**1**	29197
				Molby (53)			
9/9/87	**FINLAND**	(1)	**3**	**CZECHOSLOVAKIA**	(0)	**0**	6430
	Hjelm (29), Lius (72), Tiainen (82)						

1990/92 SERIES

GROUP MATCHES - GROUP 6

Date	Home	HT	FT	Away	HT	FT	Att
12/9/90	**FINLAND**	(0)	**0**	**PORTUGAL**	(0)	**0**	10240
25/11/90	**MALTA**	(0)	**1**	**FINLAND**	(0)	**1**	6000
	Suda (74)			*Holmgren (87)*			
17/4/91	**HOLLAND**	(1)	**2**	**FINLAND**	(0)	**0**	27000
	van Basten (9), Gullit (75)						
16/5/91	**FINLAND**	(0)	**2**	**MALTA**	(0)	**0**	5150
	Jarvinen (51), Litmanen (87)						
5/6/91	**FINLAND**	(0)	**1**	**HOLLAND**	(0)	**1**	21207
	Holmgren (60)			*de Boer (77)*			
11/9/91	**PORTUGAL**	(1)	**1**	**FINLAND**	(0)	**0**	30000
	Brito (22)						
9/10/91	**FINLAND**	(0)	**1**	**GREECE**	(0)	**1**	5225
	Ukkonen (50)			*Tsaluhidis (74)*			
30/10/91	**GREECE**	(0)	**2**	**FINLAND**	(0)	**0**	26000
	Saravakos (50), Borbokis (52)						

1994/96 SERIES

GROUP MATCHES - GROUP 8

Date	Home	HT	FT	Away	HT	FT	Att
7/9/94	**FINLAND**	(0)	**0**	**SCOTLAND**	(1)	**2**	12845
				Shearer (29), Collins (66)			
12/10/94	**GREECE**	(1)	**4**	**FINLAND**	(0)	**0**	30000
	Markou (23), Batista (70), Mahlas (76, 89)						
16/11/94	**FINLAND**	(1)	**5**	**FAROE ISLANDS**	(0)	**0**	5000
	Sumiala (37), Litmanen ((Pen, 51), 71), Paatelainen (75, 85)						
14/12/94	**FINLAND**	(2)	**4**	**SAN MARINO**	(1)	**1**	3140
	Paatelainen (24, 30, 85, 90)			*Della Valle (34)*			
29/3/95	**SAN MARINO**	(0)	**0**	**FINLAND**	(1)	**2**	824
				Litmanen (45), Sumiala (67)			
26/4/95	**FAROE ISLANDS**	(0)	**0**	**FINLAND**	(0)	**4**	1000
				Hjelm (55), Paatelainen (75), Lindberg (78), Helin (83)			
11/6/95	**FINLAND**	(1)	**2**	**GREECE**	(1)	**1**	10500
	Litmanen (Pen, 45), Hjelm (54)			*Nicolaidis (6)*			
16/8/95	**FINLAND**	(0)	**0**	**RUSSIA**	(3)	**6**	14200
				Kulkov (32, 51), Karpin (42), Radchenko (42), Kolyvanov (67, 69)			
6/9/95	**SCOTLAND**	(1)	**1**	**FINLAND**	(0)	**0**	35505
	Booth (10)						
15/11/95	**RUSSIA**	(1)	**3**	**FINLAND**	(1)	**1**	3500
	Radchenko (40), Kulkov (55), Kiriakov (70)			*Suominen (45)*			

FRANCE

1958/60 SERIES

First Round

Date	Home	HT	FT	Away	HT	FT	Att
1/10/58	**FRANCE**	(3)	**7**	**GREECE**	(0)	**1**	38000
	Kopa, Fontaine (2), Cisowski (3), Vincent			*Yfantis*			
3/12/58	**GREECE**	(0)	**1**	**FRANCE**	(0)	**1**	26000
	Papaemmanuel			*Bruey*			

Quarter-Finals

Date	Home	HT	FT	Away	HT	FT	Att
13/12/59	**FRANCE**	(3)	**5**	**AUSTRIA**	(1)	**2**	43775
	Fontaine (3), Vincent (2)			*Horak, Pichler*			
27/3/60	**AUSTRIA**	(0)	**2**	**FRANCE**	(1)	**4**	38000
	Nemic, Probst			*Marcel, Rahis, Heutte, Kopa (Pen)*			

Semi-Final

Date	Home	HT	FT	Away	HT	FT	Att
6/7/60	**YUGOSLAVIA**	(0)	**2**	**FRANCE**	(0)	**0**	26370
	Jerkovic (2), Galic, Zanetic, Knez						

Third Place Match

Date	Home	HT	FT	Away	HT	FT	Att
9/7/60	**CZECHOSLOVAKIA**	(0)	**2**	**FRANCE**	(0)	**0**	9438
	Bubnik, Pavlovic			*Marseille*			

1962/64 SERIES

First Round

Date	Home	HT	FT	Away	HT	FT	Att
3/10/62	**ENGLAND**	(0)	**1**	**FRANCE**	(1)	**1**	35380
	Flowers (Pen)			*Goujon*			
27/2/63	**FRANCE**	(3)	**5**	**ENGLAND**	(0)	**2**	23986
	Wisnieski (2), Cossou (2), Douis			*Smith, Tambling*			

Second Round

Date	Home	HT	FT	Away	HT	FT	Att
29/9/63	**BULGARIA**	(1)	**1**	**FRANCE**	(0)	**0**	26000
	Diev						
26/10/63	**FRANCE**	(1)	**3**	**BULGARIA**	(0)	**1**	32223
	Goujon (2), Herbin			*Jamikov*			

Quarter-Finals

Date	Home	HT	FT	Away	HT	FT	Att
25/4/64	**FRANCE**	(0)	**1**	**HUNGARY**	(2)	**3**	35274
	Cossou			*Albert, Tichy (2)*			

24/5/64 **HUNGARY** .... (1) **2** **FRANCE** .... (1) **1** 70200
Sipos, Bene — *Combin*

1966/68 SERIES
GROUP MATCHES - GROUP 7

22/10/66 **FRANCE** .... (1) **2** **POLAND** .... (0) **1** 22000
Lech, Di Nallo — *Grzegorczyk*

11/11/66 **BELGIUM** .... (0) **2** **FRANCE** .... (0) **1** 45000
Van Himst (2) — *Lech*

27/11/66 **LUXEMBOURG** .... (0) **0** **FRANCE** .... (3) **3** 3500
Herbet, Revelli, Lech

17/9/67 **POLAND** .... (1) **1** **FRANCE** .... (2) **4** 51000
Brychczy — *Herbin, Di Nallo (2), Guy*

28/10/67 **FRANCE** .... (0) **1** **BELGIUM** .... (1) **1** 18000
Herbin — *Claessen*

23/12/67 **FRANCE** .... (1) **3** **LUXEMBOURG** .... (0) **1** 7500
Loubet (3) — *Klein*

Quarter-Finals

6/4/68 **FRANCE** .... (0) **1** **YUGOSLAVIA** .... (0) **1** 45000
Di Nallo — *Musemic*

24/4/68 **YUGOSLAVIA** .... (4) **5** **FRANCE** .... (1) **1** 47747
Petkovic (2), Musemic (2), Dzajic — *Di Nallo*

1970/72 SERIES
GROUP MATCHES - GROUP 2

11/11/70 **FRANCE** .... (1) **3** **NORWAY** .... (0) **1** 20000
Floch, Lech, Mezy — *Nielsen*

25/4/71 **HUNGARY** .... (0) **1** **FRANCE** .... (0) **1** 45000
Kocsis (Pen) — *Revelli*

8/9/71 **NORWAY** .... (0) **1** **FRANCE** .... (2) **3** 16544
A. Olsen — *Loubet, Vergnes, Blanchet*

10/10/71 **FRANCE** .... (0) **0** **HUNGARY** .... (2) **2** 25000
Bene, Zambo

10/11/71 **FRANCE** .... (0) **2** **BULGARIA** .... (0) **1** 10000
Loubet (2) — *Bonev (Pen)*

4/12/71 **BULGARIA** .... (0) **2** **FRANCE** .... (0) **1** 15000
Zhekov, Michailov — *Blanchet*

1974/76 SERIES
GROUP MATCHES - GROUP 7

12/10/74 **BELGIUM** .... (1) **2** **FRANCE** .... (1) **1** 50000
Martens, Van Der Elst — *Coste*

16/11/74 **FRANCE** .... (0) **2** **EAST GERMANY** ..... (1) **2** 50000
Guillou, Gallice — *Sparwasser, Kreische*

25/5/75 **ICELAND** .... (0) **0** **FRANCE** .... (0) **0** 11000

3/9/75 **FRANCE** .... (1) **3** **ICELAND** .... (0) **0** 29000
Guillou (2), Berdoll

11/10/75 **EAST GERMANY** ..... (0) **2** **FRANCE** .... (0) **1** 30000
Streich, Vogel (Pen) — *Bathenay*

15/11/75 **FRANCE** .... (0) **0** **BELGIUM** .... (0) **0** 45000

1978/80 SERIES
GROUP MATCHES - GROUP 5

2/9/78 **FRANCE** .... (0) **2** **SWEDEN** .... (0) **2** 44703
Berdoll (72), Six (83) — *Nordgren (54), L. Larsson (90)*

7/10/78 **LUXEMBOURG** .... (0) **1** **FRANCE** .... (1) **3** 12000
Michaux (73) — *Six (14), Tresor (62), Gemmrich (79)*

25/2/79 **FRANCE** .... (1) **3** **LUXEMBOURG** .... (0) **0** 25000
Petit (38), Emon (62), Larios (80)

4/4/79 **CZECHOSLOVAKIA** .... (0) **2** **FRANCE** .... (0) **0** 50000
Panenka (Pen, 67), Stambachr (72)

5/9/79 **SWEDEN** .... (1) **1** **FRANCE** .... (1) **3** 14395
Backe (24) — *Lacombe (14), Platini (55), Battiston (71)*

14/11/79 **FRANCE** .... (0) **2** **CZECHOSLOVAKIA** .... (0) **1** 39973
Pecout (67), Rampillon (75) — *Kozak (89)*

1982/84 SERIES
FINALS - GROUP 1

12/6/84 **FRANCE** .... (0) **1** **DENMARK** .... (0) **0** 47750
Platini (77)

16/6/84 **FRANCE** .... (3) **5** **BELGIUM** .... (0) **0** 51287
Platini (3, (Pen, 74), 88), Giresse (32), Fernandez (43)

19/6/84 **FRANCE** .... (0) **3** **YUGOSLAVIA** .... (1) **2** 5000
Platini (59, 61, 76) — *Sestic (31), D. Stoikovic (Pen, 80)*

Semi-Final

23/6/84 **FRANCE** .... (1) **3** **PORTUGAL** .... (0) **2** 5500
Domergue (23, 114), Platini (119) — *Jordao (73, 97)* — Marseill

(After Extra Time)

Final

27/6/84 **FRANCE** .... (0) **2** **SPAIN** .... (0) **0** 4736
Platini (56), Bellone (90) — Paris

1986/88 SERIES
GROUP MATCHES - GROUP 3

10/9/86 **ICELAND** .... (0) **0** **FRANCE** .... (0) **0** 1370

11/10/86 **FRANCE** .... (0) **0** **USSR** .... (0) **2** 4049
Belanov (67), Rats (73)

19/11/86 **EAST GERMANY** ..... (0) **0** **FRANCE** .... (0) **0** 5200

29/4/87 **FRANCE** .... (1) **2** **ICELAND** .... (0) **0** 3000
Micciche (38), Stopyra (65)

16/6/87 **NORWAY** .... (0) **2** **FRANCE** .... (0) **0** 826
Mordt (71), Andersen (80)

9/9/87 **USSR** .... (0) **1** **FRANCE** .... (1) **1** 10000
Mikhailichenko (77) — *Toure (13)*

14/10/87 **FRANCE** .... (0) **1** **NORWAY** .... (0) **1** 1200
Fargeon (63) — *Sundby (76)*

18/11/87 **FRANCE** .... (0) **0** **EAST GERMANY** ..... (0) **1** 2000
Ernst (89)

1990/92 SERIES
GROUP MATCHES - GROUP 1

5/9/90 **ICELAND** .... (0) **1** **FRANCE** .... (1) **2** 8000
Edvaldsson (85) — *Papin (12), Cantona (74)*

13/10/90 **FRANCE** .... (0) **2** **CZECHOSLOVAKIA** ... (0) **1** 38249
Papin (60, 83) — *Skuhravy (89)*

17/11/90 **ALBANIA** .... (0) **0** **FRANCE** .... (1) **1** 1500
Boli (25)

22/2/91 **FRANCE** .... (1) **3** **SPAIN** .... (1) **1** 45000
Sauzee (15), Papin (58), Blanc (77) — *Baquero (11)*

30/3/91 **FRANCE** .... (4) **5** **ALBANIA** .... (0) **0** 24181
Sauzee (1, 19), Papin (pen 34, 43), Lekbello (o.g. 82)

4/9/91 **CZECHOSLOVAKIA** .... (1) **1** **FRANCE** .... (0) **2** 50000
Nemecek (19) — *Papin (53, 89)*

12/10/91 **SPAIN** .... (1) **1** **FRANCE** .... (2) **2** 27500
Abelardo (34) — *Fernandez (13), Papin (16)*

20/11/91 **FRANCE** .... (1) **3** **ICELAND** .... (0) **1** 35000
Simba (42), Cantona (60, 68) — *Sverrisson (71)*

FINALS - GROUP 1

10/6/92 **SWEDEN** .... (1) **1** **FRANCE** .... (0) **1** 29000
Eriksson (24) — *Papin (58)*

14/6/92 **FRANCE** .... (0) **0** **ENGLAND** .... (0) **0** 26535

17/6/92 **FRANCE** .... (0) **1** **DENMARK** .... (1) **2** 25763
Papin (60) — *Larsen (8), Elstrup (78)*

1994/96 SERIES
GROUP MATCHES - GROUP 1

7/9/94 **SLOVAKIA** .... (0) **0** **FRANCE** .... (0) **0** 17000

8/10/94 **FRANCE** .... (0) **0** **ROMANIA** .... (0) **0** 31744

16/11/94 **POLAND** .... (0) **0** **FRANCE** .... (0) **0** 21000

13/12/94 **AZERBAIJAN** .... (0) **0** **FRANCE** .... (1) **2** 4000
Papin (24), Loko (55)

29/3/95 **ISRAEL** .... (0) **0** **FRANCE** .... (0) **0** 43000

26/4/95 **FRANCE** .... (2) **4** **SLOVAKIA** .... (0) **0** 26000
Kristofik (Og, 27), Ginola (43), Blanc (57), Guerin (61)

16/8/95 **FRANCE** .... (0) **1** **POLAND** .... (1) **1** 40426
Djorkaeff (86) — *Juskowiak (35)*

6/9/95 **FRANCE** .... (3) **10** **AZERBAIJAN** .... (0) **0** 15000
Desailly (13), Djorkaeff (18, 79), Guerin (33), Pedros (49), Leboeuf (53, 70), Dugarry (66), Zidane (68), Cocard (90)

11/10/95 **ROMANIA** .... (0) **1** **FRANCE** .... (2) **3** 25000
Lacatus (51) — *Karembeu (28), Djorkaeff (42), Zidane (75)*

15/11/95 **FRANCE** .... (0) **2** **ISRAEL** .... (0) **0** 21500
Djorkaeff (69), Lizarazu (88)

GEORGIA

1994/96 SERIES

GROUP MATCHES - GROUP 7

7/9/94 **GEORGIA** (0) **0** **MOLDOVA** (1) **1** 40000
Oprya (40)

12/10/94 **BULGARIA** (0) **2** **GEORGIA** (0) **0** 45000
Kostadinov (56, 62)

16/11/94 **GEORGIA** (2) **5** **WALES** (0) **0** 45000
Ketsbaya (31, 49), Kinkladze (41), Goglichigani (59), Arveladze (67)

14/12/94 **ALBANIA** (0) **0** **GEORGIA** (1) **1** 15000
Arveladze (17)

29/3/95 **GEORGIA** (0) **0** **GERMANY** (2) **2** 75000
Klinsmann (24, 45)

26/4/95 **GEORGIA** (2) **2** **ALBANIA** (0) **0** 25000
S. Arveladze (3), Ketsbaya (42)

7/6/95 **WALES** (0) **0** **GEORGIA** (1) **1** 6500
Kinkladze (73)

6/9/95 **GERMANY** (1) **4** **GEORGIA** (1) **1** 40000
Moller (39), Ziege (57), Kirsten (62), Babbel (72) — *Ketsbaya (28)*

11/10/95 **GEORGIA** (1) **2** **BULGARIA** (0) **1** 45000
Arveladze (3), Kinkladze (48) — *Stoichkov (88)*

15/11/95 **MOLDOVA** (2) **3** **GEORGIA** (0) **2** 9000
Testemicianu (3), Miterev (20, 61) — *Dzyamashia (65), Kulibaba (Og, 79)*

GERMANY (UNIFIED)

1990/92 SERIES

GROUP MATCHES - GROUP 5

31/10/90 **LUXEMBOURG** (0) **2** **GERMANY** (2) **3** 9500
Girres (57), Langers (65) — *Klinsmann (16), Bein (30), Voller (49)*

1/5/91 **GERMANY** (1) **1** **BELGIUM** (0) **0** 56000
Matthaus (3)

5/6/91 **WALES** (0) **1** **GERMANY** (0) **0** 38000
Rush (66)

16/10/91 **GERMANY** (3) **4** **WALES** (0) **1** 46000
Moller (4), Voller (38), Riedle (45) Doll (72) — *Bodin (pen 83)*

20/11/91 **BELGIUM** (0) **0** **GERMANY** (1) **1** 26000
Voller (15)

17/12/91 **GERMANY** (2) **4** **LUXEMBOURG** (0) **0** 24500
Matthaus (pen 15), Buchwald (44) Riedle (51), Hassler (62)

FINALS - GROUP 2

12/6/92 **CIS** (0) **1** **GERMANY** (0) **1** 17410
Dobrovolsky (pen 62) — *Hassler (89)*

15/6/92 **SCOTLAND** (0) **0** **GERMANY** (1) **2** 17638
Riedle (28), Effenberg (46)

18/6/92 **HOLLAND** (2) **3** **GERMANY** (0) **1** 37725
Rijkaard (2), Witschge (14) Bergkamp (71) — *Klinsmann (53)*

Semi-final

21/6/92 **SWEDEN** (0) **2** **GERMANY** (1) **3** 28827
Brolin (pen 64), Andersson (89) — *Hassler (10), Riedle (58, 88)*

Final

26/6/92 **GERMANY** (0) **0** **DENMARK** (1) **2** 37800
Jensen (18), Vilfort (78)

1994/96 SERIES

GROUP MATCHES - GROUP 7

16/11/94 **ALBANIA** (1) **1** **GERMANY** (1) **2** 23000
Zmijani (32) — *Klinsmann (18), Kirsten (46)*

14/12/94 **MOLDOVA** (0) **0** **GERMANY** (2) **3** 22000
Kirsten (6), Klinsmann (38), Matthaus (72)

18/12/94 **GERMANY** (2) **2** **ALBANIA** (0) **1** 20310
Matthaus (Pen, 8), Klinsmann (17) — *Rrakli (58)*

29/3/95 **GEORGIA** (0) **0** **GERMANY** (2) **2** 75000
Klinsmann (24, 45)

26/4/95 **GERMANY** (1) **1** **WALES** (1) **1** 43461
Herrlich (42) — *Saunders (8)*

7/6/95 **BULGARIA** (1) **3** **GERMANY** (2) **2** 60000
Stoichkov (Pens (45, 66)), Kostadinov (69) — *Klinsmann (18), Strunz (44)*

6/9/95 **GERMANY** (1) **4** **GEORGIA** (1) **1** 40000
Moller (39), Ziege (57), Kirsten (62), Babbel (72) — *Ketsbaya (28)*

8/10/95 **GERMANY** (3) **6** **MOLDOVA** (0) **1** 18500
Stroyenko (Og, 16), Helmer (18), Sammer (24, 71), Moller (47, 61) — *Rebesha (82)*

11/10/95 **WALES** (0) **1** **GERMANY** (0) **2** 25000
Helmer (Og, 78) — *Melville (Og, 75), Klinsmann (80)*

15/11/95 **GERMANY** (0) **3** **BULGARIA** (0) **1** 75841
Klinsmann (50, (Pen, 76)), Hassler (56) — *Stoichkov (47)*

GREECE

1958/60 SERIES

First Round

1/10/58 **FRANCE** (3) **7** **GREECE** (0) **1** 38000
Kopa, Fontaine (2), Cisowski (3), Vincent — *Yfantis*

3/12/58 **GREECE** (0) **1** **FRANCE** (0) **1** 26000
Papaemmanuel — *Bruey*

1962/64 SERIES

First Round

ALBANIA WALK OVER GREECE (WITHDREW)

GREECE & ALBANIA TECHNICALLY AT WAR SINCE 1912

1966/68 SERIES

GROUP MATCHES - GROUP 3

16/10/66 **GREECE** (1) **2** **FINLAND** (0) **1** 32000
Alexiades (2) — *Makipaa*

10/5/67 **FINLAND** (1) **1** **GREECE** (1) **1** 14038
Peltonen — *Haitas*

16/7/67 **USSR** (0) **4** **GREECE** (0) **0** 45000
Banischevsky (2), Sabo, Chislenko

4/10/67 **GREECE** (2) **4** **AUSTRIA** (0) **1** 45000
Sideris (3, 1 Pen), Papaioannou — *Grausam*

31/10/67 **GREECE** (0) **0** **USSR** (0) **1** 40000
Chislenko

5/11/67 **AUSTRIA** (1) **1** **GREECE** (0) **1** 25000
Siber — *Sideris*

1970/72 SERIES

GROUP MATCHES - GROUP 3

11/10/70 **MALTA** (0) **1** **GREECE** (0) **1** 15000
Vassallo — *Papaioannou*

16/12/70 **GREECE** (0) **0** **SWITZERLAND** (0) **1** 38000
Muller

21/4/71 **ENGLAND** (1) **3** **GREECE** (0) **0** 55000
Chivers, Hurst, Lee

12/5/71 **SWITZERLAND** (0) **1** **GREECE** (0) **0** 37000
Odermatt

20/6/71 **GREECE** (0) **2** **MALTA** (0) **0** 12000
Davourlis, Aidiniou

1/12/71 **GREECE** (0) **0** **ENGLAND** (0) **2** 45000
Hurst, Chivers

1974/76 SERIES

GROUP MATCHES - GROUP 8

13/10/74 **BULGARIA** (3) **3** **GREECE** (1) **3** 35000
Bonev, Denev (2) — *Antoniadis, Papaioannou, Glezos*

20/11/74 **GREECE** (1) **2** **WEST GERMANY** (0) **2** 11000
Delikaris, Eleftherakis — *Cullmann, Wimmer*

18/12/74 **GREECE** (2) **2** **BULGARIA** (0) **1** 30000
Sarafis, Antoniadis — *Kolev*

23/2/75 **MALTA** (1) **2** **GREECE** (0) **0** 20000
Aquilina, Magro

4/6/75 **GREECE** (2) **4** **MALTA** (0) **0** 15000
Mavros, Antoniadis (Pen), Iosifidis, Papaioannou

11/10/75 **WEST GERMANY** (0) **1** **GREECE** (0) **1** 65000
Heynckes — *Delikaris*

1978/80 SERIES

GROUP MATCHES - GROUP 8

24/5/78 **FINLAND** (1) **3** **GREECE** (0) **0** 6000
Ismail Atik (35, 82), Nieminen (80)

20/9/78 **USSR** (1) **2** **GREECE** (0) **0** 55000
Chesnokov (20), Bessonov (53)

11/10/78 **GREECE** (5) **8** **FINLAND** (0) **1** 8000
Mavros (14, 39, 44, (Pen, 72), Nikoloudis (20), Delikaris (23, 47), Galakos (80) — *Heiskanen (60)*

29/10/78 **GREECE** (0) **4** **HUNGARY** (0) **1** 10000
Galakos (59, 68), Ardizoglu (71), Mavros (89) — *Martos (90)*

2/5/79 **HUNGARY** (0) **0** **GREECE** (0) **0** 25000

12/9/79 **GREECE** (1) **1** **USSR** (0) **0** 25000
Nikoloudis (25)

FINALS - GROUP 1

11/6/80 **HOLLAND** (0) **1** **GREECE** (0) **0** 10000
Kist (Pen, 55)

14/6/80 **CZECHOSLOVAKIA** (2) **3** **GREECE** (1) **1**
Panenka (5), Visek (35), Nehoda (63) — *Anastopoulos (11)*

17/6/80 **WEST GERMANY** (0) **0** **GREECE** (0) **0** 13901

1982/84 SERIES

GROUP MATCHES - GROUP 3

9/10/82 **LUXEMBOURG** (0) **0** **GREECE** (2) **2** 3500
Dimopoulos (Pen, 8), Anastopoulos (25)

17/11/82 **GREECE** (0) **0** **ENGLAND** (1) **3** 45000
Woodcock (2, 63), Lee (68)

30/3/83 **ENGLAND** (0) **0** **GREECE** (0) **0** 48500

27/4/83 **DENMARK** (0) **1** **GREECE** (0) **0** 45000
Busk (76)

15/5/83 **HUNGARY** (1) **2** **GREECE** (2) **3** 12500
Nyilasi (25), Hajszan (89) — *Anastopoulos (16), Kostikos (33), Papaioannou (52)*

16/11/83 **GREECE** (0) **0** **DENMARK** (1) **2** 30000
Elkjaer (16), Simonsen (47)

3/12/83 **GREECE** (1) **2** **HUNGARY** (2) **2** 1500
Anastopoulos (9, 55) — *Kardos (11), Torocsik (39)*

14/12/83 **GREECE** (1) **1** **LUXEMBOURG** (0) **0** 5000
Saravakos (18)

1986/88 SERIES

GROUP MATCHES - GROUP 5

15/10/86 **POLAND** (1) **2** **GREECE** (1) **1** 32500
Dziekanowski ((Pen, 5), (Pen, 40)) — *Anastopoulos (13)*

12/11/86 **GREECE** (1) **2** **HUNGARY** (0) **1** 15000
Mitropoulos (39), Anastopoulos (65) — *Boda (72)*

3/12/86 **CYPRUS** (2) **2** **GREECE** (1) **4** 10000
Christofi (28), Savvides (41) — *Antoniou (13), Papaioannou (48), Batsinilas (73), Anastopoulos (Pen, 86)*

14/1/87 **GREECE** (0) **3** **CYPRUS** (0) **1** 35000
Anastopoulos (54, 66), Bonovas (63) — *Savva (60)*

25/3/87 **HOLLAND** (0) **1** **GREECE** (1) **1** 56000
Van Basten (55) — *Saravakos (6)*

29/4/87 **GREECE** (0) **1** **POLAND** (0) **0** 70000
Saravakos (57)

14/10/87 **HUNGARY** (3) **3** **GREECE** (0) **0** 8000
Detari (4), Bognar (12), Meszaros (15)

16/12/87 **GREECE** (0) **0** **HOLLAND** (1) **3** 7000
R. Koeman (19), Gillhaus (75, 81)

1990/92 SERIES

GROUP MATCHES - GROUP 6

31/10/90 **GREECE** (2) **4** **MALTA** (0) **0** 17500
Tsiantakis (37), Karapialis (40) Saravakos (59), Borbokis (88)

21/11/90 **HOLLAND** (2) **2** **GREECE** (0) **0** 26000
Bergkamp (7), van Basten (18)

23/1/91 **GREECE** (1) **3** **PORTUGAL** (1) **2** 30000
Borbokis (7), Manolas (68) Tsaluhidis (85) — *Aguas (18), Futre (62)*

9/10/91 **FINLAND** (0) **1** **GREECE** (0) **1** 5225
Ukkonen (50) — *Tsaluhidis (74)*

30/10/91 **GREECE** (0) **2** **FINLAND** (0) **0** 26000
Saravakos (50), Borbokis (52)

20/11/91 **PORTUGAL** (1) **1** **GREECE** (0) **0** 2000
Joao Pinto II (17)

4/12/91 **GREECE** (0) **0** **HOLLAND** (1) **2** 32500
Bergkamp (38), Blind (87)

22/12/91 **MALTA** (1) **1** **GREECE** (0) **1** 8000
Sultana (42) — *Marinakis (67)*

1994/96 SERIES

GROUP MATCHES - GROUP 8

7/9/94 **FAROE ISLANDS** (0) **1** **GREECE** (2) **5** 2412
Rasmussen (89) — *Saravakos (12), Tsalouhidis (16, 86), Alexandris (55, 65)*

12/10/94 **GREECE** (1) **4** **FINLAND** (0) **0** 30000
Markou (23), Batista (70), Mahlas (76, 89)

16/11/94 **GREECE** (1) **2** **SAN MARINO** (0) **0** 13500
Mahlas (21), Frantzekos (84)

18/12/94 **GREECE** (1) **1** **SCOTLAND** (0) **0** 20000
Apostolakis (Pen, 18)

26/4/95 **GREECE** (0) **0** **RUSSIA** (1) **3** 45000
Nikiforov (36), Zagorakis (Og, 78), Beschastnykh (79)

11/6/95 **FINLAND** (1) **2** **GREECE** (1) **1** 10500
Litmanen (Pen, 45), Hjelm (54) — *Nicolaidis (6)*

16/8/95 **SCOTLAND** (0) **1** **GREECE** (0) **0** 34910
McCoist (72)

6/9/95 **SAN MARINO** (0) **0** **GREECE** (2) **4** 1000
Tsalouhidis (5), G. Georgiadis (31), Alexandris (61), Monis (81)

11/10/95 **RUSSIA** (1) **2** **GREECE** (0) **1** 65000
Kovtun (36), Onopko (71) — *Tsalouhidis (64)*

15/11/95 **GREECE** (0) **5** **FAROE ISLANDS** (0) **0** 11000
Alexandris (58), Nikolaides (62), Mahlas (66), Donis (75), Tsartas (80)

HOLLAND

1962/64 SERIES

First Round

11/11/62 **HOLLAND** (1) **3** **SWITZERLAND** (1) **1** 60000
Van Der Linden, Swart, Groot — *Hertig*

31/3/63 **SWITZERLAND** (0) **1** **HOLLAND** (1) **1** 31800
Allemann — *Kruijver*

Second Round

11/9/63 **HOLLAND** (1) **1** **LUXEMBOURG** (1) **1** 36000
Nuninga — *May*

30/10/63 **LUXEMBOURG** (1) **2** **HOLLAND** (1) **1** 42400
Dimmer (2) — *Kruiver*

1966/68 SERIES

GROUP MATCHES - GROUP 5

7/9/66 **HOLLAND** (1) **2** **HUNGARY** (0) **2** 65000
Pijs, Cruyff — *Molnar, Albert*

30/11/66 **HOLLAND** (0) **2** **DENMARK** (0) **0** 23000
Van De Kuyen, Swart

5/4/67 **EAST GERMANY** (0) **4** **HOLLAND** (2) **3** 40000
Vogel, Frenzel (3) — *Keizer (2), Mulder*

10/5/67 **HUNGARY** (2) **2** **HOLLAND** (0) **1** 25000
Meszoly (Pen), Farkas — *Suurbier*

13/9/67 **HOLLAND** (0) **1** **EAST GERMANY** (0) **0** 45000
Cruyff

4/10/67 **DENMARK** (1) **3** **HOLLAND** (0) **2** 34500
Bjerre (2, 1 Pen), Sondergaard — *Suurbier, Israel*

1970/72 SERIES

GROUP MATCHES - GROUP 7

11/10/70 **HOLLAND** (0) **1** **YUGOSLAVIA** (1) **1** 60000
Israel (Pen) — *Dzajic*

11/11/70 **EAST GERMANY** (0) **1** **HOLLAND** (0) **0** 36000
Ducke

24/2/71 **HOLLAND** (4) **6** **LUXEMBOURG** (0) **0** 40000
Cruyff (2), Keizer (2), Lippens, Suurbier

5/4/71 **YUGOSLAVIA** (1) **2** **HOLLAND** (0) **0** 20000
Jerkovic, Dzajic

10/10/71 **HOLLAND** (1) **3** **EAST GERMANY** (1) **2** 50000
Keizer (2), Hulshoff — *Vogel (2)*

17/11/71 **LUXEMBOURG** (0) **0** **HOLLAND** (5) **8** 17500
Cruyff (3), Keizer, Pahlplatz, Hulshoff, Hoekema, Israel

1974/76 SERIES

GROUP MATCHES - GROUP 5

25/9/74 **FINLAND** (1) **1** **HOLLAND** (2) **3** 20379
Rahja — *Cruyff (2), Neeskens*

20/11/74 **HOLLAND** (1) **3** **ITALY** (1) **1** 62000
Rensenbrink, Cruyff (2) — *Boninsegna*

20/8/75 **HOLLAND** (2) **4** **FINLAND** (1) **1** 28000
Van Der Kuylen (3), Lubse — *Paatelainen*

10/9/75 **POLAND** .... (2) **4** **HOLLAND** .... (0) **1** 100000
Lato, Gadocha, Szarmach (2) — *Van Der Kerkhoff*

15/10/75 **HOLLAND** .... (1) **3** **POLAND** .... (0) **0** 60000
Neeskens, Geels, Thijssen

22/11/75 **ITALY** .... (1) **1** **HOLLAND** .... (0) **0** 80000
Capello

Quarter-Finals

25/4/76 **HOLLAND** .... (2) **5** **BELGIUM** .... (0) **0** 58000
Rijsbergen, Rensenbrink (3), Neeskens (Pen)

22/5/76 **BELGIUM** .... (1) **1** **HOLLAND** .... (0) **2** 45000
Van Gool — *Rep, Cruyff*

Semi-Final

16/6/76 **CZECHOSLOVAKIA** .... (1) **3** **HOLLAND** .... (0) **1** 40000 Zabreb
Ondrus, Nehoda, Moder — *Ondrus (og)*

(After Extra Time)

Third Place Match

19/6/76 **HOLLAND** .... (2) **3** **YUGOSLAVIA** .... (1) **2** 18000 Zagreb
Geels (2), W. Van Der Kerkhoff — *Katalinski, Dzajic*

(After Extra Time)

1978/80 SERIES

GROUP MATCHES - GROUP 4

20/9/78 **HOLLAND** .... (1) **3** **ICELAND** .... (0) **0** 14500
Krol (33), Brandts (53), Rensenbrink (63)

11/10/78 **SWITZERLAND** .... (1) **1** **HOLLAND** .... (1) **3** 23000
Tanner (29) — *Wildschut (19), Brandts (65), Geels (89)*

15/11/78 **HOLLAND** .... (1) **3** **EAST GERMANY** ..... (0) **0** 47000
Kische (og, 17), Geels ((Pen, 73), 88)

28/3/79 **HOLLAND** .... (0) **3** **SWITZERLAND** .... (0) **0** 27000
Kist (55), Metgod (84), Peters (89)

2/5/79 **POLAND** .... (1) **2** **HOLLAND** .... (0) **0** 100000
Boniek (19), Mazur (Pen, 64)

5/9/79 **ICELAND** .... (0) **0** **HOLLAND** .... (0) **4** 12000
Metgod (49), W. Van Der Kerkhoff (70), Nanninga (73, 88)

17/10/79 **HOLLAND** .... (0) **1** **POLAND** .... (1) **1** 53000
Stevens (64) — *Rudy (38)*

21/11/79 **EAST GERMANY** ...... (2) **2** **HOLLAND** .... (1) **3** 99000
Schnuphase (17), Streich (Pen, 34) — *Thijssen (44), Kist (50), R. Van Der Kerkhoff (67)*

FINALS - GROUP 1

11/6/80 **HOLLAND** .... (0) **1** **GREECE** .... (0) **0** 10000
Kist (Pen, 55)

14/6/80 **WEST GERMANY** ..... (1) **3** **HOLLAND** .... (0) **2** 50000
Allofs (15, 60, 67) — *Rep (Pen, 65), W. Van Der Kerkhoff (86)*

17/6/80 **CZECHOSLOVAKIA** .... (1) **1** **HOLLAND** .... (0) **1** 11889
Nehoda (38) — *Kist (59)*

1982/84 SERIES

GROUP MATCHES - GROUP 7

1/9/82 **ICELAND** .... (0) **1** **HOLLAND** .... (0) **1** 4500
Edvaldsson (49) — *Schoenaker (51)*

22/9/82 **HOLLAND** .... (1) **2** **EIRE** .... (0) **1** 19000
Schoenaker (1), Gullit (65) — *Daly (80)*

19/12/82 **MALTA** .... (0) **0** **HOLLAND** .... (4) **6** 13000
Ophof (Pen, 22), Van Kooten (25, 70), Hovenkamp (34), Schoenaker (39, 51)

17/2/83 **SPAIN** .... (1) **1** **HOLLAND** .... (0) **0** 45000
Senor (Pen, 43)

7/9/83 **HOLLAND** .... (3) **3** **ICELAND** .... (0) **0** 10000
R. Koeman (16), Gullit (18), Houtman (21)

12/10/83 **EIRE** .... (2) **2** **HOLLAND** .... (0) **3** 35000
Waddock (6), Brady (Pen, 34) — *Gullit (51, 76), Van Basten (67)*

16/11/83 **HOLLAND** .... (1) **2** **SPAIN** .... (1) **1** 58000
Houtman (26), Gullit (63) — *Santillana (41)*

17/12/83 **HOLLAND** .... (2) **5** **MALTA** .... (0) **0** 59000
Vanenburg (18), Wijnstekers (29), Rijkaard (71, 87), Houtman (81)

1986/88 SERIES

GROUP MATCHES - GROUP 5

15/10/86 **HUNGARY** .... (0) **0** **HOLLAND** .... (0) **1** 15000
Van Basten (68)

19/11/86 **HOLLAND** .... (0) **0** **POLAND** .... (0) **0** 65000

21/12/86 **CYPRUS** .... (0) **0** **HOLLAND** .... (1) **2** 10000
Gullit (19), Bosman (73)

25/3/87 **HOLLAND** .... (0) **1** **GREECE** .... (1) **1** 56000
Van Basten (55) — *Saravakos (6)*

29/4/87 **HOLLAND** .... (2) **2** **HUNGARY** .... (0) **0** 53000
Gullit (37), A. Muhren (40)

14/10/87 **POLAND** .... (0) **0** **HOLLAND** .... (2) **2** 21500
Gullit (30, 38)

28/10/87 **HOLLAND** .... (4) **8** **CYPRUS** .... (0) **0** 55000
Bosman (1, 38, 52, 60, 67), Gullit (20), Spelbos (3), Vant Schip (46)

GAME DECLARED VOID DUE TO ATTACK ON CYPRIOT GOALKEEPER

Replay : -

9/12/87 **HOLLAND** .... (2) **4** **CYPRUS** .... (0) **0** Closed Doors
Bosman (35, 44, 66), R. Koeman (Pen, 63)

16/12/87 **GREECE** .... (0) **0** **HOLLAND** .... (1) **3** 7000
R. Koeman (19), Gillhaus (75, 81)

FINALS - GROUP 2

12/6/88 **HOLLAND** .... (0) **0** **USSR** .... (0) **1** 60000
Rats (53)

15/6/88 **ENGLAND** .... (0) **1** **HOLLAND** .... (1) **3** 65000
Robson (53) — *Van Basten (23, 71, 75)*

18/6/88 **EIRE** .... (0) **0** **HOLLAND** .... (0) **1** 70800
Kieft (81)

Semi-Final

21/6/88 **WEST GERMANY** ..... (0) **1** **HOLLAND** .... (0) **2** 60000 Hamburg
Matthaus (Pen, 54) — *R. Koeman (Pen, 73),* Van Basten (88)

Final

25/6/88 **HOLLAND** .... (1) **2** **USSR** .... (0) **0** 72308 Munich
Gullit (32), Van Basten (53)

1990/92 SERIES

GROUP MATCHES - GROUP 6

17/10/90 **PORTUGAL** .... (0) **1** **HOLLAND** .... (0) **0** 35000
Aguas (54)

21/11/90 **HOLLAND** .... (2) **2** **GREECE** .... (0) **0** 26000
Bergkamp (7), Van Basten (18)

19/12/90 **MALTA** .... (0) **0** **HOLLAND** .... (3) **8** 11000
van Basten (9, 20, 23, 64, pen 80), Winter (53) Bergkamp (58, 70)

13/3/91 **HOLLAND** .... (1) **1** **MALTA** .... (0) **0** 36383
van Basten (pen 31)

17/4/91 **HOLLAND** .... (1) **2** **FINLAND** .... (0) **0** 27000
van Basten (9), Gullit (75)

5/6/91 **FINLAND** .... (0) **1** **HOLLAND** .... (0) **1** 21207
Holmgren (60) — *de Boer (77)*

16/10/91 **HOLLAND** .... (1) **1** **PORTUGAL** .... (0) **0** 50000
Witschge (20)

4/12/91 **GREECE** .... (0) **0** **HOLLAND** .... (1) **2** 32500
Bergkamp (38), Blind (87)

FINALS - GROUP 2

12/6/92 **HOLLAND** .... (0) **1** **SCOTLAND** .... (0) **0** 35720
Bergkamp (76)

15/6/92 **HOLLAND** .... (0) **0** **CIS** .... (0) **0** 34440

18/6/92 **HOLLAND** .... (2) **3** **GERMANY** .... (0) **1** 37725
Rijkaard (2), Witschge (14) Bergkamp (71) — *Klinsmann (53)*

Semi-final

22/6/92 **HOLLAND** .... (1) **2** **DENMARK** .... (2) **2** 37450
Bergkamp (23), Rijkaard (85) — *Larsen (5, 32)*

Denmark won on penalties after extra-time

1994/96 SERIES

GROUP MATCHES - GROUP 5

7/9/95 **LUXEMBOURG** .... (0) **0** **HOLLAND** .... (1) **4** 8200
Roy (23), R. De Boer (65, 67), Jonk (90)

12/10/94 **NORWAY** .... (0) **1** **HOLLAND** .... (1) **1** 22293
Rekdal (52) — *Roy (22)*

16/11/94 **HOLLAND** .... (0) **0** **CZECH REPUBLIC** .... (0) **0** 45000

14/12/94 **HOLLAND** (3) **5** **LUXEMBOURG** (0) **0** 30000
Mulder (6), Roy (16), Jonk (39), R. De Boer (51), Seedorf (90)

29/3/95 **HOLLAND** (1) **4** **MALTA** (0) **0** 37000
Seedorf (38), Bergkamp (Pen, 75), Winter (78), Kluivert (84)

26/4/95 **CZECH REPUBLIC** (0) **3** **HOLLAND** (1) **1** 17463
Skuhravy (49), Nemecek (57), Berger (62) — *Jonk (7)*

7/6/95 **BYELORUSSIA** (1) **1** **HOLLAND** (0) **0** 22000
Gerasimets (27)

6/9/95 **HOLLAND** (0) **1** **BYELORUSSIA** (0) **0** 17000
Mulder (83)

11/10/95 **MALTA** (0) **0** **HOLLAND** (0) **4** 8000
Overmars (52, 61, 65), Seedorf (80)

15/11/95 **HOLLAND** (0) **3** **NORWAY** (0) **0** 49000
Seedorf (59), Mulder (86), Overmars (89)

Play-Off Match

13/12/95 **EIRE** (0) **0** **HOLLAND** (1) **2** 40000 Liverpool
Kluivert (29, 88)

HUNGARY

1958/60 SERIES

First Round

28/9/58 **USSR** (3) **3** **HUNGARY** (0) **1** 100572
Ilyin, Metreveli, Ivanov — *Gorocs*

27/9/58 **HUNGARY** (0) **0** **USSR** (0) **1** 78000
Voinov

1962/64 SERIES

First Round

7/11/62 **HUNGARY** (2) **3** **WALES** (1) **1** 35000
Albert, Tichy, Sandor — *Medwin*

20/3/63 **WALES** (1) **1** **HUNGARY** (0) **1** 30300
Jones (Pen) — *Tichy (Pen)*

Second Round

20/10/63 **EAST GERMANY** (0) **1** **HUNGARY** (1) **2** 33400
Noeldner — *Bene, Rakosi*

3/11/63 **HUNGARY** (2) **3** **EAST GERMANY** (2) **3** 35400
Bene, Sandor, Solymosi (Pen) — *Heine, Ducke, Erier*

Quarter-Finals

25/4/64 **FRANCE** (0) **1** **HUNGARY** (2) **3** 35274
Cossou — *Albert, Tichy (2)*

24/5/64 **HUNGARY** (1) **2** **FRANCE** (1) **1** 70200
Sipos, Bene — *Combin*

Semi-Final

17/6/64 **SPAIN** (1) **2** **HUNGARY** (0) **1** 50000 Madrid
Pereda, Amancio — *Bene*

Third Place Match

20/6/64 **HUNGARY** (1) **3** **DENMARK** (0) **1** 4000
Bene, Novak (2, 1 Pen) — *Berthelsen*
(After Extra Time)

1966/68 SERIES

GROUP MATCHES - GROUP 5

7/9/66 **HOLLAND** (1) **2** **HUNGARY** (0) **2** 65000
Pijs, Cruyff — *Molnar, Albert*

21/9/66 **HUNGARY** (5) **6** **DENMARK** (0) **0** 20000
Albert (2), Meszoly (Pen), Bene, Farkas, Varga

10/5/67 **HUNGARY** (2) **2** **HOLLAND** (0) **1** 25000
Meszoly (Pen), Farkas — *Suurbier*

25/5/67 **DENMARK** (0) **0** **HUNGARY** (1) **2** 35200
Sandvad (og), Bene

27/9/67 **HUNGARY** (1) **3** **EAST GERMANY** (0) **1** 72000
Farkas (3) — *Frenzel*

29/10/67 **EAST GERMANY** (0) **1** **HUNGARY** (0) **0** 60000
Frenzel

Quarter-Finals

4/5/68 **HUNGARY** (1) **2** **USSR** (0) **0** 80000
Farkas, Gorocs

11/5/68 **USSR** (1) **3** **HUNGARY** (0) **0** 103000
Solymosi (og), Khurtsilava, Byshovets

1970/72 SERIES

GROUP MATCHES - GROUP 2

7/10/70 **NORWAY** (0) **1** **HUNGARY** (2) **3** 18000
Iversen — *Bene, Farkas, Kocsis*

25/4/71 **HUNGARY** (0) **1** **FRANCE** (0) **1** 45000
Kocsis (Pen) — *Revelli*

19/5/71 **BULGARIA** (1) **3** **HUNGARY** (0) **0** 45000
Kolev, Petkov, Velickov

22/9/71 **HUNGARY** (0) **2** **BULGARIA** (0) **0** 70000
Juhasz, Vidats

10/10/71 **FRANCE** (0) **0** **HUNGARY** (2) **2** 25000
Bene, Zambo

27/10/71 **HUNGARY** (3) **4** **NORWAY** (0) **0** 30000
Bene (2), Dunai, Szucs

Quarter-Finals

29/4/72 **HUNGARY** (1) **1** **ROMANIA** (0) **1** 70000
Branikovits — *Satmareanu*

14/5/72 **ROMANIA** (1) **2** **HUNGARY** (2) **2** 75000
Dobrin, Neagu — *Szoeke, Kocsis*

17/5/72 **HUNGARY** (1) **2** **ROMANIA** (1) **1** 45000
Kocsis, Szoeke — *Neagu*

Semi-Final

14/6/72 **USSR** (0) **1** **HUNGARY** (0) **0** 3500
Konkov — Brussels

Third Place Match

17/6/72 **BELGIUM** (1) **2** **HUNGARY** (0) **1** 10000 Liege
Lambert, Van Himst — *Ku (Pen)*

1974/76 SERIES

GROUP MATCHES - GROUP 2

13/10/74 **LUXEMBOURG** (2) **2** **HUNGARY** (2) **4** 3000
Dussier (2, 1 Pen) — *Horvath, Nagy (2), Balint*

30/10/74 **WALES** (0) **2** **HUNGARY** (0) **0** 8445
Griffiths, Toshack

2/4/75 **AUSTRIA** (0) **0** **HUNGARY** (0) **0** 70000

16/4/75 **HUNGARY** (0) **1** **WALES** (1) **2** 35000
Branikovits — *Toshack, Mahoney*

24/9/75 **HUNGARY** (2) **2** **AUSTRIA** (1) **1** 30000
Nyilasi, Pusztai — *Krankl (Pen)*

19/10/75 **HUNGARY** (4) **8** **LUXEMBOURG** (0) **1** 15000
Pinter, Nyilasi (5), Wollek, Varadi — *Dussier*

1978/80 SERIES

GROUP MATCHES - GROUP 6

20/9/78 **FINLAND** (1) **2** **HUNGARY** (0) **1** 4797
Ismail Atik (30), Pyykko (53) — *Tieber (74)*

11/10/78 **HUNGARY** (1) **2** **USSR** (0) **0** 40000
Varadi (26), Szokolai (58)

29/10/78 **GREECE** (0) **4** **HUNGARY** (0) **1** 10000
Galakos (59, 68), Ardizoglu (71), Mavros (89) — *Martos (90)*

2/5/79 **HUNGARY** (0) **0** **GREECE** (0) **0** 25000

19/5/79 **USSR** (1) **2** **HUNGARY** (1) **2** 80000
Chesnokov (23), Shengelia (75) — *Tatar (33), Pusztai (63)*

17/10/79 **HUNGARY** (2) **3** **FINLAND** (0) **1** 15000
Fekete (23, 43), Tatar (51) — *Toivola (50)*

1982/84 SERIES

GROUP MATCHES - GROUP 3

27/3/83 **LUXEMBOURG** (1) **2** **HUNGARY** (2) **6** 3000
Reiter (3), R. Schreiner (55) — *Poczik (31, 59, 70), Nyilasi (41), Poloskei (51), Hannich (Pen, 57)*

27/4/83 **HUNGARY** (3) **6** **LUXEMBOURG** (0) **2** 8000
Hajszan (23), Nyilasi (34, 63), Kiss (37), Szentees (61), Burcsa (65) — *Reiter (57), Malget (58)*

17/4/83 **ENGLAND** (1) **2** **HUNGARY** (0) **0** 55000
Francis (31), Withe (70)

15/5/83 **HUNGARY** (1) **2** **GREECE** (2) **3** 12500
Nyilasi (25), Hajszan (89) — *Anastopoulos (16), Kostikos (33), Papaioannu (52)*

1/6/83 **DENMARK** (1) **3** **HUNGARY** (1) **1** 44800
Elkjaer (4), J. Olsen (81), Simonsen (Pen, 85) — *Nyilasi (30)*

12/10/83 **HUNGARY** (0) **0** **ENGLAND** (3) **3** 15000
Hoddle (14), Lee (19), Mariner (40)

26/10/83 **HUNGARY** .... (0) **1** **DENMARK** .... (0) **0** 10000
Kiss (56)

3/12/83 **GREECE** .... (1) **2** **HUNGARY** .... (2) **2** 1500
Anastopoulos (9, 55) — *Kardos (11), Torocsik (39)*

1986/88 SERIES

GROUP MATCHES - GROUP 5

15/10/86 **HUNGARY** .... (0) **0** **HOLLAND** .... (0) **1** 15000
Van Basten (68)

12/11/86 **GREECE** .... (1) **2** **HUNGARY** .... (0) **1** 15000
Mitropoulos (39), Anastopoulos (65) — *Boda (72)*

8/2/87 **CYPRUS** .... (0) **0** **HUNGARY** .... (0) **1** 8000
Boda (49)

29/4/87 **HOLLAND** .... (2) **2** **HUNGARY** .... (0) **0** 53000
Gullit (37), A. Muhren (40)

17/5/87 **HUNGARY** .... (1) **5** **POLAND** .... (1) **3** 8000
Vincze (39), Detari ((Pen, 62), 76), Peter (66), Preszeller (83) — *Marziniak (27), Smolarek (52), Wojcicki (81)*

23/9/87 **POLAND** .... (1) **3** **HUNGARY** .... (1) **2** 10000
Dziekanowski (6), Tarasiewicz (57), Lesniak (61) — *Bognar (10), Meszaros (72)*

14/10/87 **HUNGARY** .... (3) **3** **GREECE** .... (0) **0** 8000
Detari (4), Bognar (12), Meszaros (15)

2/12/87 **HUNGARY** .... (0) **1** **CYPRUS** .... (0) **0** 2000
Kiprich (89)

1990/92 SERIES

GROUP MATCHES - GROUP 3

10/10/90 **NORWAY** .... (0) **0** **HUNGARY** .... (0) **0** 6304

17/10/90 **HUNGARY** .... (1) **1** **ITALY** .... (0) **1** 25000
Disztl (16) — *Baggio (pen 54)*

31/10/90 **HUNGARY** .... (3) **4** **CYPRUS** .... (1) **2** 3000
Lorincz (1), Christodolou (o.g. 19) Kiprich (pen 20, pen 67) — *Xiurupas (13), Tsolakis (89)*

3/4/91 **CYPRUS** .... (0) **0** **HUNGARY** .... (2) **2** 3000
Szalma (15), Kiprich (40)

17/4/91 **HUNGARY** .... (0) **0** **USSR** .... (1) **1** 40000
Mikhailichenko (30)

1/5/91 **ITALY** .... (2) **3** **HUNGARY** .... (0) **1** 45000
Donadoni (4, 16), Vialli (56) — *Bognar (pen 66)*

25/9/91 **USSR** .... (1) **2** **HUNGARY** .... (1) **2** 50000
Shalimov (pen 37), Kanchelskis (50) — *Kiprich (16, 84)*

30/10/91 **HUNGARY** .... (0) **0** **NORWAY** .... (0) **0** 10000

1994/96 SERIES

GROUP MATCHES - GROUP 3

7/9/94 **HUNGARY** .... (2) **2** **TURKEY** .... (0) **2** 20000
Kiprich (5), Halmai (45) — *Hakan (65), Bulent (71)*

16/11/94 **SWEDEN** .... (1) **2** **HUNGARY** .... (0) **0** 27571
Brolin (44), Dahlin (70)

29/3/95 **HUNGARY** .... (0) **2** **SWITZERLAND** .... (0) **2** 15000
Kiprich (51), Illes (70) — *Subiat (72, 84)*

26/4/95 **HUNGARY** .... (1) **1** **SWEDEN** .... (0) **0** 8000
Halmai (2)

11/6/95 **ICELAND** .... (0) **2** **HUNGARY** .... (1) **1** 3573
Bergsson (63), Sigurdur Jonsson (66) — *Vincze (19)*

6/9/95 **TURKEY** .... (2) **2** **HUNGARY** .... (0) **0** 30000
Hakan (9, 31)

11/10/95 **SWITZERLAND** .... (1) **3** **HUNGARY** .... (0) **0** 20000
Turkyilmaz (23), Sforza (56), Ohrel (89)

11/11/95 **HUNGARY** .... (0) **1** **ICELAND** .... (0) **0** 5000
Illes (55)

ICELAND

1962/64 SERIES

First Round

12/8/62 **EIRE** .... (2) **4** **ICELAND** .... (1) **2** 25000
Cantwell (2), Tuohy, Fogarty — *Jonsson (2)*

2/9/62 **ICELAND** .... (0) **1** **EIRE** .... (1) **1** 9100
Arnason — *Tuohy*

DID NOT COMPETE IN THE 1966/68 SERIES OR THE 1970/72 SERIES

1974/76 SERIES

GROUP MATCHES - GROUP 7

8/9/74 **ICELAND** .... (0) **0** **BELGIUM** .... (1) **2** 10000
Van Moer (2, 1 Pen)

12/10/74 **EAST GERMANY** ..... (1) **1** **ICELAND** .... (1) **1** 15000
Hoffmann — *Hallgrimsson*

25/5/75 **ICELAND** .... (0) **0** **FRANCE** .... (0) **0** 11000

5/6/75 **ICELAND** .... (2) **2** **EAST GERMANY** ..... (0) **1** 4500
Edvaldsson, Sigurvinsson — *Pommerenke*

3/9/75 **FRANCE** .... (1) **3** **ICELAND** .... (0) **0** 29000
Guillou (2), Berdoll

6/9/75 **BELGIUM** .... (1) **1** **ICELAND** .... (0) **0** 9000
Lambert

1978/80 SERIES

GROUP MATCHES - GROUP 4

6/9/78 **ICELAND** .... (0) **0** **POLAND** .... (1) **2** 7000
Kusto (22), Lato (72)

20/9/78 **HOLLAND** .... (1) **3** **ICELAND** .... (0) **0** 14500
Krol (33), Brandts (53), Rensenbrink (63)

4/10/78 **EAST GERMANY** ..... (2) **3** **ICELAND** .... (1) **1** 12000
Peter (6), Riedieger (29), Hoffman (72) — *P. Pettursson (Pen, 14)*

22/5/79 **SWITZERLAND** .... (1) **2** **ICELAND** .... (0) **0** 25000
H. Hermann (27), Zappa (53)

9/6/79 **ICELAND** .... (0) **1** **SWITZERLAND** .... (0) **2** 10400
Gudlaugsson (50) — *Ponte (58), Heinz Hermann (61)*

5/9/79 **ICELAND** .... (0) **0** **HOLLAND** .... (0) **4** 12000
Metgod (49), W. Van Der Kerkhof (70), Nanninga (73, 88)

12/9/79 **ICELAND** .... (0) **0** **EAST GERMANY** ..... (0) **3** 10000
Weber ((Pen, 64), 70), Streich (77)

10/10/79 **POLAND** .... (0) **2** **ICELAND** .... (0) **0** 25000
Ogaza (55, (Pen, 74))

1982/84 SERIES

GROUP MATCHES - GROUP 7

5/6/82 **MALTA** .... (1) **2** **ICELAND** .... (0) **1** 3000
Spiteri-Gonzi (43), Fabri (48) — *Geirsson (Pen, 51)*

1/9/82 **ICELAND** .... (0) **1** **HOLLAND** .... (0) **1** 4500
Edvaldsson (49) — *Schoenaker (51)*

13/10/82 **EIRE** .... (1) **2** **ICELAND** .... (0) **0** 20000
Stapleton (35), Grealish (63)

27/10/82 **SPAIN** .... (0) **1** **ICELAND** .... (0) **0** 25000
Pedraza (59)

29/5/83 **ICELAND** .... (0) **0** **SPAIN** .... (1) **1** 10000
Maceda (9)

5/6/83 **ICELAND** .... (1) **1** **MALTA** .... (0) **0** 5718
Edvaldsson (44)

7/9/83 **HOLLAND** .... (3) **3** **ICELAND** .... (0) **0** 10000
R. Koeman (16), Gullit (18), Houtman (21)

21/9/83 **ICELAND** .... (0) **0** **EIRE** .... (2) **3** 12000
Waddock (17), Robinson (21), Walsh (82)

1986/88 SERIES

GROUP MATCHES - GROUP 3

10/9/86 **ICELAND** .... (0) **0** **FRANCE** .... (0) **0** 13700

24/9/86 **ICELAND** .... (1) **1** **USSR** .... (1) **1** 7000
Gudjohnsen (29) — *Sulakvelidze (44)*

29/10/86 **EAST GERMANY** ..... (1) **2** **ICELAND** .... (0) **0** 18000
Thom (4, 89)

29/4/87 **FRANCE** .... (1) **2** **ICELAND** .... (0) **0** 30000
Micciche (38), Stopyra (65)

3/6/87 **ICELAND** .... (0) **0** **EAST GERMANY** ..... (2) **6** 10000
Minge (15), Thom (37, 69, 88), Doll (49), Doschner (85)

9/9/87 **ICELAND** .... (1) **2** **NORWAY** .... (1) **1** 6500
Petursson (28), Ormslev (60) — *J. Andersen*

23/9/87 **NORWAY** .... (0) **0** **ICELAND** .... (1) **1** 3540
Edvaldsson (31)

28/10/87 **USSR** .... (1) **2** **ICELAND** .... (0) **0** 40000
Belanov (15), Portasov (50)

1990/92 SERIES

GROUP MATCHES - GROUP 1

30/5/90 **ICELAND** .... (1) **2** **ALBANIA** .... (0) **0** 6500
Gudjohnsen (41), Edvaldsson (82)

5/9/90 **ICELAND** .... (0) **1** **FRANCE** .... (1) **2** 8000
Edvaldsson (85) — *Papin (12), Cantona (74)*

26/9/90 **CZECHOSLOVAKIA** .... (1) **1** **ICELAND** .... (0) **0** 35000
Danek

10/10/90 **SPAIN** .... (1) **2** **ICELAND** .... (0) **1** 46000
Butragueno (44), Carlos (63) — *Jonsson (66)*

26/5/91 **ALBANIA** .... (0) **1** **ICELAND** .... (0) **0** 5000
Abazi (65)

5/6/91 **ICELAND** .... (0) **0** **CZECHOSLOVAKIA** .... (1) **1** 5000
Hasek (15)

25/9/91 **ICELAND** (0) **2** **SPAIN** (0) **0** 8900
Orlygsson (71), Sverrisson (79)

20/11/91 **FRANCE** (1) **3** **ICELAND** (0) **1** 35000
Simba (42), Cantona (60, 68) — *Sverrisson (71)*

1994/96 SERIES

GROUP MATCHES - GROUP 3

7/9/94 **ICELAND** (0) **0** **SWEDEN** (1) **1** 12000
Ingesson (36)

12/10/94 **TURKEY** (3) **5** **ICELAND** (0) **0** 20000
Saffet (11, 28), Hakan (30, 62), Sergen (65)

16/11/94 **SWITZERLAND** (1) **1** **ICELAND** (0) **0** 15800
Bickel (45)

1/6/95 **SWEDEN** (1) **1** **ICELAND** (1) **1** 26676
Brolin (Pen, 16) — *A. Gunnlaugsson (3)*

11/6/95 **ICELAND** (0) **2** **HUNGARY** (1) **1** 3573
Bergsson (63), Sigurdur Jonsson (66) — *Vincze (19)*

16/8/95 **ICELAND** (0) **0** **SWITZERLAND** (2) **2** 9034
Knup (3), Turkyilmaz (13)

11/10/95 **ICELAND** (0) **0** **TURKEY** (0) **0** 2308

11/11/95 **HUNGARY** (0) **1** **ICELAND** (0) **0** 5000
Illes (55)

ISRAEL

1994/96 SERIES

GROUP MATCHES - GROUP 1

4/9/94 **ISRAEL** (1) **2** **POLAND** (0) **1** 3500
R. Harazi (43, 58) — *Kosecki (80)*

12/10/94 **ISRAEL** (2) **2** **SLOVAKIA** (2) **2** 10000
Harazi (26), Gaibanin (Pen, 35) — *Rusnak (7), Moravcik (16)*

16/11/94 **AZERBAIJAN** (0) **0** **ISRAEL** (1) **2** 3000
R. Harazi (29), Rosenthal (51)

14/12/94 **ISRAEL** (0) **1** **ROMANIA** (0) **1** 42500
Rosenthal (83) — *Lacatus (70)*

29/3/95 **ISRAEL** (0) **0** **FRANCE** (0) **0** 43000

25/4/95 **POLAND** (1) **4** **ISRAEL** (2) **3** 5500
Nowak (1), Juskowiak (50), Kowalczyk (55), Kosecki (62) — *Rosenthal (37), Revivo (42), Zohar (77)*

7/6/95 **ROMANIA** (1) **2** **ISRAEL** (0) **1** 28000
Lacatus (16), Munteanu (65) — *Bercovitz (50)*

6/9/95 **SLOVAKIA** (0) **1** **ISRAEL** (0) **0** 10000
Jancula (54)

11/10/95 **ISRAEL** (1) **2** **AZERBAIJAN** (0) **0** 5000
R. Harazi (30, 50)

15/11/95 **FRANCE** (0) **2** **ISRAEL** (0) **0** 21500
Djorkaeff (69), Lizarazu (88)

ITALY

1962/64 SERIES

First Round

2/12/62 **ITALY** (4) **6** **TURKEY** (0) **0** 26600
Orlando (4), Rivera (2)

27/3/63 **TURKEY** (0) **0** **ITALY** (0) **1** 27300
Sotmani

Second Round

13/10/63 **USSR** (2) **2** **ITALY** (0) **0** 102400
Ponedelnik, Chislenko

10/11/63 **ITALY** (0) **1** **USSR** (1) **1** 69600
Rivera — *Gusarov*

1966/68 SERIES

GROUP MATCHES - GROUP 6

16/11/66 **ITALY** (2) **3** **ROMANIA** (1) **1** 75000
Mazzola (2), De Paoli — *Pircalab*

22/3/67 **CYPRUS** (0) **0** **ITALY** (0) **2** 11105
Domenghini, Facchetti

25/6/67 **ROMANIA** (0) **0** **ITALY** (0) **1** 70000
Bertini

1/11/67 **ITALY** (2) **5** **CYPRUS** (0) **0** 24000
Fogli, Mazzola, Riva (3)

18/11/67 **SWITZERLAND** (1) **2** **ITALY** (0) **2** 57000
Quentin, Kunzli — *Riva (2)*

23/12/67 **ITALY** (3) **4** **SWITZERLAND** (0) **0** 28000
Mazzola (2), Riva, Domenghini

Quarter-Finals

6/4/68 **BULGARIA** (1) **3** **ITALY** (0) **2** 55000
Jekov (2, 1 Pen), Dermendjiev — *Penev (og), Prati*

20/4/68 **ITALY** (1) **2** **BULGARIA** (0) **0** 84000
Prati, Domenghini

Semi-Finals

5/6/68 **ITALY** (0) **0** **USSR** (0) **0** 70000
Naples

ITALY WON ON THE TOSS OF A COIN

Final

8/6/68 **ITALY** (0) **1** **YUGOSLAVIA** (1) **1** 88000 Rome
Domenghini — *Dzajic*

Final Replay

10/6/68 **ITALY** (2) **2** **YUGOSLAVIA** (0) **0** 70000 Rome
Riva, Anastasi

1970/72 SERIES

GROUP MATCHES - GROUP 6

1/11/70 **AUSTRIA** (1) **1** **ITALY** (2) **2** 60000
Parits — *De Sisti, Mazzola*

9/12/70 **ITALY** (2) **3** **EIRE** (0) **0** 55000
De Sisti (Pen), Boninsegna, Prati

11/5/71 **EIRE** (1) **1** **ITALY** (1) **2** 25000
Conway — *Boninsegna, Prati*

9/6/71 **SWEDEN** (0) **0** **ITALY** (0) **0** 40000

10/10/71 **ITALY** (2) **3** **SWEDEN** (0) **0** 70000
Riva (2), Boninsegna

20/11/71 **ITALY** (1) **2** **AUSTRIA** (2) **2** 85000
Riva, De Sisti — *Jara, Santarini (og)*

Quarter-Finals

29/4/72 **ITALY** (0) **0** **BELGIUM** (0) **0** 70000

13/5/72 **BELGIUM** (1) **2** **ITALY** (0) **1** 38000
Van Moer, Van Himst — *Riva (Pen)*

1974/76 SERIES

GROUP MATCHES - GROUP 5

20/11/74 **HOLLAND** (1) **3** **ITALY** (1) **1** 62000
Rensenbrink, Cruyff (2) — *Boninsegna*

19/4/75 **ITALY** (0) **0** **POLAND** (0) **0** 90000

5/6/75 **FINLAND** (0) **0** **ITALY** (0) **1** 17700
Chinaglia (Pen)

27/9/75 **ITALY** (0) **0** **FINLAND** (0) **0** 29000

25/10/75 **POLAND** (0) **0** **ITALY** (0) **0** 70000

22/11/75 **ITALY** (1) **1** **HOLLAND** (0) **0** 80000
Capello

1978/80 SERIES

FINALS - GROUP 2

12/6/80 **SPAIN** (0) **0** **ITALY** (0) **0** 55000

15/6/80 **ITALY** (0) **1** **ENGLAND** (0) **0** 59649
Tardelli (83)

18/6/80 **ITALY** (0) **0** **BELGIUM** (0) **0** 69000

Third Place Match

21/6/80 **CZECHOSLOVAKIA** (0) **1** **ITALY** (0) **1** 25000
Jurkemik — *Graziani*

CZECHOSLOVAKIA WON 9-8 ON PENALTIES

1982/84 SERIES

GROUP MATCHES - GROUP 5

13/11/82 **ITALY** (1) **2** **CZECHOSLOVAKIA** (1) **2** 80000
Altobelli (13), Kapko (og, 66) — *Sloup (26), Chaloupka (72)*

4/12/82 **ITALY** (0) **0** **ROMANIA** (0) **0** 52000

12/2/83 **CYPRUS** (0) **1** **ITALY** (0) **1** 25000
Mavris (47) — *Patikis (og, 57)*

16/4/83 **ROMANIA** (1) **1** **ITALY** (0) **0** 80000
Boloni

29/5/83 **SWEDEN** (1) **2** **ITALY** (0) **0** 35000
Sandberg (31), Stromberg (56)

15/10/83 **ITALY** .... (0) **0** **SWEDEN** .... (2) **3** 69086
Stromberg (20, 27), Sunesson (71)

16/11/83 **CZECHOSLOVAKIA** .... (0) **2** **ITALY** .... (0) **0** 40000
Rada (64, (Pen, 77))

22/12/83 **ITALY** .... (0) **3** **CYPRUS** .... (0) **1** 20773
Altobelli (53), Cabrini (82), Rossi (Pen, 86) — *Tsinghis (Pen, 68)*

1986/88 SERIES

GROUP MATCHES - GROUP 2

15/11/86 **ITALY** .... (1) **3** **SWITZERLAND** .... (1) **2** 75000
Donadoni (1), Altobelli (52, 85) — *Brigger (31), Weber (89)*

6/12/86 **MALTA** .... (0) **0** **ITALY** .... (2) **2** 30000
Ferri (11), Altobelli (19)

24/1/87 **ITALY** .... (5) **5** **MALTA** .... (0) **0** 35000
Bagni (4), Bergomi (9), Altobelli (24, 35), Vialli (44)

8/2/87 **PORTUGAL** .... (0) **0** **ITALY** .... (1) **1** 32500
Altobelli (40)

3/6/87 **SWEDEN** .... (1) **1** **ITALY** .... (0) **0** 40000
P. Larsson (25)

17/10/87 **SWITZERLAND** .... (0) **0** **ITALY** .... (0) **0** 35000

14/11/87 **ITALY** .... (2) **2** **SWEDEN** .... (1) **1** 35000
Vialli (27, 45) — *Larsson (38)*

5/12/87 **ITALY** .... (1) **3** **PORTUGAL** .... (0) **0** 20000
Vialli (8), Giannini (88), De Agostini (89)

FINALS - GROUP 1

10/6/88 **WEST GERMANY** ..... (0) **1** **ITALY** .... (0) **1** 68400
Brehme (55) — *Mancini (51)*

14/6/88 **ITALY** .... (0) **1** **SPAIN** .... (0) **0** 51790
Vialli (73)

17/6/88 **ITALY** .... (0) **2** **DENMARK** .... (0) **0** 60500
Altobelli (65), De Agostini (87)

Semi-Final

22/6/88 **USSR** .... (0) **2** **ITALY** .... (0) **0** 70000
Litovchenko (59), Protasov (62)

1990/92 SERIES

GROUP MATCHES - GROUP 3

17/10/90 **HUNGARY** .... (1) **1** **ITALY** .... (0) **1** 25000
Disztl (16) — *Baggio (pen 54)*

3/11/90 **ITALY** .... (0) **0** **USSR** .... (0) **0** 52500

22/12/90 **CYPRUS** .... (0) **0** **ITALY** .... (3) **4** 10000
Vierchowod (15), Serena (22, 50), Lombardo (44)

1/5/91 **ITALY** .... (2) **3** **HUNGARY** .... (0) **1** 45000
Donadoni (4, 16), Vialli (56) — *Bognar (pen 66)*

5/6/91 **NORWAY** .... (2) **2** **ITALY** .... (0) **1** 27500
Dahlum (4), Bohinen (25) — *Schillachi (77)*

12/10/91 **USSR** .... (0) **0** **ITALY** .... (0) **0** 92000

13/11/91 **ITALY** .... (0) **1** **NORWAY** .... (0) **1** 30000
Rizzitelli (82) — *Jakobsen (60)*

21/12/91 **ITALY** .... (1) **2** **CYPRUS** .... (0) **0** 26000
Vialli (27), Baggio (55)

1994/96 SERIES

GROUP MATCHES - GROUP 4

7/9/94 **SLOVENIA** .... (1) **1** **ITALY** .... (1) **1** 18000
Udovic (14) — *Costacurta (16)*

8/10/94 **ESTONIA** .... (0) **0** **ITALY** .... (1) **2** 4000
Panucci (20), Casiraghi (77)

16/11/94 **ITALY** .... (0) **1** **CROATIA** .... (1) **2** 39000
D. Baggio (90) — *Suker (32, 60)*

25/3/95 **ITALY** .... (1) **4** **ESTONIA** .... (0) **1** 33000
Zola (45, 65), Albertini (58), Ravanelli (82) — *Reim (72)*

29/3/95 **UKRAINE** .... (0) **0** **ITALY** .... (2) **2** 20000
Lombardo (12), Zola (38)

26/4/95 **LITHUANIA** .... (0) **0** **ITALY** .... (1) **1** 15000
Zola (11)

6/9/95 **ITALY** .... (1) **1** **SLOVENIA** .... (0) **0** 30000
Ravanelli (13)

8/10/95 **CROATIA** .... (0) **1** **ITALY** .... (1) **1** 40000
Suker (Pen, 47) — *Albertini (29)*

11/11/95 **ITALY** .... (1) **3** **UKRAINE** .... (1) **1** 44000
Ravanelli (21, 48), Maldini (54) — *Polunin (19)*

15/11/95 **ITALY** .... (0) **4** **LITHUANIA** .... (0) **0** 26000
Stonkus (Og, 51), Zola (65, 80, 82)

LATVIA

1994/96 SERIES

GROUP MATCHES - GROUP 6

7/9/94 **LATVIA** .... (0) **0** **EIRE** .... (2) **3** 3000
Aldridge (16, (Pen, 75)), Sheridan (29)

9/10/94 **LATVIA** .... (0) **1** **PORTUGAL** .... (1) **3** 1900
Milevsky (88) — *Joao Pinto (33, 72), Figo (73)*

15/11/94 **LIECHTENSTEIN** ...... (0) **0** **LATVIA** .... (1) **1** 1300
Babichev (13)

29/3/95 **AUSTRIA** .... (2) **5** **LATVIA** .... (0) **0** 4000
Herzog (17, 59), Pfeifenberger (40), Polster ((Pen, 70), 90)

26/4/95 **LATVIA** .... (0) **0** **NORTHERN IRELAND** . (0) **1** 1500
Dowie (Pen, 69)

3/6/95 **PORTUGAL** .... (3) **3** **LATVIA** .... (0) **2** 40000
Figo (5), Secretario (19), Domingos (20) — *Babichev (51), Rimkus (85)*

7/6/95 **NORTHERN IRELAND** . (1) **1** **LATVIA** .... (0) **2** 6000
Dowie (44) — *Zeiberlins (58), Astasjevs (62)*

16/8/95 **LATVIA** .... (1) **3** **AUSTRIA** .... (0) **2** 2000
Rimkus (13, 59), Zeiberlins (88) — *Polster (68), Ramusch (78)*

6/9/95 **LATVIA** .... (0) **1** **LIECHTENSTEIN** ...... (0) **0** 3800
A. Zeiberlins (83)

11/10/95 **EIRE** .... (0) **2** **LATVIA** .... (0) **1** 33000
Aldridge ((Pen, 61), 64) — *Rimkus (78)*

LIECHTENSTEIN

1994/96 SERIES

GROUP MATCHES - GROUP 6

20/4/94 **NORTHERN IRELAND** . (3) **4** **LIECHTENSTEIN** ...... (0) **1** 4500
J. Quinn (5, 33), Lomas (23), Dowie (48) — *Hasler (84)*

7/9/94 **LIECHTENSTEIN** ...... (0) **0** **AUSTRIA** .... (3) **4** 5800
Polster (21, 45, 83), Aigner (22)

12/10/94 **EIRE** .... (3) **4** **LIECHTENSTEIN** ...... (0) **0** 32980
Coyne (2, 4), Quinn (30, 82)

15/11/94 **LIECHTENSTEIN** ...... (0) **0** **LATVIA** .... (1) **1** 1300
Babichev (13)

18/12/94 **PORTUGAL** .... (3) **8** **LIECHTENSTEIN** ...... (0) **0** 32000
Domingos Oliveira (2, 11), Oceano (44), Joao Pinto (57), Fernando Couto (73), Folha (74), Alves (75, 79)

26/4/95 **AUSTRIA** .... (3) **7** **LIECHTENSTEIN** ...... (0) **0** 5500
Kuhbauer (7), Polster (10, (Pen, 54)), Sabitzer (17), Purk (84), Hutter (87, 89)

3/6/95 **LIECHTENSTEIN** ...... (0) **0** **EIRE** .... (0) **0** 4500

15/8/95 **LIECHTENSTEIN** ...... (0) **0** **PORTUGAL** .... (3) **7** 2500
Domingos (25), Paulinho (33), Rui Costa (41, 71), Paulo Alves (67, 73, 90)

6/9/95 **LATVIA** .... (0) **1** **LIECHTENSTEIN** ...... (0) **0** 3800
A. Zeiberlins (83)

11/10/95 **LIECHTENSTEIN** ...... (0) **0** **NORTHERN IRELAND** . (1) **4** 1100
O'Neil (36), McMahon (49), Quinn (55), Gray (72)

LITHUANIA

1994/96 SERIES

GROUP MATCHES - GROUP 4

7/9/94 **UKRAINE** .... (0) **0** **LITHUANIA** .... (0) **2** 25000
Ivanauskas (53), Skarbalius (61)

9/10/94 **CROATIA** .... (0) **2** **LITHUANIA** .... (0) **0** 12000
Jerkan (56), Kozniku (61)

16/11/94 **SLOVENIA** .... (0) **1** **LITHUANIA** .... (0) **2** 6000
Zahovic (55) — *Surkistovas (64), Zuta (87)*

29/3/95 **LITHUANIA** .... (0) **0** **CROATIA** .... (0) **0** 9000

26/4/95 **LITHUANIA** .... (0) **0** **ITALY** .... (1) **1** 15000
Zola (11)

7/6/95 **LITHUANIA** .... (0) **2** **SLOVENIA** .... (0) **1** 7000
Stonkus (47), Shuika (69) — *Gliha (82)*

16/8/95 **ESTONIA** .... (0) **0** **LITHUANIA** .... (0) **1** 1750
Maciulevicius (48)

6/9/95 **LITHUANIA** .... (1) **1** **UKRAINE** .... (0) **3** 11500
Maciulevicius (16) — *Huseinov (66, 71), Gusin (84)*

11/10/95 **LITHUANIA** .... (4) **5** **ESTONIA** .... (0) **0** 2500
Maciulevicius (8), Shuka (13, 39), Slekys (44), Ivanauskas (61)

15/11/95 **ITALY** .... (0) **4** **LITHUANIA** .... (0) **0** 26000
Stonkus (Og, 51), Zola (65, 80, 82)

LUXEMBOURG

1962/64 SERIES

First Round

LUXEMBOURG RECEIVED A BYE

Second Round

11/9/63 **HOLLAND** (1) **1** **LUXEMBOURG** (1) **1** 36000
Nuninga
May

30/10/63 **LUXEMBOURG** (1) **2** **HOLLAND** (1) **1** 42400
Dimmer (2)
Kruiver

Quarter-Finals

4/12/63 **LUXEMBOURG** (2) **3** **DENMARK** (2) **3** 6921
Pilot, H. Klein (2)
O. Madsen (3)

10/12/63 **DENMARK** (1) **2** **LUXEMBOURG** (1) **2** 39400
O. Madsen (2)
Leonard, H. Schmidt

18/12/63 **DENMARK** (1) **1** **LUXEMBOURG** (0) **0** 5700
O. Madsen

1966/68 SERIES
GROUP MATCHES - GROUP 7

2/10/66 **POLAND** (0) **4** **LUXEMBOURG** (0) **0** 22000
Jarosik, Liberda, Grzegorczyk, Sadek

27/11/66 **LUXEMBOURG** (0) **0** **FRANCE** (3) **3** 3500
Herbet, Revelli, Lech

16/3/67 **LUXEMBOURG** (0) **0** **POLAND** (0) **0** 8000

19/3/67 **LUXEMBOURG** (0) **0** **BELGIUM** (3) **5** 10000
Van Himst (2), Stockman (3)

22/11/67 **BELGIUM** (0) **3** **LUXEMBOURG** (0) **0** 8000
Thio (2), Claessen

23/12/67 **FRANCE** (1) **3** **LUXEMBOURG** (0) **1** 7500
Loubet (3)
Klein

1970/72 SERIES
GROUP MATCHES - GROUP 7

15/11/70 **LUXEMBOURG** (0) **0** **EAST GERMANY** (4) **5** 3000
Vogel, Kreische (4)

24/2/71 **HOLLAND** (4) **6** **LUXEMBOURG** (0) **0** 40000
Cruyff (2), Keizer (2), Lippens, Suurbier

25/4/71 **EAST GERMANY** (1) **2** **LUXEMBOURG** (0) **1** 15000
Kreische, Frenzel
Dussier

8/10/71 **LUXEMBOURG** (0) **0** **YUGOSLAVIA** (1) **2** 9000
Bukal (2)

27/10/71 **YUGOSLAVIA** (0) **0** **LUXEMBOURG** (0) **0** 20000

17/11/71 **LUXEMBOURG** (0) **0** **HOLLAND** (5) **8** 17500
Cruyff (3), Keizer, Pahlplatz, Hulshoff, Hoekema, Israel

1974/76 SERIES
GROUP MATCHES - GROUP 2

13/10/74 **LUXEMBOURG** (2) **2** **HUNGARY** (2) **4** 3000
Dussier (2, 1 Pen)
Horvath, Nagy (2), Balint

20/11/74 **WALES** (1) **5** **LUXEMBOURG** (0) **0** 10530
Toshack, England, Roberts, Griffiths, Yorath

16/3/75 **LUXEMBOURG** (1) **1** **AUSTRIA** (0) **2** 6000
Braun
Koglberger, Krankl

1/5/75 **LUXEMBOURG** (1) **1** **WALES** (2) **3** 5000
Phillipp (Pen)
Reece, James (2)

15/10/75 **AUSTRIA** (3) **6** **LUXEMBOURG** (2) **2** 14500
Welzl (2), Krankl (2), Jara, Prohaska
Braun, Phillipp

19/10/75 **HUNGARY** (4) **8** **LUXEMBOURG** (0) **1** 15000
Pinter, Nyilasi (5), Wollek, Varadi
Dussier

1978/80 SERIES
GROUP MATCHES - GROUP 5

7/10/78 **LUXEMBOURG** (0) **1** **FRANCE** (1) **3** 12000
Michaux (73)
Six (14), Tresor (62), Gemmrich (79)

25/2/79 **FRANCE** (1) **3** **LUXEMBOURG** (0) **0** 25000
Petit (38), Emon (62), Larios (80)

1/5/79 **LUXEMBOURG** (0) **0** **CZECHOSLOVAKIA** (1) **3** 3500
Masny (22), Gajdusek (67), Stambachr (68)

7/6/79 **SWEDEN** (2) **3** **LUXEMBOURG** (0) **0** 7300
Gronhagen (15), Cervin (29), Borg (Pen, 54)

23/10/79 **LUXEMBOURG** (1) **1** **SWEDEN** (0) **1** 2000
Braun (Pen, 5)
Gronhagen (63)

24/11/79 **CZECHOSLOVAKIA** (3) **4** **LUXEMBOURG** (0) **0** 15000
Panenka (37), Masny (39, 44), Vizek (60)

1982/84 SERIES
GROUP MATCHES - GROUP 3

9/10/82 **LUXEMBOURG** (0) **0** **GREECE** (2) **2** 3500
Dimopoulos (Pen, 8), Anastopoulos (25)

10/11/82 **LUXEMBOURG** (0) **1** **DENMARK** (1) **2** 2057
Di Domenico (54)
Lerby (Pen, 29), Berggren (67)

15/12/82 **ENGLAND** (4) **9** **LUXEMBOURG** (0) **0** 35000
Moes (Og, 17), Coppell (21), Woodcock (34), Blissett (43, 63, 86), Chamberlain (72), Hoddle (88), Neal (89)

27/3/83 **LUXEMBOURG** (1) **2** **HUNGARY** (2) **6** 3000
Reiter (3), R. Schreiner (55)
Poczik (31, 59, 70), Nyilasi (41), Poloskei (51), Hannich (Pen, 57)

17/4/83 **HUNGARY** (3) **6** **LUXEMBOURG** (0) **2** 8000
Hajszan (23), Nyilasi (34, 63), Kiss (37), Szentes (61), Burcsa (65)
Reiter (57), Malget (58)

12/10/83 **DENMARK** (4) **6** **LUXEMBOURG** (0) **0** 44700
Laudrup (17, 24, 69), Elkjaer (37, 58), Simonsen (42)

16/11/83 **LUXEMBOURG** (0) **0** **ENGLAND** (2) **4** 12000
Robson (11, 56), Mariner (39), Butcher (50)

14/12/83 **GREECE** (1) **1** **LUXEMBOURG** (0) **0** 5000
Saravakos (18)

1986/88 SERIES
GROUP MATCHES - GROUP 7

14/10/86 **LUXEMBOURG** (0) **0** **BELGIUM** (3) **6** 15000
Gerets (6), Claesen (9, 54, (Pen, 88)), Vercauteren (41), Ceulemans (87)

12/11/86 **SCOTLAND** (2) **3** **LUXEMBOURG** (0) **0** 35078
Cooper ((Pen, 24), 38), Johnston (70)

30/4/87 **LUXEMBOURG** (0) **1** **BULGARIA** (0) **4** 1500
Langers (59)
Sadkov (49), Sirakov (55), Tanev (62), Kolev (82)

20/5/87 **BULGARIA** (2) **3** **LUXEMBOURG** (0) **0** 20000
Sirakov (35), Vordanov (Pen, 41), Kolev (57)

28/5/87 **LUXEMBOURG** (0) **0** **EIRE** (1) **2**
Galvin (44), Whelan (64)

9/9/87 **EIRE** (1) **2** **LUXEMBOURG** (1) **1** 18000
Stapleton (31), McGrath (74)
Krings (28)

11/11/87 **BELGIUM** (1) **3** **LUXEMBOURG** (0) **0** 15000
Ceulemans (17), Degryse (55), Creve (81)

2/12/87 **LUXEMBOURG** (0) **0** **SCOTLAND** (0) **0** 1999

1990/92 SERIES
GROUP MATCHES - GROUP 5

31/10/90 **LUXEMBOURG** (0) **2** **GERMANY** (2) **3** 9500
Girres (57), Langers (65)
Klinsmann (16), Bein (30), Voller (49)

14/11/90 **LUXEMBOURG** (0) **0** **WALES** (1) **1** 7000
Rush (15)

27/2/91 **BELGIUM** (3) **3** **LUXEMBOURG** (0) **0** 24500
Vandenbergh (7), Ceulemans (17) Scifo (36)

11/9/91 **LUXEMBOURG** (0) **0** **BELGIUM** (1) **2** 9000
Scifo (25), Degryse (49)

13/11/91 **WALES** (0) **1** **LUXEMBOURG** (0) **0** 20000
Bodin (pen 82)

17/12/91 **GERMANY** (2) **4** **LUXEMBOURG** (0) **0** 24500
Matthaus (pen 15), Buchwald (44) Riedle (51), Hassler (62)

1994/96 SERIES
GROUP MATCHES - GROUP 5

7/9/94 **LUXEMBOURG** (0) **0** **HOLLAND** (1) **4** 8200
Roy (23), R. De Boer (65, 67), Jonk (90)

12/10/94 **BYELORUSSIA** (0) **2** **LUXEMBOURG** (0) **0** 8500
Romashchenko (67), Gerasimets (76)

14/12/94 **HOLLAND** (3) **5** **LUXEMBOURG** (0) **0** 30000
Mulder (6), Roy (15), Jonk (39), R. De Boer (51), Seedorf (90)

22/2/95 **MALTA** (0) **0** **LUXEMBOURG** (0) **1** 6000
Langers (54)

29/3/95 **LUXEMBOURG** (0) **0** **NORWAY** (1) **2** 3031
Leonhardsen (35), Aase (80)

26/4/95 **NORWAY** (3) **5** **LUXEMBOURG** (0) **0** 15124
J.I. Jakobsen (11), Fjortoft (12), Brattbakk (24), Berg (46), Rekdal (52)

7/6/95 **LUXEMBOURG** (0) **1** **CZECH REPUBLIC** (0) **0** 1500
Hellers (89)

6/9/95 **LUXEMBOURG** (1) **1** **MALTA** (0) **0** 4700
Holtz (44)

11/10/95 **LUXEMBOURG** (0) **0** **BYELORUSSIA** (0) **0** 4500

15/11/95 **CZECH REPUBLIC** (1) **3** **LUXEMBOURG** (0) **0** 22530
Drulak (35, 46), Berger (57)

MACEDONIA

1994/96 SERIES

GROUP MATCHES - GROUP 2

7/9/94 **MACEDONIA** (1) **1** **DENMARK** (0) **1** 25000
Stojkovski (4) — Povlsen (87)

12/10/94 **MACEDONIA** (0) **0** **SPAIN** (2) **2** 30000
Slinas (16, 25)

16/11/94 **BELGIUM** (1) **1** **MACEDONIA** (0) **1** 17000
Verheyen (31) — Boskovski (54)

17/12/94 **MACEDONIA** (2) **3** **CYPRUS** (0) **0** 16000
Bosko Djurovski (15, 29, 90)

26/4/95 **DENMARK** (0) **1** **MACEDONIA** (0) **0** 38888
P. Nielsen (70)

10/5/95 **ARMENIA** (1) **2** **MACEDONIA** (0) **2** 12500
Grigorian (23), Shakhgeldyan (50) — Hristov (60), Markovski (69)

7/6/95 **MACEDONIA** (0) **0** **BELGIUM** (4) **5**
Grun (15), Scifo (18, 59), Schepens (27), Versavel (43)

Match played behind closed doors as a disciplinary punishment

6/9/95 **MACEDONIA** (1) **1** **ARMENIA** (0) **2** 10000
Micevski (10) — Razmik (61), Armen (78)

11/10/95 **CYPRUS** (0) **1** **MACEDONIA** (1) **1** 12000
Agathocleous (90) — Perides (Og, 30)

15/11/95 **SPAIN** (1) **3** **MACEDONIA** (0) **0** 21350
Narvaez (8), Manjarin (73), Caminero (79)

MALTA

1962/64 SERIES

First Round

28/6/62 **DENMARK** (3) **6** **MALTA** (0) **1** 11200
O. Madsen (3), Enoksen, Berthelsen, Clausen — Theobald

16/12/62 **MALTA** (1) **1** **DENMARK** (2) **3** 6987
Urpani — Madsen, Christiansen, Berthelsen

DID NOT COMPETE IN THE 1966/68 COMPETITION

1970/72 SERIES

GROUP MATCHES - GROUP 3

11/10/70 **MALTA** (0) **1** **GREECE** (0) **1** 15000
Vassallo — Papaioannou

20/12/70 **MALTA** (0) **1** **SWITZERLAND** (0) **2** 8000
Theobald (Pen) — Quentin, Kunzli

3/2/71 **MALTA** (0) **0** **ENGLAND** (1) **1** 30000
Peters

21/4/71 **SWITZERLAND** (4) **5** **MALTA** (0) **0** 18000
Blattler, Kunzli, Quentin, Citherlet, Muller

12/5/71 **ENGLAND** (2) **5** **MALTA** (0) **0** 35000
Chivers (2), Lee, Clarke (Pen), Lawler

20/6/71 **GREECE** (0) **2** **MALTA** (0) **0** 12000
Davourlis, Aidiniou

1974/76 SERIES

GROUP MATCHES - GROUP 8

29/12/74 **MALTA** (0) **0** **WEST GERMANY** (1) **1** 12535
Cullmann

23/2/75 **MALTA** (1) **2** **GREECE** (0) **0** 20000
Aquilina, Magro

4/6/75 **GREECE** (2) **4** **MALTA** (0) **0** 15000
Mavros, Antoniadis (Pen), Iosifidis, Papaioannou

11/6/75 **BULGARIA** (3) **5** **MALTA** (0) **0** 35000
Dimitrov, Denev, Panov, Bonev (Pen), Milanov

21/12/75 **MALTA** (0) **0** **BULGARIA** (0) **2** 7000
Panov, Jordanov

28/2/76 **WEST GERMANY** (4) **8** **MALTA** (0) **0** 54000
Worm (2), Heynckes (2), Beers (2), Holzenbein, Vogts

1978/80 SERIES

GROUP MATCHES - GROUP 7

25/10/78 **WALES** (3) **7** **MALTA** (0) **0** 11475
O. Sullivan (19), Edwards (22, 50, 53), Thomas (69), Flynn (72)

25/2/79 **MALTA** (0) **0** **WEST GERMANY** (0) **0** 13000

18/3/79 **TURKEY** (1) **2** **MALTA** (0) **1** 30000
Sedat (34), Fatih (56) — Spiteri-Gonzi (54)

2/6/79 **MALTA** (0) **0** **WALES** (1) **2** 9000
Nicholas (15), Flynn (50)

28/10/79 **MALTA** (0) **1** **TURKEY** (2) **2** 5000
Lelifarrugia (62) — Sedat (17), Mustafa (30)

27/2/80 **WEST GERMANY** (3) **8** **MALTA** (0) **0** 38000
Allofs (14, 55), Bonhof (Pen, 19), Fischer (40, 89), Holland (Og, 61), Kelsch (70), Rummenigge (74)

1982/84 SERIES

GROUP MATCHES - GROUP 7

5/6/82 **MALTA** (1) **2** **ICELAND** (0) **1** 3000
Spiteri-Gonzi (43), Fabri (48) — Geirsson (Pen, 51)

19/12/82 **MALTA** (0) **0** **HOLLAND** (4) **6** 13000
Ophof (Pen, 22), Van Kooten (25, 70), Hovenkamp (34), Schoenaker (39, 51)

30/3/83 **MALTA** (0) **0** **EIRE** (0) **1** 10000
Stapleton (89)

15/5/83 **MALTA** (1) **2** **SPAIN** (1) **3** 11000
Busuttil (30, 47) — Senor (23), Carrasco (60), Gordillo (85)

5/6/83 **ICELAND** (1) **1** **MALTA** (0) **0** 5718
Edvaldsson (44)

16/11/83 **EIRE** (3) **8** **MALTA** (0) **0** 10000
Lawrenson (24, 64), Stapleton (Pen, 27), O'Callaghan (33), Sheedy (77), Brady (78, 86), Daly (87)

17/12/83 **HOLLAND** (2) **5** **MALTA** (0) **0** 59000
Vanenburg (18), Wijnstekers (29), Rijkaard (71, 87), Houtman (81)

21/12/83 **SPAIN** (3) **12** **MALTA** (1) **1** 25000
Santillana (16, 26, 29, 76), Rincon (47, 57, 64, 78), Merceda (62, 63), Sarabia (80), Senor (86) — Degiorgio (24)

1986/88 SERIES

GROUP MATCHES - GROUP 2

16/11/86 **MALTA** (0) **0** **SWEDEN** (1) **5** 15000
Hysen (38), Magnusson (67), Fredriksson (69), Ekstrom (81), Palmer (84)

6/12/86 **MALTA** (0) **0** **ITALY** (2) **2** 30000
Ferri (11), Altobelli (19)

24/1/87 **ITALY** (5) **5** **MALTA** (0) **0** 35000
Bagni (4), Bergomi (9), Altobelli (24, 35), Vialli (44)

29/3/87 **PORTUGAL** (1) **2** **MALTA** (1) **2** 12000
J. Placido (12, 76) — Mizzi (Pen, 23), Busuttil (66)

15/4/87 **SWITZERLAND** (3) **4** **MALTA** (0) **1** 5000
Egli (5), Bregy (16, (Pen, 38), 87) — Busuttil (71)

24/5/87 **SWEDEN** (1) **1** **MALTA** (0) **0** 16165
Ekstrom (13)

15/11/87 **MALTA** (0) **1** **SWITZERLAND** (1) **1** 5000
Busuttil (89) — Zwicker (3)

20/12/87 **MALTA** (0) **0** **PORTUGAL** (0) **1** 4000
Frederico

1990/92 SERIES

GROUP MATCHES - GROUP 6

31/10/90 **GREECE** (2) **4** **MALTA** (0) **0** 17500
Tsiantakis (37), Karapialis (40), Saravakos (59), Borbokis (88)

25/11/90 **MALTA** (0) **1** **FINLAND** (0) **1** 6000
Suda (74) — Holmgren (87)

19/12/90 **MALTA** (0) **0** **HOLLAND** (3) **8** 11000
van Basten (9, 20, 23, 64, pen 80), Winter (53), Bergkamp (58, 70)

9/2/91 **MALTA** (0) **0** **PORTUGAL** (1) **1** 10000
Futre (27)

20/2/91 **PORTUGAL** (3) **5** **MALTA** (0) **0** 10000
Aguas (5), Leal (33), Paneira (pen 40), Scerri (o.g. 48), Cadete (81)

13/3/91 **HOLLAND** (1) **1** **MALTA** (0) **0** 36383
van Basten (pen 31)

16/5/91 **FINLAND** (0) **2** **MALTA** (0) **0** 5150
Jarvinen (51), Litmanen (87)

22/12/91 **MALTA** (1) **1** **GREECE** (0) **1** 8000
Sultana (42) — Marinakis (67)

1994/96 SERIES

GROUP MATCHES - GROUP 5

6/9/94 **CZECH REPUBLIC** (3) **6** **MALTA** (0) **1** 10226
Smejkal (6), Kubik (33), Siegl (35, 49, 81), Berger (89) — Laferla (75)

12/10/94 **MALTA** (0) **0** **CZECH REPUBLIC** (0) **0** 4000

14/12/94 **MALTA** (0) **0** **NORWAY** (1) **1** 3000
Fjortoft (10)

22/2/95 **MALTA** (0) **0** **LUXEMBOURG** (0) **1** 6000
Langers (54)

29/3/95 **HOLLAND** (1) **4** **MALTA** (0) **0** 37000
Seedorf (38), Bergkamp (Pen, 75), Winter (78), Kluivert (84)

26/4/95 **BYELORUSSIA** (0) **1** **MALTA** (0) **1** 9250
Taikov (57) — *Carabott (71)*

7/6/95 **NORWAY** (1) **2** **MALTA** (0) **0** 15180
Fjortoft (43), Flo (88)

6/9/95 **LUXEMBOURG** (1) **1** **MALTA** (0) **0** 4700
Holtz (44)

11/10/95 **MALTA** (0) **0** **HOLLAND** (0) **4** 8000
Overmars (52, 61, 65), Seedorf (80)

12/11/95 **MALTA** (0) **0** **BYELORUSSIA** (0) **2** 4000
Gerasimets (82, 85)

MOLDOVA

1994/96 SERIES

GROUP MATCHES - GROUP 7

7/9/94 **GEORGIA** (0) **0** **MOLDOVA** (1) **1** 40000
Oprya (40)

12/10/94 **MOLDOVA** (2) **3** **WALES** (1) **2** 12000
Belous (9), Seku (29), Pogorelov (79) — *Speed (6), Blake (70)*

16/11/94 **BULGARIA** (1) **4** **MOLDOVA** (0) **1** 50000
Stoichkov (45, 85), Balakov (64), Kostadinov (87) — *Kleshchenko (59)*

14/12/94 **MOLDOVA** (0) **0** **GERMANY** (2) **3** 22000
Kirsten (6), Klinsmann (38), Matthaus (72)

29/3/95 **ALBANIA** (2) **3** **MOLDOVA** (0) **0** 15000
Kushta (32, 79), Kacaj (42)

26/4/95 **MOLDOVA** (0) **0** **BULGARIA** (1) **3** 20500
Balakov (29), Stoichkov (54, 67)

7/6/95 **MOLDOVA** (2) **2** **ALBANIA** (2) **3** 7000
Curteanu (10), Kleshchenko (15) — *Kushta (8), Bellai (25), Vata (71)*

6/9/95 **WALES** (0) **1** **MOLDOVA** (0) **0** 5000
Speed (55)

8/10/95 **GERMANY** (3) **6** **MOLDOVA** (0) **1** 18500
Stroyenko (Og, 16), Helmer (18), Sammer (24, 71), Moller (47, 61) — *Rebesha (82)*

15/11/95 **MOLDOVA** (2) **3** **GEORGIA** (0) **2** 9000
Testemicianu (3), Miterev (20, 61) — *Dzyamashia (65), Kulibaba (Og, 79)*

NORTHERN IRELAND

1962/64 SERIES

First Round

10/10/62 **POLAND** (0) **0** **NORTHERN IRELAND** (1) **2** 31500
Dougan, Humphries

25/11/62 **NORTHERN IRELAND** (1) **2** **POLAND** (0) **0** 28900
Crossan, Bingham

Second Round

30/5/63 **SPAIN** (0) **1** **NORTHERN IRELAND** (0) **1** 28000
Rivilla — *W. Irvine*

30/10/63 **NORTHERN IRELAND** (0) **0** **SPAIN** (0) **1** 45900
Gento

1966/68 SERIES

GROUP MATCHES - GROUP 8

22/10/66 **NORTHERN IRELAND** (0) **0** **ENGLAND** (1) **2** 48600
Hunt, Peters

16/11/66 **SCOTLAND** (2) **2** **NORTHERN IRELAND** (1) **1** 45281
Murdoch, Lennox — *Nicholson*

12/4/67 **NORTHERN IRELAND** (0) **0** **WALES** (0) **0** 17000

21/10/67 **NORTHERN IRELAND** (0) **1** **SCOTLAND** (0) **0** 55000
Clements

22/11/67 **ENGLAND** (1) **2** **NORTHERN IRELAND** (0) **0** 85000
Hurst, R. Charlton

28/2/68 **WALES** (0) **2** **NORTHERN IRELAND** (0) **0** 17500
Rees, W. Davies

1970/72 SERIES

GROUP MATCHES - GROUP 4

11/11/70 **SPAIN** (1) **3** **NORTHERN IRELAND** (0) **0** 48000
Rexach, Pirri, Luis

3/2/71 **CYPRUS** (0) **0** **NORTHERN IRELAND** (0) **3** 12000
Nicholson, Dougan, Best (Pen)

21/4/71 **NORTHERN IRELAND** (2) **5** **CYPRUS** (0) **0** 35000
Best (3), Dougan, Nicholson

22/9/71 **USSR** (1) **1** **NORTHERN IRELAND** (0) **0** 100000
Muntjan (Pen)

13/10/71 **NORTHERN IRELAND** (1) **1** **USSR** (1) **1** 15000
Nicholson — *Byshovets*

16/2/72 **NORTHERN IRELAND** (0) **1** **SPAIN** (1) **1** 19925
Morgan — *Rojo*

1974/76 SERIES

GROUP MATCHES - GROUP 3

4/9/74 **NORWAY** (0) **2** **NORTHERN IRELAND** (1) **1** 7200
Lund (2) — *Finney*

30/10/74 **SWEDEN** (0) **0** **NORTHERN IRELAND** (2) **2** 16657
Nicholl, O'Neill

16/3/75 **NORTHERN IRELAND** (1) **1** **YUGOSLAVIA** (0) **0** 30000
Hamilton

3/9/75 **NORTHERN IRELAND** (1) **1** **SWEDEN** (1) **2** 12000
Hunter — *Sjoberg, Torstensson*

29/10/75 **NORTHERN IRELAND** (2) **3** **NORWAY** (0) **0** 8000
Morgan, McIlroy, Hamilton

19/11/75 **YUGOSLAVIA** (1) **1** **NORTHERN IRELAND** (0) **0** 30000
Oblak

1978/80 SERIES

GROUP MATCHES - GROUP 1

20/9/78 **EIRE** (0) **0** **NORTHERN IRELAND** (0) **0** 55000

25/10/78 **NORTHERN IRELAND** (0) **2** **DENMARK** (0) **1** 30000
Spence (63), Anderson (85) — *Jensen (51)*

29/11/78 **BULGARIA** (0) **0** **NORTHERN IRELAND** (1) **2** 30000
Armstrong (17), J. Nicholl (83)

7/2/79 **ENGLAND** (1) **4** **NORTHERN IRELAND** (0) **0** 92000
Keegan (24), Latchford (46, 63), Watson (49)

2/5/79 **NORTHERN IRELAND** (2) **2** **BULGARIA** (0) **0** 18700
C. Nicholl (16), Armstrong (33)

6/6/79 **DENMARK** (2) **4** **NORTHERN IRELAND** (0) **0** 16800
Elkjaer (30, 33, 83), Simonsen (63)

17/10/79 **NORTHERN IRELAND** (0) **1** **ENGLAND** (2) **5** 25000
Moreland (Pen, 50) — *Francis (18, 62), Woodcock (34), J. Nicholl (Og, 74)*

21/11/79 **NORTHERN IRELAND** (0) **1** **EIRE** (0) **0** 15000
Armstrong (54)

1982/84 SERIES

GROUP MATCHES - GROUP 6

13/10/82 **AUSTRIA** (2) **2** **NORTHERN IRELAND** (0) **0** 11500
Schachner (3, 39)

17/11/82 **NORTHERN IRELAND** (1) **1** **WEST GERMANY** (0) **0** 30000
Stewart (18)

15/12/82 **ALBANIA** (0) **0** **NORTHERN IRELAND** (0) **0** 30000

30/3/83 **NORTHERN IRELAND** (2) **2** **TURKEY** (0) **1** 20000
M. O'Neill (5), McClelland (17) — *Hassan (55)*

27/4/83 **NORTHERN IRELAND** (0) **1** **ALBANIA** (0) **0** 14000
Stewart (54)

21/9/83 **NORTHERN IRELAND** (1) **3** **AUSTRIA** (0) **1** 25000
Hamilton (28), Whiteside (65), O'Neill (89) — *Gasselich (82)*

12/10/83 **TURKEY** (1) **1** **NORTHERN IRELAND** (0) **0** 38000
Selcuk (17)

16/11/83 **WEST GERMANY** (0) **0** **NORTHERN IRELAND** (0) **1** 61418
Whiteside (50)

1986/88 SERIES

GROUP MATCHES - GROUP 4

15/10/86 **ENGLAND** (1) **3** **NORTHERN IRELAND** (0) **0** 35300
Lineker (33, 80), Waddle (78)

12/11/86 **TURKEY** (0) **0** **NORTHERN IRELAND** (0) **0** 25000

1/4/87 **NORTHERN IRELAND** (0) **0** **ENGLAND** (2) **2** 23000
Robson (19), Waddle (43)

29/4/87 **NORTHERN IRELAND** (1) **1** **YUGOSLAVIA** (0) **2** 5000
Clarke (39) — *Stojkovic (48), Zlatkovvjovic (79)*

14/10/87 **YUGOSLAVIA** (2) **3** **NORTHERN IRELAND** (0) **0** 22500
Vokri (13, 35), Hadzibegic (Pen, 73)

11/11/87 **NORTHERN IRELAND** (0) **1** **TURKEY** (0) **0** 5000
Quinn (47)

1990/92 SERIES
GROUP MATCHES - GROUP 4

12/9/90	**N. IRELAND**	(0) **0**	**YUGOSLAVIA** *Pancev (36), Prosinecki (86)*	(1) **2**	10000
7/10/90	**N. IRELAND** *Clarke (58)*	(0) **1**	**DENMARK** *Bartram (pen 11)*	(1) **1**	10000
4/11/90	**AUSTRIA**	(0) **0**	**N. IRELAND**	(0) **0**	7000
27/3/91	**YUGOSLAVIA** *Binic (35), Pancev (40, 60, 61)*	(1) **4**	**N. IRELAND** *Hill (45)*	(1) **1**	10750
1/5/91	**N. IRELAND** *Clarke (44)*	(1) **1**	**FAROE ISLANDS** *Reynheim (65)*	(0) **1**	10000
11/9/91	**FAROE ISLANDS**	(0) **0**	**N. IRELAND** *Wilson (8), Clarke (12, 51, pen 68), McDonald (14)*	(3) **5**	1623
6/10/91	**N. IRELAND** *Dowie (17), Black (40)*	(2) **2**	**AUSTRIA** *Lainer (44)*	(1) **1**	8000
3/11/91	**DENMARK** *Povlsen (22, 36)*	(2) **2**	**N. IRELAND** *Taggart (71)*	(0) **1**	10881

1994/96 SERIES
GROUP MATCHES - GROUP 6

20/4/94	**NORTHERN IRELAND** *J. Quinn (5, 33), Lomas (23), Dowie (48)*	(3) **4**	**LIECHTENSTEIN** *Hasler (84)*	(0) **1**	4500
7/9/94	**NORTHERN IRELAND** *Quinn (Pen, 58)*	(0) **1**	**PORTUGAL** *Costa (8), Oliviera (81)*	(1) **2**	6000
12/10/94	**AUSTRIA** *Polster (Pen, 25)*	(1) **1**	**NORTHERN IRELAND** *Gillespie (3), P. Gray (36)*	(2) **2**	20000
16/11/94	**NORTHERN IRELAND**	(0) **0**	**EIRE** *Aldridge (6), Keane (11), Sheridan (38), Townsend (54)*	(3) **4**	10336
29/3/95	**EIRE** *Quinn (47)*	(0) **1**	**NORTHERN IRELAND** *Dowie (72)*	(0) **1**	32200
26/4/95	**LATVIA**	(0) **0**	**NORTHERN IRELAND** *Dowie (Pen, 69)*	(0) **1**	1500
7/6/95	**NORTHERN IRELAND** *Dowie (44)*	(1) **1**	**LATVIA** *Zeiberlins (58), Astasjevs (62)*	(0) **2**	6000
3/9/95	**PORTUGAL** *Domingos (47)*	(0) **1**	**NORTHERN IRELAND** *Hughes (66)*	(0) **1**	50000
11/10/95	**LIECHTENSTEIN**	(0) **0**	**NORTHERN IRELAND** *O'Neil 36, McMahon (49), Quinn (55), Gray (72)*	(1) **4**	1100
15/11/95	**NORTHERN IRELAND** *Dowie (Pen, 32), Gray (64), Hunter (53), O'Neill (27, 78)*	(2) **5**	**AUSTRIA** *Schopp (56), Stumpf (70), Wetl (81)*	(0) **3**	8400

NORWAY

1958/60 SERIES

First Round

20/5/59	**NORWAY**	(0) **0**	**AUSTRIA** *Hof*	(1) **1**	27566
23/9/59	**AUSTRIA** *Nemec (2), Hof (2), Skerlan*	(3) **5**	**NORWAY** *Odegaard (2)*	(2) **2**	37000

1962/64 SERIES

First Round

21/6/62	**NORWAY**	(0) **0**	**SWEDEN** *Martinsson (2)*	(2) **2**	28551
4/11/62	**SWEDEN** *Eriksson*	(0) **1**	**NORWAY** *Krogh*	(0) **1**	8726

1966/68 SERIES
GROUP MATCHES - GROUP 2

13/11/66	**BULGARIA** *Tzanev (2), Jekov (2)*	(3) **4**	**NORWAY** *Hasund (2)*	(0) **2**	20000
8/6/67	**NORWAY** *Iversen*	(1) **1**	**PORTUGAL** *Eusebio (2)*	(1) **2**	31000
29/6/67	**NORWAY**	(0) **0**	**BULGARIA**	(0) **0**	20000
3/9/67	**NORWAY** *Berg (2), Birjeland*	(1) **3**	**SWEDEN** *Nordahl*	(1) **1**	32000
5/11/67	**SWEDEN** *Turesson (2), Eriksson (2), Danielsson*	(2) **5**	**NORWAY** *Iversen (Pen), Hasund*	(0) **2**	14000
12/11/67	**PORTUGAL** *Torres, Graca*	(1) **2**	**NORWAY** *Nilsen*	(1) **1**	40000

1970/72 SERIES
GROUP MATCHES - GROUP 2

7/10/70	**NORWAY** *Iversen*	(0) **1**	**HUNGARY** *Bene, Fazekas, Kocsis*	(2) **3**	18000
11/11/70	**FRANCE** *Floch, Lech, Mezy*	(1) **3**	**NORWAY** *Nielsen*	(0) **1**	20000
15/11/70	**BULGARIA** *Atanasov*	(1) **1**	**NORWAY** *Fuglset*	(0) **1**	25000
9/6/71	**NORWAY** *Iversen*	(0) **1**	**BULGARIA** *Bonev (2, 1 Pen), Zhekov, Vassilev*	(4) **4**	22000
8/9/71	**NORWAY** *A. Olsen*	(0) **1**	**FRANCE** *Loubet, Vergnes, Blanchet*	(2) **3**	16544
27/10/71	**HUNGARY** *Bene (2), Dunai, Szucs*	(3) **4**	**NORWAY**	(0) **0**	30000

1974/76 SERIES
GROUP MATCHES - GROUP 3

4/9/74	**NORWAY** *Lund (2)*	(0) **2**	**NORTHERN IRELAND** *Finney*	(1) **1**	7200
30/10/74	**YUGOSLAVIA** *Vukotic, Katalinski*	(1) **3**	**NORWAY** *Lund*	(1) **1**	12000
9/6/75	**NORWAY** *Thunberg*	(0) **1**	**YUGOSLAVIA** *Buljan, Bogicevic, Surjak*	(3) **3**	25000
30/6/75	**SWEDEN** *Nordahl (2), Grahn (Pen)*	(1) **3**	**NORWAY** *Olsen (Pen)*	(0) **1**	9580
13/8/75	**NORWAY**	(0) **0**	**SWEDEN** *Sandberg, Andersson*	(1) **2**	18000
29/10/75	**NORTHERN IRELAND** *Morgan, McIlroy, Hamilton*	(2) **3**	**NORWAY**	(0) **0**	8000

1978/80 SERIES
GROUP MATCHES - GROUP 2

30/8/78	**NORWAY**	(0) **0**	**AUSTRIA** *Pezzey (23), Krankl (43)*	(2) **2**	1200
20/9/78	**BELGIUM** *Cools (65)*	(0) **1**	**NORWAY** *Larsen (8)*	(1) **1**	7000
25/10/78	**SCOTLAND** *Dalglish (30, 81), Gemmill (Pen, 87)*	(1) **3**	**NORWAY** *E. Aas (3), Okland (64)*	(1) **2**	60000
9/5/79	**NORWAY**	(0) **0**	**PORTUGAL** *Alves (35)*	(1) **1**	9800
7/6/79	**NORWAY**	(0) **0**	**SCOTLAND** *Jordan (32), Dalglish (39), Robertson (43), McQueen (54)*	(3) **4**	17268
29/8/79	**AUSTRIA** *Jara (42), Prohaska (Pen, 46), Kreuz (75), Krankl (86)*	(1) **4**	**NORWAY**	(0) **0**	37000
12/9/79	**NORWAY** *Jacobsen (7)*	(1) **1**	**BELGIUM** *Janssens (31), Van Der Elst (75)*	(1) **2**	11665
1/11/79	**PORTUGAL** *Artur (28), Nene (59, 69)*	(1) **3**	**NORWAY** *Georg Hammer*	(1) **1**	25000

1982/84 SERIES
GROUP MATCHES - GROUP 4

22/9/82	**WALES** *Nygard (Og, 31)*	(1) **1**	**NORWAY**	(0) **0**	4340
13/10/82	**NORWAY** *Lund (5), Oekland (69), Hareide (89)*	(1) **3**	**YUGOSLAVIA** *Savic (74)*	(0) **1**	12264
27/10/82	**BULGARIA** *Velichkov (13), Nikolov (68)*	(1) **2**	**NORWAY** *Thoresen (17), Oekland (67)*	(1) **2**	37500
7/9/83	**NORWAY** *Hareide (4)*	(1) **1**	**BULGARIA** *Mladenov (12), Sirakov (50)*	(1) **2**	15515
21/9/83	**NORWAY**	(0) **0**	**WALES**	(0) **0**	17575
12/10/83	**YUGOSLAVIA** *Vujovic (21), Susic (40)*	(2) **2**	**NORWAY** *Thoresen (88)*	(0) **1**	12500

1986/88 SERIES
GROUP MATCHES - GROUP 3

24/9/86	**NORWAY**	(0) **0**	**EAST GERMANY**	(0) **0**	10142
29/10/86	**USSR** *Litovchenko (25), Belanov (Pen, 27), Blokhin, Khidiatulin (52)*	(3) **4**	**NORWAY**	(0) **0**	35000
3/6/87	**NORWAY**	(0) **0**	**USSR** *Zavarov (15)*	(1) **1**	10473
16/6/87	**NORWAY** *Mordt (71), Andersen (80)*	(0) **2**	**FRANCE**	(0) **0**	8268
9/9/87	**ICELAND** *Petursson (28), Ormslev (60)*	(1) **2**	**NORWAY** *Jorn Andersen*	(1) **1**	6500
23/9/87	**NORWAY**	(0) **0**	**ICELAND** *Edvaldsson (31)*	(1) **1**	3540
14/10/87	**FRANCE** *Fargeon (63)*	(0) **1**	**NORWAY** *Sundby (76)*	(0) **1**	12000
28/10/87	**EAST GERMANY** *Kirsten (15, 53), Thom (34)*	(2) **3**	**NORWAY** *Fjaerestad (32)*	(1) **1**	10000

1990/92 SERIES

GROUP MATCHES - GROUP 3

12/9/90 **USSR** .... (1) **2** **NORWAY** .... (0) **0** 23000
Kanchelskis (22), Kuznetsov (60)

10/10/90 **NORWAY** .... (0) **0** **HUNGARY** .... (0) **0** 6304

14/11/90 **CYPRUS** .... (0) **0** **NORWAY** .... (1) **3** 3000
Sorloth (39), Bohinen (50), Brandhaug (64)

1/5/91 **NORWAY** .... (0) **3** **CYPRUS** .... (0) **0** 7800
Lydersen (pen 49), Dahlum (65)
Sorloth (90)

5/6/91 **NORWAY** .... (2) **2** **ITALY** .... (0) **1** 27500
Dahlum (4), Bohinen (25) *Schillachi (77)*

28/8/91 **NORWAY** .... (0) **0** **USSR** .... (0) **1** 25427
Mostovoi (74)

30/10/91 **HUNGARY** .... (0) **0** **NORWAY** .... (0) **0** 10000

13/11/91 **ITALY** .... (0) **1** **NORWAY** .... (0) **1** 30000
Rizzitelli (82) *Jakobsen (60)*

1994/96 SERIES

GROUP MATCHES - GROUP 5

7/9/94 **NORWAY** .... (0) **1** **BYELORUSSIA** .... (0) **0** 16739
Frigaard (88)

12/10/94 **NORWAY** .... (0) **1** **HOLLAND** .... (1) **1** 22293
Rekdal (52) *Roy (22)*

16/11/94 **BYELORUSSIA** .... (0) **0** **NORWAY** .... (2) **4** 7500
Berg (34), Leonhardsen (39), Bohinen (52), Rekdal (Pen, 83)

14/12/94 **MALTA** .... (0) **0** **NORWAY** .... (1) **1** 3000
Fjortoft (10)

29/3/95 **LUXEMBOURG** .... (0) **0** **NORWAY** .... (1) **2** 3031
Leonhardsen (35), Aase (80)

26/4/95 **NORWAY** .... (3) **5** **LUXEMBOURG** .... (0) **0** 15124
J.I. Jakobsen (11), Fjortoft (12), Brattbakk (24), Berg (46), Rekdal (52)

7/6/95 **NORWAY** .... (1) **2** **MALTA** .... (0) **0** 15180
Fjortoft (43), Flo (88)

16/8/95 **NORWAY** .... (1) **1** **CZECH REPUBLIC** ..... (0) **1** 22054
Berg (27) *Suchoparek (84)*

6/9/95 **CZECH REPUBLIC** ..... (1) **2** **NORWAY** .... (0) **0** 19522
Skuhravy (Pen, 6), Drulak (87)

15/11/95 **HOLLAND** .... (0) **3** **NORWAY** .... (0) **0** 49000
Seedorf (59), Mulder (86), Overmars (89)

POLAND

1958/60 SERIES

First Round

28/6/59 **POLAND** .... (1) **2** **SPAIN** .... (2) **4** 71000
Pol, Brychczy *Di Stefano (2), Suarez (2)*

14/10/59 **SPAIN** .... (1) **3** **POLAND** .... (0) **0** 62000
Di Stefano, Gensana, Gento

1962/64 SERIES

First Round

10/10/62 **POLAND** .... (0) **0** **NORTHERN IRELAND** (1) **2** 31500
Dougan, Humphries

25/11/62 **NORTHERN IRELAND** . (1) **2** **POLAND** .... (0) **0** 28900
Crossan, Bingham

1966/68 SERIES

GROUP MATCHES - GROUP 7

2/10/66 **POLAND** .... (0) **4** **LUXEMBOURG** .... (0) **0** 30000
Jarosik, Liberda, Grzegorczyk, Sadek

22/10/66 **FRANCE** .... (1) **2** **POLAND** .... (0) **1** 22000
Lech, Di Nallo *Grzegorczyk*

16/3/67 **LUXEMBOURG** .... (0) **0** **POLAND** .... (0) **0** 8000

21/5/67 **POLAND** .... (2) **3** **BELGIUM** .... (0) **1** 70000
Lubanski (2), Szoltysik *Puis*

17/9/67 **POLAND** .... (1) **1** **FRANCE** .... (2) **4** 51000
Brychczy *Herbin, Di Nallo (2), Guy*

8/10/67 **BELGIUM** .... (2) **2** **POLAND** .... (2) **4** 30000
Devrindt (2) *Smijevski (3), Brychczy*

1970/72 SERIES

GROUP MATCHES - GROUP 8

14/10/70 **POLAND** .... (1) **3** **ALBANIA** .... (0) **0** 15000
Gadocha, Lubanski, Szoltysik

12/5/71 **ALBANIA** .... (1) **1** **POLAND** .... (1) **1** 20000
Zegha *Banas*

22/9/71 **POLAND** .... (1) **5** **TURKEY** .... (0) **1** 4000
Bula, Lubanski (3), Gadocha *Nihat*

10/10/71 **POLAND** .... (1) **1** **WEST GERMANY** .... (1) **3** 10000
Gadocha *Muller (2), Grabowski*

17/11/71 **WEST GERMANY** .... (0) **0** **POLAND** .... (0) **0** 6200

5/12/71 **TURKEY** .... (0) **1** **POLAND** .... (0) **0** 7000
Cemil

1974/76 SERIES

GROUP MATCHES - GROUP 5

1/9/74 **FINLAND** .... (1) **1** **POLAND** .... (1) **2** 1900
Rahja *Szarmach, Lato*

9/10/74 **POLAND** .... (2) **3** **FINLAND** .... (0) **0** 5000
Kasperczak, Gadocha (Pen), Lato

19/4/75 **ITALY** .... (0) **0** **POLAND** .... (0) **0** 9000

10/9/75 **POLAND** .... (2) **4** **HOLLAND** .... (0) **1** 10000
Lato, Gadocha, Szarmach (2) *R. Van Der Kerkhoff*

25/10/75 **POLAND** .... (0) **0** **ITALY** .... (0) **0** 7000

15/10/75 **HOLLAND** .... (1) **3** **POLAND** .... (0) **0** 6000
Neeskens, Geels, Thijssen

1978/80 SERIES

GROUP MATCHES - GROUP 4

6/9/78 **ICELAND** .... (0) **0** **POLAND** .... (1) **2** 7000
Kusto (22), Lato (72)

15/11/78 **POLAND** .... (1) **2** **SWITZERLAND** ...... (0) **0** 45000
Boniek (30), Ogaza (57)

18/4/79 **EAST GERMANY** ..... (0) **2** **POLAND** .... (1) **1** 55000
Streich (50), Lindemann (63) *Boniek (8)*

2/5/79 **POLAND** .... (1) **2** **HOLLAND** .... (0) **0** 100000
Boniek (19), Mazur (Pen, 64)

12/9/79 **SWITZERLAND** ...... (0) **0** **POLAND** .... (1) **2** 25000
Terlecki (34, 63)

26/9/79 **POLAND** .... (0) **1** **EAST GERMANY** ..... (0) **1** 90000
Wieczorek (77) *Hafner (61)*

10/10/79 **POLAND** .... (0) **2** **ICELAND** .... (0) **0** 25000
Ogaza (55, (Pen, 74))

17/10/79 **HOLLAND** .... (0) **1** **POLAND** .... (1) **1** 53000
Stevens (64) *Rudy (38)*

1982/84 SERIES

GROUP MATCHES - GROUP 2

8/9/82 **FINLAND** .... (0) **2** **POLAND** .... (2) **3** 3526
Valvee (84), Kousa (85) *Smolarek (Pen, 16), Dziekanowski (20), Kupcewicz (73)*

10/10/82 **PORTUGAL** .... (1) **2** **POLAND** .... (0) **1** 75000
Nene (2), Gomes (81) *Janas (89)*

17/4/83 **POLAND** .... (1) **1** **FINLAND** .... (1) **1** 8000
Smolarek (Pen, 2) *Janes (Og, 5)*

22/5/83 **POLAND** .... (1) **1** **USSR** .... (0) **1** 75000
Boniek (20) *Wojcicki (Og, 63)*

9/10/83 **USSR** .... (1) **2** **POLAND** .... (0) **0** 72500
Demianenko (10), Blokhin (62)

28/10/83 **POLAND** .... (0) **0** **PORTUGAL** .... (1) **1** 15000
Carlos Manuel (31)

1986/88 SERIES

GROUP MATCHES - GROUP 5

15/10/86 **POLAND** .... (1) **2** **GREECE** .... (1) **1** 32500
Dziekanowski (Pens 5, 40) *Anastopoulos (13)*

19/11/86 **HOLLAND** .... (0) **0** **POLAND** .... (0) **0** 65000

12/4/87 **POLAND** .... (0) **0** **CYPRUS** .... (0) **0** 25000

29/4/87 **GREECE** .... (0) **1** **POLAND** .... (0) **0** 70000
Saravakos (57)

17/5/87 **HUNGARY** .... (1) **5** **POLAND** .... (1) **3** 8000
Vincze (39), Detari ((Pen, 62), 76), Peter (66), Preszeller (83) *Marziniak (27), Smolarek (52), Wojcicki (81)*

23/9/87 **POLAND** .... (1) **3** **HUNGARY** .... (1) **2** 10000
Dziekanowski (6), Tarasiewicz (57), Lesniak (61) *Bognar (10), Meszaros (72)*

14/10/87 **POLAND** .... (0) **0** **HOLLAND** .... (2) **2** 21500
Gullit (30, 38)

11/11/87 **CYPRUS** .... (0) **0** **POLAND** .... (0) **1** 8000
Lesniak (74)

1990/92 SERIES

GROUP MATCHES - GROUP 7

7/10/90 **ENGLAND** .... (1) **2** **POLAND** .... (0) **0** 77040
Lineker (pen 39), Beardsley (89)

4/11/90 **TURKEY** (0) **0** **POLAND** (1) **1** 25000
Dziekanowski (37)

17/4/91 **POLAND** (0) **3** **TURKEY** (0) **0** 1500
Tarasiewicz (75), Urban (81), Kosecki (88)

1/5/91 **EIRE** (0) **0** **POLAND** (0) **0** 48000

6/10/91 **POLAND** (0) **3** **EIRE** (1) **3** 17000
Czachowski (55), Furtok (77), Urban (86) — *McGrath (10), Townsend (62), Cascarino (68)*

3/11/91 **POLAND** (1) **1** **ENGLAND** (0) **1** 15000
Szewczyk (32) — *Lineker (77)*

1994/96 SERIES
GROUP MATCHES - GROUP 1

4/9/94 **ISRAEL** (1) **2** **POLAND** (0) **1** 3500
R. Harazi (43, 58) — *Kosecki (80)*

2/10/94 **POLAND** (1) **1** **AZERBAIJAN** (0) **1** 10000
Juskowiak (45)

6/11/94 **POLAND** (0) **0** **FRANCE** (0) **0** 21000

29/3/95 **ROMANIA** (1) **2** **POLAND** (1) **1** 25500
Raducioiu (44), Wandzik (Og, 55) — *Juskowiak (Pen, 42)*

25/4/95 **POLAND** (1) **4** **ISRAEL** (2) **3** 5500
Nowak (1), Juskowiak (50), Kowalczyk (55), Kosecki (62) — *Rosenthal (37), Revivo (42), Zohar (77)*

7/6/95 **POLAND** (1) **5** **SLOVAKIA** (0) **0** 17000
Juskowiak (9, 73), Swierczewski (59), Kosecki (63), Nowak (70)

16/8/95 **FRANCE** (0) **1** **POLAND** (1) **1** 40426
Djorkaeff (86) — *Juskowiak (35)*

6/9/95 **POLAND** (0) **0** **ROMANIA** (0) **0** 19000

11/10/95 **SLOVAKIA** (1) **4** **POLAND** (1) **1** 11000
Dubovsky (Pen, 32), Jancula (68), Ujlaky (77), Simon (83) — *Juskowiak (19)*

15/11/95 **AZERBAIJAN** (0) **0** **POLAND** (0) **0** 1000

PORTUGAL

1958/60 SERIES

First Round

21/6/59 **EAST GERMANY** (0) **0** **PORTUGAL** (1) **2** 25000
Matateu, Coluna

28/6/59 **PORTUGAL** (1) **3** **EAST GERMANY** (0) **2** 35000
Coluna (2), Cavem — *Vogt, Kohle*

Quarter-Finals

8/5/60 **PORTUGAL** (1) **2** **YUGOSLAVIA** (0) **1** 50000
Santana, Matateu — *Kostic*

22/5/60 **YUGOSLAVIA** (2) **5** **PORTUGAL** (1) **1** 55000
Kostic (2), Sekularac, Cebinac, Galic — *Cavem*

1962/64 SERIES

First Round

7/11/62 **BULGARIA** (0) **3** **PORTUGAL** (0) **1** 50000
Asparoukhov (2), Diev — *Eusebio*

16/12/62 **PORTUGAL** (2) **3** **BULGARIA** (0) **1** 25900
Hernani (2), Coluna — *Iliev*

23/1/63 **BULGARIA** (0) **1** **PORTUGAL** (0) **0** 15000
Asparoukhov

1966/68 SERIES
GROUP MATCHES - GROUP 2

13/11/66 **PORTUGAL** (1) **1** **SWEDEN** (1) **2** 20000
Graca — *Danielsson (2)*

1/6/67 **SWEDEN** (0) **1** **PORTUGAL** (1) **1** 49689
Svensson — *Pinto*

8/6/67 **NORWAY** (1) **1** **PORTUGAL** (1) **2** 31000
Iversen — *Eusebio (2)*

12/11/67 **PORTUGAL** (1) **2** **NORWAY** (1) **1** 40000
Torres, Graca — *Nilsen*

26/11/67 **BULGARIA** (0) **1** **PORTUGAL** (0) **0** 60000
Dermendijev

17/12/67 **PORTUGAL** (0) **0** **BULGARIA** (0) **0** 20000

1970/72 SERIES
GROUP MATCHES - GROUP 5

14/10/70 **DENMARK** (0) **0** **PORTUGAL** (1) **1** 18000
Joao Jacinto

17/2/71 **BELGIUM** (2) **3** **PORTUGAL** (0) **0** 25000
Lambert, Van Himst, Denul

21/4/71 **PORTUGAL** (1) **2** **SCOTLAND** (0) **0** 35000
Stanton (Og), Eusebio

12/5/71 **PORTUGAL** (2) **5** **DENMARK** (0) **0** 20000
Rodrigues, Eusebio, Baptista (2), Sandvad (Og)

13/10/71 **SCOTLAND** (1) **2** **PORTUGAL** (0) **1** 50000
O'Hare, Gemmill — *Rodrigues*

21/11/71 **PORTUGAL** (0) **1** **BELGIUM** (0) **1** 53600
Peres (Pen) — *Lambert*

1974/76 SERIES
GROUP MATCHES - GROUP 1

20/11/74 **ENGLAND** (0) **0** **PORTUGAL** (0) **0** 85700

30/4/75 **CZECHOSLOVAKIA** (3) **5** **PORTUGAL** (0) **0** 25000
Bicovsky (2), Nehoda (2), Petras

8/6/75 **CYPRUS** (0) **0** **PORTUGAL** (1) **2** 11000
Nene (2)

12/11/75 **PORTUGAL** (1) **1** **CZECHOSLOVAKIA** (1) **1** 45000
Nene — *Ondrus*

19/11/75 **PORTUGAL** (1) **1** **ENGLAND** (1) **1** 40000
Rodrigues — *Channon*

3/12/75 **PORTUGAL** (1) **1** **CYPRUS** (0) **0** 4000
Alves

1978/80 SERIES
GROUP MATCHES - GROUP 2

11/10/78 **PORTUGAL** (1) **1** **BELGIUM** (1) **1** 35000
Gomes (31) — *Vercauteren (37)*

15/11/78 **AUSTRIA** (0) **1** **PORTUGAL** (1) **2** 62000
Schachner (71) — *Nene (30), Alberto (90)*

29/11/78 **PORTUGAL** (1) **1** **SCOTLAND** (0) **0** 60000
Alberto (29)

9/5/79 **NORWAY** (0) **0** **PORTUGAL** (1) **1** 9800
Alves (35)

17/10/79 **BELGIUM** (0) **2** **PORTUGAL** (0) **0** 10000
Van Moer (46), Van Der Elst (55)

1/11/79 **PORTUGAL** (1) **3** **NORWAY** (1) **1** 25000
Artur (28), Nene (59, 69) — *Georg Hammer*

21/11/79 **PORTUGAL** (1) **1** **AUSTRIA** (1) **2** 80000
Reinaldo (42) — *Welzl (36), Schachner (51)*

6/2/80 **SCOTLAND** (2) **4** **PORTUGAL** (0) **1** 20233
Dalglish (7), Gray (25), Archibald (68), Gemmill (Pen, 83) — *Gomes (75)*

1982/84 SERIES
GROUP MATCHES - GROUP 2

22/9/82 **FINLAND** (0) **0** **PORTUGAL** (1) **2** 3132
Nene (15), Oliveira (89)

10/10/82 **PORTUGAL** (1) **2** **POLAND** (0) **1** 75000
Nene (2), Gomes (81) — *Janas (89)*

27/4/83 **USSR** (2) **5** **PORTUGAL** (0) **0** 100000
Cherenkov (18, 64), Rodionov (40), Demianenko (50), Lorianov (87)

21/9/83 **PORTUGAL** (2) **5** **FINLAND** (0) **0** 7500
Jordad (18), Carlos Manuel (23), Ikalainen (Og, 46), Jose Luis (48), Oliveira (51)

28/10/83 **POLAND** (0) **0** **PORTUGAL** (1) **1** 15000
Carlos Manuel (31)

13/11/83 **PORTUGAL** (1) **1** **USSR** (0) **0** 70000
Jordao (Pen, 44)

FINALS - GROUP 2

14/6/84 **WEST GERMANY** (0) **0** **PORTUGAL** (0) **0** 47950

17/6/84 **PORTUGAL** (0) **1** **SPAIN** (0) **1** 30000
Sousa (51) — *Santillana (72)*

20/6/84 **PORTUGAL** (0) **1** **ROMANIA** (0) **0** 20000
Nene (80)

Semi-Final

23/6/84 **FRANCE** (1) **3** **PORTUGAL** (0) **2** 55000 Marseille
Domergue (24, 114), Platini (119) — *Jordao (73, 97)*
(After Extra Time)

1986/88 SERIES
GROUP MATCHES - GROUP 2

12/10/86 **PORTUGAL** (0) **1** **SWEDEN** (0) **1** 15000
Coelho (66) — *Stromberg (50)*

29/10/86 **SWITZERLAND** (1) **1** **PORTUGAL** (0) **1** 11000
Bergy (6) — *Fernandes (86)*

8/2/87 **PORTUGAL** .... (0) **0** **ITALY** .... (1) **1** 32500
Altobelli (40)

29/3/87 **PORTUGAL** .... (1) **2** **MALTA** .... (1) **2** 12000
Jorge Placido (12, 76) — *Mizzi (Pen, 23), Busuttil (66)*

23/9/87 **SWEDEN** .... (0) **0** **PORTUGAL** .... (1) **1** 28916
Gomes

11/11/87 **PORTUGAL** .... (0) **0** **SWITZERLAND** .... (0) **0** 12500

5/12/87 **ITALY** .... (1) **3** **PORTUGAL** .... (0) **0** 20000
Vialli (8), Giannini (88), De Agostini (89)

20/12/87 **MALTA** .... (0) **0** **PORTUGAL** .... (0) **1** 4000
Frederico

1990/92 SERIES

GROUP MATCHES - GROUP 6

12/9/90 **FINLAND** .... (0) **0** **PORTUGAL** .... (0) **0** 10240

17/10/90 **PORTUGAL** .... (0) **1** **HOLLAND** .... (0) **0** 35000
Aguas (54)

23/1/91 **GREECE** .... (1) **3** **PORTUGAL** .... (1) **2** 30000
Borbokis (7), Manalos (68), Tsaluhidis (85) — *Aguas (18), Futre (62)*

9/2/91 **MALTA** .... (0) **0** **PORTUGAL** .... (1) **1** 10000
Futre (27)

22/2/91 **PORTUGAL** .... (3) **5** **MALTA** .... (0) **0** 10000
Aguas (5), Leal (33), Paneira (pen 40), Scerri (o.g. 48), Cadete (81)

11/9/91 **PORTUGAL** .... (1) **1** **FINLAND** .... (0) **0** 30000
Brito (22)

16/10/91 **HOLLAND** .... (1) **1** **PORTUGAL** .... (0) **0** 50000
Witschge (20)

20/11/91 **PORTUGAL** .... (1) **1** **GREECE** .... (0) **0** 2000
Joao Pinto II (17)

1994/96 SERIES

GROUP MATCHES - GROUP 6

7/9/94 **NORTHERN IRELAND** . (0) **1** **PORTUGAL** .... (1) **2** 6000
Quinn (Pen, 58) — *Costa (8), Oliviera (81)*

9/10/94 **LATVIA** .... (0) **1** **PORTUGAL** .... (1) **3** 1900
Milevsky (88) — *Joao Pinto (33, 72), Figo (73)*

13/11/94 **PORTUGAL** .... (1) **1** **AUSTRIA** .... (0) **0** 46000
Figo (37)

18/12/94 **PORTUGAL** .... (3) **8** **LIECHTENSTEIN** ...... (0) **0** 32000
Oliviera (2, 11), Oceano (44), Joao Pinto (57), Fernando Couto (73), Folha (74), Alves (75, 79)

26/4/95 **EIRE** .... (1) **1** **PORTUGAL** .... (0) **0** 25000
Vitor Baia (Og, 44)

3/6/95 **PORTUGAL** .... (3) **3** **LATVIA** .... (0) **2** 40000
Figo (5), Secretario (19), Domingos (20) — *Babichev (51), Rimkus (85)*

15/8/95 **LIECHTENSTEIN** ..... (0) **0** **PORTUGAL** .... (3) **7** 2500
Domingos (25), Paulinho (33), Rui Costa (41, 71), Paulo Alves (67, 73, 90)

3/9/95 **PORTUGAL** .... (0) **1** **NORTHERN IRELAND** . (0) **1** 50000
Domingos (47) — *Hughes (66)*

11/10/95 **AUSTRIA** .... (1) **1** **PORTUGAL** .... (0) **1** 44000
Stoger (21) — *Paulinho Santos (49)*

15/11/95 **PORTUGAL** .... (0) **3** **EIRE** .... (0) **0** 80000
Rui Costa (59), Helder (78), Cadete (89)

ROMANIA

1958/60 SERIES

First Round

2/11/58 **ROMANIA** .... (0) **3** **TURKEY** .... (0) **0** 67000
Oaida, Constantin, Dinulescu

26/4/59 **TURKEY** .... (1) **2** **ROMANIA** .... (0) **0** 24000
Lefter (2, 1 Pen)

Quarter-Finals

22/5/60 **ROMANIA** .... (0) **0** **CZECHOSLOVAKIA** .... (2) **2** 100000
Masopust, Bubnik

29/5/60 **CZECHOSLOVAKIA** .... (3) **3** **ROMANIA** .... (0) **0** 45000
Bubernik (2), Bubnik

1962/64 SERIES

First Round

1/11/62 **SPAIN** .... (4) **6** **ROMANIA** .... (0) **0** 51700
Guillot (3), Veloso, Collar, Macri (Og)

25/11/62 **ROMANIA** .... (2) **3** **SPAIN** .... (0) **1** 72800
Manolache (2), Tataru — *Veloso*

1966/68 SERIES

GROUP MATCHES - GROUP 6

2/11/66 **ROMANIA** .... (4) **4** **SWITZERLAND** ...... (0) **2** 300
Dridea (3), Fratila — *Kunzli, Odermatt*

26/11/66 **ITALY** .... (2) **3** **ROMANIA** .... (1) **1** 750
Mazzola (2), De Paoli — *Pircalab*

3/12/66 **CYPRUS** .... (1) **1** **ROMANIA** .... (0) **5** 200
Kostakis — *Dridea (2), Lucescu, Fratila (2)*

23/4/67 **ROMANIA** .... (3) **7** **CYPRUS** .... (0) **0** 200
Dimitriu (3), Ionescu (2), Martinovic, Lucescu

24/5/67 **SWITZERLAND** ...... (3) **7** **ROMANIA** .... (0) **1** 230
Kunzli (2), Quentin (2), Blattler (2), Odermatt — *Dobrin*

25/6/67 **ROMANIA** .... (0) **0** **ITALY** .... (0) **1** 700
Bertini

1970/72 SERIES

GROUP MATCHES - GROUP 1

10/10/70 **ROMANIA** .... (2) **3** **FINLAND** .... (0) **0** 5000
Dumitrache (2), Nunweiller

11/11/70 **WALES** .... (0) **0** **ROMANIA** .... (0) **0** 2000

16/5/71 **CZECHOSLOVAKIA** .... (0) **1** **ROMANIA** .... (0) **0** 5000
Vesely

22/9/71 **FINLAND** .... (0) **0** **ROMANIA** .... (2) **4** 208
Jordanescu, Lupescu, Dembrovski, Lucescu (Pen)

14/11/71 **ROMANIA** .... (1) **2** **CZECHOSLOVAKIA** ... (0) **1** 10000
Dembrovski, Dobrin — *Capkovic*

24/11/71 **ROMANIA** .... (1) **2** **WALES** .... (0) **0** 7000
Lupescu, Lucescu

Quarter-Finals

29/4/72 **HUNGARY** .... (1) **1** **ROMANIA** .... (0) **1** 7000
Branikovits — *Satmareanu*

14/5/72 **ROMANIA** .... (1) **2** **HUNGARY** .... (2) **2** 7500
Dobrin, Neagu — *Szoeke, Kocsis*

17/5/72 **HUNGARY** .... (1) **2** **ROMANIA** .... (1) **1** 45000
Kocsis, Szoeke — *Neagu*

1974/76 SERIES

GROUP MATCHES - GROUP 4

13/10/74 **DENMARK** .... (0) **0** **ROMANIA** .... (0) **0** 15700

17/4/75 **SPAIN** .... (1) **1** **ROMANIA** .... (0) **1** 100000
Velazquez — *Crisan*

11/5/75 **ROMANIA** .... (2) **6** **DENMARK** .... (0) **1** 60000
Georgescu (2), Crisan (2), Lucescu, Dinu — *Dahl*

1/6/75 **ROMANIA** .... (1) **1** **SCOTLAND** .... (0) **1** 80000
Georgescu — *McQueen*

16/11/75 **ROMANIA** .... (0) **2** **SPAIN** .... (1) **2** 50000
Georgescu (Pen), Jordanescu — *Villar, Santillana*

17/12/75 **SCOTLAND** .... (1) **1** **ROMANIA** .... (0) **1** 11000
Rioch — *Lucescu*

1978/80 SERIES

GROUP MATCHES - GROUP 3

25/10/78 **ROMANIA** .... (0) **3** **YUGOSLAVIA** .... (1) **2** 25000
Sames (62, 68), Jordanescu (Pen, 75) — *Petrovic (Pen, 22), Desnica (90)*

15/11/78 **SPAIN** .... (1) **1** **ROMANIA** .... (0) **0** 46000
Asensi (9)

4/4/79 **ROMANIA** .... (0) **2** **SPAIN** .... (0) **2** 40000
Georgescu ((Pen, 57), 65) — *Dani (59,70)*

13/5/79 **CYPRUS** .... (1) **1** **ROMANIA** .... (1) **1** 8000
Kaiafas (31) — *Ankustia (30)*

31/10/79 **YUGOSLAVIA** .... (0) **2** **ROMANIA** .... (0) **1** 35000
Vujovic (48), Sliskovic (50) — *Radacanu (79)*

18/11/79 **ROMANIA** .... (1) **2** **CYPRUS** .... (0) **0** 10000
Multescu (40), Radacanu (75)

1982/84 SERIES

GROUP MATCHES - GROUP 5

1/5/82 **ROMANIA** .... (2) **3** **CYPRUS** .... (1) **1** 20000
Vaetus (16), Camataru (19), Boloni (71) — *Vrachimis (29)*

8/9/82 **ROMANIA** .... (1) **2** **SWEDEN** .... (0) **0** 60000
Andone (25), Klein (52)

4/12/82 **ITALY** .... (0) **0** **ROMANIA** .... (0) **0** 52000

16/4/83 **ROMANIA** .... (1) **1** **ITALY** .... (0) **0** 80000
Boloni

15/5/83 **ROMANIA** (0) **0** **CZECHOSLOVAKIA** (1) **1** 60000
Visek (Pen, 40)

9/6/83 **SWEDEN** (0) **0** **ROMANIA** (1) **1** 31474
Camataru (29)

12/11/83 **CYPRUS** (0) **0** **ROMANIA** (0) **1** 13000
Boloni (77)

30/11/83 **CZECHOSLOVAKIA** (0) **1** **ROMANIA** (0) **1** 48000
Luhovy (85) — *Geolgau (63)*

FINALS - GROUP 2

14/6/84 **SPAIN** (1) **1** **ROMANIA** (1) **1** 15000
Carrasco (Pen, 20) — *Boloni (34)*

17/6/84 **WEST GERMANY** (1) **2** **ROMANIA** (0) **1** 35000
Voller (24, 65) — *Coras (46)*

20/6/84 **PORTUGAL** (0) **1** **ROMANIA** (0) **0** 20000
Nene (80)

1986/88 SERIES

GROUP MATCHES - GROUP 1

10/9/86 **ROMANIA** (1) **4** **AUSTRIA** (0) **0** 20000
Iovan (44, 63), Lacatus (61), Hagi (89)

12/11/86 **SPAIN** (0) **1** **ROMANIA** (0) **0** 47500
Michel (57)

25/3/87 **ROMANIA** (3) **5** **ALBANIA** (1) **1** 15000
Piturca (1), Holoni (42), Hagi (Pen, 44), Belodedici (54), Bumbescu (69) — *Muca (34)*

29/4/87 **ROMANIA** (3) **3** **SPAIN** (0) **1** 30000
Piturca (37), Mateut (45), Ungureanu (48) — *Caldere (81)*

28/10/87 **ALBANIA** (0) **0** **ROMANIA** (0) **1** 18000
Klein (61)

18/11/87 **AUSTRIA** (0) **0** **ROMANIA** (0) **0** 6200

1990/92 SERIES

GROUP MATCHES - GROUP 2

12/9/90 **SCOTLAND** (1) **2** **ROMANIA** (1) **1** 12801
Robertson (37), McCoist (76) — *Camataru (13)*

17/10/90 **ROMANIA** (0) **0** **BULGARIA** (1) **3** 25000
Sirakov (28), Todorov (48, 76)

5/12/90 **ROMANIA** (3) **6** **SAN MARINO** (0) **0** 24000
Sabau (2), Mateut (18), Raducioiu (43) Lupescu (56), Badea (77), Petrescu (85)

27/3/91 **SAN MARINO** (1) **1** **ROMANIA** (2) **3** 745
Pasolini (pen 30) — *Hagi (pen 17), Raducioiu (45), Matteoni (og 86)*

3/4/91 **SWITZERLAND** (0) **0** **ROMANIA** (0) **0** 16000

16/10/91 **ROMANIA** (0) **1** **SCOTLAND** (0) **0** 30000
Hagi (pen 73)

13/11/91 **ROMANIA** (0) **1** **SWITZERLAND** (0) **0** 35000
Mateut (72)

20/11/91 **BULGARIA** (0) **1** **ROMANIA** (1) **1** 20000
Sirakov (56) — *Popescu (30)*

1994/96 SERIES

GROUP MATCHES - GROUP 1

7/9/94 **ROMANIA** (1) **3** **AZERBAIJAN** (0) **0** 10000
Belodedici (43), Petrescu (58), Raducioiu (88)

8/10/94 **FRANCE** (0) **0** **ROMANIA** (0) **0** 31744

12/11/94 **ROMANIA** (1) **3** **SLOVAKIA** (0) **2** 16000
Popescu (7), Hagi (46), Prodan (81) — *Dubrovsky (56), Chvila (78)*

14/12/94 **ISRAEL** (0) **1** **ROMANIA** (0) **1** 42500
Rosenthal (83) — *Lacatus (70)*

29/3/95 **ROMANIA** (1) **2** **POLAND** (1) **1** 25500
Raducioiu (44), Wandzik (Og, 55) — *Juskowiak (Pen, 42)*

26/4/95 **AZERBAIJAN** (1) **1** **ROMANIA** (2) **4** 1000
Suleimanov (35) — *Raducioiu (2, 69, 76), Dumitrescu (39)*

7/6/95 **ROMANIA** (1) **2** **ISRAEL** (0) **1** 28000
Lacatus (16), Munteanu (65) — *Bercovitz (50)*

6/9/95 **POLAND** (0) **0** **ROMANIA** (0) **0** 19000

11/10/95 **ROMANIA** (0) **1** **FRANCE** (2) **3** 25000
Lacatus (51) — *Karembeu (28), Djorkaeff (42), Zidane (75)*

15/11/95 **SLOVAKIA** (0) **0** **ROMANIA** (0) **2** 7500
Hagi (68), Munteanu (83)

RUSSIA

1994/96 SERIES

GROUP MATCHES - GROUP 8

12/10/94 **RUSSIA** (1) **4** **SAN MARINO** (0) **0** 20000
Karpin (43), Kolyvanov (63), Nikiforov (64), Radchenko (66)

16/11/94 **SCOTLAND** (1) **1** **RUSSIA** (1) **1** 31254
Booth (19) — *Radchenko (25)*

29/3/95 **RUSSIA** (0) **0** **SCOTLAND** (0) **0** 27500

26/4/95 **GREECE** (0) **0** **RUSSIA** (1) **3** 45000
Nikiforov (36), Zagorakis (Og, 78), Beschastnikh (79)

6/5/95 **RUSSIA** (0) **3** **FAROE ISLANDS** (0) **0** 9500
Kechinov (63), Pisarev (72), Moukhamadiev (80)

7/6/95 **SAN MARINO** (0) **0** **RUSSIA** (2) **7** 1450
Dobrovolski (Pen, 20), Gobbi (Og, 38), Kiriakov (48), Shalimov (49), Beschastnikh (59), Kolyvanov (64), Chernishev (86)

16/8/95 **FINLAND** (0) **0** **RUSSIA** (3) **6** 14200
Kulkov (32, 51), Karpin (42), Radchenko (32), Kolyvanov (67, 69)

6/9/95 **FAROE ISLANDS** (1) **2** **RUSSIA** (1) **5** 1852
H. Jarnskor (12), T. Jonsson (55) — *Mostovoi (10), Kiriakov (60), Kolyvanov (65), Tsimbalar (84), Shalimov (87)*

11/10/95 **RUSSIA** (1) **2** **GREECE** (0) **1** 65000
Kovtun (36), Onopko (71) — *Tsalouhidis (64)*

15/11/95 **RUSSIA** (1) **3** **FINLAND** (1) **1** 3500
Radchenko (40), Kulkov (55), Kiriakov (70) — *Suominen (45)*

SAN MARINO

1990/92 SERIES

GROUP MATCHES - GROUP 2

14/11/90 **SAN MARINO** (0) **0** **SWITZERLAND** (3) **4** 931
Sutter (7), Chapuisat (27), Knup (43), Chassot (87)

5/12/90 **ROMANIA** (3) **6** **SAN MARINO** (0) **0** 24000
Sabau (2), Mateut (18), Raducioiu (43) Lupescu (56), Badea (77), Petrescu (85)

27/3/91 **SAN MARINO** (1) **1** **ROMANIA** (2) **3** 745
Pasolini (pen 30) — *Hagi (pen 17), Raducioiu (45), Matteoni (o.g. 86)*

1/5/91 **SAN MARINO** (0) **0** **SCOTLAND** (0) **2** 3512
Strachan (pen 63), Durie (66)

22/5/91 **SAN MARINO** (0 **0** **BULGARIA** (2) **3** 612
Ivanov (13), Sirakov (20), Penev (70)

5/6/91 **SWITZERLAND** (3) **7** **SAN MARINO** (0) **0** 12000
Knup (3, 87), Hottiger (13), Sutter (29) Hermann (55), Ohrel (78), Turkyilmaz (90)

16/10/91 **BULGARIA** (3) **4** **SAN MARINO** (0) **0** 8000
Valentini (o.g. 20), Stoichkov (pen 37) Yankov (41), Iliev (85)

13/11/91 **SCOTLAND** (3) **4** **SAN MARINO** (0) **0** 35170
McStay, Gough, Durie, McCoist

1994/96 SERIES

GROUP MATCHES - GROUP 8

12/10/94 **RUSSIA** (1) **4** **SAN MARINO** (0) **0** 20000
Karpin (42), Kolyvanov (63), Nikiforov (64), Radchenko (66)

16/11/94 **GREECE** (1) **2** **SAN MARINO** (0) **0** 13500
Mahlas (21), Frantzekos (84)

14/12/94 **FINLAND** (2) **4** **SAN MARINO** (1) **1** 3140
Paatelainen (24, 30, 85, 90) — *Della Valle (34)*

29/3/95 **SAN MARINO** (0) **0** **FINLAND** (1) **2** 824
Litmanen (45), Sumiala (67)

26/4/95 **SAN MARINO** (0) **0** **SCOTLAND** (1) **2** 1738
Collins (19), Calderwood (85)

25/5/95 **FAROE ISLANDS** (2) **3** **SAN MARINO** (0) **0** 3450
J.C. Hansen (6), J.E. Rasmussen (9), J. Johnsson (62)

7/6/95 **SAN MARINO** (0) **0** **RUSSIA** (2) **7** 1450
Dobrovolski (Pen, 20), Gobbi (Og, 38), Kiriakov (48), Shalimov (49), Beschastnikh (59), Kolyvanov (64), Chernishev (86)

6/9/95 **SAN MARINO** (0) **0** **GREECE** (2) **4** 1000
Tsalouhidis (5), G. Georgiadis (31), Alexandris (61), Donis (81)

11/10/95 **SAN MARINO** (0) **1** **FAROE ISLANDS** (2) **3** 1000
Valentini (52) — *Todi Jonsson (42, 45, 59)*

15/11/95 **SCOTLAND** (2) **5** **SAN MARINO** (0) **0** 30306
Booth (45), Jess (30), McCoist (49), Nevin (71), Francini (Og, 90)

SCOTLAND

1966/68 SERIES

GROUP MATCHES - GROUP 8

22/10/66 **WALES** (0) **1** **SCOTLAND** (0) **1** 32500
R. Davies — *Law*

16/11/66	**SCOTLAND**	(2)	**2**	**NORTHERN IRELAND**	(1)	**1**	45281
	Murdoch, Lennox			*Nicholson*			
15/4/67	**ENGLAND**	(0)	**2**	**SCOTLAND**	(1)	**3**	100000
	J. Charlton, Hurst			*Law, Lennox, McCalliog*			
21/10/67	**NORTHERN IRELAND**	(0)	**1**	**SCOTLAND**	(0)	**0**	55000
	Clements						
22/11/67	**SCOTLAND**	(1)	**3**	**WALES**	(1)	**2**	57000
	Gilzean (2), McKinnon			*R. Davies, Durban*			
24/2/68	**SCOTLAND**	(1)	**1**	**ENGLAND**	(1)	**1**	134000
	Hughes			*Peters*			

1970/72 SERIES

GROUP MATCHES - GROUP 5

11/11/70	**SCOTLAND**	(1)	**1**	**DENMARK**	(0)	**0**	24000
	O'Hare						
3/2/71	**BELGIUM**	(1)	**3**	**SCOTLAND**	(0)	**0**	25000
	Van Himst (3, 1 Pen)						
21/4/71	**PORTUGAL**	(1)	**2**	**SCOTLAND**	(0)	**0**	35000
	Stanton (Og), Eusebio						
9/6/71	**DENMARK**	(1)	**1**	**SCOTLAND**	(0)	**0**	38600
	Laudrup						
13/10/71	**SCOTLAND**	(1)	**2**	**PORTUGAL**	(0)	**1**	50000
	O'Hare, Gemmill			*Rodrigues*			
10/11/71	**SCOTLAND**	(1)	**1**	**BELGIUM**	(0)	**0**	36000
	O'Hare						

1974/76 SERIES

GROUP MATCHES - GROUP 4

20/11/74	**SCOTLAND**	(1)	**1**	**SPAIN**	(1)	**2**	92000
	Bremner			*Quini (2)*			
5/2/75	**SPAIN**	(0)	**1**	**SCOTLAND**	(1)	**1**	60000
	Megido			*Jordan*			
1/6/75	**ROMANIA**	(1)	**1**	**SCOTLAND**	(0)	**1**	80000
	Georgeescu			*McQueen*			
3/9/75	**DENMARK**	(0)	**0**	**SCOTLAND**	(0)	**1**	40300
				Harper			
29/10/75	**SCOTLAND**	(0)	**3**	**DENMARK**	(1)	**1**	48021
	Dalglish, Rioch, McDougall			*Bastrup*			
17/12/75	**SCOTLAND**	(1)	**1**	**ROMANIA**	(0)	**1**	11000
	Rioch			*Lucescu*			

1978/80 SERIES

GROUP MATCHES - GROUP 2

20/9/78	**AUSTRIA**	(1)	**3**	**SCOTLAND**	(0)	**2**	70000
	Pezzey (27), Schachner (47), Kreuz (63)			*McQueen (64), Gray (78)*			
25/10/78	**SCOTLAND**	(1)	**3**	**NORWAY**	(1)	**2**	60000
	Dalglish (30, 81), Gemmill (Pen, 87)			*E. Aas (3), Okland (64)*			
29/11/78	**PORTUGAL**	(1)	**1**	**SCOTLAND**	(0)	**0**	60000
	Alberto (29)						
7/6/79	**NORWAY**	(0)	**0**	**SCOTLAND**	(3)	**4**	17268
				Jordan (32), Dalglish (39), Robertson (43), McQueen (54)			
17/10/79	**SCOTLAND**	(0)	**1**	**AUSTRIA**	(1)	**1**	72700
	Gemmill (75)			*Krankl (40)*			
21/11/79	**BELGIUM**	(1)	**2**	**SCOTLAND**	(0)	**0**	12000
	Van Der Elst (5), Voordeckers (47)						
19/12/79	**SCOTLAND**	(0)	**1**	**BELGIUM**	(3)	**3**	30000
	Robertson (55)			*Van Den Bergh (18), Van Der Elst (23, 28)*			
6/2/80	**SCOTLAND**	(2)	**4**	**PORTUGAL**	(0)	**1**	20233
	Dalglish (7), Gray (25), Archibald (68), Gemmill (Pen, 83)			*Gomes (75)*			

1982/84 SERIES

GROUP MATCHES - GROUP 1

13/10/82	**SCOTLAND**	(0)	**2**	**EAST GERMANY**	(0)	**0**	40300
	Wark (53), Sturrock (75)						
17/11/82	**SWITZERLAND**	(0)	**2**	**SCOTLAND**	(0)	**0**	30500
	Sulser (50), Egli (60)						
15/12/82	**BELGIUM**	(2)	**3**	**SCOTLAND**	(2)	**2**	48877
	Van Den Bergh (25), Van Der Elst (38, 63)			*Dalglish (13, 35)*			
30/3/83	**SCOTLAND**	(0)	**2**	**SWITZERLAND**	(1)	**2**	36923
	Wark (70), Nicholas (75)			*Egli (15), Hermann (58)*			
12/10/83	**SCOTLAND**	(0)	**1**	**BELGIUM**	(1)	**1**	23000
	Nicholas (50)			*Vercauteren (30)*			
16/11/83	**EAST GERMANY**	(2)	**2**	**SCOTLAND**	(0)	**1**	18000
	Kreer (33), Streich (42)			*Bannon (78)*			

1986/88 SERIES

GROUP MATCHES - GROUP 7

10/9/86	**SCOTLAND**	(0)	**0**	**BULGARIA**	(0)	**0**	3507
15/10/86	**EIRE**	(0)	**0**	**SCOTLAND**	(0)	**0**	4800
12/11/86	**SCOTLAND**	(2)	**3**	**LUXEMBOURG**	(0)	**0**	3507
	Cooper ((Pen, 24), 38), Johnston (70)						
18/2/87	**SCOTLAND**	(0)	**0**	**EIRE**	(1)	**1**	4508
				Lawrenson (8)			
1/4/87	**BELGIUM**	(1)	**4**	**SCOTLAND**	(1)	**1**	2665
	Claesen (8, 55, 85), Vercauteren (75)			*McStay (13)*			
14/10/87	**SCOTLAND**	(1)	**2**	**BELGIUM**	(0)	**0**	2005
	McCoist (14), McStay (79)						
11/11/87	**BULGARIA**	(0)	**0**	**SCOTLAND**	(0)	**1**	6000
				MacKay			
2/12/87	**LUXEMBOURG**	(0)	**0**	**SCOTLAND**	(0)	**0**	199

1990/92 SERIES

GROUP MATCHES - GROUP 2

12/9/90	**SCOTLAND**	(1)	**2**	**ROMANIA**	(1)	**1**	12801
	Robertson (37), McCoist (76)			*Camataru (13)*			
17/10/90	**SCOTLAND**	(1)	**2**	**SWITZERLAND**	(0)	**1**	27740
	Robertson (pen 34), McAllister (53)			*Knup (pen 66)*			
14/11/90	**BULGARIA**	(0)	**1**	**SCOTLAND**	(1)	**1**	42000
	Todorov (74)			*McCoist (9)*			
27/3/91	**SCOTLAND**	(0)	**1**	**BULGARIA**	(0)	**1**	33119
	Collins (84)			*Kostadinov (89)*			
1/5/91	**SAN MARINO**	(0)	**0**	**SCOTLAND**	(0)	**2**	3512
				Strachan (pen 63), Durie (66)			
11/9/91	**SWITZERLAND**	(2)	**2**	**SCOTLAND**	(0)	**2**	48000
	Chapuisat (30), Hermann (39)			*Durie (47), McCoist (83)*			
16/10/91	**ROMANIA**	(0)	**1**	**SCOTLAND**	(0)	**0**	30000
	Hagi (pen 73)						
13/11/91	**SCOTLAND**	(3)	**4**	**SAN MARINO**	(0)	**0**	35170
	McStay, Gough, Durie, McCoist						

FINALS - GROUP 2

12/6/92	**HOLLAND**	(0)	**1**	**SCOTLAND**	(0)	**0**	35720
	Bergkamp (76)						
15/6/92	**SCOTLAND**	(0)	**0**	**GERMANY**	(1)	**2**	17638
				Riedle (28), Effenberg (46)			
18/6/92	**SCOTLAND**	(2)	**3**	**CIS**	(0)	**0**	14660
	McStay (6), McClair (17), McAllister (pen 83)						

1994/96 SERIES

GROUP MATCHES - GROUP 8

7/9/94	**FINLAND**	(0)	**0**	**SCOTLAND**	(1)	**2**	12845
				Shearer (29), Collins (66)			
12/10/94	**SCOTLAND**	(3)	**5**	**FAROE ISLANDS**	(0)	**1**	20885
	McGinlay (4), Booth (34), Collins (40, 72), McKinlay (61)			*Muller (75)*			
16/11/94	**SCOTLAND**	(0)	**1**	**RUSSIA**	(1)	**1**	31254
	Booth (19)			*Radchenko (25)*			
18/12/94	**GREECE**	(1)	**1**	**SCOTLAND**	(0)	**0**	20000
	Apostolakis (Pen, 18)						
29/3/95	**RUSSIA**	(0)	**0**	**SCOTLAND**	(0)	**0**	27500
26/4/95	**SAN MARINO**	(0)	**0**	**SCOTLAND**	(1)	**2**	1738
				Collins (19), Calderwood (85)			
7/6/95	**FAROE ISLANDS**	(0)	**0**	**SCOTLAND**	(2)	**2**	3881
				McKinlay (25), McGinlay (29)			
16/8/95	**SCOTLAND**	(0)	**1**	**GREECE**	(0)	**0**	34910
	McCoist (72)						
6/9/95	**SCOTLAND**	(1)	**1**	**FINLAND**	(0)	**0**	35505
	Booth (10)						
15/11/95	**SCOTLAND**	(2)	**5**	**SAN MARINO**	(0)	**0**	30306
	Booth (45), Jess (30), McCoist (49), Nevin (71), Francini (Og, 90)						

SLOVAKIA

1994/96 SERIES

GROUP MATCHES - GROUP 1

7/9/94	**SLOVAKIA**	(0)	**0**	**FRANCE**	(0)	**0**	17000
12/10/94	**ISRAEL**	(2)	**2**	**SLOVAKIA**	(2)	**2**	10000
	Harazi (26), Gaibanin (Pen, 35)			*Rusnak (7), Moravcik (16)*			
12/11/94	**ROMANIA**	(1)	**3**	**SLOVAKIA**	(0)	**2**	16000
	Popescu (7), Hagi (46), Prodan (81)			*Dubovsky (56), Chvila (78)*			
29/3/95	**SLOVAKIA**	(3)	**4**	**AZERBAIJAN**	(0)	**1**	12450
	Tittel (35), Timko (40, 52), Dubovsky (Pen, 45)			*Suleimanov (Pen, 80)*			

26/4/95 **FRANCE** (2) **4** **SLOVAKIA** (0) **0** 26000
Kristofik (Og, 27), Ginola (43), Blanc (57), Guerin (61)

7/6/95 **POLAND** (1) **5** **SLOVAKIA** (0) **0** 17000
Juskowiak (9, 73), Swierczewski (59), Kosecki (63), Nowak (70)

16/8/95 **AZERBAIJAN** (0) **0** **SLOVAKIA** (0) **1** 1000
Jancula (60)

6/9/95 **SLOVAKIA** (0) **1** **ISRAEL** (0) **0** 10000
Jancula (54)

11/10/95 **SLOVAKIA** (1) **4** **POLAND** (1) **1** 11000
Dubovsky (Pen, 32), Jancula (68), Ujlaky (77), Simon (83) — *Juskowiak (19)*

15/11/95 **SLOVAKIA** (0) **0** **ROMANIA** (0) **2** 7500
Hagi (68), Munteanu (83)

SLOVENIA

1994/96 SERIES

GROUP MATCHES - GROUP 4

7/9/94 **SLOVENIA** (1) **1** **ITALY** (1) **1** 18000
Udovic (14) — *Costacurta (16)*

12/10/94 **UKRAINE** (0) **0** **SLOVENIA** (0) **0** 12000

16/11/94 **SLOVENIA** (0) **1** **LITHUANIA** (0) **2** 6000
Zahovic (55) — *Surkistovas (64), Zuta (87)*

29/3/95 **SLOVENIA** (1) **3** **ESTONIA** (0) **0** 12000
Zahvic (40), Gliha (53), Kokol (90)

26/4/95 **CROATIA** (1) **2** **SLOVENIA** (0) **0** 25000
Prosinecki (17), Suker (90)

7/6/95 **LITHUANIA** (0) **2** **SLOVENIA** (0) **1** 7000
Stonkus (47), Shuika (69) — *Gliha (82)*

11/6/95 **ESTONIA** (1) **1** **SLOVENIA** (1) **3** 2000
Reim (26) — *Novak (38, 69), Zahovic (79)*

6/9/95 **ITALY** (1) **1** **SLOVENIA** (0) **0** 30000
Ravanelli (13)

11/10/95 **SLOVENIA** (0) **3** **UKRAINE** (2) **2** 11000
Udovic (50, 90), Zahovic (73) — *Skrypnyk (24), Guseinov (44)*

15/11/95 **SLOVENIA** (1) **1** **CROATIA** (1) **2** 10000
Gliha (36) — *Suker (41), Jurcevic (55)*

SPAIN

1958/60 SERIES

First Round

28/6/59 **POLAND** (1) **2** **SPAIN** (2) **4** 71000
Pol, Brychczy — *Di Stefano (2), Suarez (2)*

14/10/59 **SPAIN** (1) **3** **POLAND** (0) **0** 62000
Di Stefano, Gensana, Gento

Second Round

USSR WALKOVER SPAIN (WITHDREW)

1962/64 SERIES

First Round

1/11/62 **SPAIN** (4) **6** **ROMANIA** (0) **0** 51700
Guillot (3), Veloso, Collar, Macri (Og)

25/11/62 **ROMANIA** (2) **3** **SPAIN** (0) **1** 72800
Manolache (2), Tataru — *Veloso*

Second Round

30/5/63 **SPAIN** (0) **1** **NORTHERN IRELAND** (0) **1** 28000
Rivilla — *W. Irvine*

30/10/63 **NORTHERN IRELAND** (0) **0** **SPAIN** (0) **1** 45900
Gento

Quarter-Finals

11/3/64 **SPAIN** (4) **5** **EIRE** (1) **1** 27200
Amancio (2), Marcellino (2), Fuste — *McEvoy*

8/4/64 **EIRE** (0) **0** **SPAIN** (1) **2** 38100
Zaballa (2)

Semi-Final

17/6/64 **SPAIN** (1) **2** **HUNGARY** (0) **1** 50000 Madrid
Pereda, Amancio — *Bene*

Final

21/6/64 **SPAIN** (1) **2** **USSR** (1) **1** 120000 Madrid
Pereda, Marcelino — *Khusainev*

1966/68 SERIES

GROUP MATCHES - GROUP 1

23/10/66 **EIRE** (0) **0** **SPAIN** (0) **0** 38000

7/12/66 **SPAIN** (2) **2** **EIRE** (0) **0** 25000
Garcia, Pirri

1/2/67 **TURKEY** (0) **0** **SPAIN** (0) **0** 35000

31/5/67 **SPAIN** (0) **2** **TURKEY** (0) **0** 40000
Grosso, Gento

1/10/67 **CZECHOSLOVAKIA** (0) **1** **SPAIN** (0) **0** 40000
Horvath

22/10/67 **SPAIN** (1) **2** **CZECHOSLOVAKIA** (0) **1** 40000
Pirri, Garate — *Kuna*

Quarter-Finals

3/4/68 **ENGLAND** (0) **1** **SPAIN** (0) **0** 100000
R. Charlton

8/5/68 **SPAIN** (0) **1** **ENGLAND** (0) **2** 120000
Amancio — *Peters, Hunter*

1970/72 SERIES

GROUP MATCHES - GROUP 4

11/11/70 **SPAIN** (1) **3** **NORTHERN IRELAND** (0) **0** 48000
Rexach, Pirri, Luis

9/5/71 **CYPRUS** (0) **0** **SPAIN** (1) **2** 10000
Pirri, Violeta

30/5/71 **USSR** (0) **2** **SPAIN** (0) **1** 100000
Kolotov, Schevtschenko — *Rexach*

27/10/71 **SPAIN** (0) **0** **USSR** (0) **0** 58000

24/11/71 **SPAIN** (3) **7** **CYPRUS** (0) **0** 20000
Pirri (2, 1 Pen), Quino (2), Aquillar, Loro, Rojo

16/2/72 **NORTHERN IRELAND** (0) **1** **SPAIN** (1) **1** 19925
Morgan — *Rojo*

1974/76 SERIES

GROUP MATCHES - GROUP 4

25/9/74 **DENMARK** (0) **1** **SPAIN** (2) **2** 27300
Nygaard (Pen) — *Claramunt (Pen), Martinez*

20/11/74 **SCOTLAND** (1) **1** **SPAIN** (1) **2** 92000
Bremner — *Quini (2)*

5/2/75 **SPAIN** (0) **1** **SCOTLAND** (1) **1** 60000
Megido — *Jordan*

17/4/75 **SPAIN** (1) **1** **ROMANIA** (0) **1** 100000
Velazquez — *Crisan*

12/10/75 **SPAIN** (1) **2** **DENMARK** (0) **0** 20000
Pirri, Capon

16/11/75 **ROMANIA** (0) **2** **SPAIN** (1) **2** 50000
Georgeescu (Pen), Jordanescu — *Villar, Santillana*

Quarter-Finals

24/4/76 **SPAIN** (1) **1** **WEST GERMANY** (0) **1** 63000
Santillana — *Beer*

22/5/76 **WEST GERMANY** (2) **2** **SPAIN** (0) **0** 77600
Hoeness, Toppmoller

1978/80 SERIES

GROUP MATCHES - GROUP 3

4/10/78 **YUGOSLAVIA** (1) **1** **SPAIN** (2) **2** 55000
Halihodzic (44) — *Juanito (20), Santillana (32)*

15/11/78 **SPAIN** (1) **1** **ROMANIA** (0) **0** 46000
Asensi (9)

13/12/78 **SPAIN** (2) **5** **CYPRUS** (0) **0** 17500
Asensi (9), Delbosque (10), Santillana (52, 77), Ruben Cano (65)

4/4/79 **ROMANIA** (0) **2** **SPAIN** (0) **2** 40000
Georgescu ((Pen, 57), 65) — *Dani (59, 70)*

10/10/79 **SPAIN** (0) **0** **YUGOSLAVIA** (1) **1** 40000
Surjak (5)

9/12/79 **CYPRUS** (0) **1** **SPAIN** (2) **3** 15000
Vrahimis (69) — *Villar (5), Santillana (41), Saura (89)*

FINALS - GROUP 2

12/6/80 **SPAIN** (0) **0** **ITALY** (0) **0** 55000

15/6/80 **SPAIN** (1) **1** **BELGIUM** (1) **2** 11000
Quini (35) — *Gerets (17), Cools (64)*

18/6/80 **SPAIN** (0) **1** **ENGLAND** (1) **2** 14440
Dani (Pen, 48) — *Brooking (18), Woodcock (62)*

1982/84 SERIES

GROUP MATCHES - GROUP 7

27/10/82 **SPAIN** .... (0) **1** **ICELAND** .... (0) **0** 25000
Pedraza (59)

17/11/82 **EIRE** .... (1) **3** **SPAIN** .... (1) **3** 39000
Grimes (2), Stapleton (64, 76) — *Maceda (31), Martin (Og. 47), Victor (60)*

17/2/83 **SPAIN** .... (1) **1** **HOLLAND** .... (0) **0** 45000
Senor (Pen, 43)

27/4/83 **SPAIN** .... (0) **2** **EIRE** .... (0) **0** 45000
Santillana (51), Rincon (89)

15/5/83 **MALTA** .... (1) **2** **SPAIN** .... (1) **3** 11000
Busuttil (30, 47) — *Senor (23), Carrasco (60), Gordillo (85)*

29/5/83 **ICELAND** .... (0) **0** **SPAIN** .... (1) **1** 10000
Maceda (9)

16/11/83 **HOLLAND** .... (1) **2** **SPAIN** .... (1) **1** 58000
Houtman (26), Gullit (63) — *Santillana (41)*

21/12/83 **SPAIN** .... (3) **12** **MALTA** .... (1) **1** 25000
Santillana (16, 26, 29, 76), Rincon (47, 57, 64, 78), Maceda (62, 63), Sarabia (80), Senor (86) — *Degiorgio (24)*

FINALS - GROUP 2

14/6/84 **SPAIN** .... (1) **2** **ROMANIA** .... (1) **1** 15000
Carrasco (Pen, 20) — *Boloni (34)*

17/6/84 **PORTUGAL** .... (0) **1** **SPAIN** .... (0) **1** 30000
Sousa (51) — *Santillana (72)*

20/6/84 **WEST GERMANY** ..... (0) **0** **SPAIN** .... (0) **1** 40000
Maceda (89)

Semi-Final

24/6/84 **SPAIN** .... (0) **1** **DENMARK** .... (1) **1** 48000 Lyon
Maceda (66) — *Lerby (6)*

(After Extra Time)

SPAIN WON 5-4 ON PENALTIES

Final

27/6/84 **FRANCE** .... (0) **2** **SPAIN** .... (0) **0** 47368 Paris
Platini (56), Bellone (90)

1986/88 SERIES

GROUP MATCHES - GROUP 1

12/11/86 **SPAIN** .... (0) **1** **ROMANIA** .... (0) **0** 47500
Michel (57)

3/12/86 **ALBANIA** .... (1) **1** **SPAIN** .... (0) **2** 20000
Muca (27) — *Arteche (66), Joaquin (83)*

1/4/87 **AUSTRIA** .... (1) **2** **SPAIN** .... (1) **3** 41000
Linzmaier (39), Polster (64) — *Eloy (31, 58), Carrasco (89)*

29/4/87 **ROMANIA** .... (3) **3** **SPAIN** .... (0) **1** 30000
Piturca (37), Mateut (45), Ungureanu (48) — *Caldere (81)*

14/10/87 **SPAIN** .... (0) **2** **AUSTRIA** .... (0) **0** 70410
Michel (Pen, 58), Sanchis (63)

18/11/87 **SPAIN** .... (3) **5** **ALBANIA** .... (0) **0** 50000
Baquero (5, 31, 74), Michel (Pen, 36), Llorente (67)

FINALS - GROUP 1

11/6/88 **DENMARK** .... (1) **2** **SPAIN** .... (1) **3** 60000
Laudrup (25), Povlsen (85) — *Michel (5), Butragueno (52), Gordillo (67)*

14/6/88 **ITALY** .... (0) **1** **SPAIN** .... (0) **0** 51790
Vialli (73)

17/6/88 **WEST GERMANY** ..... (1) **2** **SPAIN** .... (0) **0** 72308
Voller (30, 51)

1990/92 SERIES

GROUP MATCHES - GROUP 1

10/10/90 **SPAIN** .... (1) **2** **ICELAND** .... (0) **1** 46000
Butragueno (44), Carlos (63) — *Jonsson (66)*

14/11/90 **CZECHOSLOVAKIA** .... (1) **3** **SPAIN** .... (1) **2** 35000
Danek (16, 67), Moravcik (77) — *Roberto (30), Carlos (55)*

19/12/90 **SPAIN** .... (4) **9** **ALBANIA** .... (0) **0** 27600
Amor (9), Carlos (22, 63), Butragueno (30, 57, 66, 75), Hierro (37), Baquero (86)

20/2/91 **FRANCE** .... (1) **3** **SPAIN** .... (1) **1** 45000
Sauzee (15), Papin (58), Blanc (77) — *Baquero (11)*

25/9/91 **ICELAND** .... (0) **2** **SPAIN** .... (0) **0** 8900
Orlygsson (71), Sverrisson (79)

12/10/91 **SPAIN** .... (1) **1** **FRANCE** .... (2) **2** 27500
Abelardo (34) — *Fernandez (13)*

13/11/91 **SPAIN** .... (1) **2** **CZECHOSLOVAKIA** ... (0) **1** 24500
Abelardo (10), Michel (pen 79) — *Nemecek (59)*

18/12/91 **ALBANIA** vs **SPAIN** - Cancelled

1994/96 SERIES

GROUP MATCHES - GROUP 2

7/9/94 **CYPRUS** .... (1) **1** **SPAIN** .... (2) **2** 10000
Soteriou (36) — *Higueras (15, 25)*

12/10/94 **MACEDONIA** .... (0) **0** **SPAIN** .... (2) **2** 30000
Salinas (16, 25)

16/11/94 **SPAIN** .... (1) **3** **DENMARK** .... (0) **0** 38000
Nadal (41), Donato (57), Luiz Enrique (87)

17/12/94 **BELGIUM** .... (1) **1** **SPAIN** .... (1) **4** 21000
Degryse (6) — *Hierro (29), Donato (Pen, 56), Salinas (68), Luis Enrique (89)*

29/3/95 **SPAIN** .... (1) **1** **BELGIUM** .... (1) **1** 27000
Guerrero (24) — *Degryse (26)*

26/4/95 **ARMENIA** .... (0) **0** **SPAIN** .... (0) **2** 40000
Amavisca (49), Goikoetxea (63)

7/6/95 **SPAIN** .... (0) **1** **ARMENIA** .... (0) **0** 17000
Hierro (Pen, 64)

6/9/95 **SPAIN** .... (1) **6** **CYPRUS** .... (0) **0** 16000
Guerrero (45), Alfonso (51), Pizzi (75, 80), Hierro (78), Caminero (83)

11/10/95 **DENMARK** .... (0) **1** **SPAIN** .... (1) **1** 40260
Vilfort (47) — *Hierro (Pen, 17)*

15/11/95 **SPAIN** .... (1) **3** **MACEDONIA** .... (0) **0** 21350
Narvaez (8), Manjarin (73), Caminero (79)

SWEDEN

1962/64 SERIES

First Round

21/6/62 **NORWAY** .... (0) **0** **SWEDEN** .... (2) **2** 28551
Martinsson (2)

4/11/62 **SWEDEN** .... (0) **1** **NORWAY** .... (0) **1** 8726
Eriksson — *Krogh*

Second Round

19/6/63 **YUGOSLAVIA** .... (0) **0** **SWEDEN** .... (0) **0** 25100

19/9/63 **SWEDEN** .... (1) **3** **YUGOSLAVIA** .... (1) **2** 20300
Persson (2), Bild — *Zambata, Galic*

Quarter-Finals

13/5/64 **SWEDEN** .... (0) **1** **USSR** .... (0) **1** 37000
Hamrin — *Ivanov*

27/5/64 **USSR** .... (1) **3** **SWEDEN** .... (0) **1** 99700
Ponedelnik (2), Voronin — *Hamrin*

1966/68 SERIES

GROUP MATCHES - GROUP 2

13/11/66 **PORTUGAL** .... (1) **1** **SWEDEN** .... (1) **2** 20000
Graca — *Danielsson (2)*

1/6/67 **SWEDEN** .... (0) **1** **PORTUGAL** .... (1) **1** 49689
Svensson — *Pinto*

11/6/67 **SWEDEN** .... (0) **0** **BULGARIA** .... (1) **2** 24271
Jekov, Dermendjiev

3/9/67 **NORWAY** .... (1) **3** **SWEDEN** .... (1) **1** 32000
Berg (2), Birjeland — *Nordahl*

5/11/67 **SWEDEN** .... (2) **5** **NORWAY** .... (0) **2** 14000
Turesson (2), Eriksson (2), Danielsson — *Iversen (Pen), Hasund*

12/11/67 **BULGARIA** .... (2) **3** **SWEDEN** .... (0) **0** 35000
Kotkov, Mitkov, Asparoukov

1970/72 SERIES

GROUP MATCHES - GROUP 6

14/10/70 **EIRE** .... (1) **1** **SWEDEN** .... (0) **1** 30000
Carroll (Pen) — *Brzokoupil*

28/10/70 **SWEDEN** .... (0) **1** **EIRE** .... (0) **0** 12000
Turesson

26/5/71 **SWEDEN** .... (0) **1** **AUSTRIA** .... (0) **0** 10000
Olsson

9/6/71 **SWEDEN** .... (0) **0** **ITALY** .... (0) **0** 40000

5/9/71 **AUSTRIA** .... (1) **1** **SWEDEN** .... (0) **0** 42000
Stering

10/10/71 **ITALY** .... (2) **3** **SWEDEN** .... (0) **0** 70000
Riva (2), Boninsegna

1974/76 SERIES
GROUP MATCHES - GROUP 3

30/10/74 **SWEDEN** .... (0) **0** **NORTHERN IRELAND** . (2) **2** 16657
Nicholl, O'Neill

4/6/75 **SWEDEN** .... (1) **1** **YUGOSLAVIA** .... (1) **2** 27250
Edstrom — *Katalinski, Ivejic*

30/6/75 **SWEDEN** .... (1) **3** **NORWAY** .... (0) **1** 9580
Nordahl (2), Grahn (Pen) — *Olsen (Pen)*

13/8/75 **NORWAY** .... (0) **0** **SWEDEN** .... (1) **2** 18000
Jandberg, Andersson

3/9/75 **NORTHERN IRELAND** .. (1) **1** **SWEDEN** .... (1) **2** 12000
Hunter — *Sjoberg, Torstensson*

15/10/75 **YUGOSLAVIA** .... (1) **3** **SWEDEN** .... (0) **0** 45000
Oblak, Vladic, Vebec

1978/80 SERIES
GROUP MATCHES - GROUP 5

2/9/78 **FRANCE** .... (0) **2** **SWEDEN** .... (0) **2** 44703
Berdoll (72), Six (83) — *Nordgren (54), L. Larsson (90)*

4/10/78 **SWEDEN** .... (1) **1** **CZECHOSLOVAKIA** .... (1) **3** 12000
Borg (Pen, 15) — *Kroupa (17), Masny (47), Nehoda (85)*

7/6/79 **SWEDEN** .... (2) **3** **LUXEMBOURG** .... (0) **0** 7300
Gronhagen (15), Cervin (29), Borg (Pen, 54)

5/9/79 **SWEDEN** .... (1) **1** **FRANCE** .... (1) **3** 14395
Backe (24) — *Lacombe (14), Platini (55), Battiston (71)*

10/10/79 **CZECHOSLOVAKIA** .... (3) **4** **SWEDEN** .... (0) **1** 35000
Nehoda (20), Kozak (34), Visek (41, 78) — *Jan Svensson*

23/10/79 **LUXEMBOURG** .... (1) **1** **SWEDEN** .... (0) **1** 2000
Braun (Pen, 5) — *Gronehagen (63)*

1982/84 SERIES
GROUP MATCHES - GROUP 5

8/9/82 **ROMANIA** .... (1) **2** **SWEDEN** .... (0) **0** 60000
Andone (25), Klein (52)

6/10/82 **CZECHOSLOVAKIA** .... (0) **2** **SWEDEN** .... (0) **2** 17500
Janecka (48, 53) — *Jingblad (88), Eriksson (89)*

13/11/82 **CYPRUS** .... (0) **0** **SWEDEN** .... (1) **1** 3000
Corneliusson (34)

15/5/83 **SWEDEN** .... (0) **5** **CYPRUS** .... (0) **0** 19801
Prytz (52, 75), Corneliusson (57), Hysen (60), A. Ravelli (71)

29/5/83 **SWEDEN** .... (1) **2** **ITALY** .... (0) **0** 35000
Sandberg (31), Stromberg (56)

9/6/83 **SWEDEN** .... (0) **0** **ROMANIA** .... (1) **1** 31474
Camataru (29)

21/9/83 **SWEDEN** .... (1) **1** **CZECHOSLOVAKIA** .... (0) **0** 22000
Corneliusson (14)

15/10/83 **ITALY** .... (0) **0** **SWEDEN** .... (2) **3** 69086
Stromberg (20, 27), Sunesson (71)

1986/88 SERIES
GROUP MATCHES - GROUP 2

24/9/86 **SWEDEN** .... (1) **2** **SWITZERLAND** .... (0) **0** 27751
Ekstrom (19, 79)

12/10/86 **PORTUGAL** .... (0) **1** **SWEDEN** .... (0) **1** 15000
Coelho (66) — *Stromberg (50)*

16/11/86 **MALTA** .... (0) **0** **SWEDEN** .... (1) **5** 15000
Hysen (38), Magnusson (67), Fredriksson (69), Ekstrom (81), Palmer (84)

24/8/87 **SWEDEN** .... (1) **1** **MALTA** .... (0) **0** 16165
Ekstrom (13)

3/6/87 **SWEDEN** .... (1) **1** **ITALY** .... (0) **0** 40000
P. Larsson (25)

17/6/87 **SWITZERLAND** .... (0) **1** **SWEDEN** .... (0) **1** 7000
Halter (58) — *Ekstrom (60)*

23/9/87 **SWEDEN** .... (0) **0** **PORTUGAL** .... (1) **1** 28916
Gomes

14/11/87 **ITALY** .... (2) **2** **SWEDEN** .... (1) **1** 65000
Vialli (27, 45) — *Larsson (38)*

1990/92 SERIES

Sweden Qualified as Hosts

FINALS - GROUP 1

10/6/92 **SWEDEN** .... (1) **1** **FRANCE** .... (0) **1** 29000
Eriksson (24) — *Papin (58)*

14/6/92 **SWEDEN** .... (0) **1** **DENMARK** .... (0) **0** 29902
Brolin (58)

17/6/92 **SWEDEN** .... (0) **2** **ENGLAND** .... (1) **1** 30126
Eriksson (51), Brolin (82) — *Platt (3)*

Semi-final

21/6/92 **SWEDEN** .... (0) **2** **GERMANY** .... (1) **3** 28827
Brolin (pen 64), Andersson (89) — *Hassler (10), Riedle (58, 88)*

1994/96 SERIES
GROUP MATCHES - GROUP 3

7/9/94 **ICELAND** .... (0) **0** **SWEDEN** .... (1) **1** 12000
Ingesson (36)

12/10/94 **SWITZERLAND** .... (1) **4** **SWEDEN** .... (1) **2** 24000
Ohrel (36), Sforza (79), Turkyilmaz (80), Blomqvist (Og, 63) — *K. Andersson (4), Dahlin (61)*

16/11/94 **SWEDEN** .... (1) **2** **HUNGARY** .... (0) **0** 27571
Brolin (44), Dahlin (70)

29/3/95 **TURKEY** .... (0) **2** **SWEDEN** .... (1) **1** 25000
Emre Asik (64), Sergen Yalcin (75) — *K. Andersson (Pen, 23)*

26/4/95 **HUNGARY** .... (1) **1** **SWEDEN** .... (0) **0** 8000
Halmai (2)

1/6/95 **SWEDEN** .... (1) **1** **ICELAND** .... (1) **1** 26676
Brolin (Pen, 16) — *A. Gunnlaugsson (3)*

6/9/95 **SWEDEN** .... (0) **0** **SWITZERLAND** ...... (0) **0** 18500

15/11/95 **SWEDEN** .... (1) **2** **TURKEY** .... (0) **2** 16350
Alexandersson (24), Pettersen (63) — *Hakan (62), Ertugrul (72)*

SWITZERLAND

1962/64 SERIES

First Round

11/11/62 **HOLLAND** .... (1) **3** **SWITZERLAND** ...... (1) **1** 60000
Van Der Linden, Swart, Groot — *Hertig*

31/3/63 **SWITZERLAND** .... (0) **1** **HOLLAND** .... (1) **1** 31800
Allemann — *Kruijver*

1966/68 SERIES
GROUP MATCHES - GROUP 6

2/11/66 **ROMANIA** .... (4) **4** **SWITZERLAND** ...... (0) **2** 30000
Dridea (3), Fratila — *Kunzli, Odermatt*

24/5/67 **SWITZERLAND** .... (3) **7** **ROMANIA** .... (0) **1** 23000
Kunzli (2), Quentin (2), Blattler (2), Odermatt — *Dobrin*

8/11/67 **SWITZERLAND** .... (2) **5** **CYPRUS** .... (0) **0** 4000
Blattler (2), Kunzli, Durr, Odermatt

18/11/67 **SWITZERLAND** .... (1) **2** **ITALY** .... (0) **2** 57000
Quentin, Kunzli — *Riva (2)*

23/12/67 **ITALY** .... (3) **4** **SWITZERLAND** ...... (0) **0** 28000
Mazzola (2), Riva, Domenghini

17/2/68 **CYPRUS** .... (1) **2** **SWITZERLAND** ...... (0) **1** 8000
Melis, Bamboulis — *Odermatt*

1970/72 SERIES
GROUP MATCHES - GROUP 3

16/12/70 **GREECE** .... (0) **0** **SWITZERLAND** ...... (0) **1** 38000
Muller

20/12/70 **MALTA** .... (0) **1** **SWITZERLAND** ...... (0) **2** 8000
Theobald (Pen) — *Quentin, Kunzli*

21/4/71 **SWITZERLAND** .... (4) **5** **MALTA** .... (0) **0** 18000
Blattler, Kunzli, Quentin, Citherlet, Muller

12/5/71 **SWITZERLAND** .... (0) **1** **GREECE** .... (0) **0** 37000
Odermatt

13/10/71 **SWITZERLAND** .... (2) **2** **ENGLAND** .... (2) **3** 55000
Jeandupeux, Kunzli — *Hurst, Chivers, Wiebel (Og)*

10/11/71 **ENGLAND** .... (1) **1** **SWITZERLAND** ...... (1) **1** 100000
Summerbee — *Odermatt*

1974/76 SERIES
GROUP MATCHES - GROUP 6

1/12/74 **TURKEY** .... (1) **3** **SWITZERLAND** ...... (1) **1** 51410
Ismail, Buyuk, Mehmet — *Schild*

30/4/75 **SWITZERLAND** .... (1) **1** **TURKEY** .... (0) **1** 23000
Muller — *Alpasian*

11/5/75 **EIRE** .... (2) **2** **SWITZERLAND** ...... (0) **1** 50000
Martin, Treacy — *Muller*

21/5/75 **SWITZERLAND** .... (0) **1** **EIRE** .... (0) **0** 15000
Elsener

12/10/75 **SWITZERLAND** .... (0) **0** **USSR** .... (0) **1** 18000
Muntjan

12/11/75 **USSR** .... (2) **4** **SWITZERLAND** ...... (1) **1** 40000
Konkov, Onischenko (2), Veremejev — *Risi*

1978/80 SERIES
GROUP MATCHES - GROUP 4

11/10/78 **SWITZERLAND** (1) **1** **HOLLAND** (1) **3** 23000
Tanner (29) — *Wildschut (19), Brandts (65), Geels (89)*

15/11/78 **POLAND** (1) **2** **SWITZERLAND** (0) **0** 45000
Boniek (30), Ogaza (57)

28/3/79 **HOLLAND** (0) **3** **SWITZERLAND** (0) **0** 27000
Kist (55), Metgod (84), Peters (89)

5/5/79 **SWITZERLAND** (0) **0** **EAST GERMANY** (1) **2** 9000
Lindemann (44), Streich (89)

22/5/79 **SWITZERLAND** (1) **2** **ICELAND** (0) **0** 25000
Herbert Hermann (27), Zappa (53)

9/6/79 **ICELAND** (0) **1** **SWITZERLAND** (0) **2** 10400
Gudlaugsson (50) — *Ponte (58), Heinz Hermann (61)*

12/9/79 **SWITZERLAND** (0) **0** **POLAND** (1) **2** 25000
Terlecki (34, 63)

13/10/79 **EAST GERMANY** (3) **5** **SWITZERLAND** (1) **2** 45000
Weber (1), Haffmann (9, 75, 85), Schnuphase (26) — *Barberis (19), Pfister (72)*

1982/84 SERIES
GROUP MATCHES - GROUP 1

6/10/82 **BELGIUM** (1) **3** **SWITZERLAND** (0) **0** 16808
Ludi (Og, 2), Coeck (48), Van Den Bergh (82)

17/11/82 **SWITZERLAND** (0) **2** **SCOTLAND** (0) **0** 30500
Sulser (50), Egli (60)

30/3/83 **SCOTLAND** (0) **2** **SWITZERLAND** (1) **2** 36923
Wark (70), Nicholas (75) — *Egli (15), Hermann (58)*

14/5/83 **SWITZERLAND** (0) **0** **EAST GERMANY** (0) **0** 32000

12/10/83 **EAST GERMANY** (1) **3** **SWITZERLAND** (0) **0** 12000
Richter (44), Ernst (73), Streich (89)

9/11/83 **SWITZERLAND** (1) **3** **BELGIUM** (0) **1** 10000
Schallibaum (24), Brigger (76), Geiger (82) — *Van Den Bergh (64)*

1986/88 SERIES
GROUP MATCHES - GROUP 2

24/9/86 **SWEDEN** (1) **2** **SWITZERLAND** (0) **0** 27751
Ekstrom (19, 79)

29/10/86 **SWITZERLAND** (1) **1** **PORTUGAL** (0) **1** 11000
Bergy (6) — *Fernandes (86)*

15/11/86 **ITALY** (1) **3** **SWITZERLAND** (1) **2** 75000
Donadoni (1), Altobelli (52, 85) — *Brigger (31), Weber (89)*

15/4/87 **SWITZERLAND** (3) **4** **MALTA** (0) **1** 5000
Egli (5), Bregy (16, (Pen, 38), 87) — *Busuttil (71)*

17/6/87 **SWITZERLAND** (0) **1** **SWEDEN** (0) **1** 7000
Halter (58) — *Ekstrom (60)*

17/10/87 **SWITZERLAND** (0) **0** **ITALY** (0) **0** 35000

11/11/87 **PORTUGAL** (0) **0** **SWITZERLAND** (0) **0** 12500

15/11/87 **MALTA** (0) **1** **SWITZERLAND** (1) **1** 5000
Busuttil (89) — *Zwicker (3)*

1990/92 SERIES
GROUP MATCHES - GROUP 2

12/9/90 **SWITZERLAND** (1) **2** **BULGARIA** (0) **0** 12500
Hottiger (19), Bickel (63)

17/10/90 **SCOTLAND** (1) **2** **SWITZERLAND** (0) **1** 27740
Robertson (pen 34), McAllister (53) — *Knup (pen 66)*

14/11/90 **SAN MARINO** (0) **0** **SWITZERLAND** (3) **4** 931
Sutter (7), Chapuisat (27), Knup (43), Chassot (87)

3/4/91 **SWITZERLAND** (0) **0** **ROMANIA** (0) **0** 16000

1/5/91 **BULGARIA** (2) **2** **SWITZERLAND** (0) **3** 55000
Kostadinov (11), Sirakov (25) — *Knup (58, 88), Turkyilmaz (90)*

5/6/91 **SWITZERLAND** (3) **7** **SAN MARINO** (0) **0** 12000
Knup (3, 87), Hottiger (13), Sutter (29) Hermann (55), Ohrel (78), Turkyilmaz (90)

11/9/91 **SWITZERLAND** (2) **2** **SCOTLAND** (0) **2** 48000
Chapuisat (30), Hermann (39) — *Durie (47), McCoist (83)*

13/11/91 **ROMANIA** (0) **1** **SWITZERLAND** (0) **0** 35000
Mateut (72)

1994/96 SERIES
GROUP MATCHES - GROUP 3

12/10/94 **SWITZERLAND** (1) **4** **SWEDEN** (1) **2** 24000
Ohrel (36), Sforza (79), Turkyilmaz (80), Blomqvist (Og, 63) — *K. Andersson (4), Dahlin (61)*

16/11/94 **SWITZERLAND** (1) **1** **ICELAND** (0) **0** 15800
Bickel (45)

14/12/94 **TURKEY** (1) **1** **SWITZERLAND** (2) **2** 30000
Recep Cetin (40) — *Koller (7), Bickel (16)*

29/3/95 **HUNGARY** (0) **2** **SWITZERLAND** (0) **2** 15000
Kiprich (51), Illes (70) — *Subiat (72, 84)*

26/4/95 **SWITZERLAND** (1) **1** **TURKEY** (1) **2** 24000
Hottiger (38) — *Hakan (17), Temizkanoglu (54)*

16/8/95 **ICELAND** (0) **0** **SWITZERLAND** (2) **2** 9034
Knup (3), Turkyilmaz (13)

6/9/95 **SWEDEN** (0) **0** **SWITZERLAND** (0) **0** 18500

11/10/95 **SWITZERLAND** (1) **3** **HUNGARY** (0) **0** 20000
Turkyilmaz (23), Sforza (56), Ohrel (89)

TURKEY

1958/60 SERIES

First Round

2/11/58 **ROMANIA** (0) **3** **TURKEY** (0) **0** 67000
Oaida, Constantin, Dinulescu

26/4/59 **TURKEY** (1) **2** **ROMANIA** (0) **0** 24000
Lefter (2, 1 Pen)

1962/64 SERIES

First Round

2/12/62 **ITALY** (4) **6** **TURKEY** (0) **0** 26600
Orlando (4), Rivera (2)

27/2/63 **TURKEY** (0) **0** **ITALY** (0) **1** 27300
Somani

1966/68 SERIES
GROUP MATCHES - GROUP 1

16/11/66 **EIRE** (0) **2** **TURKEY** (0) **1** 20000
O'Neill, McEvoy — *Ogun*

1/2/67 **TURKEY** (0) **0** **SPAIN** (0) **0** 35000

22/2/67 **TURKEY** (1) **2** **EIRE** (0) **1** 35000
Ayhan, Ogun — *Cantwell*

31/5/67 **SPAIN** (0) **2** **TURKEY** (0) **0** 40000
Grosso, Gento

18/6/67 **CZECHOSLOVAKIA** (1) **3** **TURKEY** (0) **0** 20000
Adamec (2), Jurkanin

15/11/67 **TURKEY** (0) **0** **CZECHOSLOVAKIA** (0) **0** 52000

1970/72 SERIES
GROUP MATCHES - GROUP 8

18/10/70 **WEST GERMANY** (1) **1** **TURKEY** (1) **1** 53000
Muller (Pen) — *Kamarun*

9/12/70 **TURKEY** (2) **2** **ALBANIA** (1) **1** 45000
Metin, Cemil — *Ziu*

25/4/71 **TURKEY** (0) **0** **WEST GERMANY** (1) **3** 45000
Muller (2), Koppel

22/9/71 **POLAND** (1) **5** **TURKEY** (0) **1** 40000
Bula, Lubanski (3), Gadocha — *Nihat*

4/11/71 **ALBANIA** (1) **3** **TURKEY** (0) **0** 15000
Pernaska (2), Pano

5/12/71 **TURKEY** (0) **1** **POLAND** (0) **0** 70000
Cemil

1974/76 SERIES
GROUP MATCHES - GROUP 6

20/11/74 **TURKEY** (0) **1** **EIRE** (0) **1** 67000
Conroy (Og) — *Givens*

1/12/74 **TURKEY** (1) **2** **SWITZERLAND** (1) **1** 51410
Ismail, Buyuk Mehmet — *Schild*

2/4/75 **USSR** (1) **3** **TURKEY** (0) **0** 100000
Kolotov (2), Blokhin

30/4/75 **SWITZERLAND** (1) **1** **TURKEY** (0) **1** 23000
Muller — *Alpasian*

29/10/75 **EIRE** (3) **4** **TURKEY** (0) **0** 25000
Givens (4)

23/11/75 **TURKEY** (1) **1** **USSR** (0) **0** 80000
Cemil

1978/80 SERIES
GROUP MATCHES - GROUP 7

29/11/78 **WALES** (0) **1** **TURKEY** (0) **0** 11794
Deacy (67)

18/3/79 **TURKEY** (1) **2** **MALTA** (0) **1** 30000
Sedat (34), Fatih (56) — *Spiteri-Gonzi (54)*

1/4/79 **TURKEY** .... (0) **0** **WEST GERMANY** ..... (0) **0** 50000

28/10/79 **MALTA** .... (0) **1** **TURKEY** .... (2) **2** 5000
Lelifarrugia (62) — *Sedat (17), Mustafa (30)*

21/11/79 **TURKEY** .... (0) **1** **WALES** .... (0) **0** 50000
Onal (79)

22/12/79 **WEST GERMANY** ..... (1) **2** **TURKEY** .... (0) **0** 73000
Fischer (16), Zimmermann (89)

1982/84 SERIES

GROUP MATCHES - GROUP 6

27/10/82 **TURKEY** .... (0) **1** **ALBANIA** .... (0) **0** 35000
Arif (86)

17/11/82 **AUSTRIA** .... (3) **4** **TURKEY** .... (0) **0** 10500
Polster (10), Pezzey (34), Prohaska (Pen, 36), Schachner (54)

30/3/83 **NORTHERN IRELAND** .. (2) **2** **TURKEY** .... (0) **1** 20000
M. O'Neill (5), McClelland (17) — *Hassan (55)*

23/4/83 **TURKEY** .... (0) **0** **WEST GERMANY** ..... (2) **3** 75000
Rummenigge ((Pen, 31), 71), Dremmlet (35)

11/5/83 **ALBANIA** .... (0) **1** **TURKEY** .... (1) **1** 30000
Rashit (Og, 73) — *Metin (34)*

12/10/83 **TURKEY** .... (1) **1** **NORTHERN IRELAND** . (0) **0** 38000
Selcuk (17)

26/10/83 **WEST GERMANY** ..... (1) **5** **TURKEY** .... (0) **1** 35000
Voller (44, 65), Rummenigge (61, (Pen, 75), Stielike (66) — *Hassan (67)*

16/11/83 **TURKEY** .... (0) **3** **AUSTRIA** .... (0) **1** 30000
Ilyas (62), Selcuk (69, (Pen, 76)) — *Baumeister (71)*

1986/88 SERIES

GROUP MATCHES - GROUP 4

29/10/86 **YUGOSLAVIA** .... (2) **4** **TURKEY** .... (0) **0** 15000
Zlatko Vujovic (25, 35, 84), Savicevic (75)

12/11/86 **TURKEY** .... (0) **0** **NORTHERN IRELAND** . (0) **0** 25000

29/4/87 **TURKEY** .... (0) **0** **ENGLAND** .... (0) **0** 25000

14/10/87 **ENGLAND** .... (4) **8** **TURKEY** .... (0) **0** 42528
Barnes (1, 28), Lineker (8, 42, 71), Robson (59), Beardsley (62), Webb (88)

11/11/87 **NORTHERN IRELAND** .. (0) **1** **TURKEY** .... (0) **0** 5000
Quinn (47)

16/12/87 **TURKEY** .... (0) **2** **YUGOSLAVIA** .... (2) **3** 10000
Yusuf (68), Feyyaz (73) — *Radanovic (5), Katanec (40), Hadzibegic (Pen, 54)*

1990/92 SERIES

GROUP MATCHES - GROUP 7

17/10/90 **EIRE** .... (2) **5** **TURKEY** .... (0) **0** 46000
Aldridge (15, 58, 73), O'Leary (40), Quinn (66)

14/11/90 **TURKEY** .... (0) **0** **POLAND** .... (1) **1** 25000
Dziekanowski (37)

17/4/91 **POLAND** .... (0) **3** **TURKEY** .... (0) **0** 1500
Tarasiewicz (75), Urban (81), Kosecki (88)

1/5/91 **TURKEY** .... (0) **0** **ENGLAND** .... (1) **1** 25000
Wise (32)

16/10/91 **ENGLAND** .... (1) **1** **TURKEY** .... (0) **0** 50896
Smith (21)

13/11/91 **TURKEY** .... (1) **1** **EIRE** .... (1) **3** 42000
Riza (pen 12) — *Byrne (7, 58), Cascarino (55)*

1994/96 SERIES

GROUP MATCHES - GROUP 3

7/9/94 **HUNGARY** .... (2) **2** **TURKEY** .... (0) **2** 20000
Kiprich (5), Halmai (45) — *Hakan (65), Bulent (71)*

12/10/94 **TURKEY** .... (3) **5** **ICELAND** .... (0) **0** 20000
Saffet (11, 28), Hakan (30, 62), Sergen (65)

14/12/94 **TURKEY** .... (1) **1** **SWITZERLAND** .... (2) **2** 30000
Recep Cetin (40) — *Koller (7), Bickel (16)*

29/3/95 **TURKEY** .... (0) **2** **SWEDEN** .... (1) **1** 25000
Emre Asik (64), Sergen Yalcin (75) — *K. Andersson (Pen, 23)*

26/4/95 **SWITZERLAND** .... (1) **1** **TURKEY** .... (1) **2** 24000
Hottiger (38) — *Hakan (17), Temizkanoglu (54)*

6/9/95 **TURKEY** .... (2) **2** **HUNGARY** .... (0) **0** 30000
Hakan (9, 31)

11/10/95 **ICELAND** .... (0) **0** **TURKEY** .... (0) **0** 2308

15/11/95 **SWEDEN** .... (1) **2** **TURKEY** .... (0) **2** 16350
Alexandersson (24), Pettersen (63) — *Hakan (62), Ertugrul (72)*

UKRAINE

1994/96 SERIES

GROUP MATCHES - GROUP 4

7/9/94 **UKRAINE** .... (0) **0** **LITHUANIA** .... (0) **2** 25000
Ivanauskas (53), Skarbalius (61)

12/10/94 **UKRAINE** .... (0) **0** **SLOVENIA** .... (0) **0** 12000

13/11/94 **UKRAINE** .... (2) **3** **ESTONIA** .... (0) **0** 500
Konovalov (30), Kirs (Og, 45), Guseinov (76)

25/3/95 **CROATIA** .... (2) **4** **UKRAINE** .... (0) **0** 25000
Boban (13), Suker (21, 76), Prosinecki (70)

29/3/95 **UKRAINE** .... (0) **0** **ITALY** .... (2) **2** 20000
Lombardo (12), Zola (38)

26/4/95 **ESTONIA** .... (0) **0** **UKRAINE** .... (1) **1** 1600
Guseinov (16)

11/6/95 **UKRAINE** .... (1) **1** **CROATIA** .... (0) **0** 10000
Kalitvintsev (13)

6/9/95 **LITHUANIA** .... (1) **1** **UKRAINE** .... (0) **3** 11500
Maciulevicius (16) — *Huseinov (66, 71), Gusin (84)*

11/10/95 **SLOVENIA** .... (0) **3** **UKRAINE** .... (2) **2** 11000
Udovic (50, 90), Zahovic (73) — *Skrypnyk (24), Guseinov (44)*

11/11/95 **ITALY** .... (1) **3** **UKRAINE** .... (1) **1** 44000
Ravanelli (21, 48), Maldini (54) — *Polunin (19)*

USSR

1958/60 SERIES

First Round

28/9/58 **USSR** .... (3) **3** **HUNGARY** .... (0) **1** 100572
Ilyin, Metreveli, Ivanov — *Gorocs*

27/9/59 **HUNGARY** .... (0) **0** **USSR** .... (0) **1** 78000
Voinov

Quarter-Finals

USSR WALK OVER SPAIN (WITHDREW)

Semi-Final

6/7/60 **USSR** .... (1) **3** **CZECHOSLOVAKIA** .... (0) **0** 25184 Marseille
Ivanov (2), Ponedelnik

Final

10/7/60 **USSR** .... (0) **2** **YUGOSLAVIA** .... (1) **1** 17966
Metreveli, Ponedelnik — *Galic*

(After Extra Time)

1962/64 SERIES

First Round

USSR RECEIVED A BYE

Second Round

13/10/63 **USSR** .... (2) **2** **ITALY** .... (0) **0** 102400
Ponedelnik, Chislenko

10/11/63 **ITALY** .... (0) **1** **USSR** .... (1) **1** 69600
Rivera — *Gusarov*

Quarter-Finals

13/5/64 **SWEDEN** .... (0) **1** **USSR** .... (0) **1** 37000
Hamrin — *Ivanov*

27/5/64 **USSR** .... (1) **3** **SWEDEN** .... (0) **1** 99700
Ponedelnik (2), Voronin — *Hamrin*

Semi-Final

17/6/64 **USSR** .... (2) **3** **DENMARK** .... (0) **0** 38000 Barcelona
Voronin, Ponedelnik, Ivanov

Final

21/6/64 **SPAIN** .... (1) **2** **USSR** .... (1) **1** 120000 Madrid
Pereda, Marcelino — *Khusainev*

1966/68 SERIES

GROUP MATCHES - GROUP 3

10/6/67 **USSR** .... (3) **4** **AUSTRIA** .... (1) **3** 103000
Malafeev, Byshovets, Chislenko, Streltzov — *Hof, Wolny, Sieber*

16/7/67 **USSR** .... (0) **4** **GREECE** .... (0) **0** 45000
Banischevsky (2), Sabo, Chislenko

30/8/67 **USSR** .... (1) **2** **FINLAND** .... (0) **0** 20597
Khurtsilava, Chislenko

6/9/67 **FINLAND** (2) **2** **USSR** (3) **5** 7793
Peltonen, Kilponen — *Sabo (2), Masslov, Banischevsky, Malafeev*

15/10/67 **AUSTRIA** (0) **1** **USSR** (0) **0** 37400
Grausam

31/10/67 **GREECE** (0) **0** **USSR** (0) **1** 40000
Chislenko

Quarter-Finals

4/5/68 **HUNGARY** (1) **2** **USSR** (0) **0** 80000
Farkas, Gorocs

11/5/68 **USSR** (1) **3** **HUNGARY** (0) **0** 103000
Solymosi (Og), Khurtsilava, Byshovets

Semi-Final

5/6/68 **ITALY** (0) **0** **USSR** (0) **0** 70000 Naples

ITALY WON ON TOSS OF COIN

Third Place Match

8/6/68 **ENGLAND** (1) **2** **USSR** (0) **0** 50000 Rome
R. Charlton, Hurst

1970/72 SERIES
GROUP MATCHES - GROUP 4

15/11/71 **CYPRUS** (1) **1** **USSR** (2) **3** 8000
Charalambos — *Kolotov, Evryuzhikhin, Sherchenko*

30/5/71 **USSR** (0) **2** **SPAIN** (0) **1** 100000
Kolotov, Schevtschenko — *Rexach*

7/6/71 **USSR** (3) **6** **CYPRUS** (0) **1** 50000
Fedotov (2), Evryuzhikhin (2), Kolotov, Banischevsky — *Mikail*

22/9/71 **USSR** (1) **1** **NORTHERN IRELAND** (0) **0** 100000
Muntjan (Pen)

13/10/71 **NORTHERN IRELAND** (1) **1** **USSR** (1) **1** 15000
Nicholson — *Byshovets*

27/10/71 **SPAIN** (0) **0** **USSR** (0) **0** 58000

Quarter-Finals

29/4/72 **YUGOSLAVIA** (0) **0** **USSR** (0) **0** 95000

13/5/72 **USSR** (0) **3** **YUGOSLAVIA** (0) **0** 103000
Kolotov, Banischevsky, Kozinkevich

Semi-Final

14/6/72 **USSR** (0) **1** **HUNGARY** (0) **0** 3500 Brussels
Konkov

Final

18/6/72 **WEST GERMANY** (1) **3** **USSR** (0) **0** 43437 Brussels
Muller (2), Wimmer

1974/76 SERIES
GROUP MATCHES - GROUP 6

30/10/74 **EIRE** (2) **3** **USSR** (0) **0** 32000
Givens (3)

2/4/75 **USSR** (1) **3** **TURKEY** (0) **0** 100000
Kolotov (2), Blokhin

18/5/75 **USSR** (2) **2** **EIRE** (0) **1** 100000
Blokhin, Kolotov — *Hand*

12/10/75 **SWITZERLAND** (0) **0** **USSR** (0) **1** 18000
Muntjan

12/11/75 **USSR** (2) **4** **SWITZERLAND** (1) **1** 40000
Konkov, Onischenko (2), Veremejev — *Risi*

23/11/75 **TURKEY** (1) **1** **USSR** (0) **0** 80000
Cemil

Quarter-Finals

24/4/76 **CZECHOSLOVAKIA** (1) **2** **USSR** (0) **0** 52000
Moder, Panenka

22/5/76 **USSR** (0) **2** **CZECHOSLOVAKIA** (1) **2** 100000
Burjak, Blokhin — *Moder (2)*

1978/80 SERIES
GROUP MATCHES - GROUP 6

20/9/78 **USSR** (1) **2** **GREECE** (0) **0** 55000
Chesnokov (20), Bessonov (53)

11/10/78 **HUNGARY** (1) **2** **USSR** (0) **0** 40000
Varadi (26), Szokolai (58)

19/5/79 **USSR** (1) **2** **HUNGARY** (1) **2** 80000
Chesnokov (23), Shengelia (75) — *Tatar (33), Pusztai (63)*

4/7/79 **FINLAND** (0) **1** **USSR** (1) **1** 12000
Ismail Atik (55) — *Khapsalis (25)*

12/9/79 **GREECE** (1) **1** **USSR** (0) **0** 25000
Nikoloudis (25)

31/10/79 **USSR** (0) **2** **FINLAND** (0) **2** 1000
Andreyev (50), Gavrilov (68) — *Himanka (75), Haskivi (82)*

1982/84 SERIES
GROUP MATCHES - GROUP 2

13/10/82 **USSR** (1) **2** **FINLAND** (0) **0** 20000
Baltacha (2), Andreyev (59)

27/4/83 **USSR** (2) **5** **PORTUGAL** (0) **0** 100000
Cherenkov (18, 64), Rodionov (40), Demianenko (50), Lorianov (87)

22/5/83 **POLAND** (1) **1** **USSR** (0) **1** 75000
Boniek (20) — *Wojcicki (Og, 63)*

1/6/83 **FINLAND** (0) **0** **USSR** (1) **1** 16996
Blokhin (75)

9/10/83 **USSR** (1) **2** **POLAND** (0) **0** 72500
Demianenko (10), Blokhin (62)

13/11/83 **PORTUGAL** (1) **1** **USSR** (0) **0** 70000
Jordao (Pen, 44)

1986/88 SERIES
GROUP MATCHES - GROUP 3

24/9/86 **ICELAND** (1) **1** **USSR** (1) **1** 7000
Gudjohnsen (29) — *Sulakvelidze (44)*

11/10/86 **FRANCE** (0) **0** **USSR** (0) **2** 40496
Belanov (67), Rats (73)

29/10/86 **USSR** (3) **4** **NORWAY** (0) **0** 35000
Litovchenko (25), Belanov (Pen, 27), Blokhin, Khidiatulin (52)

29/4/87 **USSR** (1) **2** **EAST GERMANY** (0) **0** 95000
Zavarov (41), Belanov (49)

3/6/87 **NORWAY** (0) **0** **USSR** (1) **1** 10473
Zavarov (15)

9/9/87 **USSR** (0) **1** **FRANCE** (1) **1** 100000
Mikhailichenko (77) — *Toure (13)*

10/10/87 **EAST GERMANY** (1) **1** **USSR** (0) **1** 25000
Kirsten (44) — *Aleinikov (80)*

28/10/87 **USSR** (1) **2** **ICELAND** (0) **0** 40000
Belanov (15), Protasov (50)

FINALS - GROUP 2

12/6/88 **HOLLAND** (0) **0** **USSR** (0) **1** 60000
Rats (53)

15/6/88 **EIRE** (1) **1** **USSR** (0) **1** 52000
Whelan (38) — *Protasov (74)*

18/6/88 **ENGLAND** (1) **1** **USSR** (2) **3** 53000
Adams (16) — *Aleinikov (3), Mikhailichenko (28), Pasulko (72)*

Semi-Final

22/6/88 **USSR** (0) **2** **ITALY** (0) **0** 70000
Litovchenko (59), Protasov (62)

Final

25/6/88 **HOLLAND** (1) **2** **USSR** (0) **0** 72308
Gullit (32), Van Basten (53)

1990/92 SERIES
GROUP MATCHES - GROUP 3

12/9/90 **USSR** (1) **2** **NORWAY** (0) **0** 23000
Kanchelskis (22), Kuznetsov (60)

3/11/90 **ITALY** (0) **0** **USSR** (0) **0** 52500

17/4/91 **HUNGARY** (0) **0** **USSR** (1) **1** 40000
Mikhailichenko (30)

29/5/91 **USSR** (1) **4** **CYPRUS** (0) **0** 20000
Mostovoi (29), Mikhailichenko (51), Korneyev (84), Aleinikov (88)

28/8/91 **NORWAY** (0) **0** **USSR** (0) **1** 25427
Mostovoi (74)

25/9/91 **USSR** (1) **2** **HUNGARY** (1) **2** 50000
Shalimov (pen 37), Kanchelskis (50) — *Kiprich (16, 84)*

12/10/91 **USSR** (0) **0** **ITALY** (0) **0** 92000

13/11/91 **CYPRUS** (0) **0** **USSR** (1) **3** 4000
Protasov (27), Yuran (79), Kanchelskis (82)

FINALS - GROUP 2

USSR - changed name to CIS (Confederation of Independent States) following the breakup of the union and played the Final Series under that title.

12/6/92 **CIS** (0) **1** **GERMANY** (0) **1** 17410
Dobrovolsky (pen 62) — *Hassler (89)*

15/6/92 **HOLLAND** (0) **0** **CIS** (0) **0** 34440

18/6/92 **SCOTLAND** (2) **3** **CIS** (0) **0** 14660
McStay (6), McClair (17), McAllister (pen 83)

WALES

1962/64 SERIES

First Round

7/11/62 **HUNGARY** (2) **3** **WALES** (1) **1** 35000
Albert, Tichy, Sandor — *Medwin*

20/3/63 **WALES** (1) **1** **HUNGARY** (0) **1** 30300
Jones (Pen) — *Tichy (Pen)*

1966/68 SERIES
GROUP MATCHES - GROUP 8

22/10/66 **WALES** (0) **1** **SCOTLAND** (0) **1** 32500
R. Davies — *Law*

16/11/66 **ENGLAND** (3) **5** **WALES** (1) **1** 76000
Hurst (2), J. Charlton, R. Charlton, Hennessey (Og) — *W. Davies*

12/4/67 **NORTHERN IRELAND** (0) **0** **WALES** (0) **0** 17000

21/10/67 **WALES** (0) **0** **ENGLAND** (1) **3** 45000
Peters, R. Charlton, Ball

22/11/67 **SCOTLAND** (1) **3** **WALES** (1) **2** 57000
Gilzean (2), McKinnon — *R. Davies, Durban*

28/2/68 **WALES** (0) **2** **NORTHERN IRELAND** (0) **0** 17500
Rees, W. Davies

1970/72 SERIES
GROUP MATCHES - GROUP 1

11/11/70 **WALES** (0) **0** **ROMANIA** (0) **0** 20000

21/4/71 **WALES** (0) **1** **CZECHOSLOVAKIA** (0) **3** 20000
R. Davies (Pen) — *Capkovic (2), Taborsky*

26/5/71 **FINLAND** (0) **0** **WALES** (0) **1** 6000
Toshack

13/10/71 **WALES** (1) **3** **FINLAND** (0) **0** 10000
Durban, Toshack, Reece

27/10/71 **CZECHOSLOVAKIA** (0) **1** **WALES** (0) **0** 32000
Kuna

24/11/71 **ROMANIA** (1) **2** **WALES** (0) **0** 70000
Lupescu, Lucescu

1974/76 SERIES
GROUP MATCHES - GROUP 2

4/9/74 **AUSTRIA** (0) **2** **WALES** (1) **1** 35000
Kreuz, Krankl — *Griffiths*

30/10/74 **WALES** (0) **2** **HUNGARY** (0) **0** 8445
Griffiths, Toshack

20/11/74 **WALES** (1) **5** **LUXEMBOURG** (0) **0** 10530
Toshack, England, Roberts, Griffiths, Yorath

16/4/75 **HUNGARY** (0) **1** **WALES** (1) **2** 35000
Branikovits — *Toshack, Mahoney*

1/5/75 **LUXEMBOURG** (1) **1** **WALES** (2) **3** 5000
Phillipp (Pen) — *Reece, James (2)*

19/11/75 **WALES** (1) **1** **AUSTRIA** (0) **0** 30000
Griffiths

Quarter-Finals

24/4/76 **YUGOSLAVIA** (1) **2** **WALES** (0) **0** 55000
Vukotic, Popivoda

22/5/76 **WALES** (1) **1** **YUGOSLAVIA** (1) **1** 30000
Evans — *Katalinski (Pen)*

1978/80 SERIES
GROUP MATCHES - GROUP 7

25/10/78 **WALES** (3) **7** **MALTA** (0) **0** 11475
O' Sullivan (19), Edwards (22, 50, 53), Thomas (69), Flynn (72)

29/11/78 **WALES** (0) **1** **TURKEY** (0) **0** 11794
Deacy (67)

2/5/79 **WALES** (0) **0** **WEST GERMANY** (1) **2** 30000
Zimmermann (29), Fischer (52)

2/6/79 **MALTA** (0) **0** **WALES** (1) **2** 9000
Nicholas (15), Flynn (50)

17/10/79 **WEST GERMANY** (4) **5** **WALES** (0) **1** 60000
Fischer (22, 39), Kaltz (33), Rummenigge (42), Forster (82) — *Curtis (83)*

21/11/79 **TURKEY** (0) **1** **WALES** (0) **0** 50000
Onal (79)

1982/84 SERIES
GROUP MATCHES - GROUP 4

22/9/82 **WALES** (1) **1** **NORWAY** (0) **0** 4340
Nygard (Og, 31)

15/12/82 **YUGOSLAVIA** (3) **4** **WALES** (2) **4** 20000
Cvetkovic (14), Zivkov (17), Kranjcar (36), Jesic (66) — *Flynn (5), Rush (39), Jones (70), R. James (80)*

27/4/83 **WALES** (0) **1** **BULGARIA** (0) **0** 9006
Charles (79)

21/9/83 **NORWAY** (0) **0** **WALES** (0) **0** 17575

16/11/83 **BULGARIA** (0) **1** **WALES** (0) **0** 8000
Gochev (54)

14/12/83 **WALES** (0) **1** **YUGOSLAVIA** (0) **1** 24000
James (54) — *Bazdarevic (80)*

1986/88 SERIES
GROUP MATCHES - GROUP 6

10/9/86 **FINLAND** (1) **1** **WALES** (0) **1** 9840
Hjelm (11) — *Slatter (68)*

1/4/87 **WALES** (2) **4** **FINLAND** (0) **0** 7696
Rush, Hodges, Phillips (64), Andy Jones

29/4/87 **WALES** (0) **1** **CZECHOSLOVAKIA** (0) **1** 14150
Rush (83) — *Knoflicek (74)*

9/9/87 **WALES** (1) **1** **DENMARK** (0) **0** 20535
Hughes (19)

14/10/87 **DENMARK** (0) **1** **WALES** (0) **0** 44500
Elkjaer (49)

11/11/87 **CZECHOSLOVAKIA** (1) **2** **WALES** (0) **0** 6443
Knoflicek (32), Bilek (89)

1990/92 SERIES
GROUP MATCHES - GROUP 5

17/10/90 **WALES** (1) **3** **BELGIUM** (1) **1** 12000
Rush (29), Saunders (86), Hughes (88) — *Versavel (24)*

14/11/90 **LUXEMBOURG** (0) **0** **WALES** (0) **1** 7000
Rush (15)

27/3/91 **BELGIUM** (0) **1** **WALES** (0) **1** 27500
Degryse (47) — *Saunders (58)*

5/6/91 **WALES** (0) **1** **GERMANY** (0) **0** 38000
Rush (66)

16/10/91 **GERMANY** (3) **4** **WALES** (0) **1** 46000
Moller (4), Voller (38), Riedle (45), Doll (72) — *Bodin (pen 83)*

13/11/91 **WALES** (0) **1** **LUXEMBOURG** (0) **0** 20000
Bodin (pen 82)

1994/96 SERIES
GROUP MATCHES - GROUP 7

7/9/94 **WALES** (1) **2** **ALBANIA** (0) **0** 6500
Coleman (9), Giggs (67)

12/10/94 **MOLDOVA** (2) **3** **WALES** (1) **2** 12000
Belovs (9), Seku (29), Pogorelov (79) — *Speed (6), Blake (70)*

16/11/94 **GEORGIA** (2) **5** **WALES** (0) **0** 45000
Ketsbaya (31, 49), Kinkladze (41), Goglichigani (59), Arveladze (67)

14/12/94 **WALES** (0) **0** **BULGARIA** (2) **3** 20000
Ivanov (5), Kostadinov (15), Stoichkov (51)

29/3/95 **BULGARIA** (1) **3** **WALES** (1) **1** 65000
Balakov (37), Penev (70, 82) — *Saunders (83)*

26/4/95 **GERMANY** (1) **1** **WALES** (1) **1** 43461
Herrlich (42) — *Saunders (8)*

7/6/95 **WALES** (0) **0** **GEORGIA** (1) **1** 6500
Kinkladze (73)

6/9/95 **WALES** (0) **1** **MOLDOVA** (0) **0** 5000
Speed (55)

11/10/95 **WALES** (0) **1** **GERMANY** (0) **2** 25000
Helmer (Og, 78) — *Melville (Og, 75), Klinsmann (80)*

15/11/95 **ALBANIA** (1) **1** **WALES** (1) **1** 5500
Kushta (Pen, 4) — *Pembridge (43)*

WEST GERMANY

1966/68 SERIES
GROUP MATCHES - GROUP 4

9/4/67 **WEST GERMANY** ..... (2) **6** **ALBANIA** .... (0) **0** 30000
Muller (4), Lohr (2)

3/5/67 **YUGOSLAVIA** .... (0) **1** **WEST GERMANY** ..... (0) **0** 50000
Skoblar

7/10/67 **WEST GERMANY** ..... (1) **3** **YUGOSLAVIA** .... (0) **1** 72000
Lohr, Muller, Seeler — *Zambata*

17/12/67 **ALBANIA** .... (0) **0** **WEST GERMANY** ..... (0) **0** 21889

1970/72 SERIES
GROUP MATCHES - GROUP 8

18/10/70 **WEST GERMANY** ..... (1) **1** **TURKEY** .... (1) **1** 53000
Muller (Pen) — *Kamarun*

17/2/71 **ALBANIA** .... (0) **0** **WEST GERMANY** ..... (1) **1** 20000
Muller

25/4/71 **TURKEY** .... (0) **0** **WEST GERMANY** ..... (1) **3** 45000
Muller (2), Koppel

12/6/71 **WEST GERMANY** ..... (2) **2** **ALBANIA** .... (0) **0** 46000
Netzer, Grabowski

10/10/71 **POLAND** .... (1) **1** **WEST GERMANY** ..... (1) **3** 100000
Gadocha — *Muller (2), Grabowski*

17/11/71 **WEST GERMANY** ..... (0) **0** **POLAND** .... (0) **0** 62000

Quarter-Finals

29/4/72 **ENGLAND** .... (0) **1** **WEST GERMANY** ..... (1) **3** 100000
Lee — *Hoeness, Netzer (Pen), Muller*

13/5/72 **WEST GERMANY** ..... (0) **0** **ENGLAND** .... (0) **0** 72000

Semi-Final

14/6/72 **WEST GERMANY** ..... (1) **2** **BELGIUM** .... (0) **1** 60000 Antwerp
Muller (2) — *Polleunis*

Final

18/6/72 **WEST GERMANY** ..... (1) **3** **USSR** .... (0) **0** 43437 Brussels
Muller (2), Wimmer

1974/76 SERIES
GROUP MATCHES - GROUP 8

20/11/74 **GREECE** .... (1) **2** **WEST GERMANY** ..... (0) **2** 11000
Delikaris, Eleftherakis — *Cullmann, Wimmer*

29/12/74 **MALTA** .... (0) **0** **WEST GERMANY** ..... (1) **1** 12535
Cullmann

27/4/75 **BULGARIA** .... (0) **1** **WEST GERMANY** ..... (0) **1** 50000
Kolev (Pen) — *Ritschel (Pen)*

11/10/75 **WEST GERMANY** ..... (0) **1** **GREECE** .... (0) **1** 65000
Heynckes — *Delikaris*

19/11/75 **WEST GERMANY** ..... (0) **1** **BULGARIA** .... (0) **0** 73000
Heynckes

28/2/76 **WEST GERMANY** ..... (4) **8** **MALTA** .... (0) **0** 54000
Worm (2), Heynckes (2), Beers (2), Holzenbein, Vogts

Quarter-Finals

24/4/76 **SPAIN** .... (1) **1** **WEST GERMANY** ..... (0) **1** 63000
Santillana — *Beer*

22/5/76 **WEST GERMANY** ..... (2) **2** **SPAIN** .... (0) **0** 77600
Hoeness, Toppmoller

Semi-Final

17/6/76 **WEST GERMANY** ..... (0) **4** **YUGOSLAVIA** .... (2) **2** 75000 Belgrade
Holzenbein, Muller (3) — *Popivoda, Dzajic*

(After Extra Time)

Final

20/6/76 **CZECHOSLOVAKIA** .... (2) **2** **WEST GERMANY** ..... (1) **2** 45000 Belgrade
Svehlik, Dobias — *Muller, Holzenbein*

(After Extra Time)

CZECHOSLOVAKIA WON 5-3 ON PENALTIES

1978/80 SERIES
GROUP MATCHES - GROUP 7

25/2/79 **MALTA** .... (0) **0** **WEST GERMANY** ..... (0) **0** 13000

1/4/79 **TURKEY** .... (0) **0** **WEST GERMANY** .... (0) **0** 500

2/5/79 **WALES** .... (0) **0** **WEST GERMANY** .... (1) **2** 300
Zimmermann (29), Fischer (52)

17/10/79 **WEST GERMANY** .... (4) **5** **WALES** .... (0) **1** 600
Fischer (22, 39), Kaltz (33), Rummenigge (42), Forster (82) — *Curtis (83)*

22/12/79 **WEST GERMANY** .... (1) **2** **TURKEY** .... (0) **0** 730
Fischer (16), Zimmermann (89)

27/2/80 **WEST GERMANY** .... (3) **8** **MALTA** .... (0) **0** 380
K. Allofs (14, 55), Bonhof (Pen, 19), Fischer (40, 89), Holland (Og, 61), Kelsch (70), Rummenigge (74)

FINALS - GROUP 1

11/6/80 **WEST GERMANY** .... (0) **1** **CZECHOSLOVAKIA** ... (0) **0** 150
Rummenigge (55)

14/6/80 **WEST GERMANY** .... (1) **3** **HOLLAND** .... (0) **2** 500
Allofs (15, 60, 67) — *Rep (Pen, 65), W. Van Der Kerkhof (86)*

17/6/80 **WEST GERMANY** .... (0) **0** **GREECE** .... (0) **0** 139

Final

22/6/80 **WEST GERMANY** .... (1) **2** **BELGIUM** .... (0) **1** 4786 Rom
Hrubesch (10, 89) — *Van Der Eychen (Pen, 71)*

1982/84 SERIES
GROUP MATCHES - GROUP 6

17/11/82 **NORTHERN IRELAND** . (1) **1** **WEST GERMANY** .... (0) **0** 3000
Stewart (18)

30/3/83 **ALBANIA** .... (0) **1** **WEST GERMANY** .... (0) **2** 3000
Targaj (Pen, 81) — *Voeller (54), Rummenigge (Pen, 67)*

23/4/83 **TURKEY** .... (0) **0** **WEST GERMANY** .... (2) **3** 7500
Rummenigge ((Pen, 31), 71), Dremmlet (35)

27/4/83 **AUSTRIA** .... (0) **0** **WEST GERMANY** .... (0) **0** 6000

5/10/83 **WEST GERMANY** .... (3) **3** **AUSTRIA** .... (0) **0** 7000
Rummenigge (4), Voller (19, 21)

26/10/83 **WEST GERMANY** .... (1) **5** **TURKEY** .... (0) **1** 4000
Voller (44, 65), Rummenigge (61, (Pen, 75)), Stielike (66) — *Hassan (67)*

16/11/83 **WEST GERMANY** .... (0) **0** **NORTHERN IRELAND** . (0) **1** 61418
Whiteside (50)

20/11/83 **WEST GERMANY** .... (1) **2** **ALBANIA** .... (1) **1** 40000
Rummenigge (24), Strack (80) — *Tomori (23)*

FINALS - GROUP 1

14/6/84 **WEST GERMANY** .... (0) **0** **PORTUGAL** .... (0) **0** 47950

17/6/84 **WEST GERMANY** .... (1) **2** **ROMANIA** .... (0) **1** 35000
Voller (24, 65) — *Coras (46)*

20/6/84 **WEST GERMANY** .... (0) **0** **SPAIN** .... (0) **1** 40000
Maceda (89)

1986/88 SERIES
FINALS - GROUP 1

10/6/88 **WEST GERMANY** .... (0) **1** **ITALY** .... (0) **1** 68400
Brehme (55) — *Mancini (51)*

14/6/88 **WEST GERMANY** .... (1) **2** **DENMARK** .... (0) **0** 70000
Klinsmann (9), Thon (85)

17/6/88 **WEST GERMANY** .... (1) **2** **SPAIN** .... (0) **0** 72308
Voller (30, 51)

Semi-Final

21/6/88 **WEST GERMANY** .... (0) **1** **HOLLAND** .... (0) **2** 60000 Hamburg
Matthaus (Pen, 54) — *R. Koeman (Pen, 73), Van Basten (88)*

YUGOSLAVIA

1958/60 SERIES

First Round

31/5/59 **YUGOSLAVIA** .... (1) **2** **BULGARIA** .... (0) **0** 40000
Galic, Tasic

25/10/59 **BULGARIA** .... (0) **1** **YUGOSLAVIA** .... (0) **1** 45000
Diev — *Mujic*

Quarter-Finals

8/5/60 **PORTUGAL** .... (1) **2** **YUGOSLAVIA** .... (0) **1** 50000
Santana, Matateu — *Kostic*

22/5/60 **YUGOSLAVIA** .... (2) **5** **PORTUGAL** .... (1) **1** 55000
Kostic (2), Sekularac, Cebinac, Galic — *Cavem*

Semi-Finals

6/7/60 **YUGOSLAVIA** (1) **5** **FRANCE** (2) **4** 26370 Paris
Jerkovic (2), Galic, Zanetic, Knez — *Vincent, Heutte (2), Wisnieski*

Final

10/7/60 **USSR** (0) **2** **YUGOSLAVIA** (1) **1** 17966 Paris
Metreveli, Ponedelnik — *Galic*

1962/64 SERIES

First Round

4/11/62 **YUGOSLAVIA** (2) **3** **BELGIUM** (2) **2** 25500
Skoblar (2), Vasovic — *Stockman, Jurion*

31/3/63 **BELGIUM** (0) **0** **YUGOSLAVIA** (1) **1** 24600
Samardzic

Second Round

10/6/63 **YUGOSLAVIA** (0) **0** **SWEDEN** (0) **0** 25100

19/9/63 **SWEDEN** (1) **3** **YUGOSLAVIA** (1) **2** 20300
Persson (2), Bild — *Zambata, Galic*

1966/68 SERIES

GROUP MATCHES - GROUP 4

3/5/67 **YUGOSLAVIA** (0) **1** **WEST GERMANY** (0) **0** 50000
Skoblar

14/5/67 **ALBANIA** (0) **0** **YUGOSLAVIA** (1) **2** 35000
Zambata (2)

7/10/67 **WEST GERMANY** (1) **3** **YUGOSLAVIA** (0) **1** 72000
Lohr, Muller, Seeler — *Zambata*

12/11/67 **YUGOSLAVIA** (1) **4** **ALBANIA** (0) **0** 30000
Sprecic, Osim (2), Lazarevic

Quarter-Finals

6/4/68 **FRANCE** (0) **1** **YUGOSLAVIA** (0) **1** 45000
Di Nallo — *Musemic*

24/4/68 **YUGOSLAVIA** (4) **5** **FRANCE** (1) **1** 47747
Petkovic (2), Musemic (2), Dzajic — *Di Nallo*

Semi-Final

5/6/68 **YUGOSLAVIA** (0) **1** **ENGLAND** (0) **0** 21834 Florence
Dzajic

Final

8/6/68 **ITALY** (0) **1** **YUGOSLAVIA** (1) **1** 88000 Rome
Domenghini — *Dzajic*

Final Replay

10/6/68 **ITALY** (2) **2** **YUGOSLAVIA** (0) **0** 70000 Rome
Riva, Anastasi

1970/72 SERIES

GROUP MATCHES - GROUP 7

11/10/70 **HOLLAND** (0) **1** **YUGOSLAVIA** (1) **1** 60000
Israel (Pen) — *Dzajic*

5/4/71 **YUGOSLAVIA** (1) **2** **HOLLAND** (0) **0** 20000
Jerkovic, Dzajic

9/5/71 **EAST GERMANY** (0) **1** **YUGOSLAVIA** (2) **2** 100000
Lowe — *Filipovic, Dzajic*

8/10/71 **LUXEMBOURG** (0) **0** **YUGOSLAVIA** (1) **2** 9000
Bukal (2)

17/10/71 **YUGOSLAVIA** (0) **0** **EAST GERMANY** (0) **0** 4000

27/10/71 **YUGOSLAVIA** (0) **0** **LUXEMBOURG** (0) **0** 20000

Quarter-Finals

29/4/72 **YUGOSLAVIA** (0) **0** **USSR** (0) **0** 95000

13/5/72 **USSR** (0) **3** **YUGOSLAVIA** (0) **0** 103000
Kolotov, Banischevsky, Kozinkevich

1974/76 SERIES

GROUP MATCHES - GROUP 3

30/10/74 **YUGOSLAVIA** (1) **2** **NORWAY** (1) **1** 12000
Vukotic, Katalinski — *Lund*

16/3/75 **NORTHERN IRELAND** (1) **1** **YUGOSLAVIA** (0) **0** 30000
Hamilton

4/6/75 **SWEDEN** (1) **1** **YUGOSLAVIA** (1) **2** 27250
Edstrom — *Katalinski, Ivejic*

9/6/75 **NORWAY** (0) **1** **YUGOSLAVIA** (3) **3** 25000
Thunberg — *Buljan, Bogicevic, Surjak*

15/10/75 **YUGOSLAVIA** (1) **3** **SWEDEN** (0) **0** 45000
Oblak, Vladic, Vebec

19/11/75 **YUGOSLAVIA** (1) **1** **NORTHERN IRELAND** (0) **0** 30000
Oblak

Quarter-Finals

24/4/76 **YUGOSLAVIA** (1) **2** **WALES** (0) **0** 55000
Vukotic, Popivoda

22/5/76 **WALES** (1) **1** **YUGOSLAVIA** (1) **1** 30000
Evans — *Katalinski (Pen)*

Semi-Final

17/6/76 **WEST GERMANY** (0) **4** **YUGOSLAVIA** (2) **2** 75000 Belgrade
Holzenbein, Muller (3) — *Popivoda, Dzajic*

Third Place Match

19/6/76 **HOLLAND** (2) **3** **YUGOSLAVIA** (1) **2** 18000
Geels (2), Van Der Kerkhof — *Katalinski, Dzajic*
(After Extra Time)

1978/80 SERIES

GROUP MATCHES - GROUP 3

4/10/78 **YUGOSLAVIA** (1) **1** **SPAIN** (2) **2** 55000
Halilhodzic (44) — *Juanito (20), Santillana (32)*

25/10/78 **ROMANIA** (0) **3** **YUGOSLAVIA** (1) **2** 25000
Sames (62, 68), Jordanescu (Pen, 75) — *Petrovic (Pen, 22), Desnica (90)*

1/4/79 **CYPRUS** (0) **0** **YUGOSLAVIA** (1) **3** 4500
Vujovic (40, 79), Surjak (82)

10/10/79 **SPAIN** (0) **0** **YUGOSLAVIA** (1) **1** 40000
Surjak (5)

31/10/79 **YUGOSLAVIA** (0) **2** **ROMANIA** (0) **1** 35000
Vujovic (48), Sliskovic (50) — *Radacanu (79)*

14/11/79 **YUGOSLAVIA** (1) **5** **CYPRUS** (0) **0** 22500
Kranjcar (32, 50), Vujovic (60), Petrovic (75), Savic (87)

1982/84 SERIES

GROUP MATCHES - GROUP 4

13/10/82 **NORWAY** (1) **3** **YUGOSLAVIA** (0) **1** 12264
Lund (5), Oekland (69), Hareide (89) — *Savic (74)*

17/11/82 **BULGARIA** (0) **0** **YUGOSLAVIA** (1) **1** 25000
Stojkovic (36)

15/12/82 **YUGOSLAVIA** (3) **4** **WALES** (2) **4** 20000
Cvetkovic (14), Zivkov (17), Kranjcar (36), Jesic (66) — *Flynn (5), Rush (39), Jones (70), R. James (80)*

12/10/83 **WALES** (2) **2** **NORWAY** (0) **1** 12500
Zlatko Vujovic (21), Susic (40) — *Thoresen (88)*

14/12/83 **WALES** (0) **1** **YUGOSLAVIA** (0) **1** 24000
James (54) — *Bazdarevic (80)*

21/12/83 **YUGOSLAVIA** (1) **3** **BULGARIA** (1) **2** 37500
Susic (30, 52), Radanovic (90) — *Iskrenov (28), Dimitrov (60)*

FINALS - GROUP 1

13/6/84 **BELGIUM** (2) **2** **YUGOSLAVIA** (0) **0** 45000
Van Den Bergh (27), Grun (44)

16/6/84 **DENMARK** (2) **5** **YUGOSLAVIA** (0) **0** 25000
Ivkovic (Og, 7), Berggren (16), Arnesen (Pen, 68), Elkjaer (81), Lauridsen (83)

19/6/84 **FRANCE** (0) **3** **YUGOSLAVIA** (1) **2** 50000
Platini (59, 61, 76) — *Sestic (31), D. Stojkovic (Pen, 80)*

1986/88 SERIES

GROUP MATCHES - GROUP 4

29/10/86 **YUGOSLAVIA** (2) **4** **TURKEY** (0) **0** 15000
Zlatko Vujovic (25, 35, 84), Savicevic (75)

12/11/86 **ENGLAND** (1) **2** **YUGOSLAVIA** (0) **0** 60000
Mabbutt (21), Anderson (57)

29/4/87 **NORTHERN IRELAND** (1) **1** **YUGOSLAVIA** (0) **2** 5000
Clarke (39) — *Stojkovic (48), Zlatko Vujovic (79)*

14/10/87 **YUGOSLAVIA** (2) **3** **NORTHERN IRELAND** (0) **0** 22500
Vokrri (13, 35), Hadzibegic (Pen, 73)

11/11/87 **YUGOSLAVIA** (0) **1** **ENGLAND** (4) **4** 70000
Katanec (80) — *Beardsley (4), Barnes (17), Robson (20), Adams (25)*

16/12/87 **TURKEY** (0) **2** **YUGOSLAVIA** (2) **3** 10000
Yusuf (68), Feyyaz (73) — *Radanovic (5), Katanec (40), Hadzibegic (Pen, 54)*

1990/92 SERIES

GROUP MATCHES - GROUP 4

Date	Home			Away			Att.
12/9/90	**N. IRELAND**	(0)	**0**	**YUGOSLAVIA**	(1)	**2**	10000
				Pancev (36), Prosinecki (86)			
31/10/90	**YUGOSLAVIA**	(2)	**4**	**AUSTRIA**	(1)	**1**	17500
	Pancev (32, 52, 85), Katanec (43)			*Ogris (15)*			
14/11/90	**DENMARK**	(0)	**0**	**YUGOSLAVIA**	(0)	**2**	39700
				Bazdarevic (77), Jarni (84)			
27/3/91	**YUGOSLAVIA**	(1)	**4**	**N. IRELAND**	(1)	**1**	26000
	Binic (35), Pancev (40, 60, 61)			*Hill (45)*			
1/5/91	**YUGOSLAVIA**	(0)	**1**	**DENMARK**	(1)	**2**	26000
	Pancev (50)			*Christensen (31, 62)*			
16/5/91	**YUGOSLAVIA**	(2)	**7**	**FAROE ISLANDS**	(0)	**0**	8000
	Najdoski (21), Prosinecki (24), Pancev (51, 72) Vulic (65), Boban (68), Suker (85)						
16/10/91	**FAROE ISLANDS**	(0)	**0**	**YUGOSLAVIA**	(1)	**2**	2485
				Yugovic (17), Savicevic (79)			
13/11/91	**AUSTRIA**	(0)	**0**	**YUGOSLAVIA**	(2)	**2**	8000
				Lukic (19), Savicevic (39)			

YUGOSLAVIA qualified for the Finals but were excluded because of United Nations sanctions against Serbia.

THE 1996 FINALS - THE STADIA

GROUP A — WEMBLEY

Games Scheduled			
June 8th 1996	—	**England vs Switzerland**	*3.00pm*
June 15th 1996	—	**Scotland vs England**	*3.00pm*
June 18th 1996	—	**Holland vs England**	*7.30pm*
June 23rd 1996	—	**Quarter Final – Runners-Up 'B' vs Winners 'A'**	*3.00pm*
June 26th 1996	—	**Semi-Final – Q.F. 2 Winners vs Q.F. 3 Winners**	*7.30pm*
June 30th 1996	—	**FINAL**	*7.00pm*

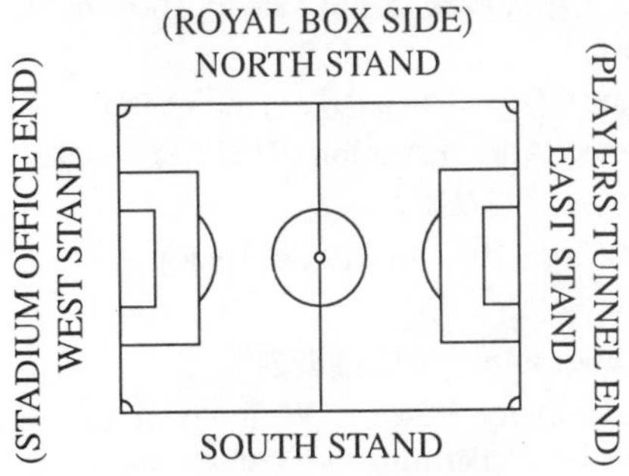

DISABLED INFORMATION

Wheelchairs: 40 spaces in the North Stand and 40 spaces in the South Stand

Disabled Toilets: Available in the North and South Stands

Blind: No Special Facilities

GROUND INFORMATION

Address: Wembley Stadium, Wembley, Middlesex HA9 0DW

Telephone: Box Office (0181) 900-1234

Telephone: Administration (0181) 902-8833

Fax: (0181) 900-1055

Ground Capacity: 80,000 (all seats)

Pitch Size: 115 x 75 yds

Police Telephone: (0181) 900-7212

Nearest Railway Stations: Wembley Central (Euston line) & Wembley Complex (Marylebone line) – both 10 minutes walk

Nearest Tube Station: Wembley Park (Jubilee and Metropolitan lines) – 5 minutes walk

Car Parking: Car Park at Stadium for over 7,000 vehicles

THE 1996 FINALS - THE STADIA

GROUP A — VILLA PARK

Games Scheduled

June 10th 1996	—	**Holland vs Scotland**	*4.30pm*
June 13th 1996	—	**Switzerland vs Holland**	*7.30pm*
June 18th 1996	—	**Scotland vs Switzerland**	*7.30pm*
June 23rd 1996	—	**Quarter-Final – Runners-Up 'C' vs Winners 'D'**	*6.30pm*

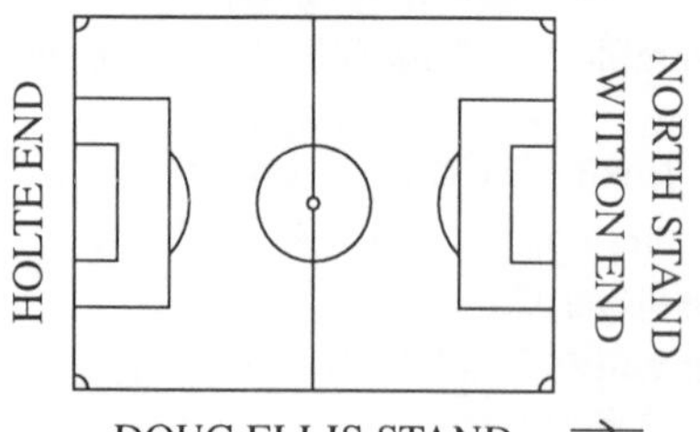

DISABLED INFORMATION

Wheelchairs: 56 spaces available in Trinity Road Stand
Disabled Toilets: Available in the Trinity Road Stand
Blind: Commentaries available

GROUND INFORMATION

Address: Villa Park, Trinity Road, Birmingham B6 6HE

Telephone: Box Office (0121) 327-5353

Telephone: Administration (0121) 327-2299

Fax: (0121) 322-2107

Ground Capacity: 40,310 (all seats)

Pitch Size: 115 x 75 yds

Police Telephone: (0121) 322-6010

Nearest Railway Station: Witton or Aston – both 5 minutes walk (Birmingham New Street line)

Car Parking: Aston Villa Leisure Centre Car Park, Aston Hall Road

Alternatives: Park at Perry Barr Greyhound Stadium (1.25 miles) or at Bescot Stadium, Walsall and take train to Witton to avoid traffic jams

THE 1996 FINALS - THE STADIA

GROUP B — ST. JAMES' PARK

Games Scheduled

June 10th 1996	—	**Romania vs France**	*7.30pm*
June 13th 1996	—	**Bulgaria vs Romania**	*4.30pm*
June 18th 1996	—	**France vs Bulgaria**	*4.30pm*

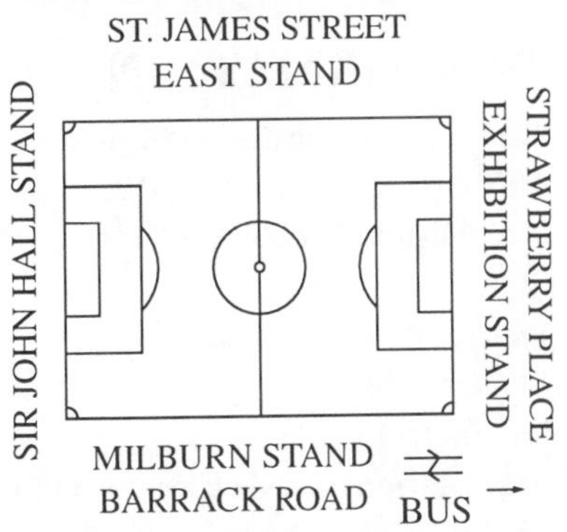

DISABLED INFORMATION

Wheelchairs: Approximately 100 spaces in the Sir John Hall Stand

Disabled Toilets: Available in the Sir John Hall Stand

Blind: Commentaries available for 20 blind people

GROUND INFORMATION

Address: St. James' Park, Newcastle-upon-Tyne, NE1 4ST

Telephone: Box Office (0191) 261-1571

Telephone: Administration (0191) 232-8361

Fax: (0191) 232-9875

Ground Capacity: 36,649 (all seats)

Pitch Size: 110 x 73 yds

Police Telephone: (0191) 232-3451

Nearest Railway Station: Newcastle Central (0.5 mile)

Nearest Metro Station: St. James' (adjacent)

Car Parking: City Centre multi-storey car parks within 0.5 mile. Try to avoid street parking

THE 1996 FINALS - THE STADIA

GROUP B — ELLAND ROAD

Games Scheduled			
June 9th 1996	—	**Spain vs Bulgaria**	*2.30pm*
June 15th 1996	—	**France vs Spain**	*6.00pm*
June 18th 1996	—	**Romania vs Spain**	*4.30pm*

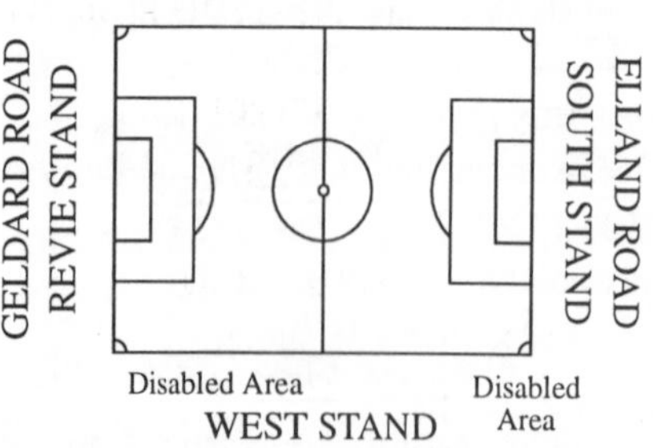

DISABLED INFORMATION

Wheelchairs: 40 spaces in the West Stand, 25 spaces in the North Stand and 34 spaces in the South Stand

Disabled Toilets: Adjacent to each disabled section

Blind: Commentaries available

GROUND INFORMATION

Address: Elland Road, Leeds, LS11 0ES

Telephone: Box Office (0113) 271-0710

Telephone: Administration (0113) 271-6037

Fax: (0113) 272-0370

Ground Capacity: 40,204 (all seats)

Pitch Size: 117 x 76 yds

Police Telephone: (0113) 243-5353

Nearest Railway Station: Leeds City – 1.5 miles

Car Parking: Car Park for about 1,000 vehicles adjacent. Also street parking and various car parks around Lowfields Road area.

THE 1996 FINALS - THE STADIA

GROUP C — OLD TRAFFORD

Games Scheduled

June 9th 1996	—	**Germany vs Czech Republic**	*5.00pm*
June 16th 1996	—	**Russia vs Germany**	*3.00pm*
June 19th 1996	—	**Italy vs Germany**	*7.30pm*
June 23rd 1996	—	**Quarter-Final – Winners 'C' vs Runners-Up 'D'**	*3.00pm*
June 26th 1996	—	**Semi-Final – Q.F.1 Winners vs Q.F. 4 Winners**	*4.00pm*

NORTH STAND

WEST STAND STRETFORD END

EAST STAND

SOUTH STAND

DISABLED INFORMATION

Wheelchairs: 32 spaces in the South East corner

Disabled Toilets: Adjacent to the disabled area

Blind: Commentaries available for 20 blind people

GROUND INFORMATION

Address: Sir Matt Busby Way, Old Trafford, Manchester, M16 0RA

Telephone: Box Office (0161) 872-0199

Telephone: Administration (0161) 872-1661

Fax: (0161) 896-5502

Ground Capacity: 45,000 (all seats – rising to 55,300 when building work completed)

Pitch Size: 116 x 76 yds

Police Telephone: (0161) 872-5050

Nearest Railway Station: Old Trafford (0.5 mile) - on the line from Manchester Oxford Road Station

Car Parking: Spaces for 1,200 cars at Lancashire Cricket Ground and also at Industrial sites down Trafford Park Road

THE 1996 FINALS - THE STADIA

GROUP C — ANFIELD

Games Scheduled

June 11th 1996	—	**Italy vs Russia**	*4.30pm*
June 14th 1996	—	**Czech Republic vs Italy**	*7.30pm*
June 19th 1996	—	**Russia vs Czech Republic**	*7.30pm*
June 22nd 1996	—	**Quarter-Final – Winners 'B' vs Runners-Up 'A'**	*6.30pm*

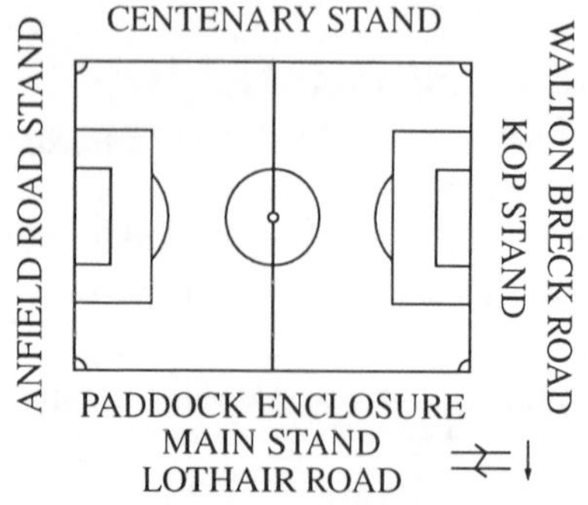

DISABLED INFORMATION

Wheelchairs: 27 spaces available in the Kop Stand

Disabled Toilets: Available in the Kop Stand

Blind: Commentaries available

GROUND INFORMATION

Address: Anfield Road, Liverpool L4 0TH

Telephone: Box Office (0151) 260-8680

Telephone: Administration (0151) 263-2361

Fax: (0151) 261-1416

Ground Capacity: 41,000 (all seats)

Pitch Size: 110 x 74 yds

Police Telephone: (0151) 709-6010

Nearest Railway Station: Kirkdale (0.75 mile) – on the line from Liverpool Lime Street

Car Parking: Stanley Park Car Park adjacent – 1,000 spaces available or Goodison Park car park. Street parking can be risky

Alternative: Park at Albert Dock and take Merseyrail to Sandhills Station

THE 1996 FINALS - THE STADIA

GROUP D — HILLSBOROUGH

Games Scheduled			
June 9th 1996	—	**Denmark vs Portugal**	*7.30pm*
June 16th 1996	—	**Croatia vs Denmark**	*6.00pm*
June 19th 1996	—	**Turkey vs Denmark**	*4.30pm*

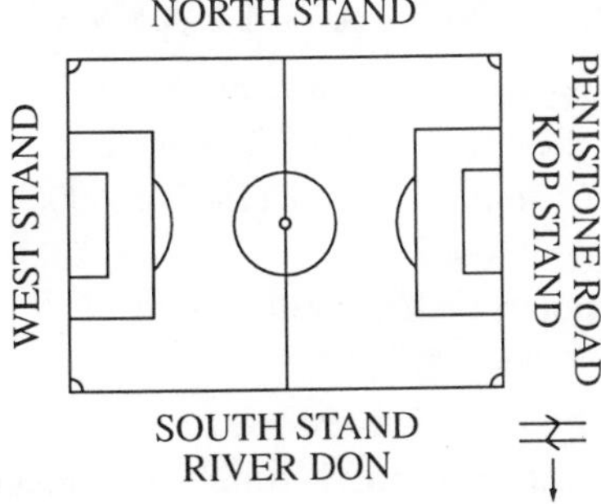

GROUND INFORMATION

Address: Hillsborough, Sheffield S6 1SW
Telephone: Box Office (0114) 233-7233
Telephone: Administration (0114) 234-3122
Fax: (0114) 233-7145
Ground Capacity: 36,020 (all seats)
Pitch Size: 115 x 75 yds
Police Telephone: (0114) 234-3131
Nearest Railway Station: Sheffield Midland (4 miles)
Car Parking: Owlerton Greyhound Stadium nearby and street parking – possibly over one mile away!

DISABLED INFORMATION

Wheelchairs: 56 spaces in the North Stand
Disabled Toilets: Available in the North Stand
Blind: Commentaries available in the North Stand

THE 1996 FINALS - THE STADIA

GROUP D — CITY GROUND

Games Scheduled			
June 11th 1996	—	**Turkey vs Croatia**	*7.30pm*
June 14th 1996	—	**Portugal vs Turkey**	*4.30pm*
June 19th 1996	—	**Croatia vs Portugal**	*4.30pm*

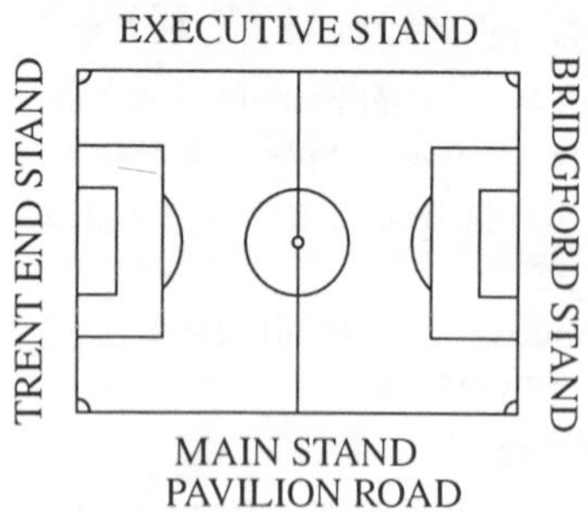

DISABLED INFORMATION

Wheelchairs: Approximately 40 spaces in the Bridgford Stand

Disabled Toilets: Available in the Bridgford Stand

Blind: No Special Facilities

GROUND INFORMATION

Address: City Ground, Nottingham NG2 5FJ

Telephone: Box Office (0115) 952-6002

Telephone: Administration (0115) 952-6000

Fax: (0115) 952-6003

Ground Capacity: 30,564 (all seats)

Pitch Size: 115 x 78 yds

Police Telephone: (0115) 948-1888

Nearest Railway Station: Nottingham Midland (0.5 mile)

Car Parking: Car Park for 300 cars at the Ground and street parking off Radcliffe Road. Also along the Trent Embankment

THE 1996 FINALS - DIRECTIONS

GROUP A — WEMBLEY

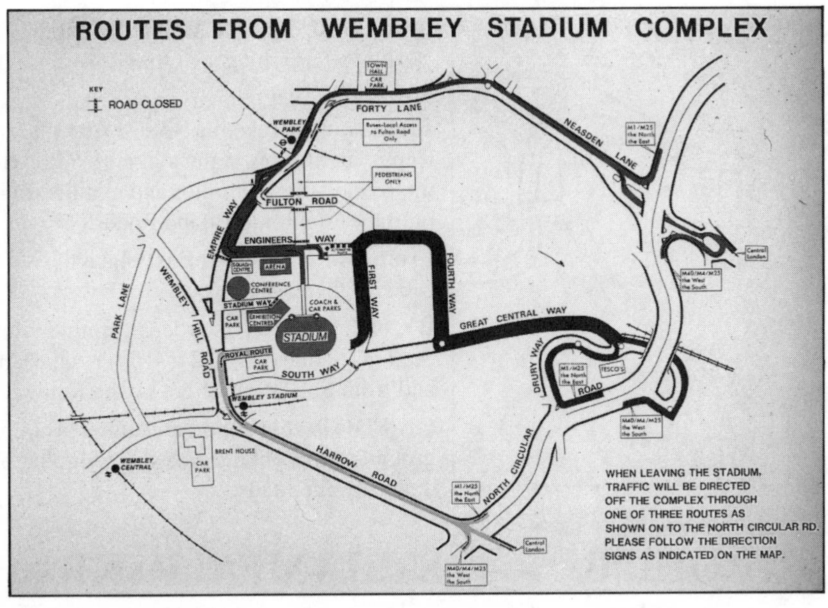

GROUP A — VILLA PARK

(Home of Aston Villa F.C.)

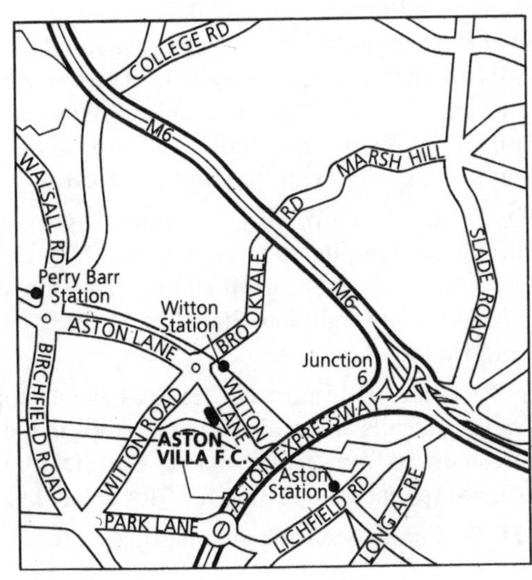

BY CAR:

From All Parts: Exit the M6 at Junction 6 (Spaghetti Junction) and follow the signs for Birmingham (N.E.). Take the 4th exit at the roundabout onto the A38(M) signposted Aston. After 0.5 mile turn right into Aston Hall Road for the ground.

BY BUS: Special Buses depart from Birmingham Central Bus Station in Midland Road (phone (0121) 200-2700 for details). The Nº 7 bus service runs from Corporation Street in the City Centre to Witton Square.

ON FOOT: It is a 5 minute walk from Witton Station. Turn left after Witton Arms to the roundabout then left again into Witton Lane.

THE 1996 FINALS - DIRECTIONS

GROUP B — ELLAND ROAD

(Home of Leeds United F.C.)

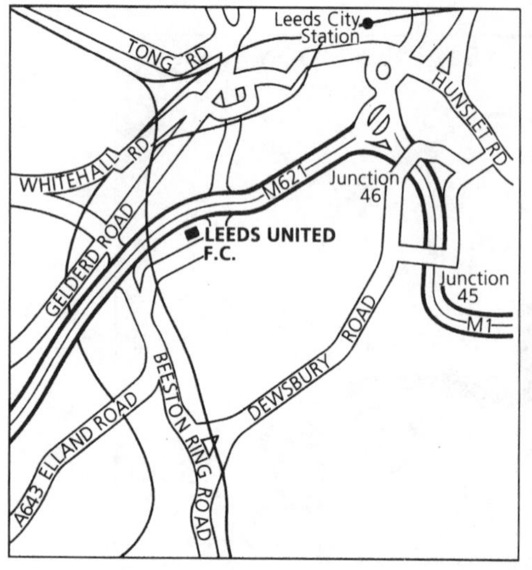

BY CAR:

From West: Exit the M62 at Junction 27 onto the M621. After 3 miles exit the M621 onto the A643 into Elland Road for the Ground.

From North: Take the A58 or A61 into the City Centre and follow signs to the M621. Leave the motorway after 1.5 miles and exit the roundabout onto the A643 into Elland Road.

From South & South East: Take the M1 to the M621 – then as North.

BY BUS: Special buses depart from Swinegate Bus Station (phone (0113) 245-1601) in the City Centre and from Sovereign Street by the Railway Station.

ON FOOT: It is not practicable to walk to the ground as this entails crossing a number of busy dual carriage roads.

GROUP B — ST. JAMES' PARK

(Home of Newcastle United F.C.)

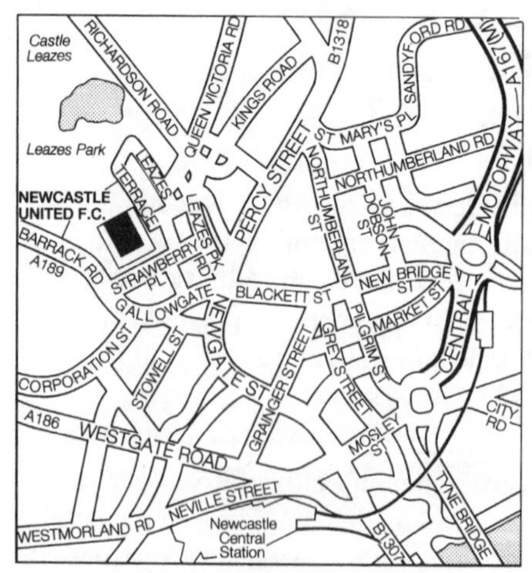

BY CAR:

From North: Follow A1 into Newcastle, then Hexham signs into Percy Street. Turn right into Leazes Park Road

From South: Take A1M, then after Birtley Granada Services take A69 Gateshead Western Bypass (bear left on Motorway). Follow the Airport signs for approximately 3 miles then take A692 (Newcastle) sign, crossing the Redheugh Bridge. At the roundabout take the 3rd exit (Blenheim Street). Proceed over two sets of traffic lights crossing Westmorland Road and Westgate Road. Turn left into Bath Lane. traffic lights to next roundabout and take third exit into Barrack Road

From West: Take A69 towards City Centre. Pass Newcastle General Hospital. At traffic lights immediately after Hospital turn left into Brighton Grove and after 70 yards turn right into Stanhope Street. Proceed into Barrack Road.

BY BUS: There are 10 or more bus services which stop at Gallowgate – details are available at bus stops in the City Centre and also from the Haymarket Bus Station in the City Centre (phone (0191) 232-4211 for details).

BY FOOT: St. James' Metro Station is adjacent to Ground.

GROUP C — ANFIELD

(Home of Liverpool F.C.)

BY CAR:

(See Car Parking information for an alternative)

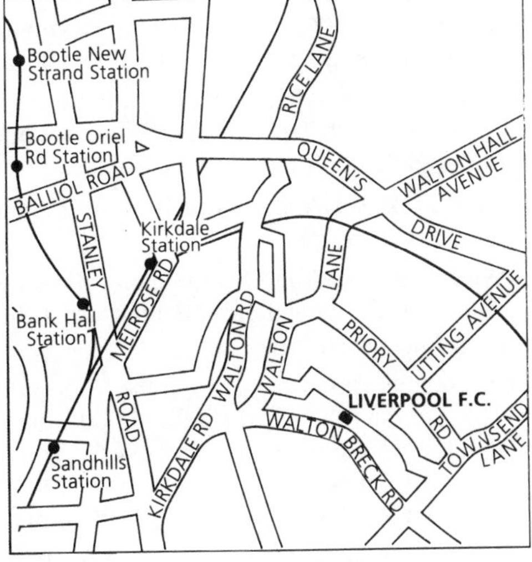

From North: Exit M6 junction 28 and follow Liverpool A58 signs into Walton Hall Avenue, pass Stanley Park and turn left into Anfield Road

From South & East: Take M62 to end of motorway then turn right into Queen's Drive (A5058) and turn left (3 miles) into Utting Avenue, after 1 mile turn right into Anfield Road

From North Wales: Take Mersey Tunnel into City Centre and follow signs to Preston (A580) into Walton Hall Avenue, turn right into Anfield Road before Stanley Park.

BY BUS: Special buses depart from Central Bus Station, Lime Street (phone (0151) 709-8600 for details) and City Centre. Services 17, 26, 27 & 217 run to Anfield.

ON FOOT: Liverpool Lime Street Railway Station is 3 to 4 miles and is a hard and not very pleasant walk. Better to take Merseyrail to Kirkdale Station which is 10 to 15 minutes walk.

GROUP C — OLD TRAFFORD

(Home of Manchester United F.C.)

BY CAR: (Note that Sir Matt Busby Way is closed to traffic about 3 hours before kick-off)

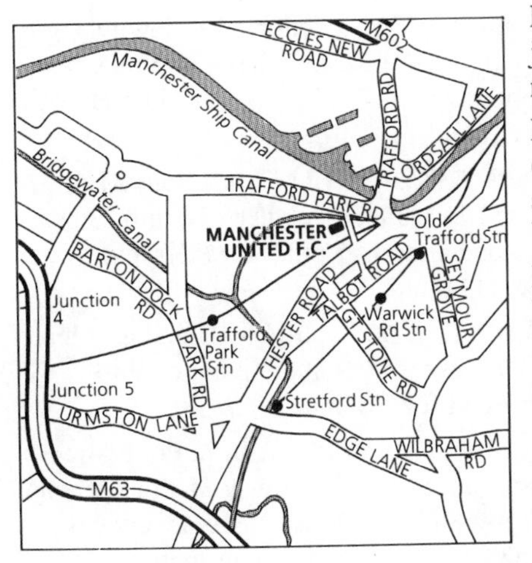

From North & West: Take M61 to M63 and exit junction 4 and follow Manchester signs (A5081). Turn right (2.5 miles) into Warwick Road.

From South: Exit M6 junction 19 take Stockport (A556) then Altrincham (A56). From Altrincham follow signs for Manchester. After 6 miles turn left into Warwick Road.

From East: Exit M62 junction 17 then A56 to Manchester. Follow signs for South then Chester (Chester Road), after 2 miles turn right into Warwick Road.

BY BUS: Special Buses depart from Aytown Street bus station (phone (0161) 228-7811 for details). Any service from the City Centre to Stretford (services 252 to 257) will go to Old Trafford.

ON FOOT: From Old Trafford Metrolink Station, go along Warwick Road, pass Cricket Ground on left and Kelloggs building on right. Go straight on at crossroads past Old Trafford pub and into Sir Matt Busby Way.

THE 1996 FINALS - DIRECTIONS

GROUP D — CITY GROUND

(Home of Nottingham Forest F.C.)

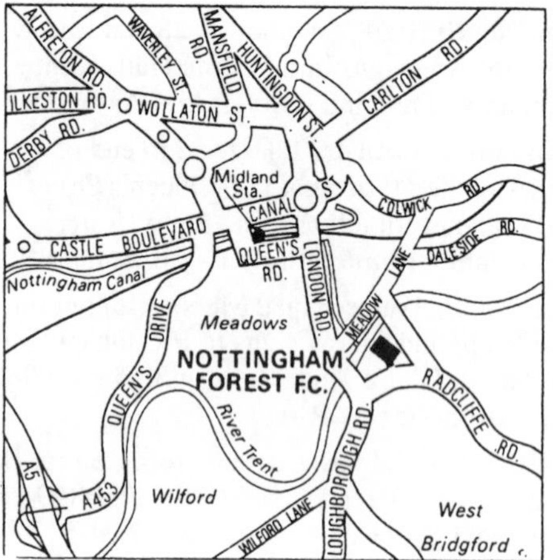

BY CAR:

From North: Exit the M1 at Junction 26 following Nottingham signs (A610) then Melton Mowbray and Trent Bridge (A606) signs. Cross River Trent, left into Radcliffe Road then left into Colwick Road.

From South: Exit M1 Junction 24 following signs Nottingham (South) to Trent Bridge. Turn right into Radcliffe Road then left into Colwick Road.

From East: Take the A52 to West Bridgford, then turn right into Colwick Road.

From West: Take A52 into Nottingham following signs Melton Mowbray and Trent Bridge, cross the River Trent (then as North).

BY BUS: Special Buses depart from the Victoria Centre Bus Station (phone (0115) 924-0000). In addition, all regular services which cross the Trent Bridge from the City Centre (Services 1, 6, 9, 10, 12, 61, 62, 63, 68, 70 and 88) will get to the ground.

ON FOOT: From the Railway Station, turn left then left again into Queen's Road. At the T-junction turn right along London Road and continue across Trent Bridge. Bear left either along the embankment or follow the road round past the Cricket Ground.

GROUP D — HILLSBOROUGH

(Home of Sheffield Wednesday F.C.)

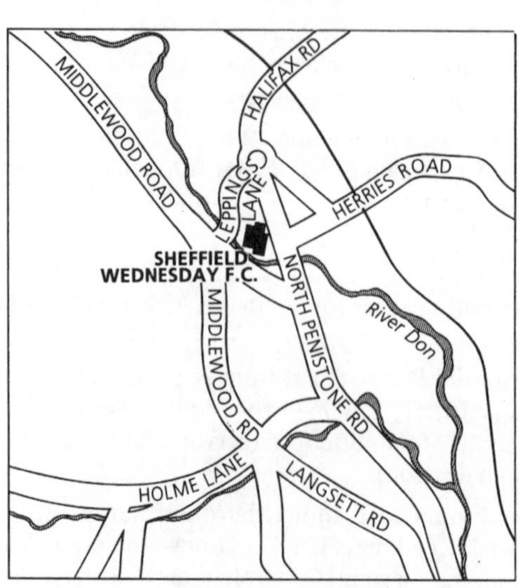

BY CAR:

From North: Exit M1 junction 34 following signs for Sheffield (A6109), take 3rd exit (1.5 miles) at roundabout and in 3.25 miles turn left into Herries Road for Ground.

From South & East: Exit M1 junctions 31 or 33 and take A57 to roundabout, take exit into Prince of Wales Road after 5.75 miles turn left into Herries Road South.

From West: Take A57 until A6101 and turn left. After 3.75 miles turn left at 'T' junction into Penistone Road for Ground.

BY BUS: Special Buses depart from Pond Street Bus Station (opposite the Railway Station) (phone (0114) 276-8688) for details). Regular services Nos. 42, 53 and 77 also pass the ground.

ON FOOT: The Railway Station is around 4 miles away and it is not practicable to walk to the ground.

THE 1996 FINALS - THE FINALISTS

BULGARIA

Population: 8,997,000 **Registered Clubs**: 23,000
Area Square Km.: 110,994 **Registered Players**: 441,300

National Colours:
Shirts: White with green & red trim
Shorts: Green with red trim
Socks: White

National Coach: Dimitar Penev (born 12.07.45) appointed July 1991

Squad Used in the Qualifying Competition

Goal	**Club**	**D.O.B.**	**Caps**	**Goals**
Dimitar Popov	CSKA Sofia	27.02.70	12	0
Borislav Mihailov	Reading (England)	12.02.63	90	0
Plamen Nikolov	Levski Sofia	20.08.91	6	0
Defence				
Emil Kremenliev	Olympiakos (Greece)	13.08.69	23	0
Zlatko Iyankov	KFC Uerdingen (Germany)	07.06.66	47	4
Tszanko Tzvetanov	Waldhof-Mannheim (Germany)	06.01.70	33	0
Ilian Kiriakov	Anorthosis Famagusta (Cyprus)	04.08.67	51	0
Trifon Ivanov	Rapid Vienna (Austria)	27.07.65	57	5
Petar Houbtchev	Hamburg (Germany)	26.02.64	29	0
Midfield				
Yordan Letchkov	Hamburg (Germany)	09.07.67	31	3
Krassimir Balakov	Stuttgart (Germany)	29.03.66	50	7
Daniel Borimirov	1860 Munich (Germany)	15.01.70	19	2
Ivailo Iordanov	Sporting (Portugal)	12.01.61	20	0
Vladko Shalamanov	Sporting Sofia	25.04.67	5	0
Forwards				
Emil Kostadinov	Bayern Munich (Germany)	12.08.67	48	16
Luboslav Penev	Atletico Madrid (Spain)	31.08.66	48	11
Hristo Stoichkov	Parma (Italy)	08.02.66	59	29
Nasko Sirakov	Slavia Sofia	26.04.62	77	22
Petar Alexandrov	Lucerne (Switzerland)	07.12.62	27	5
Petar Mihtarski	Campomaiorense (Portugal)	15.07.66	8	0
Boncho Guentchev	Luton Town (England)	07.07.64	8	0
Ilian Iliev	Benfica (Portugal)	02.07.68	5	0

THE 1996 FINALS - THE FINALISTS

CROATIA

Population: 4,683,000
Area Square Km.: 56,538

Registered Clubs: 1,579
Registered Players: 78,000

National Colours:
Shirts: Red and white
Shorts: White
Socks: Blue

National Coach: Miroslav Blazevic (born 10.02.35) appointed 1994

Squad Used in the Qualifying Competition

Goal	**Club**	**D.O.B.**	**Caps**	**Goals**
Drazen Ladic	Croatia Zagreb	01.01.63	20	0
Tonci Gabric	Hajduk Split	11.03.61	4	0
Marijan Mrmic	Varteks Varazdin	06.05.65	2	0
Defence				
Robert Jarni	Real Betis (Spain)	26.10.68	16	0
Igor Stimac	Derby County (England)	06.09.67	13	1
Nikola Jerkan	Oviedo (Spain)	08.12.64	15	1
Dubravko Pavlicic	Hercules (Spain)	28.11.67	11	0
Elvis Brajkovic	1860 Munich (Germany)	12.06.69	4	0
Slaven Bilic	Karlsruhe (Germany)	11.09.68	16	0
Zvonimir Soldo	Croatia Zagreb	02.11.67	6	0
Niko Ceko	Zagreb	13.02.69	2	0
Dzevad Turkovic	Croatia Zagreb	17.08.72	6	0
Midfield				
Zvonimir Boban	Milan (Italy)	08.10.68	14	2
Aljosa Asanovic	Valladolid (Spain)	14.12.65	14	1
Robert Prosinecki	Barcelona (Spain)	12.01.69	10	3
Mladen Mladenovic	Salzburg (Austria)	13.09.64	15	3
Nenad Pralija	Hajduk Split	11.12.70	3	0
Forwards				
Davor Suker	Sevilla (Spain)	01.01.68	15	16
Alen Boksic	Lazio (Italy)	31.01.70	11	1
Ardian Kozniku	Cannes (France)	27.10.67	4	1
Nikola Jurkevic	Freiburg (Germany)	14.09.66	10	2
Goran Vlaovic	Padova (Italy)	07.08.72	4	0
Mario Stanic	Club Brugge (Belgium)	10.04.72	3	0

THE 1996 FINALS - THE FINALISTS

CZECH REPUBLIC

Population: 10,328,000 **Registered Clubs**: 3,562
Area Square Km.: 78,864 **Registered Players**: 237,000

National Colours:
Shirts: Red **Shorts**: White **Socks**: Blue

National Coach: Dusan Uhrin (born 05.02.43) appointed 1993

Squad Used in the Qualifying Competition

Goal	**Club**	**D.O.B.**	**Caps**	**Goals**
Pavel Srnicek	Newcastle United (England)	10.03.68	3	0
Petr Kouba	Sparta Praha	28.01.69	27	0
Ludek Miklosko	West Ham United (England)	09.12.61	40	0
Defence				
Jan Suchoparek	Slavia Praha	23.09.69	28	2
Miroslav Kadlec	Kaiserslautern (Germany)	22.06.64	49	2
Tomas Repka	Sparta Praha	02.01.74	13	0
Radoslav Latal	Schalke (Germany)	06.01.70	24	3
Vaclav Nemecek	Servette (Switzerland)	25.01.67	53	6
Michal Hornak	Sparta Praha	28.04.70	2	0
Jiri Lerch	Slavia Praha	17.10.71	1	0
Petr Gabriel	Viktoria Zizkov	17.05.73	1	0
Midfield				
Martin Frydek	Sparta Praha	09.03.69	21	2
Jiri Nemec	Schalke (Germany)	15.05.66	33	0
Pavel Nedved	Sparta Praha	30.08.72	5	0
Karel Poborsky	Slavia Praha	30.03.72	11	0
Patrik Berger	Borussia Dortmund (Germany)	10.11.73	12	8
Pavel Hapal	Tenerife (Spain)	27.07.69	29	1
Michal Bilek	Viktoria Zizkov	13.04.65	34	11
Forwards				
Pavel Kuka	Kaiserslautern (Germany)	19.07.68	39	12
Tomas Skuhravy	Genoa (Italy)	07.09.65	49	17
Radek Drulak	Drnovice	12.01.62	9	3
Vratislav Lokvenic	Sparta Praha	27.09.73	2	0
Petr Samec	Hradec Kralove	14.02.64	9	2
Vladimir Smicer	Slavia Praha	24.05.73	2	0

THE 1996 FINALS - THE FINALISTS

DENMARK

Population: 5,180,000 **Registered Clubs**: 1,555
Area Square Km.: 43,092 **Registered Players**: 338,000

National Colours:
Shirts: Red **Shorts**: White **Socks**: Red

National Coach: Richard Moller Nielsen (born 19.08.37) appointed 1990

Squad Used in the Qualifying Competition

Goal	**Club**	**D.O.B.**	**Caps**	**Goals**
Mogens Krogh	Brondby	31.10.63	4	0
Peter Schmeichel	Manchester United (England)	18.11.63	81	0
Lars Hogh	Odense	14.01.59	8	0
Defence				
Jakob Kjeldbjerg	Chelsea (England)	21.10.69	14	0
Lars Olsen	Basel (Switzerland)	02.02.61	83	4
Jes Hogh	Fenerbahce (Turkey)	07.05.66	20	1
Jacob Laursen	Silkeborg	06.10.71	10	0
Marc Rieper	West Ham United (England)	05.06.68	35	0
Jens Risager	Brondby	09.04.71	9	0
Jacob Friis-Hansen	Bordeaux (France)	06.03.67	15	0
Thomas Helveg	Udinese (Italy)	24.06.71	10	0
Torben Piechnik	AGF Aarhus	21.05.63	13	0
Midfield				
Brian Steen Nielsen	Odense	28.12.68	32	0
John Jensen	Arsenal (England)	03.05.65	69	4
Allan Nielsen	Brondby	13.03.71	1	1
Michael Schjonberg	Odense	19.01.67	10	2
Michael Laudrup	Real Madrid (Spain)	15.06.64	85	34
Morten Wieghorst	Dundee FC (Scotland)	25.02.71	5	2
Claus Thomsen	Ipswich Town (England)	31.05.70	3	0
Kim Vilfort	Brondby	15.11.62	74	14
Forwards				
Mikkel Beck	Fortuna Koln (Germany)	12.05.73	6	3
Bent Christensen	Compostela (Spain)	04.01.67	26	8
Peter Rasmussen	Aalborg	16.05.67	12	2
Brian Laudrup	Rangers (Scotland)	22.02.69	60	10
Erik Bo Andersen	Aalborg	14.11.70	4	0
Mark Strudal	Naestved	29.04.68	9	3

THE 1996 FINALS - THE FINALISTS

ENGLAND

Population: 47,254,000
Area Square Km.: 130,439
Registered Clubs: 41,750
Registered Players: 3,258,000

National Colours:
Shirts: White with blue trim
Shorts: Blue
Socks: White

National Coach: Terry Venables (born 06.01.43) appointed 1994

Squad at the time of the Final Draw

	Club	D.O.B.	Caps	Goals
Goal				
David Seaman	Arsenal	19.09.63	20	0
Tim Flowers	Blackburn Rovers	03.02.67	7	0
Ian Walker	Tottenham Hotspur	31.10.71	0	0
Defence				
Gary Neville	Manchester United	18.02.75	5	0
Rob Jones	Liverpool	05.11.71	8	0
Tony Adams	Arsenal	10.10.66	38	4
Steve Howey	Newcastle United	26.10.71	2	0
Gareth Southgate	Aston Villa	03.09.70	0	0
Gary Pallister	Manchester United	30.06.65	20	0
Stuart Pearce	Nottingham Forest	24.04.62	61	5
Graeme Le Saux	Blackburn Rovers	17.10.68	11	1
Midfield				
Trevor Sinclair	Queens Park Rangers	02.03.73	0	0
Steve Stone	Nottingham Forest	20.08.71	2	1
Jamie Redknapp	Liverpool	25.06.73	3	0
David Platt	Arsenal	10.06.66	55	26
Paul Gascoigne	Rangers (Scotland)	27.05.67	34	6
Robert Lee	Newcastle United	01.02.66	5	1
Steve McManaman	Liverpool	11.02.72	6	0
Dennis Wise	Chelsea	16.12.66	10	1
Forwards				
Les Ferdinand	Newcastle United	18.12.66	7	3
Peter Beardsley	Newcastle United	18.01.61	57	9
Teddy Sheringham	Tottenham Hotspur	02.04.66	12	2
Alan Shearer	Blackburn Rovers	13.08.70	20	5
Darren Anderton	Tottenham Hotspur	03.03.72	9	3

THE 1996 FINALS - THE FINALISTS

FRANCE

Population: 57,700,000 **Registered Clubs**: 21,186
Area Square Km.: 543,965 **Registered Players**: 1,915,836

National Colours:
Shirts: Blue **Shorts**: White **Socks**: Red

National Coach: Aime Jacquet (born 27.11.41) appointed 1993

Squad Used in the Qualifying Competition

	Club	D.O.B.	Caps	Goals
Goal				
Fabien Barthez	Monaco	28.06.71	2	0
Bernard Lama	Paris Saint-Germain	07.04.63	23	0
Defence				
Jocelyn Angloma	Torino (Italy)	07.08.65	29	0
Laurent Blanc	Auxerre	19.11.65	46	8
Eric Di Meco	Monaco	07.09.63	18	0
Frank Leboeuf	Strasbourg	22.01.68	5	2
Bixente Lizarazu	Bordeaux	09.12.69	17	1
Alain Roche	Paris Saint-Germain	14.10.67	21	1
Lilian Thuram	Monaco	01.01.72	6	0
Midfield				
Marcel Desailly	Milan (Italy)	07.09.68	18	1
Didier Deschamps	Juventus (Italy)	15.10.68	45	3
Youri Djorkaeff	Paris Saint-Germain	09.03.68	13	8
Jean-Michel Ferri	Nantes	07.02.69	4	0
Vincent Guerin	Paris Saint-Germain	22.11.65	9	2
Christian Karembeu	Sampdoria (Italy)	03.12.70	11	1
Paul Le Guen	Paris Saint-Germain	01.03.64	17	0
Corentin Martins	Auxerre	11.07.69	11	1
Reynald Pedros	Nantes	10.10.71	14	1
Zinedine Zidane	Bordeaux	23.06.72	8	4
Forwards				
Eric Cantona	Manchester United (England)	24.05.66	45	20
Christophe Cocard	Auxerre	23.11.67	9	1
Christophe Dugarry	Bordeaux	24.03.72	8	1
David Ginola	Newcastle United (England)	25.01.67	17	3
Patrice Loko	Paris Saint-Germain	06.02.70	9	2
Marc Keller	Strasbourg	14.01.68	1	0
Nicolas Oudec	Nantes	28.10.71	5	0
Jean-Pierre Papin	Bayern Munich (Germany)	05.11.63	54	30
Michael Madar	Monaco	08.05.68	2	0

GERMANY

Population: 81,100,000
Area Square Km.: 356,046
Registered Clubs: 26,162
Registered Players: 5,373,183

National Colours:
Shirts: White **Shorts**: Black **Socks**: White

National Coach: Berti Vogts (born 30.12.46) appointed 1990

Squad Used in the Qualifying Competition

Goal	**Club**	**D.O.B.**	**Caps**	**Goals**
Oliver Kahn	Bayern Munich	15.06.69	2	0
Andreas Köpke	Eintracht Frankfurt	12.03.62	28	0
Stefan Klos	Borussia Dortmund	16.08.71	0	0
Defence				
Markus Babbel	Bayern Munich	08.09.72	10	1
Thomas Helmer	Bayern Munich	21.04.65	41	2
Jürgen Kohler	Borussia Dortmund	06.10.65	77	0
Lothar Matthäus	Bayern Munich	21.03.61	122	22
Stefan Reuter	Borussia Dortmund	16.10.66	48	2
Matthias Sammer *	Borussia Dortmund	05.09.67	37	5
Midfield				
Mario Basler	Werder Bremen	18.12.68	13	1
Dieter Eilts	Werder Bremen	13.12.64	12	0
Steffen Freund	Borussia Dortmund	19.01.70	10	0
Thomas Hässler	Karlsruhe	30.05.66	68	8
Jörg Heinrich	Freiburg	06.12.69	2	0
Andreas Möller	Borussia Dortmund	02.09.67	56	20
Thomas Strunz	Bayern Munich	25.04.68	25	1
Christian Ziege	Bayern Munich	01.02.72	10	1
Forwards				
Heikko Herrlich	Borussia Dortmund	03.12.71	5	1
Ulf Kirsten *	Bayer Leverkusen	04.12.65	17	6
Fredi Bobic	Stuttgart	30.10.71	5	1
Jürgen Klinsmann	Bayern Munich	30.07.64	78	34
Stefan Kuntz	Besiktas (Turkey)	30.10.62	13	2
Karlheinz Riedle	Borussia Dortmund	16.09.65	42	16

** Sammer played 23 internationals and Kirsten 49 for the former East Germany*

THE 1996 FINALS - THE FINALISTS

HOLLAND

Population: 15,280,000 **Registered Clubs**: 5,900
Area Square Km.: 41,500 **Registered Players**: 973,348

National Colours:
Shirts: Orange **Shorts**: White **Socks**: Orange

National Coach: Guus Hiddink (born 08.11.46) appointed 1994

Squad Used in the Qualifying Competition

Goal	Club	D.O.B.	Caps	Goals
Ed De Goey	Feyenoord	20.10.66	27	0
Edwin Van Der Sar	Ajax	29.10.70	4	0
Defence				
Arthur Numan	PSV Eindhoven	14.12.69	13	0
Frank De Boer	Ajax	15.05.70	38	1
Danny Blind	Ajax	01.08.61	35	1
Michael Reiziger	Ajax	03.05.73	5	0
Johann De Kock	Roda	15.10.64	5	0
Midfield				
Richard Witschge	Bordeaux (France)	20.09.69	22	1
Clarence Seedorf	Sampdoria (Italy)	01.04.76	7	4
Ronald De Boer	Ajax	15.05.70	22	6
Edgar Davids	Ajax	13.03.73	4	0
Glenn Helder	Arsenal (England)	28.10.68	3	0
Eric Van De Lur	Roda	18.08.65	2	0
Orlando Trustfull	Feyenoord	04.08.70	2	0
Arnold Scholten	Ajax	05.12.62	0	0
Stan Valckx	PSV Eindhoven	20.10.63	19	0
Forwards				
Marc Overmars	Ajax	29.03.73	34	7
Dennis Bergkamp	Arsenal (England)	10.05.69	41	23
Yuri Mulder	Schalke (Germany)	23.03.69	5	3
Aron Winter	Lazio (Italy)	01.03.67	51	4
Bryan Roy	Nottingham Forest (England)	12.02.70	32	9
Patrick Kluivert	Ajax	01.07.76	5	1
Gaston Taument	Feyenoord	01.10.70	10	2

ITALY

Population: 57,837,000 **Registered Clubs**: 19,966
Area Square Km.: 301,277 **Registered Players**: 1,143,998

National Colours:
Shirts: Blue **Shorts**: White **Socks**: Blue

National Coach: Arrigo Sacchi (born 01.04.46) appointed 1991

Squad Used in the Qualifying Competition

Goal	**Club**	**D.O.B.**	**Caps**	**Goals**
Angelo Peruzzi	Juventus	16.02.70	5	0
Francesco Toldo	Fiorentina	02.12.71	1	0
Defence				
Antonio Benarrivo	Parma	21.08.68	20	0
Amedeo Carboni	Roma	06.04.65	9	0
Alessandro Costacurta	Milan	24.04.66	34	2
Ciro Ferraro	Juventus	11.02.67	30	0
Paolo Maldini	Milan	26.06.68	67	4
Roberto Mussi	Parma	25.08.63	7	0
Paolo Negro	Lazio	16.04.72	3	0
Midfield				
Demetrio Albertini	Milan	23.08.71	33	2
Dino Baggio	Parma	24.07.71	29	7
Massimo Crippa	Parma	17.05.65	15	1
Angelo Di Livio	Juventus	26.07.66	2	0
Roberto Di Matteo	Lazio	29.05.70	10	0
Francesco Statuto	Roma	13.07.71	3	0
Forwards				
Pierluigi Casiraghi	Lazio	04.03.69	28	6
Alessandro Del Piero	Juventus	09.11.74	7	1
Fabrizio Ravanelli	Juventus	11.12.68	6	2
Marco Simone	Milan	07.01.69	2	0
Gianfranco Zola	Parma	05.07.66	18	7

THE 1996 FINALS - THE FINALISTS

PORTUGAL

Population: 10,380,000 **Registered Clubs**: 1,420
Area Square Km.: 92,389 **Registered Players**: 81,382

National Colours:
Shirts: Red **Shorts**: Green **Socks**: Red

National Coach: Antonio Luis Alves Ribeiro de Oliveira (born 10.06.52) appointed 1994

Squad Used in the Qualifying Competition

Goal	**Club**	**D.O.B.**	**Caps**	**Goals**
Vitor Baia	FC Porto	15.10.69	38	0
Adelino Barros "Neno"	Vitoria	27.01.62	7	0
Alfredo Castro	Boavista	05.10.62	3	0
Rui Correia	Braga	22.10.67	1	0
Defence				
Joao Pinto	FC Porto	21.11.61	69	1
Fernando Nelson Alves	Sporting	05.11.71	2	0
Dimas Teixeira	Benfica	16.02.69	1	0
Paulo Madeira	Belenenses	06.09.70	11	0
Helder Cristovao	Benfica	21.03.71	14	2
Jorge Costa Almeida	FC Porto	14.10.71	13	0
Jose Barroso	Braga	26.08.70	1	0
Fernando Couto	Parma (Italy)	02.08.69	28	2
Rui Bento	Boavista	14.10.72	4	0
Joao Santos "Paulinho Santos"	FC Porto	21.11.70	10	2
Midfield				
Oceano Cruz	Sporting	29.07.62	37	7
Jose Calado Silva	Benfica	01.03.74	2	0
Manuel Guimarades "Nelo"	Boavista	25.08.67	11	0
Paulo Bento	Benfica	20.06.69	3	0
Rui Costa	Fiorentina (Italy)	29.03.72	19	6
Paulo Sousa	Juventus (Italy)	30.08.70	22	0
Carlos Secretario	Porto	12.05.70	9	1
Manuel Cruz Tulipa	Belenenses	16.10.72	2	0
Luis Figo	Barcelona (Spain)	04.11.72	25	4
Forwards				
Rui Barros	FC Porto	24.11.65	34	4
Domingos Oliveira	FC Porto	02.01.69	26	7
Ricardo Sa Pinto	Sporting	10.10.72	6	0
Jose Dominguez	Sporting	16.02.74	1	0
Joao Vieira Pinto	Benfica	19.08.71	21	6
Pedro Barbosa	Sporting	06.08.70	7	1
Paulo Futre	Milan (Italy)	28.02.66	41	6
Antonio Folha	FC Porto	21.05.71	14	3
Paulo Alves	Sporting	10.12.69	7	6

THE 1996 FINALS - THE FINALISTS

ROMANIA

Population: 23,260,000 **Registered Clubs**: 4,956
Area Square Km.: 237,500 **Registered Players**: 207,526

National Colours:
Shirts: Yellow **Shorts**: Blue **Socks**: Red

National Coach: Anghel Iordanescu (born 04.03.50) appointed 1993

Squad Used in the Qualifying Competition

	Club	D.O.B.	Caps	Goals
Goal				
Bogdan Stelea	Steaua Bucharest	05.12.67	31	0
Floria Prunea	Dinamo Bucharest	08.08.68	28	0
Florin Alexandru Tene	Rapid Bucharest	10.11.68	3	0
Dumitru Stingaciu	Vanspor (Turkey)	09.08.64	2	0
Defence				
Miodrag Belodedici	Villareal (Spain)	20.05.64	45	5
Gheorghe Mihali	Guincamp (France)	09.12.65	28	0
Dan Vasile Petrescu	Chelsea (England)	22.12.67	49	5
Daniel Claudiu Prodan	Steaua Bucharest	23.03.72	29	1
Gheorghe Popescu	Barcelona (Spain)	09.10.67	60	3
Tibor Selymes	Cercle Bruges (Belgium)	14.05.70	25	0
Anton Dobos	Steaua Bucharest	13.10.65	4	0
Corneliu Papura	Universitatea Craiova	05.09.73	9	0
Midfield				
Gheorghe Hagi	Barcelona (Spain)	05.02.65	94	27
Angelo Ioan Lupescu	Bayer Leverkusen (Germany)	09.12.68	45	5
Dorinel Ionel Munteanu	Koln (Germany)	25.06.68	43	4
Ovidiu Ioan Sabau	Brescia (Italy)	12.02.68	45	8
Nica Basarab Panduru	Benfica (Portugal)	11.07.70	21	1
Ovidiu Stinga	Salamanca (Spain)	15.12.72	11	0
Daniel Timofte	Samsunspor (Turkey)	01.10.67	22	2
Ion Timofte II	Boavista (Portugal)	16.12.67	10	1
Horia Radu Niculescu	National Bucharest	02.03.75	8	1
Dorin Mateut	Dinamo Bucharest	05.08.65	56	10
Constantin Galca	Steaua Bucharest	08.03.72	14	0
Iulian Chirita	Rapid Bucharest	02.02.67	3	0
Forwards				
Ilie Dumitrescu	West Ham United (England)	06.01.69	54	19
Florin Valeriu Raducioiu	Barcelona (Spain)	17.03.70	36	20
Marius Mihai Lacatus	Steaua Bucharest	05.04.64	73	12
Ion Vladoiu	Steaua Bucharest	05.11.68	15	0
Gheorghe Craioveanu	Real Sociedad (Spain)	14.02.68	6	0
Viorel Dinu Moldovan	Neuchatel Xamax (Switzerland)	08.08.72	5	0
Florin Cirstea	Universitatea Craiova	13.10.72	3	0
Adrian Bucurel Ilie	Steaua Bucharest	20.04.74	1	0

THE 1996 FINALS - THE FINALISTS

RUSSIA

Population: 149,000,000 **Registered Clubs**: 43,700
Area Square Km.: 17,075,400 **Registered Players**: 2,174,000

National Colours:
Shirts: White **Shorts**: Sky Blue **Socks**: Red

National Coach: Oleg Romantsev (born 04.01.54) appointed 1994

Squad Used in the Qualifying Competition

Goal	**Club**	**D.O.B.**	**Caps**	**Goals**
Stanislav Tcherchessov	Spartak Moscow	02.09.63	28	0
Dmitri Kharine	Chelsea (England)	16.08.68	30	0
Sergui Ovchinnikov	Lokomotiv Moscow	11.10.70	2	0
Defence				
Yuri Kovtoun	Dynamo Moscow	05.01.70	10	0
Vladislav Radimov	CSKA Moscow	26.11.75	3	0
Yuri Nikiforov	Spartak Moscow	16.09.70	25	4
Omar Tetradze	Spartak Vladikavkaz	13.10.69	17	0
Ilia Tsymbalar	Spartak Moscow	17.02.69	13	3
Dmitri Khlestov	Spartak Moscow	21.01.71	22	0
Ramiz Mamedov	Spartak Moscow	21.06.72	8	0
Midfield				
Valeri Karpine	Real Sociedad (Spain)	02.02.69	23	4
Igor Shalimov	Udinese (Italy)	02.02.69	40	5
Victor Onopko	Spartak Moscow	14.10.69	40	2
Evgueni Boushmanov	CSKA Moscow	02.11.71	1	0
Vassili Koulkov	Millwall (England)	11.06.66	41	5
Andrei Kanchelskis	Everton (England)	23.01.69	37	4
Andrei Afanasiev	Spartak Moscow	15.05.64	4	1
Nikolai Pissarev	Merida (Spain)	23.11.68	3	1
Andrei Piatnitski	Spartak Moscow	27.09.67	18	4
Valeri Ketchinov	Spartak Moscow	05.08.74	2	1
Dmitri Cheryshev	Dynamo Moscow	11.05.69	9	1
Forwards				
Alexander Mostovoi	Strasbourg (France)	22.08.68	27	6
Vladimir Besteastnykh	Werder Bremen (Germany)	01.04.74	13	1
Oleg Veretennikov	Rotor Volgograd	05.01.70	1	0
Igor Dobrovolski	Dynamo Moscow	27.08.67	41	10
Sergui Yuran	Millwall (England)	11.06.69	20	7
Dmitri Radchenko	La Coruna (Spain)	02.12.70	28	9
Sergui Kiriakov	Karlsruhe (Germany)	01.01.70	29	12
Vladimir Lebed	CSKA Moscow	17.08.73	1	0
Moukhsin Mukhamadiev	Spartak Moscow	21.10.66	1	1
Igor Kolyvanov	Foggia (Italy)	06.07.70	37	6

THE 1996 FINALS - THE FINALISTS

SCOTLAND

Population: 5,094,000 **Registered Clubs**: 6,148
Area Square Km.: 78,783 **Registered Players**: 140,300

National Colours:

Shirts: Blue **Shorts**: White **Socks**: Red

National Coach: Craig Brown (born 01.07.40) appointed 1993

Squad Used in the Qualifying Competition

Goal	**Club**	**D.O.B.**	**Caps**	**Goals**
Andy Goram	Rangers	13.04.64	34	0
Jim Leighton	Hibernian	24.07.58	71	0
Nicky Walker	Partick Thistle	29.09.62	1	0
Defence				
Tommy Boyd	Celtic	24.11.65	31	0
Colin Calderwood	Tottenham Hotspur (England)	20.01.65	9	1
Colin Hendry	Blackburn Rovers (England)	07.12.65	14	1
Stewart McKimmie	Aberdeen	27.10.62	36	1
Tosh McKinlay	Celtic	03.12.64	2	0
Alan McLaren	Rangers	04.01.71	24	0
Craig Burley	Chelsea (England)	24.09.71	5	0
Midfield				
John Collins	Celtic	31.01.68	29	8
Scot Gemmill	Nottingham Forest (England)	02.01.71	4	0
Gary McAllister	Leeds United (England)	25.12.64	37	4
Stuart McCall	Rangers	10.06.64	31	1
Billy McKinlay	Blackburn Rovers (England)	22.04.69	15	4
Paul McStay	Celtic	22.10.64	72	9
Pat Nevin	Tranmere Rovers (England)	06.09.63	27	5
Forwards				
John Róbertson	Heart of Midlothian	02.10.64	16	3
Ally McCoist	Rangers	24.09.62	49	17
John McGinlay	Bolton Wanderers (England)	08.04.64	9	3
Eoin Jess	Aberdeen	13.12.70	10	1
Darren Jackson	Hibernian	25.07.66	9	0
Scott Booth	Aberdeen	16.12.71	9	5
Duncan Shearer	Aberdeen	28.08.62	7	2
John Spencer	Chelsea (England)	11.09.70	8	0

THE 1996 FINALS - THE FINALISTS

SPAIN

Population: 39,600,000 **Registered Clubs**: 12,421
Area Square Km.: 504,782 **Registered Players**: 470,598

National Colours:
Shirts: Red **Shorts**: Blue **Socks**: Black

National Coach: Javier Clemente (born 12.03.50) appointed 1992

Squad Used in the Qualifying Competition

Goal	**Club**	**D.O.B.**	**Caps**	**Goals**
Jose Santiago Canizares Ruiz	Real Madrid	18.12.69	8	0
Juan Jose Valencia de la Serna	Athletic Bilbao	18.09.71	0	0
Andoni Zubizaretta Urreta	Valencia	23.10.61	105	0
Defence				
Abelardo Fernandez Antuna	Barcelona	19.03.70	23	2
Rafael Alkorta Martinez	Real Madrid	16.09.68	34	0
Augustin Aranzabal Alkorta	Real Sociedad	15.03.73	2	0
Alberto Belsue Arias	Real Zaragoza	02.03.68	11	0
Francisco Jose Camarasa Castellar	Valencia	27.09.67	14	0
Albert Ferrer Llopis	Barcelona	06.06.70	26	0
Aitor Karanka de la Haz	Athletic Bilbao	18.09.73	1	0
Sergi Barjuan Esclusa	Barcelona	28.12.71	17	1
Salvador Gonzalez Marco Voro	La Coruna	09.10.63	9	0
Midfield				
Jose Luis Perez Caminero	Atletico Madrid	08.11.67	17	7
Donato Gama da Silva	La Coruna	30.12.62	9	3
Josep Guardiola Sala	Barcelona	18.01.71	14	2
Fernando Ruiz Hierro	Real Madrid	23.03.68	39	11
Luiz Enrique Martinez Garcia	Real Madrid	08.05.70	20	3
Miguel Angel Nadal Homar	Barcelona	28.07.66	28	2
Francisco Gonzalez Perez "Fran"	La Coruna	14.07.69	7	0
Juan Antonio Goikoetxea Lasa	Athletic Bilbao	21.10.65	35	4
Forwards				
Alfonso Perez Munoz	Real Betis	26.09.72	10	2
Jose Emilio Amavisca Garate	Real Madrid	19.06.71	10	1
Angel Manuel Cuellar Llanos	Barcelona	13.09.72	2	0
Julen Guerrero Lopez	Athletic Bilbao	07.01.74	20	7
Francisco Higuera	Real Zaragoza	30.01.65	6	2
Julio Salinas Fernandez	Sporting Gijon	11.09.62	54	22
Javier Manjarin Pereda	La Coruna	31.12.69	4	1
Pier Luigi Cherubino Loggi	Real Betis	15.10.71	1	0
Juan Antonio Pizzi Torroja	Tenerife	07.06.68	9	4
Francisco Narvaez Machon "Kiko"	Atletico Madrid	26.04.72	6	1

THE 1996 FINALS - THE FINALISTS

SWITZERLAND

Population: 6,955,000 **Registered Clubs**: 473
Area Square Km.: 41,293 **Registered Players**: 182,369

National Colours:
Shirts: Red **Shorts**: White **Socks**: Red

National Coach: Roy Hodgson (born 09.08.47) appointed 1992

Squad Used in the Qualifying Competition

	Club	D.O.B.	Caps	Goals
Goal				
Stephan Lehmann	Sion	15.08.63	6	0
Marco Pascolo	Servette	09.05.66	33	0
Pascal Zuberbuhler	Grasshopper-Club	08.01.71	3	0
Defence				
Walter Fernandez	Servette	20.08.65	3	1
Harald Gamperle	Grasshopper-Club	11.05.68	4	0
Alain Geiger	Grasshopper-Club	05.11.60	110	2
Stephane Henchoz	Hamburg (Germany)	07.09.74	13	0
Dominique Herr	Sion	25.10.65	51	4
Marc Hottiger	Everton (England)	07.11.67	57	5
Yvan Quentin	Sion	02.05.70	23	0
Pascal Thuler	Grasshopper-Club	10.01.70	5	0
Ramon Vega	Grasshopper-Club	14.06.71	6	0
Stephan Wolf	Luzern	31.01.71	1	0
Midfield				
Thomas Bickel	Vissel Kobe (Japan)	06.10.63	52	5
Christophe Bonvin	Sion	14.04.65	40	8
Christian Colombo	Lugano	24.04.68	4	0
Sebastien Fournier	Sion	27.06.71	10	1
Marcel Koller	Grasshopper-Club	11.11.60	49	3
Christophe Ohrel	Saint-Etienne (France)	07.04.68	44	6
Ciriaco Sforza	Bayern Munich (Germany)	02.03.70	38	4
Alain Sutter	Freiburg (Germany)	22.01.68	60	5
Johann Vogel	Grasshopper-Club	08.03.77	2	0
Marco Walker	Basel	02.05.70	1	0
Murat Yakin	Grasshopper-Club	15.09.74	2	0
Forwards				
Stephane Chapuisat	Borussia Dortmund (Germany)	28.06.69	44	12
Marco Grassi	Rennes (France)	08.08.65	19	2
Adrian Knup	Karlsruhe (Germany)	02.07.68	43	26
Nestor Subiat	Grasshopper-Club	23.04.66	14	5
Kubilay Turkyilmaz	Galatasaray (Turkey)	04.03.67	47	18
Raphael Wicky	Sion	26.04.77	0	0
Darlo Zuffi	Basel	07.12.64	17	3

THE 1996 FINALS - THE FINALISTS

TURKEY

Population:	56,945,000	**Registered Clubs**:	4,602
Area Square Km.:	779,452	**Registered Players**:	237,500

National Colours:

Shirts: White with red band **Shorts**: White **Socks**: Red

National Coach: Fatih Terim (born 14.09.53) appointed 1993

Squad Used in the Qualifying Competition

Goal	**Club**	**D.O.B.**	**Caps**	**Goals**
Engin Ipekoglu	Fenerbahce	07.06.61	27	0
Rustu Recber	Fenerbahce	10.05.73	13	0
Nihat Tumkaya	Trabzonspor	24.03.72	0	0
Defence				
Alpay Ozalan	Besiktas	29.05.73	15	1
Bulent Korkmaz	Galatasaray	24.11.68	42	1
Osman Ozkoyiu	Trabzonspor	26.08.71	11	0
Ogun Temizkanoglu	Trabzonspor	06.10.69	33	4
Recep Cetin	Besiktas	01.10.65	43	1
Gokhan Keskin	Besiktas	01.03.66	41	1
Emre Asik	Fenerbahce	13.12.73	9	1
Midfield				
Oguz Cetin	Fenerbahce	15.02.63	55	2
Halil Ibrahim Kara	Fenerbahce	26.09.72	2	0
Tayfun Korkut	Fenerbahce	02.04.74	1	0
Kemalettin Senturk	Fenerbahce	09.02.70	2	0
Tugay Kerimoglu	Galatasaray	24.08.70	34	0
Tolunay Kafkas	Trabzonspor	31.03.68	15	2
Abdullah Ercan	Trabzonspor	08.12.71	22	0
Sergen Yalcin	Besiktas	05.10.72	12	3
Bulent Uygun	Fenerbahce	01.08.71	9	1
Forwards				
Oktay Derelioglu	Besiktas	17.12.75	1	0
Ertugrul Saglam	Besiktas	19.11.69	19	7
Hami Mandirali	Trabzonspor	20.07.68	36	7
Arif Erdem	Galatasaray	02.01.72	7	1
Hakan Sukur	Galatasaray	01.09.71	23	13
Orhan Cikiricki	Trabzonspor	15.04.67	25	2
Aykut Kocaman	Fenerbahce	05.04.65	12	1